LIVING ABROAD IN
BRAZIL

MICHAEL SOMMERS

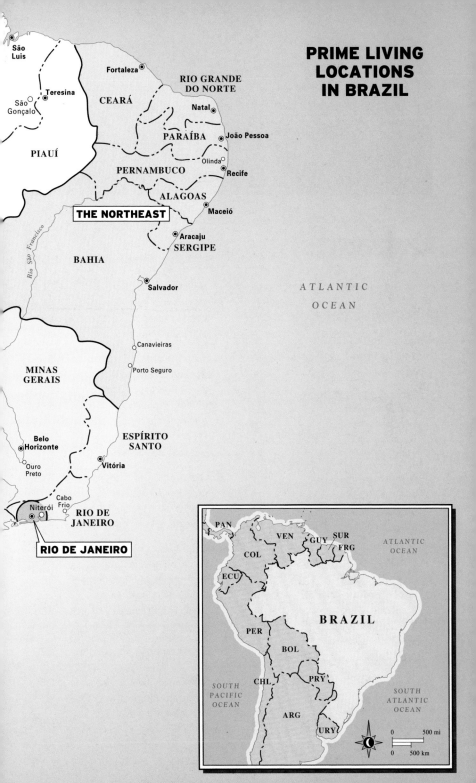

PRIME LIVING LOCATIONS IN BRAZIL

São Luis
Fortaleza
Teresina
RIO GRANDE
DO NORTE
São Gonçalo
CEARÁ
Natal
PIAUÍ
PARAÍBA
João Pessoa
Olinda
PERNAMBUCO
Recife
ALAGOAS
THE NORTHEAST
Maceió
Aracaju
SERGIPE
BAHIA
Rio São Francisco
Salvador

ATLANTIC
OCEAN

Canavieiras
Porto Seguro
MINAS
GERAIS
Belo Horizonte
ESPÍRITO
SANTO
Ouro Preto
Vitória
Cabo Frio
Niterói
RIO DE
JANEIRO
RIO DE JANEIRO

PAN
VEN
GUY
SUR
ATLANTIC
OCEAN
COL
FRG
ECU
BRAZIL
PER
BOL
CHL
PRY
SOUTH
PACIFIC
OCEAN
ARG
URY
SOUTH
ATLANTIC
OCEAN
0   500 mi
0   500 km

Contents

At Home in Brazil

The notion of moving to Brazil has often been wrapped up in a certain degree of fantasy. The South American giant was somewhere you went if you wanted to get lost in the world's largest rainforest, make a fortune mining precious gemstones, or escape extradition to live in tropical bliss after pulling off a major heist.

Mythical projections aside, in an age when earthly paradises are increasingly rare commodities, Brazil pulls off the feat of being one of the most seductive places on the planet.

Few other countries offer year-round access to natural attractions of such sheer beauty and diversity, ranging from glimmering beaches and lush jungles to rugged mountains and endless dunes. Yes, it can get a little hot, but there are no hurricanes, blizzards, or earthquakes, and you never have to wear thermal underwear.

Beyond its physical allure, you find a uniquely rich culture that seeps into every aspect of day-to-day life. Brazilians also have a flair for the visual that eschews modifiers such as "bland" or "neutral," and Brazilians' love for music if off the charts. The often unsung regional cuisines are fantastic as well; the abundance of fresh produce, especially fruit, is jaw-dropping in its variety.

Equally compelling is a lifestyle in which enjoying yourself is more of a priority than working 80-hour weeks. Brazilians do work hard, but they don't brag about it. Yes, Brazilians get stressed, but overall they have the fine art of relaxation down to a C (as in caipirinha).

Of course settling in Brazil also means dealing with the flip side of the fantasy. Brazil's recent economic boom has ushered in a period of

expanding markets, countless entrepreneurial opportunities, and major demand for qualified and specialized workers that the Brazilian labor force can't supply. While many Brazilians have benefited from the economic upturn, poverty—not to mention crime and urban violence—are still major issues.

Although financial opportunities are myriad, many expats who take up residence in Brazil do so for reasons that are more romantic than rational. They fall in love with a Brazilian—or with Brazil itself. Fed up with rat races, stress, cold weather (and cold people), many are inspired to construct simpler, but more satisfying lives in Edenic spots that keep friends and family members back home drooling with envy.

I count myself among the romantics. I came to Brazil out of love for a Brazilian and ended up staying out of love for the country and, even more so, for the people. This "romantic" characteristic is telling since I believe that to live happily in Brazil, one has to be open, adventurous, adaptable, and a bit of a dreamer. Brazil is not a rational place. "Order and progress" might be the motto stitched onto Brazil's flag, but in reality, a certain degree of chaos reigns.

A combination of patience, wiles, and charm, not to mention a decent command of Portuguese, goes a long way. If you can surrender yourself to its sometimes maddening, but never less-than-fascinating paradoxes, Brazil is a place that seeps into your soul, and living in Brazil can last a lifetime.

▶ WHAT I LOVE ABOUT BRAZIL

- Luminous blue skies.
- All the crazy, wonderful stories that people tell (Brazilians are great raconteurs).
- Tropical fruits such as *cupuaçu, mangaba,* and *bacuri.*
- Keeping the windows open 365 days of the year.
- Nursing a hangover with *água* from a freshly machete-cut coconut.
- How frequently and easily I can go barefoot.
- How frequently and easily I can go dancing in the streets.
- Once in a while a hummingbird flies into my living room.
- Brazilian music provides the soundtrack to my life.
- I never have to rush.

- The lyrical, colorful, and impossible-to-remember idiomatic expressions of the Portuguese language.
- Dozing off in a hammock.
- The heady perfume that rises from the earth after a sudden tropical downpour.
- Easy getaways to unspoiled, natural paradises.
- Breezes rustling in palm fronds.
- The number of *beijos* (kisses) and *abraços* (hugs) I can rack up on any given day.
- Brazilians' disarming ability to take a dire, dark situation and make it seem lighter: all about life and living.
- Knowing that when I'm burned out, stressed out, down and out, I can walk down the street and hurl myself into the embrace of a perpetually warm, blue ocean.

WELCOME TO BRAZIL

INTRODUCTION

*We were so right to come. The minute the plane landed I felt differ-
ent: driving through the streets and coming into the hotel, as if something wonderful were going to happen.... Ahh! It's something in the air
of Brazil—that's what it is. And whatever it is, they should bottle it.*

from the 1953 film *Latin Lovers,* spoken by wealthy American Nora Taylor
(Lana Turner) upon arriving in Rio de Janeiro

During the many years I've lived in Brazil, I've made numerous trips to North America.
Whenever the topic of my residence comes up, people are always invariably mystified,
curious, freaked out, and/or envious of the fact that I live in Brazil. While many inevitably express a great interest in traveling to Brazil (especially once I do my Brazilian
sales pitch—admittedly Brazil is not a difficult place to sell), very few are convinced
that they should up and move to Brazil as well.

In truth, visiting Brazil and moving here are two immensely different propositions.
When it comes to first impressions, the "South American giant" can do a real number
on unsuspecting foreigners. Even discounting all the myths and fantasies that swirl
around Brazil, the reality of the place can be utterly seductive. However, deciding to

© MICHAEL SOMMERS

make Brazil a temporary or permanent home means discovering a whole other set of much more complex realities, some of which can be wonderful, others problematic.

On some levels, Brazil has a lot in common with the United States. Both are massive countries—in terms of territory and population—that dominate their respective neighbors and hemispheres, politically, economically, and to some extent, culturally. Both possess a strong sense of nationalism while preserving pronounced regional identities. There are many historical parallels as well. Both countries began life as Atlantic coast colonies from which brave, enterprising settlers gradually moved west to open new frontiers. The two nations' early cash crop economies (sugar in Brazil and cotton in the United States) were based on slavery, resulting in societies that not only are racially diverse but also have racism as a major social issue. Somewhat related is the fact that both nations have traditionally possessed a historical and socioeconomic divide between the North and South. Built by immigrants, Brazil and the United States are two of the world's most successful examples of melting pot countries that, to this day, openly embrace people from different cultures. Both are also societies prone to extremes, such as the extreme divide between rich and poor (admittedly Brazil's are much greater), and the extreme violence that so often makes newspaper headlines. At the same time, Americans and Brazilians share in common the fact that they are great optimists with a fervent belief in the future (although, lately, while Brazil's faith in its destiny is at a heady high, belief in the American Dream has taken somewhat of a hit).

In other aspects, however, North Americans will find Brazil to be an alien place. Even in the most sophisticated, cosmopolitan, First World enclaves of Rio and São Paulo, life is different even if the external trappings appear to be the same. Brazil is less organized, more complex, less defined, more chaotic. If in North America, things tend to be literal, straightforward, and in-your-face, in Brazil, they're more lyrical, circuitous, curvy, and nuanced, sometimes to the point of puzzling. It's often difficult to get a straight answer or to pin things (or people) down. Unlike Americans, Brazilians tend to be less transparent, more indirect, and nonconfrontational. Lines are often blurry: between professional and personal, between white and black (and *mulato*), between now and soon and later. When a Brazilian makes plans with you, it's understood that they might actually never materialize. At the same time, getting together last minute, or on the spur of the moment, is very common. Brazil isn't a place where a lot of advance planning occurs—it is, however, a place where improvisation, flexibility, and spontaneity rule, opening up endless possibilities and opportunities.

Opportunity is a major reason why many foreigners choose to come to Brazil. The country's growing economy combined with its lack of qualified labor means there are many opportunities for foreigners that aren't available in North America. From construction sites and oil rigs to financial companies and technology startups, there are an unprecedented number of openings available. Considering the historic lack of investment in education, they aren't likely to be filled by Brazilians for at least a generation. If you're just starting out in life, moving to Brazil can help you get on the fast track. By providing you with invaluable professional experience, and sometimes serious financial compensation, working in Brazil can constitute a major investment in the rest of your career—and your life. And if you're farther on in your career or life, it might just present you with the essential change that you need or crave.

I wouldn't advise moving to Brazil if comfort, ease, routine, and stability are of prime importance to you. However, if you're open to challenges and yearn for something different, Brazil could end up fulfilling some deep desires.

Ultimately, in Brazil, life has the potential to be more exciting—and more fun. Despite their often tough existences (and many do lead difficult lives), Brazilians have a great knack for cutting through the extraneous and superfluous and getting down to the business of enjoying themselves and life, which is ultimately a very affirming—and refreshing—attitude to embrace. If you can find something to do and someone to do it with (Brazil is a very hard place without friends, family, or community), you can manage to enjoy a quality of life that's sometimes more difficult to encounter in North America.

Many foreigners are unable to pin down exactly what it is that hooks them on Brazil. Inevitably they refer to the tropical climate and the immense warmth, generosity, good humor, and openness of Brazilians. But for most die-hard Brazilianists (including myself), there's some ineffable, indescribable, but very deep essence about Brazil that surreptitiously takes hold of you, gets inside of you, and before you know it, you're hooked—maybe even for life. During the 14 years I've lived in Brazil, I've experienced moments when I contemplated returning to North America—and even a couple of occasions when I started to do so. However, all my efforts have been in vain. To date, I've never been able to kick the habit.

The Lay of the Land

The fifth-largest country in the world in terms of both territory and population (with 194 million inhabitants), Brazil is also the largest country in South America, occupying roughly half the continent. It shares borders with every South American country except Chile and Ecuador and also boasts an Atlantic coastline that stretches for 7,500 kilometers (4,655 miles).

Brazil's landscapes are quite diverse and include hills, plains, mountains, and highlands. Most of the northeastern region consists of low rolling hills and flat plains while the south and southeastern regions contain rugged mountain ranges such as the Serra do Espinhaço, Serra da Mantiqueira, and Serra do Mar. The country's highest peak, however, Pico da Neblina (2,994 meters or 8,923 feet), is located in the state of Amazonas, on Brazil's frontier with Venezuela. In the center and western parts of the country, the land rises into elevated plains known as *planaltos*. Brazil has one of the world's most complex system of rivers, all of which drain into the Atlantic. Aside from the Rio São Francisco, Brazil's longest national river, which weaves its way up from Minas Gerais through the arid Sertão of the Northeast, the most famous is the mighty Amazon, the world's second longest river and largest in terms of volume of water.

The Instituto Brasileiro do Meio Ambiente (IBAMA) is the federal agency in charge of studying and monitoring Brazil's natural environment. IBAMA's researchers have recognized seven distinct ecosystems within Brazil: the Amazonian rain forest, the Caatinga, the Atlantic rain forest, the coastal region, the Cerrado, the Pantanal wetlands, and the southern plains. In theory, a good chunk of Brazil's natural treasures—covering around 15 percent of Brazil's national territory—are protected by national and state parks as well as some reserves operated by private individuals and nongovernmental organizations (NGOs). In practice, though, the immense spaces and difficult access, coupled with limited resources, make it difficult for government watchdogs such as IBAMA to protect endangered ecosystems from illegal farming, ranching, logging, and poaching.

To this day, Brazil has vast amounts of territory that are sparsely or not at all inhabited, especially in the Interior. Indeed, Brazil is known as a "crab culture" because more than 70 percent of Brazilians live within 200 kilometers (125 miles) of the coast. Currently, around 83 percent of the population is urban.

STATES AND REGIONS

Like the United States, Brazil is a federal republic composed of 26 states and a federal district. Aside from the federal government, each state also has its own government. Brazil's states are distributed among five territorial regions that have been grouped together by the Brazilian Institute of Geography and Statistics (IBGE) based on criteria that includes shared geographical, socioeconomic, and cultural similarities. Since 1970, the five regions are Norte, Nordeste, Sudeste, Sul, and Centro-Oeste.

The Norte (North) is made up of the Amazonian states of Amazonas, Pará, Amapá, Rondônia, Acre, Roraima, and Tocantins. Geographically, it is the largest of Brazil's regions (covering 42 percent of national territory), but it's smallest in terms of population density, with only 16 million inhabitants spread out amidst a vast wilderness. Much of the region is covered by the world's largest tropical rain forest, the majority of which is uninhabited by humans (although it's home to an estimated 40,000 plant, 2,000 mammal and bird, 3,000 fish, and 2.5 million insect species). The North is where indigenous influence—in terms of population and culture—is the strongest.

The Nordeste (Northeast) contains the states of Bahia, Sergipe, Alagoas,

© MICHAEL SOMMERS

Much of Brazil is tropical rainforest.

Pernambuco, Paraíba, Rio Grande do Norte, Ceará, Piauí and Maranhão. The Northeast was the first region of Brazil to be colonized. To this day, it maintains some of the country's richest historical and cultural treasures, not to mention a strong Afro-Brazilian influence. The state capitals along the coast all have colonial origins, although those who have best preserved their pasts are Salvador (Bahia) and Recife (Pernambuco), the region's two largest and most economically and culturally dynamic cities. The majority of the Northeast's 53 million residents live in urban centers along the coast, which isn't surprising as the region boasts Brazil's longest and most stunning coastline with thousands of miles of paradise-worthy tropical beaches that make the region a tourist hot spot. The vast parched Interior, however, known as the Sertão, is partially responsible for the Northeast's legacy as one of Brazil's poorest regions.

The four states of the Sudeste (Southeast)—Rio de Janeiro, São Paulo, Minas Gerais, and Espírito Santo—concentrate Brazil's biggest economies, industries, and cities (São Paulo, Rio de Janeiro, and Belo Horizonte) as well as 40 percent (or 80 million) of the country's exceptionally diverse population. This region boasts the majestic mountain ranges of the Serra do Espinhaço, Serra da Mantiqueira, and Serra do Mar.

The last two ranges continue into the neighboring Sul (South). Less than 7 percent of Brazil's territory, but with a population of 27 million, this compact region consists of three small and southernmost coastal states: Paraná, Santa Catarina, and Rio Grande do Sul. Together they boast the country's highest standard of living, highest literacy rate, and lowest poverty and crime rates. The European influence of the South's 19th- and 20th-century immigrant settlers is quite pronounced.

The booming Centro-Oeste (Central-West) is Brazil's only completely landlocked region. The country's second largest region, covering around 19 percent of national territory, it also has its smallest population (14 million people, most of them clustered in medium-sized towns). Largely rural, with most of its topography consisting of elevating plains (*planaltos*), the Central-West embraces the sprawling states of Goiás, Mato Grosso, and Mato Grosso do Sul, where agribusiness is thriving, as well as the Distrito Federal (Federal District), home to the nation's capital of Brasília.

WEATHER

With its immense size, Brazil's climate is extremely varied. The Equator runs through the northern part of the country while the Tropic of Capricorn crosses through the south, running parallel to São Paulo. As you head from north to south, temperatures, humidity, and precipitation levels change greatly. Brazil boasts four distinctive climatic zones: subtropical, equatorial, tropical, and semiarid. Ninety percent of the country is situated in the tropical zone, where there is very little seasonal variation. Rain is frequent and temperatures range 25–35°C (77–95°F). However, as you head south, seasonal variations become more distinct, resembling those of the continental United States and Europe, with hot, steamy summers and cool winters. In the southern states of Santa Catarina and Rio Grande do Sul, temperatures can plunge low enough to produce frost and even snow.

With the exception of the Sertão, which gets very little rainfall, the rest of the country receives a lot of precipitation. Although rains are common throughout the year, coastal regions have distinctive rainy seasons when downpours are daily occurrences and can even last for several days. In the Southeast, violent downpours flood the streets of Rio and São Paulo in the summer months, December–March. In the Northeast, along the coast between Bahia and Pernambuco, rainy season generally coincides with the winter months of June–August. Rain is much less frequent in the permanently sunny states of Rio Grande do Norte and Ceará, where temperatures remain constant year-round. Close to the Equator, Maranhão and especially the Amazonian state of Pará receive the most rain throughout the year, with annual averages of 3,500 millimeters (138 inches) in some parts. The rest of the Amazon, along with the Pantanal, receives a lot of rain as well, but both regions also have a more pronounced dry season that lasts March–October.

FLORA AND FAUNA

One of the things that impresses most about Brazil is the exuberance, diversity, and fantastic aspect of its nature.

Trees and Plant Life

More than a quarter of the world's known plant species can be found in Brazil. As the world's largest tropical rain forest, the Amazon boasts an astonishing range of trees, many festooned with Tarzan-worthy vines and creepers. Among the most legendary species are wild rubber trees and Brazil nut trees, capable of producing 450 kilograms (1,000 pounds) of nuts in a year, along with rosewood and mahogany trees, whose beautiful hardwood is always much in demand for fine furniture. The extremely fertile Atlantic forest is also famous for other native woods, including jacaranda and *ipê*, with their bright purple and yellow blossoms.

Other Brazilian trees are more sought-after for their fruits than for their wood. Throughout the tropical zones of the coast and the interior, Brazilians depend on diverse varieties of local palms. The Amazon is renowned for many fruit-bearing species, particularly those that yield *pupunha* and the energy-packed açai. In Ceará and Maranhão, livelihoods depend on the *carnaúba* and *babaçu* palms, whose all-purpose fruits and fibers are used to make products that include wax, cooking oil, soap, rope, timber, and thatch. Alagoas and northern Bahia are lined with swaying plantations of coconut palms, while southern Bahia is where you'll find the *dendê* palm, whose bright orange oil is used in Bahian cuisine. In the Cerrado, the fruit of the *buriti* palm is also made into various delicacies.

Fruit trees are everywhere you go, even in cities. In the Amazon, you can feast on *cupuaçu*, *bacuri*, and *muriti*, while the Northeast is rife with mango,

© MICHAEL SOMMERS

Pineapples grow wild in Brazil.

FISH AND FOWL, GREAT AND SMALL

Whether you want to catch them, eat them, or merely admire them, Brazil's waters are filled with eye-catching and mouthwatering fish. Along the Atlantic coast, sunken galleons and protective reefs offer ideal opportunities for snorkeling and diving amid gaudily hued schools. Inland, the Amazon and the Pantanal together boast close to 3,000 species living in their rivers, lakes, and tributaries. On the small end of the scale are the dozens of species of infamous fanged piranhas. Then there is the regally red- and silver-scaled *pirarucu*, the king of freshwater fish, which can grow to lengths of 3 meters (10 feet) and weigh up to 200 kilograms (440 pounds) and is a favorite Amazonian delicacy.

Brazil is also home to a fantastic diversity of winged creatures, whose plumages are often as spectacular as a Carnaval *desfile* (parade). In the Amazon and Atlantic rain forests and, in particular, the Pantanal, you'll have plenty of opportunities to be awestruck by the Technicolor hues of *araras* (macaws), *papagaios* (parrots), and cartoon-like *tucanos* (toucans). Coastal Pará and Maranhão are ideal for viewing the *guará* (scarlet ibis), whose Day-Glo crimson finery is a consequence of its fondness for pink crustaceans.

Both the largest and smallest birds in the Americas reside in Brazil. The *ema* (rhea) is an ostrich-like flightless bird that can grow to the height of 1.5 meters (5 feet) and weigh 35 kilograms (77 pounds). With a twist on expected gender roles, males not only build nests and incubate eggs, but also raise chicks as well. Meanwhile, tiny iridescent *beija-flores* (hummingbirds)—which in Portuguese means "flower kisser"—measure as little as 6 centimeters (2.3 inches), weigh only 2 grams (0.07 ounces), and can be seen fluttering their aerodynamic wings throughout the country, including in cities where people often put out feeders for them.

papaya, *cajú* (cashew), *jaca* (jackfruit), *graviola, mangaba,* and guava trees. The Cerrado boasts exotic species such as *pequi, araticum,* and *cagaíta.* Bananas are ubiquitous, and there are many types, ranging from the tiny *banana nanica* (dwarf banana) to the immense *banana pacova,* which can measure up to 50 centimeters (20 inches). In southern Brazil, you can still glimpse the umbrella-shaped *araucárias,* a variety of pine tree whose nuts were much appreciated by local indigenous people back in the days when these trees were widespread.

Although you'll rarely find them in florists' shops (when buying flowers, Brazilians weirdly prefer to go with decidedly nontropical roses, carnations, and chrysanthemums), in the wild you'll be treated to more than 200 species of delicate and brightly colored orchids as well as bright red heliconias, birds of paradise, and glossy anthuriums. In the Amazon, the giant lilies that emerge from the platter-size pads of the *Victoria amazonica* are captivating because of their size and because they change color during each day of their three-day life span. Aside from the beauty of many Brazilian plants, their leaves and roots are used extensively for medicinal and cosmetic purposes.

Mammals

Brazil has an intriguing variety of exotic mammals. The largest creatures you might see—although they're extremely elusive—are cats such as jaguars and panthers. A far more common sight is the *capivara* (capybara), the world's biggest rodent. More like a giant guinea pig than a rat, *capivaras* are at home on land and in water and can grow to lengths of 1 meter (3.3 feet) and weigh up to 70 kilograms (155 pounds).

© MICHAEL SOMMERS

Many regions, such as the Pantanal are teeming with wildlife.

Lontras (otters) are common in rivers of the South and Southeast, while the rare *ariranha* (giant otter) inhabits the lakes and rivers of the Pantanal and the Amazon. *Antas* (tapirs) are long-snouted foraging creatures that can grow to the size of a pony. Also common in forests are *caititus* (peccaries), wild boars that can reach 1 meter (3.3 feet) in length and often travel in trampling herds of up to 50. *Tamanduás* (anteaters) are surreal-looking creatures with long snouts and even longer furry tails. They spend much of their days sucking up tens of thousands of ants with their sticky tongues. Another really odd-looking beast is the *preguiça* (sloth), which lives up to its name by doing little more than dozing in trees.

Of the world's 250 primate species, more than 70 are found in Brazil. Many of these are actually unique to the country. *Macacos* or *micos* (monkeys) are a common sight, even in major cities. Cute, tuft-headed *macaco-pregos* (capuchin monkeys) are widespread throughout Brazil, including in Rio's Floresta da Tijuca.

In terms of sea mammals, Brazil's Atlantic coast is home to seven species of whales including southern right whales (in Santa Catarina) and humpback whales (in Bahia). One of the best places in the world for viewing vast schools of dolphins is on the island of Fernando de Noronha, off the coast of Pernambuco.

Of course, the first thing that comes to mind when one hears the words *Brazil* and *reptiles* together in the same sentence is the anaconda. Hero of trashy Amazonian terror movies, the anaconda does indeed live up to its fearful reputation. Adults can grow to well over 10 meters (33 feet) in length, and many live to be more than 20 years old. Because of their size, anacondas have no predators (aside from humans in search of snakeskin), so they aren't shy about wrapping themselves around large prey and squeezing them to death before swallowing them whole (this includes people, although very

JEITO BRASILEIRO (THE BRAZILIAN WAY)

Dar um jeito or *um jeitinho* is a common Brazilian expression that sums up a quintessentially Brazilian philosophy as well as an art form and a way of life. Literally (and inadequately) translated, it means "give a way," which doesn't begin to do justice to the rich and subtle inferences the expression embraces. *Dar um jeito* is a Brazilian's typical recourse when confronted with the many *pepinos* (problems, but literally "cucumbers") that daily life throws in the way. When faced with an awkward situation or a difficult problem, Brazilians rarely confront it head on—usually a futile tactic since the *pepino* is often the result of inflexible and sometimes absurd rules or government bureaucracy. Instead, they rely on a wide range of indirect *jeitos* or strategies, among them diplomacy, craftiness, flexibility, and charm, to get around an obstacle or extricate themselves from a predicament. The whole point is not to lose your cool and make a big scene, which Brazilians, a nonconfrontational people, only resort to in extremes. When they do, it's known as *um escândalo* and involves an impressive display of melodrama.

rarely). While it's rare to come across poisonous *cobras* (snakes), which usually only attack when threatened, there are quite a few such varieties, including *víboras* (vipers), *cascavéis* (rattlesnakes), and *cobras coral* (coral snakes).

Brazil possesses several species of *jacarés* (the term used for both alligators and caimans). In the Pantanal, you'll encounter *jacarés-do-Pantanal* (Paraguayan caiman) everywhere, and probably even eat a couple as well—if you're up to it, the meat is surprisingly tender.

Along the Atlantic coast, five species of formerly endangered *tartarugas marinhas* (sea turtles) are now thriving thanks to the creation of Projeto Tamar, a national project aimed at saving the turtles from humans who once hunted them for their shells and eggs.

Social Climate

Brazilians are universally famed for being welcoming, affectionate, good-natured, and fun loving, and upon arriving in Brazil, you'll find they live up to their reputation and then some. In truth, there are times when living in Brazil—with all the chaos and corruption, bureaucracy and lack of efficiency—can really get you down. The saving grace is Brazilians themselves, who will usually go way out of their way to lend a hand, suggest someone who knows someone who knows someone who can *dar um jeito* (literally "give a way," find a solution), or offer heartfelt sympathy at your trials over an icy beer (or four). The truth is that in North America people rely on authorities and institutions, but in Brazil such entities have traditionally proven corrupt or inefficient.

In Brazil, personal relations are extremely important. Brazilian society places much more emphasis on family, community, and groups than North America where the individual rules and where individual rights are enshrined by law; they are in Brazil as well, but there are glaring contradictions between theory and practice. In Brazil, it's almost impossible to get by without a little help from your friends. This explains why Brazilians are inevitably such extroverted, social animals, who love doing things en masse and are often hilariously horrified at the thought of traveling, eating dinner, or going to a movie alone. It's not just a question of the more, the merrier; it's also one of survival. As a North American, it's easy to feel incredibly enchanted by the warmth and inclusiveness of Brazilians. At the same time, for foreigners who prize solitude, privacy, and personal space, Brazilians' intense emphasis on the social might take some getting used to.

IMMIGRATION

Like the United States and Canada, Brazil has a long history of welcoming immigrants from all over the world. In fact, Brazil was built by immigrants—from Portugal and Africa during colonial times, followed by Italy, Germany, Spain and other Europeans in the 19th and early 20th centuries as well as Japanese, Lebanese and Syrians, and more recently migrants from South American neighbors such as Bolivia.

Five centuries of immigration have shaped Brazilian society and culture into one of the richest and most diverse on the planet. Bahia's capital of Salvador, for example, is the city with the second largest population of African descent after Lagos. São Paulo—60 percent of whose population can claim some Italian ancestry—is a city where the pizza rivals that munched upon in Rome (this according to Italians). Brazil also boasts the largest Japanese and Lebanese communities outside of their respective countries.

In recent decades, however, immigration to Brazil all but ground to a halt because of the political and economic turbulence that plagued the nation during much of the late 20th century. As a result, today foreigners represent a mere 1 percent of Brazil's workforce, down from 7 percent at the turn of the 20th century.

In the last several years, however, this trend has begun to change as a result of Brazil's

© MICHAEL SOMMERS

Brazil has the largest Japanese community outside of Japan.

THE NEW IMMIGRANTS

Although the number of immigrants to Brazil might be small, their number has been increasing exponentially. According to the most recent Brazilian Census carried out by the IBGE, between 2000 and 2010, the number of immigrants living in Brazil increased by 87 percent. In 2010, the largest number of foreign immigrants came from the United States. The almost 52,000 who immigrated to Brazil that year were a major increase from 2000, when only 16,695 American immigrants moved to Brazil.

States with the Most Immigrants
São Paulo (81,682)
Paraná (39,120)

Minas Gerais (27,727)
Rio de Janeiro (19,093)
Goiás (12,444)

Regions with the Most Immigrants
Southeast (62,039)
South (47,944)
Central-West (17,667)
Northeast (8,456)
North (7,538)

Countries of Origin
United States (51,933)
Japan (41,417)
Paraguay (24,666)
Portugal (21,376)
Bolivia (15,753)

growing economy coupled with a severe lack of skilled workers and the economic crises wreaking havoc (and unemployment) in the United States and Europe. Between 2006 and 2011, the number of work permits granted to foreign professionals tripled from 25,400 to 70,524. In 2011, China, which is currently Brazil's leading trade partner and main foreign investor, was the largest source of work visas, followed by the United States, Portugal, France, and Spain.

Moreover, in 2011, Brazil reprised its traditional role as a recipient country: For the first time in two decades the number of foreign immigrants entering Brazil was larger than the number of Brazilians leaving the country. Between 2010 and 2011 alone, the number of foreign-born residents increased by 50 percent. By the end of 2011, there were 2 million foreign nationals living legally in Brazil (and an estimated 600,000 undocumented foreigners). This is still minuscule when compared to neighboring Argentina, where legal foreign residents represent 14 percent of the population, and to the United States, where they account for 13 percent.

BRAZIL AND FOREIGNERS

Even though Brazil doesn't receive as many immigrants as the United States and Canada, Brazilians themselves are incredibly welcoming to foreigners—much more so, in a sense, than their North American counterparts (for instance, there is no anti-immigrant stance or movement in the country).

Brazilians are proud of their country, although they're not given to jingoism. That said, they're also understandably sensitive to criticism. Although they can dish it out—often hilariously—they can't always take it, especially coming from sometimes insensitive gringos who complain about the way things are, or aren't, done here compared with "back home."

Traditionally, Brazil had always been a country in which First World and Third World coexisted, but it was always the Third World aspects that got all the press and

LIFE AS A GRINGO

Brazilians routinely refer to all foreigners as "gringos" although it tends to apply more the fairer you are and the worse your Portuguese is. While North Americans may feel the term is pejorative, more often than not it's actually quite affectionate (many of my friends refer to me fondly as "my gringo" or "our gringo"). Gringos are invariably treated kindly by Brazilians, and if you speak Portuguese, you'll usually be accepted on equal terms as *brasileiros*.

In some contexts, however, being a gringo will set you apart from the crowd because there is a (somewhat valid) stereotype that gringos who come to Brazil are richer and more educated than your average Brazilians. In a few instances, this may result in your getting preferential treatment over Brazilians based merely on your gringo-ness (which can be either useful or embarrassing). In other instances, this could result in making you a target for thieves or scammers who may think that you're not only loaded, but naïve or easy to take advantage of.

No matter how long you live in Brazil and how assimilated you become, you'll likely never kick your "gringo" identity. However, take comfort from the fact that once you've absorbed a sufficient degree of language and culture, you'll no longer feel like a *"gringo burro"* (dumb gringo), but a *"gringo inteligente."*

defined the country on the global stage. Over the last 10 years, however, Brazil has made enormous strides. Even though poverty and its trappings still exist on a large scale, Brazilians have a new sense of pride in Brazil's achievements and promise. They no longer see their country as Third World and react defensively to those who do—particularly gringos and especially Americans. The truth is that Brazilians innately have a pretty strong anti-American streak. It's hard to blame them considering the history of U.S. paternalism and interventionism in Latin America, specifically the fact that the U.S. government was complicit in the 1964 coup that resulted in a brutal military dictatorship that lasted a quarter century. The United States' frequently heavy-handed foreign policy—particularly during the Bush years—didn't do anything to burnish the United States' reputation. Brazilians were uniformly repulsed by Bush and critical of the invasion of Iraq. This tarnished U.S. image, however, has improved considerably during the Obama years. Brazilians greeted the election of the United States' first black president with all the joy of a World Cup win. Increasing U.S. recognition of Brazil's role on the global stage has also calmed antipathy considerably.

On the flip side, Brazilians (specifically middle- and upper-class ones) are fascinated by what Americans and American media think of Brazil (whenever Brazil makes headlines in major U.S. media, it's reported in major Brazilian media as well). They are also fascinated with American pop culture, not to mention consumer goods and gadgets (Brazilian tourist/shoppers spend more money per capita on shopping sprees in the United States than any other nationality). Ultimately, however, critical views of the U.S. government and society rarely impact the way individual Americans are treated in Brazil. When it comes to personal relations, Brazilians will take pains to adopt you as one of them. Before long, they'll be paying you the ultimate compliment by calling you a *brasileiro adotivo* (an adoptive Brazilian).

HISTORY, GOVERNMENT, AND ECONOMY

History

With alternating degrees of hope and cynicism, Brazilians have long referred to their country as the *"país do futuro"* (country of the future). However, Brazil's complex identity has been shaped by a fascinating past unlike that of any other nation in the Americas.

PREHISTORY

The verdict is still unclear as to when and from where the first indigenous populations arrived in South America. Dates vary from 10,000 to 30,000 years ago, and origins range from Asia (via a land bridge over the Bering Sea) to Africa (via canoe). Regardless of these conflicting theories, the indigenous Brazilian people, commonly referred to as *índios* (Indians), never developed the sophisticated cultures of their Andean neighbors, the Incas.

When the first Portuguese explorers arrived in 1500, an estimated 5 million indigenous people lived in Brazil. Scattered in small groups and speaking well over

© MICHAEL SOMMERS

100 languages, most lived in villages, where they survived by hunting, fishing, and gathering as well as cultivating crops such as corn and manioc. One of the main groups was the Tupi-Guarani, a seminomadic people who originally spread out from the Amazon Basin, migrating south and east to the coast. It was the fierce Tupi that greeted the first Portuguese navigators and their crew.

PORTUGUESE CONQUEST

In 1500, Portuguese explorer Pedro Álvares Cabral had set sail from Portugal in search of a western trade route to India. On April 22, his fleet of 13 ships arrived on the southern coast of Bahia, where Porto Seguro now lies. Clambering ashore, the Portuguese planted a cross at the spot they baptized Terra da Vera Cruz (Land of the True Cross). They spent the next 10 days exchanging trinkets with the local Tupi and evaluating the prospects of this new land, which the native people referred to as *Pindorama* (Land of Palms). The only potential spoil that sparked their interest was a native tree with a hard, reddish-hued wood. When the expedition returned to Portugal, word got out about this exotic timber, known as *pau brasil—pau* means "wood" and *brasil* is said to be a derivation of *brasa*, a red, hot coal. It turned out that the wood yielded a deep crimson dye that was highly coveted by European weaving factories. Over the next few decades, ambitious traders sailed across the Atlantic to the land of the *brasil* wood, which soon became shortened to "Brasil."

Portugal only officially became interested in staking its claim to Brazil when French and Spanish merchants began sniffing around the new territory. In 1549, King João III named Tomé de Sousa as the first governor-general of Brazil. Accompanied by a force of soldiers, Jesuit priests, ex-convicts, and bureaucrats, Sousa arrived in Salvador da Bahia that same year and claimed the city as the capital of the Brazilian colony.

SUGAR AND SLAVERY

By the mid-1500s, *pau brasil* supplies were already drying up. However, in Pernambuco and Bahia, sugarcane had been successfully introduced to the rolling coastal hills. Tomé de Sousa incentivized the cultivation of sugar, which at the time was an exorbitantly expensive rarity in Europe. By the mid-1500s, vast plantations were springing up throughout Brazil's Northeast. To keep up with demand, Portugal brought millions of African slaves to the colony, who were forced to work grueling 16- to 17-hour days.

Sugar became the number one source of profits for the Portuguese crown and laid the foundations for the organization of Brazil's economy as well as its society. While

© MICHAEL SOMMERS

Portugal's important cultural legacy is evident throughout Brazil.

LOSS OF APPETITE

Early European travelers to Brazil were quite enthralled with the "noble savages" they encountered and chronicled their lifestyles in manners both factual and fictional. Fact proved stranger than fiction in the case of German mercenary Hans Staden. Upon being captured by a Tupi group in 1552, Staden was treated with great hospitality: He was plied with food in preparation of a great banquet – where a plumper version of himself was to be the main course. Such a fate was in keeping with Tupi tradition, that by ritually devouring one's enemies, one could absorb their courage. However, when Staden was finally ready to become stew, he started to cry; his unwarrior-like display of tears so disgusted his Tupi hosts that they released him. Although wimpy in the eyes of his captors, Staden wrote a tell-all memoir of his adventures, which became a major best seller back in Europe and considerably raised curiosity about the vast new land across the ocean.

plantation owners alternated between paternalism and brutality toward slaves, they had no compunction about fornicating with them, which resulted in the interracial mixing of Brazil's population. In modern times, this gave rise to the myth of Brazil as a country of racial harmony, but it also allowed for the perseverance of a subtle but deeply rooted racism and glaring socioeconomic inequality that continue to this day.

JESUITS AND *BANDEIRANTES*

Jesuit missionaries, who had tight connections with the Portuguese crown, were the first to work their way deep into the unknown Brazilian interior. Intent on converting and subjugating the local indigenous population, they headed west into the Amazon and south toward the Pampas. Throughout the 1600s, Jesuit influence in Brazil grew enormously. While some Jesuits exploited the native people, using them as unpaid labor and exposing them to fatal diseases, others protected them from Portuguese settlers intent on enslaving the "savages."

Equally responsible for the opening up of Brazil's vast interior were the *bandeirantes*. Rough-and-ready bands of explorers in search of riches and índios (Indians) to enslave, *bandeirantes* first began making expeditions from São Paulo into the hinterlands in the early 17th century. The distances they covered were immense, and their discoveries filled in the contours of the Brazilian map.

In 1695, a small group of *bandeirantes* happened upon some glittering nuggets in a river at the spot that is now Sabará. The find kicked off the biggest gold rush the New World had known up until that time. Although deposits were found as far west as Goiás and Mato Grosso, most of the glitter was concentrated in the central mountainous region that came to be known as Minas Gerais (General Mines). During the boom years, 1700–1750, hundreds of thousands of fortune hunters descended on the region. Many died poor of hunger and disease; others grew filthy rich. Overnight, precarious miners' outposts blossomed into wealthy mining towns such as Ouro Preto and São João del Rei. Vast numbers of slaves were brought in to work the mines, where conditions proved worse than in the sugarcane fields.

The indebted Portuguese crown was thrilled with the discovery of gold. Built by slaves, roads led through the mountains of Minas and down to the ports of Rio de

© MICHAEL SOMMERS

Brazil's first capital was Salvador.

Janeiro and Paraty, where the gold was then shipped off to Lisbon. In fact, it was Rio's newfound importance as a strategic maritime port that elevated the filthy backwater town on the shores of Guanabara Bay to capital of Brazil, a title it usurped from Salvador in 1763. The move signaled the beginning of the end of northeastern Brazil's economic and political supremacy in favor of the southeastern "triangle" formed by Minas Gerais, Rio de Janeiro, and São Paulo.

INDEPENDENCE

The gold boom was explosive but fleeting. By the mid-1700s the precious metal was increasingly hard to find. But the Portuguese crown still insisted on taxing and appropriating every last nugget. Gradually, Brazilian settlers' anger rose and culminated in the revolt known as the Inconfidência Mineira. Led by an Ouro Preto dentist known as Tiradentes (Tooth Puller), a dozen outraged Mineiro citizens conspired to rise up against the Portuguese. After their plans were discovered, all plotters were exiled except Tiradentes who was hung in public in Rio before having his severed body parts paraded around Ouro Preto as a warning to future rebels. The horrific measures only succeeded in transforming Tiradentes into a national hero and fanning the flames of independence. Indeed, the Inconfidência Mineira was only one of many popular revolts that erupted throughout the 18th century as settlers who increasingly considered themselves native Brazilians chafed under the authority of Portugal and its colonial administrators.

While citizens of all other South American nations waged battles against their colonial oppressors to achieve independence, Brazil's road to independence took a surprising and unlikely turn. In 1807, having already conquered most of Europe, Napoleon had his eye on Portugal. As the French emperor's troops descended on Lisbon, King

© MICHAEL SOMMERS

The *bandeirantes* are memorialized with a monument in São Paulo.

João VI of Portugal and his entire court fled across the ocean to Brazil. In 1808, the king and his royal retinue of 15,000 disembarked in Rio de Janeiro, which immediately became the new capital of the Portuguese empire. The court's presence transformed Rio from a rough mosquito-infested colonial town into a thriving and increasingly elegant capital with grand avenues, parks, and palaces. João VI himself was so taken with his tropical court that he was loath to relinquish it, even after the English defeated Napoleon. When he finally returned to Portugal in 1621 to quell a popular uprising, he left his son Pedro in charge as Prince Regent of Brazil.

Like his new Brazilian subjects, young Pedro quickly grew fed up with having to comply with rules set down by Portugal. This rebellious stance came to a head in 1822. On September 7, Pedro was getting ready to ride his horse on the shores of the Ipiranga River, near São Paulo, when a messenger arrived with a handful of letters from Lisbon. The demands of the Portuguese court so angered him that he uttered the famous cry "Independence or death!" thus declaring Brazil independent. On December 1, Pedro crowned himself Dom Pedro I and became the first and only New World emperor.

EMPIRE

Pedro I's imperial reign was short-lived. In 1824, he presided over the creation of Brazil's first constitution and, in theory, accepted his status as constitutional monarch. In practice, just as he had refused to cooperate with Portugal's government, he wouldn't share power with Brazilian members of parliament. In 1831, he abdicated and returned to Portugal, leaving Brazil in the hands of his five-year-old son Pedro II. Without a strong leader in charge, over the next decade revolts broke out throughout the country, from Pará and Maranhão in the north to Rio Grande do Sul. Brazilians fought against Portuguese loyalists, slaves rebelled against their masters, and the poor rose up against the privileges of wealthy landowners.

Faced with the risk of the country being torn apart, Pedro II was quickly crowned emperor in 1840. Although only 14, Dom Pedro II was a highly intelligent, progressive, and judicious leader who was admired by both the conservative elite and the more liberal republicans. His authority quickly quelled the regional uprisings, and under his long reign Brazil enjoyed growth and stability. During this time, the Southeast definitively eclipsed the Northeast in importance, spurred on by Rio's political and cultural relevance and the beginning of the lucrative coffee boom, which brought a flood of European immigrants to the fertile hills of Rio de Janeiro, São Paulo, and Paraná as well as to the cities of the South.

ABOLITION OF SLAVERY

A main reason for the demise of the Northeast was slavery, or rather, its end. Since Brazil's earliest days as a colony, an estimated 5 million slaves had been transported across the Atlantic from Africa—more than 10 times the number that were shipped to the United States. Despite the cruel punishments they faced, many slaves revolted. Countless others escaped. Throughout Brazil, the fugitives established isolated communities known as *quilombos*. Although they lived a bare subsistence, many were able to preserve the religious and cultural traditions of their African ancestors, some of which survive to this day.

It wasn't until 1888 that Pedro II's daughter Princesa Isabel signed the Lei Áurea, giving Brazil the dubious distinction of being the last of the New World nations to ban slavery. The end of slavery had several major repercussions: It brought about the demise of the northeastern sugar- and cotton-plantation economies and caused the region (and its landowning elite) to enter a long period of decadence that would take a century to recuperate from. It also created a vast population of free but poor and uneducated black Brazilians, who had to fend for themselves and find work, a phenomenon that often sadly led to a life of "paid" slavery.

Politically, abolition was the final straw that broke the Brazilian empire. For some time, fueled by Europe's republican tendencies, Brazil's growing urban intellectual classes had been clamoring for the end of the monarchy. Increasingly, Pedro II's staunchest defenders had been the conservative landowning elite. But when he had the gall to end slavery, they too turned their backs on him. The final nail in the empire's coffin was the ill-fated Paraguay War (1865–1870), in which Brazil, Argentina, and Uruguay ganged up on their puny but fierce neighbor Paraguay. Although they practically eliminated the male population of Paraguay, the powerful allies didn't emerge unscathed from battle. Brazil lost 100,000 men and racked up serious debts, and Pedro II lost the support of the military. In 1889, a group of army officers, led by Marechal (Marshall) Manuel Deodoro da Fonseca, staged a bloodless coup d'état. Dom Pedro II returned to Europe, where he died two years later in Paris.

REPUBLIC

Although the idea had been to install a liberal republic, Deodoro preferred to become the nation's first of many military dictators. Within weeks, however, he proved so incompetent that not even the military would back him, and he was forced to step down. His deputy, Marechal Floriano Peixoto, was even worse. After he too was forced to resign, Brazil finally got its first democratically elected president in the person of Prudente de Morais.

The first Brazilian republic (1890–1930) coincided with a period of economic boom spurred on by two major cash crops: coffee and rubber. By 1890, coffee represented two-thirds of Brazil's exports and was responsible for propelling the small town of São Paulo into a thriving city that gradually became the economic hub of Brazil. Coffee barons built lavish mansions along the country lane that would gradually morph into Avenida Paulista. They also wisely invested in industry (initially textiles), foreseeing the day that Brazil's coffee boom might go bust.

Like São Paulo, Minas Gerais boasted a large population and thriving economy. Although coffee grew in Minas's lush hills, the richest and most powerful interests were the landowners who raised dairy cows. Together with São Paulo's coffee barons, they formed a powerful elite and became so influential in national government that Brazilian politics came to be defined as the system of *café com leite* (coffee with milk), an allusion to the fact that not only did these local interests dominate all policies but that all presidencies during this period alternated between cronies from São Paulo and Minas.

GETÚLIO VARGAS AND THE ESTADO NOVO

Dissatisfaction with *café com leite* politics came to a head in 1930. The Great Depression knocked the bottom out of the coffee market. To save the coffee elite from ruin, the government spent millions buying coffee at a fixed rate, only to burn the harvest for lack of foreign buyers. Workers and leaders from other parts of the country were outraged. Violent revolts broke out in the Northeast, Rio, and Rio Grande do Sul, home

© MICHAEL SOMMERS

bust of Getúlio Vargas

of a charismatic and populist politician named Getúlio Vargas. When a military coup deposed the government, Vargas became Brazil's new president—for the next 15 years. An astute politician, fervent nationalist, and flamboyant populist, Vargas ushered in a new era. He jump-started Brazilian industry by nationalizing the burgeoning oil, steel, and electrical sectors. He endeared himself to the masses by creating a health and social welfare system. He implemented labor laws and a minimum wage and extended the right to vote to women. Vargas carried out these radical reforms by declaring himself dictator and establishing a regime known as the Estado Novo (New State), which went into effect in 1937. While democracy went into hiding, his centralized government broke the hold of the regional elite, and agriculture and industry thrived.

When World War II broke out, Brazil remained neutral, although Vargas flirted with both the Axis and the Allies. Vargas finally chose the Allied side in 1942, sending Brazilian soldiers to participate in the invasion of Italy. However, the contradiction between fighting for freedom abroad while running a fascist dictatorship at home proved difficult to justify. At the end of the war, military pressure convinced Vargas to relinquish his powers in 1945. Even so, Vargas always remained largely popular with the Brazilian people, who returned him to power in 1950—this time as a democratically elected president. Without his fascist powers to protect him, his tenure was marred by public accusations of corruption. The attacks against him escalated, and on the night of August 4, 1954, he went into his bedroom at the Palácio do Catete in Rio and shot himself through the heart after leaving a love letter–suicide note to the Brazilian people.

JK AND BRASÍLIA

Juscelino Kubitschek, popularly known as "JK," won the 1956 presidential elections by promising Brazilians the equivalent of 50 years of growth and change in 5 years. He set about making good on his promise by hiring a team of highly talented modernist architects, headed by Lucio Costa and Oscar Niemeyer, to build a utopian new Brazilian capital in the geographical heart of the nation. Kubitschek's ambitious goal was to open up Brazil's vast and deserted interior to settlement and development.

Before his term was over, the "bossa nova president" presided over the April 21, 1960, inauguration of the new capital, an event that was celebrated with much pomp. The only problem was the massive bill. The costs of building Brasília left the nation in serious debt, which would later play a part in the astronomic rates of inflation that gripped Brazil in the 1970s.

MILITARY RULE (1964-1985)

JK was succeeded by much lesser men. Neither Jânio Quadros (who lasted only six months in power) nor his vice president and successor, João Goulart, possessed the skill necessary to deal with rising inflation or resolve the growing social conflicts that pitted urban workers against factory owners and rural peasants against rich landowners. Moreover, with a Cold War fear of communism in the air, Goulart's leftist leanings terrified the Brazilian right, including the military. On March 31, 1964, with implicit backing of the U.S. government, led by a small group of right-wing generals, military troops carried out a quick and nonviolent coup. Goulart was deposed, and the generals set to work transforming Brazil into a military dictatorship. Humberto Castelo Branco became president—the first in a series of generals to lead the country by iron rule over the next quarter of a century. Congress was dissolved, political parties were banned, unions were outlawed, and the media was censored. The situation grew even more drastic when General Emílio Garrastazu Médici took over in 1969. The next five years proved to be the most brutal of Brazil's military regime. Thousands of people were arrested, jailed, tortured, and even killed for even the most indirect criticism, "subversive" political beliefs, or expression of ideas deemed unsuitable by the regime. Many leading artists and intellectuals went into exile during these years. Although Brazil's dictatorship was less hard-line than those of its neighbors Chile and Argentina, where hundreds of thousands were made to "disappear," there was widespread hatred of the military leaders, who were not only cruel but corrupt as well.

During the first decade of military rule, Brazil experienced phenomenal rates of economic growth that surpassed 10 percent a year. This period became known as the "Economic Miracle." Industry boomed, and an exodus of workers from the poor Northeast migrated en masse to the manufacturing hub of São Paulo, which grew to become Latin America's financial and economic powerhouse. While many found factory jobs and other low-wage employment, others clustered in shacks on the growing city outskirts. Indeed, as some Brazilians grew rich, far more remained miserable and these slums, known as favelas, began to mushroom in major cities.

The Economic Miracle came to a grinding halt with the 1973 oil crisis. By the beginning of the 1980s, as inflation soared and Brazilian currency took a nosedive, foreign investors started clamoring for Brazil to pay its enormous and constantly multiplying debts.

PERIOD OF *ABERTURA* (1979–1985)

Increasingly fed up with censorship, corruption scandals, and a crippled economy, Brazil's middle class and workers began to express widespread opposition to the military dictatorship. In São Paulo, a series of workers' strikes spread like wildfire. A leader for the illegal unions was a young worker from Pernambuco who had lost a finger in a factory accident: Luiz Inácio da Silva (who went by the nickname "Lula") was a fierce and charismatic figure. When the government sent troops to repress the striking workers, Lula and his colleagues stood their ground. The government was forced not only to back down but to legalize unions as well. Fearing mass revolts, President João Figueiredo also began to implement certain reforms, part of a gradual *"abertura"* (opening) process that would pave the way for Brazil's return to democratic rule. Censorship rules were relaxed, and political dissidents were allowed to return from exile. In 1982 the first democratic municipal and state elections were held, and in 1985 a highly respected Mineiro politician by the name of Tancredo Neves was elected Brazil's first civilian president in two decades, marking the beginning of a *Nova República* (New Republic).

RETURN OF DEMOCRACY

Tragedy struck the night before his inauguration ceremony when Tancredo Neves was rushed to the hospital with a bleeding stomach tumor. Although the tumor wasn't fatal, the hospital was. Neves caught septicemia, a bacterial infection that led to his death. After millions mourned him, they watched the televised swearing in of his vice president, José Sarney, an old-school and uninspiring former state governor from Maranhão. As Brazil's first new democratic president, Sarney quickly dashed Brazilians' hopes of a better future. Because of the ballooning foreign debt, inflation was so high that currencies were adopted and discarded with regularity. Meanwhile, an uncensored press was free to report the endless string of financial scandals that sullied the government's reputation and filled struggling Brazilians with disgust.

Things only got worse with the election of Sarney's successor: a pretty-boy millionaire and karate champ named Fernando Collor de Mello. Collor's solution to controlling hyperinflation was to freeze Brazilians' bank accounts. Feelings of outrage spread throughout the populace when it came to light that Collor and his cronies had been siphoning billions of dollars in public money into private accounts. The scandal was so great that Congress began impeachment proceedings.

Forced to step down in 1992, Collor was replaced by his vice president, Itamar Franco, a weak figure who nonetheless made the inspired decision to select as his finance minister a savvy economist named Fernando Henrique Cardoso. Known popularly as "FHC," Cardoso was a widely respected São Paulo sociologist with leftist leanings who went into exile during the military dictatorship. By the time he joined Franco's government, his politics had migrated to the center-right, as had his economics. FHC took on Brazil's floundering economy by implementing the *Plano Real* (Real Plan) in 1994. By creating a new currency, the *real,* and tying its value to the U.S. dollar, Cardoso finally brought runaway inflation to a grinding halt for the first time in decades. When elections were held the following year, he easily defeated his rival, Lula.

With FHC as president for the next eight years (1994–2002), the New Republic finally had its first serious and competent leader. Inflation remained low, and the economy began to grow in leaps and bounds, spurred on by rampant privatization of corrupt and inefficient public companies, the opening up of Brazil's frontiers to foreign capital and interests, and the relaxation of importation barriers. Massive economic reforms were accompanied by the beginnings of much-needed political and social reforms with particular focus on the critical areas of health and education. However, the eternally gaping distance between Brazil's haves and have-nots was hardly bridged at all. Moreover, during FHC's second presidential term, a series of large-scale corruption scandals once again revealed the fundamentally rotten state of Brazil's political and justice systems.

THE PT, LULA, AND DILMA

After competing and being narrowly defeated in every presidential election since 1990, in 2001 the charismatic leader of the Partido dos Trabalhadores (PT), Luiz Inácio "Lula" da Silva, finally triumphed. Lula's victory was truly a watershed moment in Brazil's political history. In a country that for 500 years had been ruled by members of the wealthy elite, it was nothing short of miraculous that a poor boy from the drought-ridden Sertão of Pernambuco, without a university education, should rise to the nation's most powerful position.

In the heady early months of his mandate, the popular and populist soccer-playing and *churrasco*-eating president was greeted as something of a messiah. Despite his past reputation for firebrand Marxist rhetoric, Lula stayed the central course mapped out by his predecessor. Economically, he continued to steer Brazil on the road to increasing globalization. More importantly, his government made headway in addressing some of Brazil's glaring social disparities. Increasing numbers of children were able to attend school with the aid of subsidies paid to parents. And for the first time, the standard of living of Brazil's poor finally rose as minimum wage increased to historic highs, interest rates fell to historic lows, and credit (and credit cards) became easily available to all Brazilians who wanted to buy homes or start small businesses. The economic situation improved the most in the Northeast and North, which were traditionally the most neglected of Brazil's regions.

On the downside, although the PT was revered for its socialist ideals and integrity during its 20-year role as the main opposition party to successive governments, once it came to power it wasn't long before scandals began to erupt. Despite the damage done to the party, Lula was elected to a second presidential term in November 2006, and when he finally left office at the end of 2010 he boasted a historic approval rating of 83 percent.

It was largely due to Lula's immense popularity that Dilma Rousseff, his chief of staff and handpicked successor, was elected Brazil's first woman president in November 2010, with the promise that she would continue to steer Brazil along the successful path toward increased economic prosperity and social equality. Less charismatic and more technocratic than Lula, "Dilma"—a former member of an underground military group who was tortured during the military dictatorship—hails from the state of Minas Gerais, but cut her political teeth in Rio Grande do Sul, where she was state minister of energy. One major focus of her new government is to improve education, an area considered a major obstacle to Brazil really taking off.

To date, Brazil has come a long way toward becoming a mature and stable democracy with a robust economy. Within Latin America, Brazil has emerged as a regional leader and an inspiration to other nations. Meanwhile, its self-sufficiency in oil, its vanguard position in terms of biodiesels, and its increasingly important role as a supplier of raw and finished products have propelled Brazil onto the world stage. It is routinely compared with other emerging powers such as China and India, although since 2011, its growth rates have been far less spectacular than those of the two other BRIC nations. At home, major problems still exist, particularly in terms of public safety, quality of public health and education, corruption, and poverty. Despite some improvements, much-needed reforms to the justice and political systems are needed to end the culture of impunity that reigns at all levels and prevents Brazil from living up to its potential and evolving into a truly significant global player. However, obstacles aside, it can safely be said that at no other time in history have the reality of Brazil's present and the promise of this *país do futuro* appeared so closely aligned.

Government

The Federal Republic of Brazil is a democratic system of government that resembles the federal system in the United States. The elected president is both the head of state and the head of the federal government. Brazil's current constitution dates from 1988.

ORGANIZATION

Brazil's national government consists of three branches: the executive, the legislative, and the judiciary. The head of the executive branch is the President of the Republic, who is elected to office by universal suffrage. Voting is done by an extremely high-tech computerized ballot system, in which error or fraud is almost impossible.

Brazil's legislative power is concentrated in the hands of the Congresso (National Congress), which consists of two houses: The Câmara dos Deputados (Chamber of Deputies) and the Senado (Senate). The Chamber of Deputies seats 513 deputies representing each of the Brazilian states in numbers proportional to their populations. Deputies are elected by popular vote for terms of four years. The Senate seats

© MICHAEL SOMMERS

Palácio do Planalto, where the President of the Republic works

81 senators—three for each of Brazil's 26 states and three for the Federal District of Brasília. Senators are elected for terms of eight years. Both deputies and senators can run for reelection as many times as they want.

The judiciary is headed by the Supremo Tribunal Federal (Federal Supreme Court), which is the highest court in the land. Its main headquarters are in Brasília, but the court's jurisdiction extends throughout the country. Its 11 judges are appointed for life by the president on approval from a Senate majority; judges in state courts are also appointed for life.

The Economy

In terms of natural resources, Brazil has always been incredibly wealthy. Until the 20th century, the economy was based on a series of cycles that exploited a single export commodity: brazilwood in the 16th century; sugarcane in the 16th and 17th centuries; gold, silver, and gemstones in the 18th century; and finally coffee and rubber in the 19th century. Apart from these boom-and-bust cycles, agriculture and raising cattle were constant activities, but both were mainly limited to local consumption. Industrialization began in the early 20th century but didn't really kick in until the 1950s, which coincided with the beginnings of Brazil's major automobile, petrochemical, and steel industries.

After a difficult sink-or-swim period that accompanied the opening up of the economy to the world in the mid-1980s, Brazil has enjoyed robust growth rates. At the beginning of 2012, the country ranked as the world's sixth largest economy in terms

POLITICAL PARTIES

Brazil's party system is fairly chaotic to an outsider. Parties are created and disappear all the time, and candidates easily and opportunistically switch from one to another without any compunction (recent reforms have tried to limit this habit). Both the party names and more commonly used acronyms are confusing to keep track of, even for Brazilians. Many have no ideological affiliation whatsoever. There are, however, a few main parties whose delegates usually compete for major positions. Presently, after years of being the country's main opposition party, the traditionally left-wing Partido dos Trabalhadores (Workers' Party), or PT, wields power in the federal government. Other major parties that hover around the center and center-right include the Partido do Movimento Democrático Brasileiro (Brazilian Democratic Movement Party), or PMDB; the Partido da Social Democrácia Brasileira (Brazilian Social Democracy Party), or PSDB; and the Democratas (Democrats) or DEM. Currently, governing Brazil is all about making strategic alliances with members of other parties in order to pass or defeat legislation. In general, reaching a consensus involves enormous amounts of time and energy (not to mention bribes—in the form of favors or money).

Ironically, in spite of the many scandals and cover-ups, in some ways the operation of the Brazilian Congress is extremely transparent. In theory, any Brazilian or visiting foreigner can sit in on the daily sessions in the Chamber of Deputies or Senate (you will often be amazed at the low attendance, particularly on a Friday). Moreover, Senate debates are broadcast live on a television station known as TV Senado. During major government scandals, this can make for quite dramatic viewing.

of GDP. Brazil's economy is larger than that of all other South American countries, and increasingly competitive, high-quality, and innovative Brazilian goods are steadily making their presence felt in international markets. As a result of its newfound clout, Brazil is able to go head-to-head with the United States and Europe during global trade talks. Rich in natural resources and capable of supplying most of its own needs in terms of food, primary resources, energy, and manufactured products, Brazil is extremely self-sufficient. Well prepared to withstand rising imported fuel and food costs that are proving devastating for other countries, Brazil also boasts a domestic market of 194 million people who have more disposable income to burn than ever before.

AGRICULTURE

Brazil's moderate climate coupled with its fertile soil and its immense territory makes it an ideal place for the cultivation of many crops. Brazil is a leading world producer of coffee, soybeans, rice, corn, sugarcane, cocoa, and citrus fruits such as limes and oranges (Brazil is the world's largest producer and exporter of OJ). It is also the planet's largest exporter of both chicken and beef. Brazilian land is some of the cheapest on the planet. In recent years, feeling crowded on their small plots, an increasing number of European farmers have invested in vast farms in the Central-West and North, where they are amazed at how fast crops grow. Indeed, over the last two decades agribusiness has become increasingly high-tech. As a result, today Brazil boasts one of the world's most productive agricultural sectors.

© MICHAEL SOMMERS

Brazil is currently the world's largest producer of beef.

INDUSTRY AND FINANCE

Brazilian industry, which is extremely diversified and well developed, currently accounts for around one-third of the country's GDP. Although major industrial activities have traditionally been concentrated in the Southeast (particularly São Paulo and Minas) and the South, in the last few years significant investments have been made in the Northeast and the North. Among Brazil's leading manufacturing industries are the automobile, aircraft, steel, mining, petrochemical, computer, and durable consumer goods sectors. Additionally, the country has a diverse and sophisticated service industry. Financial services are particularly well developed. São Paulo is Latin America's largest financial center, and its stock exchange, BM&F Bovespa, is the second largest in the Americas.

ENERGY

In late 2007, as rising oil prices sent the planet into panic, Brazil became the envy of many countries when the national oil giant Petrobras discovered a vast deepwater reserve off the coast of Rio de Janeiro. The so-called Tupi reserve is estimated to hold up to 8 billion barrels of oil and could lead to Brazil becoming the newest member of OPEC. However, it's not as if Brazil is beholden to the increasingly coveted fossil fuel. Following the first oil crisis of 1973, the government's visionary solution was to begin converting sugarcane into ethanol as a cheaper and nonpolluting fuel for all vehicles. Today, Brazil is the world's number one producer of sugarcane alcohol; all Brazilian vehicles are flex-fuel models that run on gas, alcohol, or a mixture of both.

TOURISM

In the last decade, Brazilian tourism has developed enormously. Since 2000 there has been a major spike in tourists from North America and especially Europe. The increase is largely due to the proliferation of domestic charters and air routes as well as a more sophisticated tourism infrastructure, even in unspoiled destinations far off the beaten path. However, much greater than the growth of international tourism has been the rise in the number of Brazilians themselves who are increasingly able to travel. Because of its endless natural attractions, Brazil's major tourism niche is ecotourism, which has the advantage of providing sustainable development. Particularly in the North and Northeast, tourism is playing a pivotal role in the development of local economies. In 2012, the sector is expected to account, directly and indirectly, for 8.6 percent of GDP and close to 8 percent of all jobs.

PEOPLE AND CULTURE

Life in Brazil has a lot of cons and pros, but you'll be hard-pressed to meet a foreigner who's spent any amount of time in the country and hasn't been favorably impressed, bowled over, and transformed by two of the best and most special things the country has going for it: its people and its culture. Although Brazilians share many traits of Brazilianness—being generally warm, good-humored, extroverted, and fun loving— they are an incredibly diverse bunch, and this diversity is reflected in one of the world's richest, most multifaceted, and continuously evolving cultures. A unifying character- istic of both Brazilians and their culture is the incredible ability to absorb external in- fluences while staying true to tradition: to mix things up, improvise, and create fresh and fascinating hybrids while keeping in touch with deep and complex roots.

Ethnicity, Race, and Class

Five centuries of comingling has resulted in a Brazilian population that is extremely diverse; the endless array of physical types is accompanied by an impressive openness toward biological, cultural, and religious differences.

INDIGENOUS GROUPS

When the Portuguese first arrived in Brazil in 1500, an estimated 5 million indigenous people, most belonging to the Tupi and Guarani groups, were inhabiting this vast territory. Today only about 817,000 of their descendants remain, representing 0.4 percent of the total population. Although indigenous groups live throughout Brazil, the majority reside in the least populated areas of the Central-West and the Amazon. The degree to which they have succeeded in preserving the traditions and lifestyles of their ancestors varies enormously. However, there are indeed small communities deep within the Amazon (protected by FUNAI, the federal agency of Indian affairs) that have never had contact with "civilization." Meanwhile, according to the results of a recent mitochondrial DNA survey, an estimated 60 million Brazilians can lay claim to at least one ancestor from an indigenous group. Brazilians who are descended from both indigenous groups and Europeans are known as *caboclos*.

AFRICANS

Between the early days of colonial Brazil and the abolition of slavery in 1888, it's estimated that more than 5 million slaves were brought to Brazil from Africa. The majority of them were Bantu peoples from Portugal's African colonies, such as Mozambique and Angola, as well as Yoruba from the western coastal region of what is now Benin and Nigeria. Although you'll find Brazilians of African descent throughout the country, the largest black communities are in Rio and the coastal areas of the Northeast, particularly Salvador, where 85 percent of the population boasts some African ancestry.

In the 2010 Census, for the first time ever, a majority of Brazilians—51 percent (or 97 million people)—defined themselves as *"preto"* (black) or *"pardo,"* meaning "colored" (*pardo* is actually a beige-caramel color). Due to a tradition of interracial mixing, most Brazilians are of mixed race, or *mulato;* Brazilians descended from a mixture of Africans and Indians are known as *cafuzos*. The varying shades of skin color and the way in which they are perceived and projected among different social milieus, however, is extremely complex and nuanced.

The official designation these days is *afro-descendente* or *afro-brasileiro*. Applicable to anyone with African origins, the designations afro-descendente and afro-brasileiro are based more on cultural identity than skin color. In terms of skin color, Brazilians have come up with hundreds of often extremely creative terms to designate themselves and confound racial categorization. These range from *preto retinto* (repainted black) and *jabuticaba* (a dark purple berry-like fruit), both of which refer to darker skin tones, to *jegue quando foge* (donkey when it runs away) and *formiga* (ant), on a somewhat lighter scale. Many of these euphemistic designations have their origin in a subtle yet deeply rooted racism that is still very much alive in Brazil. As a result, darker-skinned Brazilians sometimes try, often subconsciously, to *embranquecer* (to become more

© MICHAEL SOMMERS

eating traditional Afro-Bahian *vatapá* and *caruru*, in Salvador

white) by choosing a less-black identity for themselves. This phenomenon explains why only 8.2 percent of Afro-Brazilians refer to themselves as *"negro."* Instead, many mixed-race Brazilians refer to themselves as *"mulatos,"* or even *"mulatos claros"* (light-skinned *mulatos*).

EUROPEANS

The first Europeans to set foot in Brazil were the Portuguese who claimed the territory as their own. The next five centuries saw various waves of immigration; as a result the vast majority of Brazilians can lay claim to some Portuguese ancestry. It wasn't until the mid- to late 19th century that other Europeans began to arrive en masse in Brazil. Lured by the promise of vast tracts of fertile land, growing cities, and the beginnings of industry, large numbers of Italians, Germans, and Spaniards, followed by Poles and Ukrainians, flocked to the sparsely populated states of the South and to São Paulo. To this day the South has a distinctly European character, and blond hair and blue eyes are quite common.

REGIONALISM

While Brazil easily absorbs different peoples into its national melting pot, historical and geographical specificities have led to the creation of some very distinctive regional cultures. Despite the shared language, national references, and a strong national identity as "Brazilians," it's not uncommon for a Paulistano or Catarinense visiting Bahia or Maranhão, for example, to suffer from some degree of culture shock when confronted with differences in lifestyle, mentality, language, and cuisine. The reverse is equally true. While some of these regional stereotypes are somewhat cliché—and Brazilians themselves have great fun in conflating and exaggerating them for their own mirth—as with any stereotype, there often exists an underlying kernel of truth. As such, you will find that Bahians live up to their fame for being extremely laid-back, Paulistanos really are efficient workaholics, Cariocas have hedonism down to an art form, Mineiros are taciturn and reserved, Gaúchos exhibit fierce pride, and inhabitants of the northeastern Sertão possess a tough and rough-edged temperament that reflects their surroundings.

CLASS

As a consequence of its colonial system and slavery, Brazil has always been a very stratified society. Despite the recent advances of the last decade, Brazil has one of the world's worst distributions of income and widest gaps between its small group of insanely rich and large mass of very poor residents. Up until around 1990, approximately one-fifth of

RACISM IN BRAZIL

In the early 20th century, noted Brazilian anthropologist Gilberto Freyre gave rise to the official myth of Brazil as a paragon of racial harmony, whose spontaneous mixture of indigenous peoples, Africans, and Europeans stood as a utopian counterpoint to the polarized conflicts that characterized race relations in the United States. To this day, many Brazilians still believe in the myth. Foreigners are inevitably impressed by the easy mingling of people, regardless of color, and by the fact that so many African elements–samba, capoeira, Carnaval–have become icons of Brazilianness, espoused by all Brazilians.

However, dig deep enough and the myth begins to crack. Precisely what makes racism in Brazil so insidious is that, unlike racism in the United States, it isn't in your face–so it's easier to deny it exists and maintain a status quo in which the lighter your complexion, the more money, education, and opportunities you have. As you travel around in Brazil, take note of the politicians, the business leaders, the models and TV stars, the domestic tourists, the kids in private-school uniforms, and the people walking around in swanky neighborhoods, eating in upscale restaurants, staying in hotels, and flying on airplanes with you. The vast majority are white. However, you will notice that the majority of those living on the streets,

performing menial jobs, selling wares on the sidewalk, lining up for buses, or working as door attendants, cleaning persons, or nannies are inevitably black. If you're a white man in Brazil and you walk around with a black Brazilian female friend, the immediate conclusion is that you're a john and your friend is a prostitute (or else that she's a gold digger and you're rich husband material). A dark-skinned mother with a lighter-skinned child will often be assumed to be the child's nanny and treated as such.

The result of this type of racism isn't hate crimes or white supremacy groups. But the fact is that white Brazilians overwhelmingly dominate government, business, and the media. Two notable exceptions are soccer and music, where black Brazilians are revered. Fortunately, in recent years, change has finally begun to take root. The 1988 Constitution defined the practice of racism as a crime punishable by prison and, as president, Lula da Silva created the first Ministry of Racial Equality. In 2002, the Brazilian government made it mandatory to teach African and Afro-Brazilian history and culture as part of the universal school curriculum. Meanwhile, federal and state universities have been implementing quotas in an attempt to redress the fact that only 3 percent of black Brazilians have university degrees.

Brazilians (some 32 million)—many of whom lived in urban favelas or the Northeast interior—suffered from extreme poverty.

Over time, this socioeconomic inequality has led to subtle forms of segregation and discrimination. Wealthy and middle-class Brazilians live, work, and go to (private) school in centrally located, upscale neighborhoods overflowing with services and amenities. Meanwhile, poorer Brazilians live in favelas or peripheral neighborhoods, where basic services such as electricity and sanitation are nonexistent, security is precarious, and getting to low-paying menial jobs or public schools involves hours spent on crowded buses. Although everybody knows their place, a certain degree of paternalistic codependency defines the relationships between the classes. Traditionally, the fact that poorer Brazilians have not had access to government services, or even been aware of their rights as citizens, means that they have necessarily had to rely on their employers for assistance (in the case of financial or health emergencies, for example).

© MICHAEL SOMMERS

Favelas and high-rises in Rio dominate the skyline.

Meanwhile, upper-class Brazilians are dependent on poorer Brazilians to carry out all sorts of menial tasks that they feel are somehow beneath them to perform.

In between these two extremes of rich and poor lies the Brazilian middle class, which has been around since the 19th century, but which really became a force to be reckoned with in recent times. During the 2000s, Brazil's economic boom, coupled with the sweeping social policies put into place by the federal government, have seen a record number of Brazil's poor—an estimated 40 million—vault into the ranks of the middle class, also known as the C Class.

The C Class is one of five categories of an established socioeconomic classification system used to rank Brazilians according to their purchasing power. Whether you are considered to be a member of *Classe A* (the richest of the rich), *Classe B* (upper class), *Classe C* (middle class), *Classe D* (poor), and *Classe E* (extremely poor) depends on a variety of factors ranging from household income and ownership of property and key household items (electrical appliances, TVs) to level of education. Until very recently, the vast majority of Brazilians were in the D and E classes. However, this is no longer the case. For the first time ever, the majority of the population, more than 54 percent of all Brazilians—105 million—belong to the *Classe C,* which is driving the economy with its newfound purchasing power. Between 2005 and 2011 the ranks of the A and B classes have also swollen, from 15 percent to 22 percent, while the number of Brazilians in the D and E classes has shrunk, from 51 percent to 24 percent.

Conduct and Customs

Overall, Brazil is a very relaxed and casual place, although sometimes appearances can be deceiving. Underneath the freewheeling, sensual vibe, you'll sometimes find a conservative core. Brazil has the largest Roman Catholic population on the planet, and though the practice of Catholicism in Brazil is considered to be much less rigid and conservative than in other Latin American countries, many people—particularly in rural areas—take Catholic precepts, and those of the increasingly influential evangelical churches, very seriously.

DRESS CODES

In general, Brazilian dress codes are quite casual, particularly in coastal areas in which tropical temperatures and beach culture rule. However, don't make the mistake of confusing casual with slovenly or ratty (baggy, wrinkled, oversized clothes, sweats, and hole-riddled jeans don't go over that well; Brazilians actually *iron* their jeans!). Brazilians (especially women) may be firm believers in the adage "less is more," but regardless of social class, the "less" is inevitably quite stylish. As a rule, Brazilians take great care in terms of their appearance.

In some official buildings, among them the government buildings as well as municipal theaters and even libraries and archives, a certain degree of decorum applies: Women should eschew shorts or micro skirts, men should wear long pants, and flip-flops should be avoided. Such advice goes for business dress as well.

GREETINGS

Brazilians are extremely warm and friendly, and this is apparent in the way they greet each other. If you're meeting a woman—whether a long-lost friend or a stranger—you'll typically greet her with two kisses (*beijos*), one on each cheek. Women kiss men as well, but men greeting men shake hands. However, among younger men, as well as male friends and family members, back slapping, hugging (*abraços*), and other forms of friendly physical contact are quite common. When taking leave of each other, the same hugging and kissing rituals apply. If anything, they are much warmer on account of intimacies (and alcohol) shared.

SEXUALITY

Brazilians are naturally very affectionate, which can sometimes cause confusion for foreigners. A lot of friendly hugging and kissing goes on in public, and the sense of privacy and personal space is quite different than in North America. Brazilians not only love to be together (the American idea of needing time alone is a very foreign concept), but when they're together, they sit close and touch one another a great deal. In general, such behavior merely demonstrates a natural playfulness and lack of hang-ups about expressing affection, and you shouldn't treat it as sexual. When they want to be, Brazilians can be great and thoroughly effective flirts. To *jogar charme* ("cast one's charms") is often recommended, both seriously and tongue in cheek, as a way of getting something (a discount, a restaurant table, a favor).

Another thing about Brazilians is that they tend to be far less hung up about their

© MICHAEL SOMMERS

Public displays of affection are common in Brazil.

bodies (and revealing them in public) and about sexual matters in general than North Americans. However, it's a serious mistake to confuse sensuality with licentiousness or with an "anything goes" attitude. And looking sexy should not be equated with someone wanting to have sex.

WOMEN

Machismo has a strong hold in Brazil; however, it's generally a more tepid version than in other Latin American countries. Although Brazilians respect women, North American notions of political correctness have never caught on here. And the definition of what constitutes sexual harassment is far more lax in Brazil, although an increasing number of cities have a *delegacia de mulheres,* where an all-female staff specializes in crimes against women. Tragically, domestic violence against women is very common.

As a *gringa,* alone or with other women, you'll incite curiosity and inevitably receive some intense stares or come-ons, particularly in the North and the Northeast, where foreigners stand out more. For the most part, these are all harmless. The problem is that you might feel targeted if every time you go out for a drink (a woman by herself in a bar is a rarity) or to the beach, you're being bothered. If that's the case, try to join a group, or at least stick close to one (on the beach, for example). If saying a firm *"não"* and walking away isn't dissuading an insistent suitor, head immediately to a safe place such as a hotel or restaurant. Avoid deserted areas by day, and always take taxis at night.

FAMILY LIFE

In recent years, family life—along with the very definition of what constitutes a family—has undergone a small revolution in Brazil, and the changes are having a major impact on society, culture, and public policy. The nuclear family that was once the norm in Brazil is increasingly being replaced by an array of less conventional units, spurred on by the fact that marriage—both religious and civil—is losing ground to consensual unions in which partners live together. In 2010, only 43 percent of Brazilians were officially married while 36 percent were living in so-called "stable unions," based on 1996 legislation in which legal "family status" is conferred based on cohabitation. Close to 17 percent of couples are childless while 19 percent of all Brazilian families are headed by one parent only (in 88 percent of cases, the mother). Meanwhile, more Brazilians than ever before are now living alone, especially in big cities such as Rio (more than 16 percent of Cariocas are single dwellers).

Many of these changes are due to the ascent of women in Brazilian society. Increasingly, women are more educated and occupy more high-ranking and high-paying positions. This, in turn, has given them a lot more freedom. As a result, they are having far fewer children (1.86 in 2010 compared to 6 in 1960 and 4.4 in 1980) and having them much later. The majority of Brazilian women now opt to have children between the ages for 25 and 35, when they are more financially and emotionally prepared to raise them. As a result, teenage pregnancies have diminished considerably. Women also have more freedom to live with—or without—a man. Currently, 40 percent of all Brazilian families are headed by women.

GLBT

A lot of gay and lesbian foreigners associate Brazil with images of transvestites, Carnaval drag queens, and the muscle boys of Ipanema and allow themselves to think that Brazil is a very gay-friendly place. In reality, it is and it isn't. Brazil is more tolerant of gay men and lesbians than many other Latin American countries. You'll see both gay and lesbian romances played out on nightly *novelas,* and there are openly gay and lesbian celebrities (although they are hardly activists). Both Rio and São Paulo have intense gay scenes (though almost nonexistent lesbian scenes), with a wide range of bars, clubs, and even small neighborhood enclaves. Other major cities, such as Salvador, Recife, and Florianópolis, also have gay venues and gay beaches or portions of beaches. As with heterosexuals, gays and lesbians are also much more open about flirting in public. However, overall, the scene in Brazil is much more GLS (*gay, lesbica, e simpatisante;* that is, gay, lesbian, and "sympathetic") than exclusively gay and lesbian. Gay men, lesbians, and straight people mix much more, and the result is a less overt and politicized gay and lesbian presence than in North America or Europe.

Ultimately, many Brazilians don't mind if you're gay or lesbian, but they don't want to be reminded of it; i.e., they can deal with the fact of a same-sex romance in theory but don't want to see signs of it—public kissing or hand-holding—or hear you referring explicitly to your homosexuality. Two men or women living together, traveling together, or sharing a hotel room is not a problem, but the implicit agreement is that you're two friends, even if people may suspect you're not. Although the drag queen and flamboyant queen are very much an accepted part of the culture (during Carnaval, even in small rural towns, the most macho of men don wigs, miniskirts, and lipstick), there is a difference between spectacle and humor and the reality of day-to-day life. Brazil is ultimately a macho culture, and explicit signs of homosexuality can incite insults and even violence. Even in supposedly cosmopolitan cities such as Rio and São Paulo, violence against gays is not unheard of. In the more conservative Northeast and rural areas, it is even more common. Meanwhile, although gay marriage is a long way off (and violently opposed by conservative Christian groups, particularly those in government), gays and lesbians can take advantage of *união estável* (stable union) legislation that protects rights of all couples, regardless of gender and sexual orientation, that live together as a family unit. Among other benefits, *união estável* ensures that same-sex couples can share health insurance and inherit property and that a Brazilian can sponsor a foreign partner from overseas. In 2010, over 60,000 same-sex couples in Brazil were living together legally under the *união estável* regime.

Religion

Officially, Brazil is the world's largest Roman Catholic country in terms of population. In reality, however, Brazil's great talent for syncretism and diversity has resulted in a country with an amazing number of religions, sects, and communities.

ROMAN CATHOLICISM

In 2010, 65 percent of Brazilians identified themselves as Roman Catholic; a strong decline from 1991 when 83 percent of the population claimed Catholicism as their religion. Despite the strong presence of churches, endless references to *Deus* (God), various incarnations of Nossa Senhora (the Virgin), and prayers, promises, and processions offered up to saints, the majority of Brazilian Catholics aren't practicing. While Catholicism retains a strong presence in the collective culture, the Catholic Church in Brazil has a much less rigid reputation than in other Latin American countries.

Catholicism remains a strong presence in Brazilian culture.

PROTESTANTISM

Only 22 percent of Brazilians adhere to some form of Protestantism, but their numbers are increasing exponentially. In the last two decades, evangelical and Pentecostal churches have been sprouting like wildfire, particularly in poor rural and suburban neighborhoods. There, churches such as the immensely popular Igreja Assembleia de Deus (Assembly of God Church) and Igreja Universal do Reino de Deus (Universal Kingdom of God's Church), and numerous tangents thereof, have taken root, offering succor and solutions to Brazil's poor (often for a price).

AFRO-BRAZILIAN RELIGIONS

African slaves who were brought to Brazil arrived bereft of everything except their faith. Although the Portuguese strictly banned all such forms of "demon worship," slaves were particularly adept at camouflaging the worship of their deities under the guise of pretending to worship Catholic saints. The consequences of this mingling of religious symbols can be seen today in many religious rituals and celebrations that fuse Catholicism with African and even indigenous religious elements.

The end of slavery did not bring about immediate tolerance for Afro-Brazilians to openly practice purer forms of their faith. Candomblé, Brazil's largest Afro-Brazilian cult, was banned well into the 20th century, even in Salvador and parts of Bahia where *terreiros* (traditional houses of worship) are widespread. Today, less than 0.5 percent of Brazilians adhere to Candomblé and other popular Afro-Brazilian faiths, such as Umbanda, which mixes Candomblé practices with spiritualist and indigenous elements. However, in places such as Salvador, Rio, and São Luís, Afro-Brazilian religious elements have entered into mainstream culture. Notable examples include the popularization of Yoruba terms (all Candomblé ceremonies are conducted in the Yoruba language) and of ritual dances and sacred foods (such as Bahia's famous *acarajés*). Wide segments of the population participate in *festas* honoring *orixás* (deities) in which *presentes* (gifts) are offered. In Rio and Salvador, you will often find the beaches littered with flowers washed ashore after being offered to the immensely popular *orixá* Iemanjá, goddess of the seas.

OTHER FAITHS

There are numerous spiritualist and esoteric cults practiced throughout Brazil. One of the most popular forms of spiritualism is Kardecism, which was named after 19th-century spiritualist Allan Kardec. Its followers believe in multiple reincarnations and in the idea that the spirits of the dead—who can be communicated with during séances—are present among the living. Spiritualism is so popular that it often works its way into the Globo television network's nightly *novelas.*

The Arts

With so much diversity and beauty, and so many extremities packed into its immense territory, it's no wonder that artistry and creativity run rampant in Brazil. Culture, both "high" and "low," but especially *cultura popular,* is seemingly everywhere—in the masterful elaboration of a tall tale at a bar table, the intricate embroidery of a tablecloth, the expressive sculpting of a clay *figurinha,* not to mention the 45-minute choreographed spectacle of enormous floats, dazzling costumes, and thousands of sambaing singers and dancers vying for the yearly championship title during Rio's famous Carnaval. With endless sources of inspiration, there are no limits to Brazilians' creativity.

MUSIC

Of the various forms of artistic expression, the one that is most particular and reflects the very essence and soul of Brazil is its music. In terms of sheer genius and variety, it's hard to overstate the impact of Brazilian music. Between samba, bossa

© MICHAEL SOMMERS

drumming in the streets of Salvador

nova, *forró,* and MPB (Música Popular Brasileira), Brazil's contribution to the world music scene is immeasurable. Meanwhile, within Brazil itself, music is inseparable from daily life. It plays a starring role in all types of celebrations, both sacred and profane. There is music in the beach vendor's cries of shrimp for sale as well as in the samba rhythms that teenage boys pound against the metal siding of an urban bus. And it is tattooed into the collective consciousness in such a way that you'll immediately feel as if your education is very lacking (Brazilians inevitably know *all* the words to *all* the songs, and are not at all timid about singing them for you).

Music in Brazil is also inextricably linked to dance. Many music styles— samba, frevo, carimbó, baião—are accompanied by dance steps, and it's close to impossible for most Brazilians to stay inert once the music heats up. Needless to say, the effortlessness, grace, flair, and controlled abandon with which the vast majority of Brazilians cut a rug is beyond compare.

FINE ARTS AND ARCHITECTURE

The earliest known examples of "Brazilian" art were actually paintings of Edenic landscapes done by European artists who were fascinated by the new colony's profusion of exotica. For the next three centuries, artists in Brazil devoured styles that were in vogue in Europe. Although some did so mimetically, others "tropicalized" these styles, giving them a unique Brazilianness. The most remarkable instance of this tendency occurred with the rise of *barroco mineiro,* which developed in 18th-century Minas Gerais during its massive gold boom. Magnificent churches were built using local materials and decorated in a baroque style whose details, colors, and excessive flourishes were unique in reflecting their tropical surroundings. The two major figures of *barroco mineiro* were master builder and sculptor Aleijadinho and the painter Athayde, whose works are spread throughout Minas' *cidades históricas.*

It wasn't until the 1920s that Brazilian artists consciously broke with European traditions. Modernists such as Oswald and Mário de Andrade, Anita Malfatti, Emiliano Di Cavalcanti, Tarsila do Amaral, Victor Brecheret, and Lasar Segall espoused a philosophy of national art and culture that revolved around the notion of *antropofagia* (cannibalism). They created works that, while fed by what was going on in Europe, were also nourished by themes, forms, and subject matter that were distinctly Brazilian. A subsequent generation of Modernists applied their talents to adorning public buildings, particularly the government buildings of the new capital, Brasília. Designed by leading architects Lucio Costa and Oscar Niemeyer, today Brasília is considered the greatest modernist ensemble in the world.

In recent times, contemporary Brazilian art has been marked by the successive rise of pop, installation, performance, video, and digital art. Today, names such as Cildo Meireles, Adriana Varejão, Vik Muniz, Sérgio de Camargo, Jac Leirner, and Beatriz Milhazes are internationally renowned figures, and their works are included in leading museums and galleries. Although characterized by hits and misses, contemporary architecture—some of the best examples of which can be seen in São Paulo—has also stayed true to the precepts of "cannibalism," with names such as Isay Weinfeld, Ruy Ohtake, Márcio Kogan, and Marcelo Ferraz creating works that bridge cutting-edge universal technology and tendencies with a valorization of local aesthetics and materials.

CINEMA

Cinema has always been very popular in Brazil. By the 1930s, even the smallest towns in the northeastern interior had their own modest movie palaces screening Hollywood flicks. In Rio, Praça Floriano became known as Cinelândia after the elegant downtown square was lined with sumptuous art deco movie palaces. Rio was also the birthplace of the Brazilian film industry. In 1930, Cinédia studios began churning out a series of popular romances and burlesque musical comedies known as *chanchadas,* some of which satirized Hollywood fare. A few of these films featured a very young Carmen Miranda, then at the height of her fame as a recording star.

In the 1950s and '60s, dreaming of a *cinema novo* (new cinema) and inspired by Italian neorealism directors such as Nelson Pereira dos Santos, Ruy Guerra, Anselmo Duarte, and Glauber Rocha took to making low-budget films, many shot on location in the arid Sertão, which highlighted the stark realities of the Brazilian Northeast in expressive black-and-white imagery. If not wildly popular at home, these films were a hit with international critics.

In 1964, the beginning of the military dictatorship caused *cinema novo* to experience a sudden demise. Government hard-liners censored any criticism of Brazil and forced many directors into exile. Instead, in 1969 the government created Embrafilme, a state-run production company whose goal was to develop Brazilian filmmaking. Although censorship, bureaucracy, and favoritism severely limited artistic expression, Embrafilme did provide enough capital to maintain a small industry that funded the production of important films by major directors, such as Bruno Barreto's *Dona Flor e Seus Dois Maridos* (*Dona Flor and Her Two Husbands,* 1976) and Cacá Diegues's *Bye Bye Brasil* (1979).

The end of Brazil's military dictatorship also meant the end of Embrafilme and a state-subsidized film industry. By the early 1990s only 3–4 Brazilian films were being released each year. Fortunately, things improved with the introduction of new incentive laws whereby private companies that invested in film productions would receive tax breaks. Eager to see their lives depicted onscreen, Brazilians flocked to the cinema in record numbers, despite the fact that, since the 1970s, more than two-thirds of movie theaters had been closed down, often converted into evangelical churches. Not only did the number of films produced gradually grow, but the quality was on par with the best of world cinema and was recognized as such by foreign critics, who showered awards on productions such as the Oscar-winning *Central do Brasil* (*Central*

BRAZILIAN LITERARY GIANTS

Jorge Amado was one of Brazil's most beloved 20th-century writers. His picaresque novels are set in his home state of Bahia and are populated by a charismatic if somewhat caricatured cast of sensual *mulatas*, fishermen, charming tricksters, and Candomblé priestesses. There is usually a shot of magical realism involved in these highly readable tales. Among his most enduring novels are *Gabriela, Clove, and Cinnamon* and *Dona Flor and Her Two Husbands*.

Mário de Andrade was one of the leading figures of Brazil's modernist movement, and his novel *Macunaíma* (1928) is a Brazilian classic. The title character is a mutant figure from the jungle who begins life as an indigenous man and then morphs into a black man and a white man. While changing identities, he stars in a variety of comical adventures that integrate all sorts of popular Brazilian myths, folklore, and cultural elements into a highly enjoyable narrative patchwork that is utterly Brazilian.

Machado de Assis is not widely known outside Brazil, but among international literati he has earned a place with the all-time greats. This 19th-century author was extremely vanguard, bringing a modernist sensibility and style, not to mention a rapier wit, to bear upon the lifestyles of the rich and corrupt in fin de siècle Rio. His two most famous novels, *Posthumous Memoirs of Brás Cubas* and *Quincas Borba*, are both wonderfully imaginative and mordantly funny.

Clarice Lispector was one Brazil's most intelligent and elegantly witty 20th-century writers. Her depth, human insight, and sense of wordplay are displayed in numerous short stories, which are meticulously crafted. Her most famous and most accessible novel, *The Hour of the Star,* is a searing tale of a miserable and homely northeastern migrant girl's day-to-day trials and tribulations in Rio de Janeiro.

Graciliano Ramos was a novelist from Alagoas who was largely responsible for introducing social realism and regionalism into Brazilian literature in the early 20th century. Written in pared-down prose, his most famous work, *Barren Lives,* portrays the bleak lives of families trying to survive in the hard, arid Sertão of the Northeast.

Moacyr Scliar was one of Brazil's most distinguished contemporary authors. A Jewish doctor from Rio Grande do Sul, he expertly crafted short stories and novels that often touch on the issue of Jewish identity, specifically in Brazil. Apart from his short stories, his best-known novels include *The Centaur and the Garden* and *Max and the Cats.*

Station), directed by Walter Salles, and Fernando Meirelles's *Cidade de Deus* (*City of God,* 2002), which took both Brazil and the world by storm with its brilliantly acted story of survival amid the gang warfare typical of a Carioca favela.

Sports and Games

It's hardly a secret that soccer (known in Portuguese as *futebol*) is not just Brazil's national sport but a passion that borders on the fervently religious. It was introduced by Brazilian-born Charles Miller, who in 1894 returned from higher studies in England toting a soccer ball and equipment. The first soccer games played in São Paulo proved enormously popular, and *futebol* swept through the country like wildfire.

Today, Brazil is the only country in the world to have won five World Cups (1958, 1962, 1970, 1994, and 2002), and during World Cup games, the entire country shuts down to cheer on the Seleção Brasileira, or to scream advice to the coach or players. Although Brazilians are ferocious in their support of their teams, they are equally fierce at criticizing any botched play or strategy; consequently the range of emotions displayed in any stadium or around any TV set is impressive. You're as likely to witness big macho guys hugging and kissing each other for joy after a victory as you are to see them sobbing tragically following a defeat. In Brazil, *jogadores de futebol* (soccer players) rank as the country's reigning celebrities, despite the fact that many of them spend most of the year overseas playing for top European teams.

Aside from watching *futebol* (a year-round pastime since there is no "season") everywhere you go, you'll see Brazilians, mostly males, playing *futebol*. Whether it's on the floodlit sands of Copacabana, the dilapidated streets of an urban favela or a cleared makeshift field in the middle of the Amazon forest, soccer is ubiquitous. Often players are barefoot, and goal posts are rolled-up T-shirts the passion is always the same.

© MICHAEL SOMMERS

Futebol is not just a national pastime, it's a passion.

PLANNING YOUR FACT-FINDING TRIP

If you're thinking of moving to Brazil, it's wise to spend some time getting a sense of the country and the culture, not to mention housing and job possibilities, before you go ahead and take the plunge. A fact-finding trip to explore a region of the country and neighborhoods of the city in which you're interested in potentially living can be essential. Such a trip allows you to talk to both expats and Brazilians about the areas's pros and cons and ups and downs and can help open your eyes to what you're getting yourself into.

A lot of foreigners initially come to Brazil as tourists and are often seduced by its paradisiacal aspects; tropical climate, spectacular nature, warm and friendly people, rich culture, laid-back vibe, not to mention all that fresh fruit. Sometimes, the spell is so intense that they drop everything and immediately make the move without getting a sense of what lies beneath those alluring first impressions. The shock of encountering some of the tougher, but less initially apparent, realities of life in Brazil can be brutal for those who lack preparation and walk into Brazil wearing rose-colored sunglasses. While a fact-finding trip will allow you some forays into Brazil's more delicious aspects, the focus is upon gathering sufficient information that will allow you to determine whether or not a certain neighborhood, city, region, or even Brazil itself is a good fit for you.

© MICHAEL SOMMERS

Preparing to Leave

DOCUMENTS AND IMMUNIZATIONS

If your country requires Brazilians to have travel visas, you will have to get one from the nearest Brazilian consulate before entering Brazil. Currently, citizens of Canada, the United States, and Australia require visas. Citizens of the United Kingdom, other European Union countries, and New Zealand don't need visas but must have a passport that is valid for six months and a return ticket.

Brazil requires only one vaccination: for yellow fever if you are visiting the Amazon region (or arriving from certain countries)—it's an essential for that region, but otherwise only recommended. If you are going to the Amazon, make sure you bring an International Certificate of Vaccination booklet as proof of vaccination.

WHEN TO GO

There's no real season not to go to Brazil, although based on the region you're visiting, you might want to work around certain weather tendencies. For the purpose of fact finding—not to mention affordability—it's best to avoid summertime, particularly the weeks between Christmas and Carnaval (usually in February). This period coincides with summer vacation (and often very hot summer temperatures with a scalding sun that will make moving around during the day quite uncomfortable). In coastal areas (particularly the Northeast, Rio de Janeiro, and Santa Catarina), summertime is synonymous with tourism and multiple *festas* (the main one being Carnaval). Although this makes things fun for tourists, it also results in high airfares and accommodation rates. With many people vacationing, you may encounter difficulties in meeting with professionals regarding work and study possibilities. It's also more difficult to gauge what "real life" during the rest of the year is like.

Summertime in the Southeast and parts of the Central-West is often accompanied by significant rainfall. This can lead to flooding (even in downtown Rio and São Paulo) and makes getting around very difficult. Rainfall can be heavy in the Northeast (particularly in Bahia, Alagoas, and Pernambuco) between March and June. Things are even wetter in the Amazon where the rainy season lasts for six months (usually November to May).

Because most of Brazil boasts a tropical climate, the only region you'll want to avoid exploring in the winter months is the South, where temperatures can approach 0°C (32°F). São Paulo, parts of Minas, and the Central West can also experience cool temperatures during this period (particularly at night). Be aware that due to school vacations, many Brazilians also take winter holidays in July.

If your fact-finding trip is only going to last one or two weeks, it's also worth checking an online calendar of Brazilian *feriados* or holidays. There are more than a dozen national holidays (and some state and municipal ones to boot) in Brazil when most public entities and a lot of private businesses shut down. The thing to watch for is *pontes* (bridges): When a holiday falls on a Tuesday or Thursday, for example, many Brazilians will often take Monday or Friday off as well, creating a *ponte* that stretches to the weekend and results in a 4-day vacation. Aside from finding cities abandoned, you'll also find it more difficult to obtain available, not to mention affordable, accommodations and airfares.

WHAT TO PACK

Brazil's generally warm and casual climate means you can get away with packing quite lightly. Considering the heat and sun, take a tip from Brazilians and bring light colors. You might want to avoid white, which easily soaks up dirt, especially when you're perspiring a lot (yes, be prepared to perspire). Outside of São Paulo, Brazilians are not that big on black (except for evening wear). Go for lightweight, breathable fibers (such as cotton). Keep in mind that heat and humidity will wilt carefully ironed collars, folds, and pleats, so consider clothes or fabrics that don't require a lot of ironing.

As a rule Brazilians are casual, even in professional situations (unless you're circulating in business and/or government circles). In most job-related or formal social situations, men can often wear a nice pair of trousers, a jacket, a button-down shirt (with or without tie), and a good pair of shoes. Women typically wear a skirt and blouse (with a blazer to dress things up) with heels or flats. In other situations, you can go even more casual although it's preferable that men opt for pants instead of shorts when not indulging in touristic pursuits. Remember that even in the summertime, it's a good idea to have a sweater or jacket since you'll inevitably end up in an air-conditioned environment that verges on semi-Arctic. Leave attention-grabbing or expensive watches and jewelry at home.

For research and communication purposes, bring a laptop (one that can be cleverly disguised if you're walking around with it), an iPhone or smartphone with Wi-Fi capability, or both. Bring a digital camera to take pictures of neighborhoods and apartments or houses that interest you. Aside from any prescription meds, bring some good mosquito repellent, anti-diarrheal medication, Tylenol or other analgesic, and *lots* of sunscreen (which costs a small fortune in Brazil).

Currency

Although you might want to bring some U.S. dollars for an emergency (in the event you can't get cash from an ATM or if your card gets lost, cloned, or stolen), you'll usually lose money exchanging dollars at either a bank or a *casa de câmbio* (exchange house). Major hotels will also exchange dollars, as will airport banks. Since 2006, the U.S. dollar (which at one point was US$1:R$4) has declined considerably against the stable and increasingly robust *real* (which in July 2012 was around US$1:R$2). As a result, there are very few places where U.S. dollars—or travelers checks—are accepted.

The best way to deal with money concerns in Brazil is to bring an international Visa or MasterCard (or both to give you more options), so you can also withdraw cash from bank machines. Most major branches of Banco do Brasil and Bradesco have at least one ATM that accepts Visa cards, while Bradesco, HSBC, and Citibank accept MasterCard/Cirrus. Meanwhile red Banco 24 Horas ATMs accept all cards. In all cases, you need to have a four-digit PIN number. Many ATMs have an option for English.

More and more ATMs in all major and reasonably sized cities accept international cards. It's best to use banks in downtown commercial areas or at airports, bus terminals, and shopping centers. For security reasons, bank ATMs are open 6am–10pm daily. Most have a daily withdrawal limit of R$1,000 (although Bradesco's is R$800).

To avoid having your card cloned (a frequent problem in Brazil), don't use empty ATMs and make sure nobody is watching you. Never let your credit card out of your sight and keep track of your expenditures so that you can quickly notice if unaccounted withdrawals or charges occur. It's a good idea to inform your bank that you'll be traveling to Brazil prior to your departure; it's not uncommon for banks to freeze cards believing that sudden Brazilian purchases and withdrawals constitute credit card fraud.

Arriving in Brazil

CUSTOMS AND IMMIGRATION

Before entering Brazil, all foreign travelers receive a customs form and a *cartão de entrada/saida* (entry/exit card) to fill out before going through immigration and customs. Immigration officials will stamp the entry/exit card and give you a copy that you must keep with your passport and hand over upon your departure (loss of the card will result in bureaucratic hassles with the Federal Police, not to mention a possible fine). Due to Brazil's policy of diplomatic reciprocity, all U.S. citizens entering the country will need to be photographed and fingerprinted just as Brazilians are when they arrive in the United States.

Going through customs is usually a breeze for foreign travelers although all passengers can be arbitrarily pulled over for luggage inspection to ensure you're not smuggling laptops or cell phones or such. Because of high prices for everything from electronics to cosmetics, it's not uncommon for Brazilians to go way over the duty free limit of US$500—or to beseech North American friends (or strangers) to do so for them. Bringing in multiples of anything is a big giveaway. If you exceed your spending limit, you'll end up having to pay not only duty taxes of 50 percent of the full market price (unless you have an original receipt proving otherwise), but also an additional 25 percent penalty. If bringing in more than R$10,000 cash, you'll also need to declare this as well (although not for tax purposes).

TRANSPORTATION

Options for getting into town from airports (usually located some distance from city centers) include buses and taxis. Regular *convencional* buses are cheaper but slower and difficult to navigate with luggage. Many large cities, including Rio, São Paulo, and Belo Horizonte, have special airport shuttle services that connect airports with smaller domestic airports, bus terminals, and major downtown points, including hotels. Some cities also have air-conditioned *executivo* buses that offer more comfortable seating and are a better option than *convencional* buses as long as you don't have too much luggage.

The quickest and easiest but more expensive option is to take a taxi. Although major airports have prepaid taxi services, which are "safer," they are also more expensive than taking a metered cab, especially if you agree on a fixed price in advance (this can be worthwhile if you have enough wits about you to negotiate a good price; it's not always easy to bargain in Portuguese after a long flight). Do take care to make sure your cab is in an official lineup of taxis and that the driver is registered. Don't just go with any cab driver who approaches you even if that driver offers you a good deal. *Taxis clandestinos* are not uncommon and getting into one could result in your being robbed. If you're planning on renting a car, typically you'll find branches of major rental companies such as Hertz, Avis, and Localiza at the airport. Many hotels (and even some B&Bs) can arrange airport pickups although these are often fairly expensive.

Sample Itineraries

The following four itineraries—each of which coincide with one of the four *Prime Living Locations* chapters featured in this book—have been created to help you learn a little about the areas in which you're interesting in living with the aim of laying the groundwork for a possible move and making the eventual transition easier. A few local attractions have been woven into the itinerary, which will allow you to get a sense of some of the destination's culinary, cultural, and recreational options.

Keep in mind that these itineraries are conceived as flexible bases—they can be bent and molded to fit your specific needs, and you can, and should, build alternatives depending on your circumstances, priorities, and desires. This is especially the case in terms of the itineraries for the fairly vast regions of Minas, Central-West, and South and the Northeast. The itineraries developed here focus merely (and briefly) on the main regional cities and surrounding areas addressed in the *Prime Living Locations* section. Chances are you'll want to focus on only one or two cities in each region or on individual states or areas within them (which unfortunately, in light of the size of Brazil and the scope of this book, cannot be addressed specifically).

ONE WEEK IN RIO DE JANEIRO
Day 1
It's a good idea to book a flight that leaves North America on a Saturday night (most Brazil-bound flights are overnighters). This will allow you to arrive in Rio on a quiet Sunday morning when the airport is less busy and traffic will be nonexistent. For the sake of convenience, logistics, and pure pleasure, opt for a hotel in the Zona Sul: either the beach neighborhoods of Copacabana, Ipanema, or Leblon (more expensive, but with beach access and closer to Barra) or Catete, Flamengo, Botafogo, Laranjeiras, and surrounding areas (no beach, but less touristy, more affordable, and closer to Centro).

Upon arriving at your hotel, take a restorative nap if needed—either in your room or on the famous beaches of Copacabana, Ipanema, or Leblon. A pilgrimage to any of these three Zona Sul beaches provides the ideal introduction to Rio de Janeiro, particularly on a Sunday when the city's famed beach culture is in full swing (just make sure you rent a parasol and slather on plenty of high SPF sunscreen, even if you're in the shade). Go easy on the caipirinhas, but indulge in replenishing *água de coco* (coconut water) or exotic juices at the many *bares de suco* (juice bars). In the early evening, stroll around the residential streets of Ipanema and Leblon to get a sense of what living in these coveted neighborhoods—popular with expats, but also quite expensive—would be like. Take a brief stroll around part of the Lagoa de Freitas, stopping for a relaxing drink at a kiosk, before a light dinner and early return to your hotel.

Day 2
If you already have a job lined up in Rio, or have job-related contacts to visit, today's

© MICHAEL SOMMERS

Ipanema and Leblon beaches

a good day to meet with your future or potential employers, colleagues, or partners. Chances are you'll be traveling within the Zona Sul or to Centro or Barra. After getting directions, you might want to take the plunge and throw yourself into Rio's public transportation system either via bus or Metrô (or a combination of both). Schedule your meeting to avoid the worst of morning rush hour traffic (7am-9am) and then ask hotel staff for an estimate of how long it will take you to get to your destination (if you don't want to risk being late or getting lost, consider taking a cab and braving the bus or Metrô on the way back). Note that commuting between the Zona Sul and Barra will take at least 60–90 minutes.

In some cases (such as if you're employed by an oil company), you may find it necessary to visit offices in the towns of Macaé or Rio das Ostras, which involve a two-hour commute; in such cases, it might make sense to stay overnight an extra day or two investigating housing and school options. Although regular buses depart from the Rodoviário Novo bus terminal in the Zona Norte, to save time, see if your company can arrange for a driver to pick you up.

Depending on the length of your commute and the number of meetings you have, you might spend half to most of the day in meetings. When you're finished, take the opportunity to explore the area around your future work location before returning to your hotel. In the evening, consider checking out some local *botecos* to soak up ambiance (and a refreshing drink or two).

Day 3

There's no better way to get the low-down on life in Rio than by talking to some other expats who have already been living in the city. Many can be contacted via their blogs

BEACH DOS AND DON'TS

In Rio, the beach is a fundamental part of life and lifestyle. Although it all appears incredibly laid-back, in truth, Cariocas have developed a very sophisticated *cultura de praia* with habits and codes worth taking note of if you want to blend in.

- **Don't** wear a bathing suit from home. Chances are you're going to be hopelessly out of style. Rio's cutting-edge bikini and *sunga* (the male version of a bikini) styles are always light-years ahead of the rest of the world, and because prices are generally affordable, you should purchase one (or several) on location.

- If you're female, **do** know that Cariocas of all shapes and sizes are not at all shy about revealing an awful lot of flesh (although the days of the *fio dental* (dental floss) thong have mercifully passed). However, you **don't** want to take your top off. Aside from a brief headline-making phase on Ipanema a few summers ago—when a few women's toplessness led the police to enforce decades-old decency laws—topless sunbathing is a no-no. Moreover, Cariocas are very proud of their tan lines.

- If you're male, **don't** don a Speedo-style bathing suit—these are for Olympic swimmers. For the last couple of years, stylish *sungas* have been modeled after men's full briefs. **Do** know that surfing shorts are for surfing or for wearing over your bathing suit as you go to and from the beach, but definitely not for lounging around on the sand or swimming.

- On the way to and from the beach, **do** wear flip-flops (Havaianas are the coolest) and **don't** wear shoes. Females usually cover up (lightly) with a lightweight top and micro shorts or skirts. Walking to and from the beach, males sometimes flaunt their bare chests but otherwise should wear a T-shirt.

- **Don't** take any valuables to the beach and don't leave your possessions unguarded. Take a beach bag instead of a purse. If you're alone, ask a respectable-looking neighbor to keep an eye on your stuff while you take a dip.

- **Don't** bring a towel to the beach (even if you're staying in a swanky hotel with very plush ones). *Cangas* are lighter and de rigueur. They are sold all over the beaches. If you want more comfort, rent a chair.

- **Don't** schlep food or drinks to the beach. You'll look like a bag person. Rio's beaches are well serviced by *ambulantes,* vendors who sell drinks (both healthy and unhealthy).

- Rio's beaches have strong currents in places. **Don't** go swimming if a red flag is flying. Only go in the water in areas where locals are already swimming.

- **Don't** get a sunburn. Not only will you suffer and contribute to possible skin cancer, but the red lobster look is definitely uncool and will brand you as a foolish gringo.

© MICHAEL SOMMERS

biquini in a window display at a shop in Ipanema

(for a list of many, check out the Rio page of Expat Blog (www.expat-blog.com) or by joining expat sites such as InterNations (www.internation.org). Another good source is the American Society of Rio de Janeiro (www.americansocietyrio.org). Prior to coming to Brazil, it's a great idea to set up a meeting, lunch, or happy hour drink with at least a couple of different expats whose age, profession, interests, and lifestyles are similar to yours. Aside from invaluable tips that can save you a lot of potential hassle, you can often get invaluable info regarding everything from schools and employment opportunities to shopping tips. Other expats can also help you focus on where to live. Since expats are constantly coming and going, the expat grapevine may give you some great leads on apartment availabilities, not to mention the possibility of acquiring used furniture, electronic equipment, and other essential amenities (including a car). Moreover, you'll also end up with some contacts, and even some friends, which will make life less lonely when you move to Rio definitively.

In between meetings, consider fitting in some leisure and cultural activities that will allow you to explore other neighborhoods. Consider the museums and cultural centers of Centro or Catete, Flamengo, and Botafogo, all of which have great places to eat as well. The latter neighborhoods are particularly interesting in that they offer interesting housing options, which are cheaper than those in the Zona Sul beach neighborhoods.

Day 4

One of Rio's fastest growing neighborhoods is Barra de Tijuca. A lot of expats live in this sprawling, if soulless Miami-esque beachfront neighborhood because of the wide range of available housing, great amenities (including good medical care and international schools), and beach access, not to mention the fact that many businesses (including multinationals) have recently set up shop here. You might either love or hate Barra, but it's worth checking out as a potential area to live, especially if your job is located here or you have kids (otherwise the commute to Centro or even Zona Sul can be brutal). Although you can visit (a small chunk of it) by bus, keep in mind that living in Barra is nearly impossible without a car. It's worthwhile to make an appointment to check out a few apartments in the area to get the lay of the land, plus snag a ride with a real estate agent. Don't forget to take time out to chill on the beach.

Days 5 and 6

Take these two days to investigate housing options in the Zona Sul with the aid of local real estate agents (some of whom specialize in rentals and purchases for expats and speak English). In and between visiting apartments, explore these easily walkable neighborhoods and get a sense of shopping options and amenities including gyms, hospitals and clinics, restaurants and bars, and schools. Most of Rio's international and bilingual schools, as well as its best private schools, are located in these neighborhoods. During these two days, you can schedule additional meetings with both prospective job or business networking contacts and expats who live in the area.

For logistics' sake, you might want to spend one day focusing on the beach neighborhoods of Copa, Ipanema, and Leblon along with the adjacent *bairros* of Gávea, Lagoa, and Jardim Botânico, which surround the Lagoa Rodrigo de Freitas, and spend another day on the older, more affordable residential *bairros* of Catete, Flamengo, Botafogo, Laranjeiras, Cosme Velho, and Urca. In between appointments, treat yourself to some downtime by chilling out at the refreshingly leafy Jardim Botânico and adjacent Parque Lage, in the first instance, and indulging in a trip up to the top of Pão de Açúcar or Corcavado, in the second.

Day 7

Most returning flights to North America depart in the evening, which gives you some time to tie up any loose ends in the morning. Spend the afternoon packing and then lounging around the beach before checking out of your hotel. Give yourself plenty of lead time to make it to the airport on time.

ONE WEEK IN SÃO PAULO
Day 1

Fly out of North America on a Saturday night so that you can arrive in Sampa on a (rare) quiet Sunday morning, avoiding the crowds at Guarulhos airport and immediate exposure to the city's notorious traffic. It makes sense to choose a hotel with a location that is as central as possible such as the neighborhoods in and around Centro (República, Consolação, Higienópolis) or off Avenida Paulista (Jardins or Bela Vista).

After checking into your hotel, consider a long leisurely lunch at one of Sampa's famed culinary havens (you have thousands to choose from) and then combine a little bit of culture with a walk (this is the only day you won't be fighting for sidewalk space with millions of busy Paulistanos). Suggestions include a walk down Avenida Paulista with a stop at leafy Parque Trianon and Museu de Arte de São Paulo (MASP)—Sampa's landmark art museum, beneath which an antiques fair is held on Sunday—or a trip to Parque Ibirapuera, whose verdant lawns are sprinkled with some great museums. Cap off the day with a light dinner and drink in or around fashionable Jardins. Close to both Avenida Paulista and Ibirapuera, it boasts tons of restaurants and cafés that are popular with expats.

Day 2

If you already have a job lined up in São Paulo or have professional networking contacts to meet, today's a good day to take care of business. With luck, your contacts will be in and around the central area where you're staying (Centro or Avenida Paulista), and you'll be able to quickly get to where you want to go via Metrô, bus, or taxi. However, chances are you'll have to head to one of the newer and farther-flung business *bairros* of Itaim, Brooklin Novo, or Santo Amaro, where many international investment banks and multinationals are headquartered. In this instance, a taxi is pretty much the only way to go. Regardless of the mode of transportation you choose, do everything you can to avoid rush hour (the worst of which is from 7am-9:30am). To avoid being late, confirm your travel time with hotel staff. Depending on the length of your commute and the number of meetings you have, you might spend half to most of the day attending to business.

Take the opportunity to eat, drink, and explore the area around your future work location before returning to your hotel before or after rush hour is at its worst (5pm-8pm). Depending on your timing, you can eat or drink (or both) in southeast neighborhoods such as trendy, upscale Itaim Bibi or Vila Olímpia or more funky Pinheiros and Vila Madalena, or else explore more centrally located neighborhoods such as Bela

© MICHAEL SOMMERS

São Paulo's Parque Ibirapuera

Vista, Consolação, and Higienópolis from which it will be only a walk or quick bus or cab ride to your hotel.

Day 3

Given its size, importance, wealth, and cosmopolitan nature, it's not surprising that São Paulo has a large expat community representing a wide variety of professions. It can be very helpful to contact some of them in advance—particularly if their professions, backgrounds, and lifestyles are similar to yours—and then meet up when you're in town. Try doing so via their blogs, many of which are listed on the São Paulo page of Expat Blog (www.expat-blog.com), or by joining expat sites such as InterNations (www.internation.org). Another good source is the American Society of São Paulo (www.americansociety.com.br). Due to São Paulo's overwhelming density and immensity, receiving knowledgeable insider tips regarding everything from housing and health concerns to hiring a cleaning lady can end up saving you a lot of time and peace of mind, not to mention money. Expat advice can be particularly invaluable when it comes to choosing a place to live. Considering the frequency with which expats on temporary contracts come and go, you might even find a specific lead or even an available apartment by tapping into the expat grapevine.

Use your downtime to explore other potentially livable neighborhoods that are also interesting as attractions in themselves. Consider a trip to Vila Madalena, where charming bungalows sit amidst cool boutiques, cafés, bars, and artists' ateliers, or Higienópolis, whose leafy streets are lined with beautiful modernist apartment buildings. Both neighborhoods are easily reached by Metrô or bus.

Days 4-6

In light of traffic and transportation conditions, the essential consideration in choosing where to live in São Paulo is proximity to your job. If you already have one—or a prospective one—or are planning on opening a business and have a location in mind, then that somewhat narrows down the otherwise overwhelming task of choosing where to live. If you are single or a couple, don't have a job, or work as a freelancer out of your home, you might want more affordable housing in more central neighborhoods (Bela Vista, Santa Cecília, Pinheiros) that offer better public transportation and more of an urban cultural life than wealthier but farther-flung neighborhoods such as Itaim and Morumbi. That said, even with the territory narrowed down, Sampa's *bairros* are so large and dense that you'll still have your work cut out for you.

Having contacted a realtor (ideally before coming to town)—you'll find a number of English-speaking agents that specialize in housing for expats—take these three days to visit prospective apartments and get a lay of the land. If you have children, this is a chance to visit private schools in or near the neighborhood where you plan to work and live. If you're job networking or researching starting a business, you can work some meetings into your schedule. Also consider meeting up with other expats during these days; the larger your circle of personal resources, the better.

Take time out to experience the city itself and get a sense of its rhythms. While your days will be full, Sampa is no slouch when it comes to nightlife offerings. Aside from sampling the city's endless array of restaurants and bars, take in a movie at the big-screen theaters on Avenida Paulista (English language films are almost always screened in their original version), a concert at the Teatro Municipal or Sala São Paulo, or a show at any one of the fabulous SESC cultural centers.

Day 7

Since your flight will inevitably depart in the evening, take advantage of your last morning to finalize any details. Then treat yourself to a leisurely lunch followed by some boutique browsing; Rua Augusta and surrounding streets in both Jardins (more pricey) and Consolação (more affordable) are fun to poke around. Don't forget to factor in the rush hour traffic before leaving for the airport.

MINAS, CENTRAL-WEST, AND SOUTH

While Minas Gerais, the Central-West, and the South of Brazil share certain geographic, cultural, and socioeconomic similarities, they are distinctive regions and chances are you'll have specific reasons for choosing to move to one of them.

Minas

One of Brazil's largest states, Minas Gerais is also one of its wealthiest, most populous (after São Paulo), and easiest to get around because roads are generally good, bus service is frequent, and lots of domestic flights are available from the capital of Belo Horizonte (BH) to other Brazilian capitals as well as frequent service from BH and São Paulo to smaller cities within Minas such as Uberlândia and Juiz de Fora.

Most foreigners who move to Minas inevitably end up in its capital of Belo Horizonte. If you're planning a fact-finding trip here, you can count on getting a fair amount done in one week. Smaller, less chaotic, and more organized than Rio and São

© MICHAEL SOMMERS

the colonial town of Diamantina

Paulo, BH is more compact and easier to navigate. Because bus service is extensive and distances are short, you can rely on public transit and taxis, with some walking to boot, instead of renting a car.

BH caters largely to Brazilian business tourists, which means that hotels can fill up during the week (when the city buzzes and traffic can be a problem, especially during rush hour). Meanwhile, weekends are calm and quiet. It's best to base yourself in Centro (cheaper, but noisier) or Savassi (more upscale, nicer amenities). From these two downtown neighborhoods, you can easily meet with business contacts, explore different neighborhoods in the surrounding area (and check out potential apartments), and take the city's pulse in a leisurely fashion. A great source in terms of networking with other Minas-based expats is Minas International (www.minasinternational.com), a nongovernmental organization (NGO) that connects English speakers living and doing business in Minas with each other.

Although most expats who come to Minas base themselves in Belo Horizonte, the best known—not to mention the oldest—towns in Minas are the colonial gold and diamond mining towns that date back to the early 18th century. The majority of these *cidades históricas*—Ouro Preto and Mariana, São João del Rei and Tiradentes—lie 2–3 hours southeast of BH and are easily accessible by bus. More isolated but equally appealing is Diamantina, a five-hour bus ride north. Because of their rich baroque architecture and strong cultural traditions, not to mention idyllic mountain landscapes, these are major tourist draws; it's worth tacking 2–3 days on to your trip and visiting a couple of them to get a taste of traditional Mineiro culture (not to mention Mineiro food). Moreover, you might end up being sufficiently seduced to envision opening up a *pousada,* bar, or restaurant or considering a study abroad program. With the exception of Tiradentes, all of the *cidades históricas* have federal university campuses.

Brasília

Despite the fact that it's the nation's capital—and linked by air to every Brazilian city under the sun—Brasília continues to be in the middle of nowhere, i.e., far from everywhere. If you choose to travel to the city, aside from visiting the surrounding Cerrado region, rife with unusual flora and fauna and riddled with waterfalls, you'll be pretty much stranded from the rest of Brazil unless you choose to hop a plane. However, most people who plan to live in Brasília already have a clear purpose in mind.

Considering its size and relative efficiency, a one-week fact-finding trip should give you enough time to get a good sense of the city, particularly since everywhere you'll

© MICHAEL SOMMERS

Much of Brasília, like the Museu Nacional, is ultramodern.

want to go will be located within the central confines of the Plano Piloto. Moreover, the fact that everything within the Plano Piloto is organized into zones will make your fact finding extremely efficient. You can check into a hotel in the Hotel Sector (keep in mind that rates are lower and vacancies higher on the weekends when government officials head out of town), take care of any government or diplomatic job-related business in the Eixo Monumental or Embassy Sectors, look for apartments in the Residential Sectors (most expats opt for those in the Asa Sul), and chill out in the sports and recreational sectors along the shores of Lago Paranoá.

While buses do exist in Brasília, making sense of the routes amidst all the zones and sectors takes some getting used to. Walking is pretty much out of the question. As such, consider saving time and precious brain cells by resorting to cabs (which can nonetheless add up) or renting a car. The latter will come in handy if you take some time out to visit surrounding natural attractions such as the nearby Parque Nacional de Brasília, with its refreshing natural pools, the Salto de Itiquira, a spectacular 170-meter (560-foot) waterfall, or the charming colonial gold mining town of Pirenópolis.

The South

Brazil's South—comprising the small states of Paraná, Santa Catarina, and Rio Grande do Sul—is a relatively compact region with excellent infrastructure and efficient transportation options between its three capitals of Curitiba, Florianópolis, and Porto Alegre. Numerous and fairly inexpensive flights as well as buses link these three cities to each other as well as to Rio and São Paulo. Traveling south by bus, Curitiba is only 6 hours from São Paulo, Florianópolis is only 4.5 hours from Curitiba, and Porto

Alegre is 6.5 hours from Floripa. Should you be up for a road trip, you can get from one to the other even more quickly.

Like the states in which they're situated, Curitiba, Florianópolis, and Porto Alegre are all quite small and fairly easy to navigate. One of the highlights of Curitiba's famed urban planning is its inexpensive and extensive municipal bus system, an inspiration for sustainably challenged cities around the world. Porto Alegre also has a pretty good bus system along with a Metrô that links the airport and Rodoviária to the Centro, much of which can be easily explored on foot. Floripa's Centro is also easy to get around, but bus service to the rest of the island is slow and sketchy. If you plan on looking for living arrangements at different beaches or around the Lagoa, you'll want to rent a car.

A week in any of these three capitals should give you ample time to get a sense of the cities and their neighborhoods and do any preliminary housing, education, and job research necessary. Logistics are simplified by the size and efficiency of these cities. Everything you need to do and see will be in or near a circumscribed central core, and you should consider basing yourself in and around each city's Centro or surrounding upscale neighborhoods of Batel (Curitiba) or Moinhos de Vento (Porto Alegre). If it's beaches that bring you to Floripa, you'll probably need to cover more territory, and it might make more sense to base yourself in Lagoa or in one of the North or East Coast beaches.

If you tack a couple of extra days onto your itinerary, you can easily fit in a short 2–3 day getaway to each of the states' attractions. In Paraná, this could be a two-hour trip down to Paranaguá (which can be done by bus, train, or car) followed by a couple of days relaxing on the lovely island of Ilha do Mel, or a quick one-hour flight to Foz do Iguaçu and the spectacular Iguaçu Falls. In Floripa, you could explore the more remote and stunningly beautiful of the island's 42 beaches, particularly those along the East and South coasts such as Praia do Campeche, Praia do Armação, and Lagoinha do Leste. Meanwhile, from Porto Alegre, you're only a two-hour bus ride away from the popular Alpine-esque towns of Gramado and Canela, located in the Serra Gaúcha mountain range.

Should you want to visit two or all three of these cities, consider a minimum of two weeks. Add a third week, if you want to mix pleasure in with your business.

THE NORTHEAST

The Northeast of Brazil is a vast region. To get an idea of its territory, its largest state, Bahia, is roughly the same size (actually a bit larger) than France. However, unlike Europe, logistics in the Northeast are more complicated. Although regular and fairly inexpensive flights link all the state capitals to each other as well as to big cities such as Rio, São Paulo, Brasília and Belo Horizonte (not to mention a few direct connections to Miami), outside of major cities, you'll have to rely on more infrequent (and more expensive) local flights or bus service. Between the principal coastal cities, frequent bus service is supplied by major companies that operate express service with air-conditioning (often glacial enough to require sweaters), *leitos* (seats that fold into some semblance of a bed), and complimentary mineral water.

Once you start getting into the vast Interior, and away from major cities and towns along the coast, transportation can become more of a challenge. Often it's

© MICHAEL SOMMERS

Diogo, Bahia

a toss-up between taking local buses with infrequent service (sometimes at inconvenient hours) and *lots* of local stops, or renting a car and navigating roads—often either paved, but in poor condition, or dirt—where trucks can be rampant and signage can be poor.

Depending on how much territory you plan to cover on your fact-finding trip, such logistics will play a major role in devising an itinerary. If, for instance, you plan to limit your research to a particular capital—Salvador, Recife, or Fortaleza—you can probably squeeze all your fact finding into a week. Keep in mind that although these cities are smaller than Rio and São Paulo, the fact that they are spread out along coastlines (without much urban planning) means they tend to sprawl. Limited mostly to buses, public transportation is functional, but buses can get hot, crowded, and mired in increasingly prevalent traffic. Renting a car is a good option as is relying on taxis, which are quite reasonably priced (if you hit it off with a driver, it's often possible—and quite useful if you don't know the city—to make a deal to pay the driver an attractive day rate to chauffeur you around the city). That said, if you plan to settle in any of these cities, most work and education opportunities will likely be concentrated in the same small and select middle-upper class neighborhoods in which you'll probably want to live as well. This will make fact finding a more focused task.

With the exception of Teresina, the inland capital of the small state of Piauí, all the Northeast capitals from Salvador to São Luís are coastal cities with generally attractive beaches, which only become more alluring the farther out of town you get. For purposes of practicality and pleasure, it makes sense to seek out accommodations in the more central beach neighborhoods—Barra in Salvador, Boa Viagem in Recife, Meireles in Fortaleza—which also tend to be more upscale, convenient, and equipped with amenities. Most expats tend to congregate in these *bairros* (chances of meeting and talking to other expats are high), and you'll likely consider them (and the surrounding areas) as living options, regardless of whether you're planning to rent or buy. They'll also give you a chance to get a sense of the city's strong beach culture, not to mention an opportunity to mix your fact finding with some relaxing downtime.

Within 1–2 hours of these and all other Northeast capitals (Maceió, Aracaju, João Pessoa, Natal, São Luís) lie small (albeit increasingly developed) fishing villages and small towns with beautiful beaches that make for easy day-trip getaways by bus or car. It's worth exploring them if you have a day to spare (or care to add a couple more days to your trip). From Salvador, drive north along the Linha Verde and visit Arembepe, Praia do Forte, Imbassaí, or Diogo or sail across the Bay of All Saints to Ilha de Itaparica. The charming colonial city of Olinda is only 20 minutes away from downtown Recife, but also close by are the beach towns of Cabo de Santo Agostinho (to the south) and Ilha de Itamaracá (to the north).

A two-week itinerary allows you to tackle more territory. You could either do this by adding another city to your itinerary (Salvador and Recife, for example) or branching out from your chosen base city into the surrounding area. The latter is an ideal option if you're looking to set up shop in a deserted beach paradise; purchasing an idyllic property, building a second home, or opening a tourism-related business such as a *pousada* or restaurant.

Depending on how remote you want your paradise to be, you might want to consider an entire month. During this time you could travel the entire coast of Bahia, for example, from Mangue Seco down to Caravelas, or venture from Recife up to Fortaleza, investigating little fishing villages and secluded beaches along the way until you find one that feels just right. Along the way, you can stop and stay with any number of pioneering gringos who dropped out of civilization to open up *pousadas* in paradise. They are legion along the Northeast coast and are great founts of knowledge.

Practicalities

Brazil offers accommodations and eating options for all tastes and budgets, although due to the relatively low U.S. dollar and inflation within Brazil, prices these days tend to skew higher. Hotels and restaurants tend to be on par or more expensive than their comparable North American counterparts, particularly in the big cities, and especially if you're haunting middle-class and upper-middle-class or touristic neighborhoods or establishments. Brazil's wealthy classes still tend to think it's cool to pay major bucks for goods and services that in North America are considered banal (and priced accordingly) as opposed to status symbols. If you frequent such places or succumb to cravings for things deemed fashionable, imported, or exotic (such as Thai food or chocolate brownies), be prepared to bust your budget. However, if you take advantage of truly Brazilian solutions—staying at small, B&B-like *pousadas* and eating at juice bars, *quilo* restaurants, and *botecos,* your stay will be much more authentic and atmospheric, not to mention affordable.

HOTELS, *POUSADAS,* AND *ALBERGUES*

Brazilian hotels range from one-star flophouses to four-star international chains along with a small, but increasing number of small, seductive, generally quite upscale boutique hotels, a significant number of which are owned by foreigners.

In Brazil, you'll also find *pousadas,* generally the equivalent of a guesthouse or bed-and-breakfast, although the definition is as elastic as *pousadas* themselves are varied. Some are nothing more than basic hotels, with four walls, a sheet-covered mattress, a window, and that's it. Others are welcoming, intimate, family-owned lodgings where you'll be made to feel as if you've just moved in. Still others qualify as personalized and highly refined boutique hotels with creature comforts and amenities galore. Ultimately, a *pousada* distinguishes itself from a hotel by its small size—many are located in houses or bungalows as opposed to high-rise hotels—and its B&B style. *Pousadas* are rare in big cities, particularly Rio, São Paulo, and Brasília, but you'll find them everywhere else, particularly in beach areas. A terrific source for *pousadas* across the country is Hidden Pousadas Brazil (www.hiddenpousadasbrazil.com).

Pousadas tend to be more affordable than hotels, but if you're really on a tight budget you might want to consider staying in an *albergue* or hostel, which aren't just for single, teen, and 20-something backpackers anymore. Many Brazilian *albergues* often have private double and even family rooms, with amenities such as air-conditioning and bathrooms. Although traditionally they tended to oscillate between stark barracks (in urban areas) and tropically rustic (in rural and beach areas), the last few years has witnessed a bumper crop of well-designed, homey hostels, tricked out with lounges, media centers, gardens, and countless amenities, with many of them located in the central cores (and even posher *bairros*) of major cities such as Rio and São Paulo. For a list of more than 80 hostels in Brazil, consult the Federação Brasileira dos Albergues de Juventude (www.hostel.org.br). In larger cities, renting an apartment or room via online services such as Airbnb (www.airbnb.com) is also a great solution, particularly since Brazilian or expat owners can prove to be very useful contacts.

EATING OUT

Aside from your classic sit-down restaurant serving à la carte fare, Brazil has a wide variety of eating options. Highly popular and very affordable are restaurants serving *comida por quilo* where you help yourself to a self-service buffet and then pay for your food by weight. The fare served ranges from very basic to banquet worthy. Depending on where you are, you'll find buffets that feature regional dishes, particularly in Minas and the Northeast. Ideal for vegetarians, *comida natural* (health food) restaurants also usually operate on a per-kilo system. Unfortunately, most *quilo* restaurants are only open for lunch.

Also popular are *rodízios.* At a *rodízio* (which means "rotation"), you pay a set price and then choose from a rotating display of food proffered by waiters who circle endlessly between the kitchen and the dining room. *Rodízio* is most common with *churrasco* (barbecue), but other common variations include pizza, pasta, and sushi.

Simple bars known as *botecos* are another great source of delicious home-cooked grub. For the happy-hour or late-night crowd, it's common to nibble on snacks known as *petiscos* or *tira-gostos.* Options vary tremendously according to the region and the sophistication of the bar, but universal classics include *bolinhos de bacalhau* (crunchy codfish balls) and *caldo de feijão* (a thick bean soup). One or several *porções* of these snacks can easily serve as a meal, and in fact, tables of Brazilians often communally share one or more dishes in lieu of dinner. However, lots of bars do also serve full meals, which run the gamut from home-cooked *pratos fixos* (inexpensive dishes of the day) to innovative fare on par with some of Brazil's finest restaurants.

Throughout Brazil, you'll find an enormous array of cheap and delicious snacks both on the street and on the beach, which can easily serve as a light meal. Some of the best cooking you'll taste—*tacacá* in Belém, *acarajé* in Salvador, *tapiocas* in Maceió, *pastéis* in São Paulo—is made and served on the street. Although foreigners may be leery of purchasing food on the street, hygienic conditions are generally strict. That said, use your judgment and stick to places in main areas where you see a lot of people lining up or eating. Meanwhile, in cities, small beach towns, and even seemingly deserted stretches of sand—particularly in the Northeast—you'll always encounter at least one *barraca,* or rustic beach bar, that will serve up freshly grilled fish or shrimp, and often much more.

RIO DE JANEIRO
Accommodations
The **Hotel Regina** (Rua Ferreira Viana 29, tel. 21/3289-9999, www.hotelregina.com. br, R$160–190 d) conserves few features from its 1920s heyday, but its clean, decently sized guest rooms are bright and comfortable. The location, on a small street half a block from Parque do Flamengo, is quiet and convenient.

In Copacabana, a good low-frills option is the **Hotel Toledo** (Rua Domingos Ferreira 71, 21/2257-1990, www.hoteltoledo.com.br, R$165 d), which is located on a leafy street only a block from the beach. Rooms vary in size (ask to take a look) but are clean and pleasant enough. A perk is the top-floor breakfast room with smashing views of the beach.

The **Arena Copacabana** (Av. Atlântica 2064, tel. 21/3034-1501, www.arenahotel. com.br, R$370–605 d) is a glossy ultramodern affair whose guest rooms are tricked out with the latest mod cons (Wi-Fi is *not* free). The more expensive ones have sea views, but all guests can dip their toes in the tiny rooftop pool. The staff gets kudos for helpfulness.

Straddling Ipanema and Leblon beaches, **Hotel Praia Ipanema** (Av. Vieira Souto 706, tel. 21/2141-4949, www.praiaipanema.com, R$440–470 d) allows you to live it up in posh Zona Sul style without maxing out your credit card. Minimalist rooms all have private balconies with sea views.

Based in Santa Teresa, **Cama e Café** (Rua Paschoal Carlos Magno 90, tel. 21/2225-4366, www.camaecafe.com.br) is a B&B network that links travelers and (often very interesting) residents. Many hosts are artists and liberal professionals with at least a smattering of English. Most homes are in Santa Teresa, but options in Copacabana and Ipanema exist as well. Expect to pay between R$150–250.

Dining
Although **Lamas** (Rua Marquês de Abrantes 18, Flamengo, tel. 21/2556-0799, www. cafe-lamas.com.br, 9:30am–2am Sun.–Thurs., 9:30am–4am Fri.–Sat.) has changed addresses several times since it first opened in 1874, everything about the place—from the suave bow-tied waiters to the retro ambiance—is suffused with an aura of Rio's

dining past. The food is solid, affordable fare without surprises. Most famous are the succulent filets mignons.

In Copacabana, **O Caranguejo** (Rua Barata Ribeiro 771, tel. 21/2235-1249, www.restaurantecaranguejo.com.br, 8am–2am daily) is an unpretentious place to kick back with an icy beer and pig out on fresh fish and seafood. For a snack, try the *empadas* filled with shrimp and Portuguese olives or the breaded crab claws.

A mere block from Ipanema beach, **Delirio Tropical** (Rua Garcia D'Ávila 48, tel. 21/3624-8164, www.deliriotropical.com.br, 9am–9pm daily) is a great place for a healthy meal after soaking up the sun. Choose from an array of colorful and unusual salads along with hot daily specials, and then enjoy your meal by watching beach bums walking by outside.

Another laid-back Ipanema hot spot, **Alessandro e Frederico Café** (Rua Garcia D'Ávila 134, Loja D, tel. 21/2521-0828, www.alessandroefrederico.com.br, 9am–1am Mon.–Thurs., noon–2am Fri.–Sat.) has a great selection of soups, salads, pastas, paninis, and well-executed hot entrees. The veranda is ideal for people watching. At night, head down the block to **Alessandro e Frederico Pizzeria** (Rua Garcia D'Ávila 151) for delicious pizza.

Although Brazil's most traditional dish—*feijoada*—is characteristically eaten on Saturday, you can find a mean version at **Brasileirinho** (Rua Jangadeiros 10, Loja A, tel. 21/2513-5184, www.cozinhatipica.com.br, noon–midnight daily), a rustically decorated Ipanema *boteco* that also serves hearty regional fare from the state of Minas Gerais. Another great place to sample authentic regional Brazilian food is the lively collection of *botecos* in **Cobal do Leblon** food market. The most original is **Arataca** (Rua Gilberto Cardoso, Loja 4, tel. 21/2512-6249, www.portalcobal.com.br, 9am–8pm Tues.–Sat., 9am–9pm Sun.) specializing in delicacies from the Brazilian North and Northeast including *carne de sol* (sun-dried beef) and *caldo de piranha* (piranha soup).

SÃO PAULO
Accommodations

The slogan of **155** (Rua Martinho Prado 173, Consolação, tel. 11/3150-1555, www.155hotel.com.br, R$135 d) is that "price is just a detail"—but what a sweet detail when you get box spring mattresses, free Wi-Fi, silent air conditioning, flat-screen cable TV, and stark, but attractive décor, not to mention a to-die-for location within spitting distance of trendy Baixa Augusta.

Hotel Pergamon (Rua Frei Caneca 80, Consolação, tel. 11/3123-2021, www.pergamon.com.br, R$230–290 d) was the first hotel in Brazil to introduce the concept of "chic and cheap" back in 1999. This early boutique hotel, just off Avenida Paulista, is the darling of hip Rua "Gay" Caneca. Rooms on the upper level offer terrific panoramic views.

Also right off Avenida Paulista, **Porto Bay L'Hotel** (Al. Campinas 266, Bela Vista, tel. 11/2183-0500, lhotel.com.br, R$550 d) is one of Sampa's only top chain hotels to buck the trend against big soulless high rises. Small and suffused with refined European elegance, it's also decently priced.

Part of the Spanish Sol Meliá chain, **Tryp Higienópolis** (Rua Maranhão 371, tel. 11/3665-8200, www.solmelia.com, R$220–260 d) offers impressively large condo-style accommodations. The bright, warmly accessorized rooms are a great bargain, especially in view of its location in elegant residential Higienópolis.

Dining

Located on the ground floor of Oscar Niemeyer's iconic curvaceous Copan building, **Bar da Dona Onça** (Av. Ipiranga 200, Lojas 27-29, Centro, tel. 11/3257-2016, www. bardadonaonca.com.br, noon–11pm Mon.–Wed., noon–midnight Thurs.–Sat., 1pm–5pm Sun.) serves up inspired reworkings of hearty Brazilian home-cooking classics such as *cuzcuz paulitas* (a polenta-based recipe stuffed with sardines, olives, peppers, peas, and hearts of palm). Saturday afternoon *feijoadas* have a loyal following.

Sampa's restaurants offer cuisine from all over the world, but if you're curious to try some authentic Amazonian food, head to **Amazonia** (Rua Rui Barbosa 206, Bela Vista, tel. 11/3042-9264, restauranteamazonia.wordpress.com, noon–3pm, 7pm-11:30pm Wed.–Sat., noon–10pm Sun.). The Spartan cafeteria-style deco is the antithesis of lush, but trademark dishes from the state of Pará, such as *tacacá, maniçoba,* and *pato no tucupi* are expertly prepared. On weekends, try the "best of" buffet.

After close to a century of existence, **Sujinho** (Rua da Consolação 2078, Consolação, www.sujinho.com.br, 11:30am–5am daily) is still a notorious all-day and after-hours hangout where Paulistanos mingle and dig into reasonably priced and deliciously tender barbecued meat. A wide array of side dishes allows you to assemble a meal according to your appetite.

In the heart of Jardins, **Figuiera Rubaiyat** (Rua Haddock Lobo 1738, Jardim Paulista, tel. 11/3087-1399, www.rubaiyat.com.br, noon–3:30pm, 7pm–midnight Mon.–Fri., noon–1am Sat., noon–6pm Sun.) is owned by the Rubaiyat restaurant chain, which is famed for its succulent cuts of fine beef. The *figueira* refers to the immense 80-year-old fig tree that spreads its limbs throughout much of this beautiful (though pricey) restaurant. Although the menu features all the delectable meats of its Rubaiyat siblings, the specialty here is fish and seafood.

Sampa is a hotbed of contemporary Brazilian cuisine and one of the most sizzling new chefs is Helena Rizzo who heads up the unpretentious **Maní** (Rua Joaquim Antunes 210, Jardim Paulistano, tel. 11/3085-4148, www.manimanioca.com.br, noon–3pm, 8pm–midnight Tues.–Fri., 1pm-4pm, 8:30pm–12:30am Sat., 1pm-5pm Sun.). Even the caipirinhas—with ginger ice cubes—will blow your mind. Weekday lunch offers daily specials that are more moderately priced than dinner menus.

MINAS, CENTRAL WEST, AND SOUTH
Accommodations

In Belo Horizonte, **Hotel Turista** (Rua Rio de Janeiro 423, tel. 31/3222-6160, www. turista.com, R$125–150 d) is a great bargain in the busy hub of Centro. Located in a 1950s building, it offers clean and simple rooms. The only drawback is the urban background noise. In Savassi, **Hotel Boulevard Park** (Rua Bernardo Guimarães 925, tel. 31/3261-2000, www.hotelboulevardpark.com, R$200–240 d) is a pleasant option that feels more like moving into an apartment building than checking into a hotel. Offering spotless standard rooms, it's located on a quiet tree-shaded street.

In Ouro Preto, the palatial 18th-century **Pouso do Chico Rei** (Rua Brigadeiro Mosqueira 90, tel. 31/3551-1274, www.pousodochicorei.com.br, R$140–210 d) is one of the most charming and oldest *pousadas* in town. Featuring rustic antiques, the lovely guest rooms can accommodate 1–5 people.

In Brasília's hotel district, the **Bittar Monumental** (SHN, Qd. 3, Bl. B, tel.

61/3704-4000, www.hoteisbittar.com.br, R$190–240 d) is one of the capital's more attractive budget options. Sizable rooms are nicely, if innocuously decorated. Ask for a room with hardwood floors that doesn't face onto the noisy main thoroughfare.

In Curitiba, **Nikko** (Rua Barão Rio Branco 546, Centro, tel. 41/2105-1808, www.hotelnikko.com.br, R$110–150 d) is a great nontraditional budget choice. This refined and modern Japanese hotel offers a soothing atmosphere with lots of Asian touches. Guest rooms are small but relaxing. A bamboo garden and sushi complete the ode to Japan.

If you want to base yourself in Florianópolis' Centro (as opposed to the Lagoa or beaches), the **InterCity Premium Florianópolis** (Av. Paulo Fontes 1210, tel. 48/3027-2200, www.intercityhoteis.com.br, R$150–165 d) is a gleaming hotel right across from the bus station. Spacious rooms are decorated with modern panache and feature enormous windows that, from high up, afford outstanding views of the bay and mainland.

In Porto Alegre, those with sustainable sensibilities will approve of **Eko Residence** (Av. Des. André da Rocha 131, tel. 51/3225-8644, www.ekoresidence.com.br, R$180–230 d). Located in Centro, this "green" hotel's energy needs are partially met by wind and solar power, and it recycles rainwater and garbage. Rooms are spacious and feature free Wi-Fi along with kitchenettes. An in-house restaurant serves healthy fare, and the color green—from painted walls to potted plants—is pleasantly omnipresent.

Dining

Belo Horizonte has its share of top addresses where you can savor Mineiro cooking in all its robust glory. One of the most traditional is **Dona Lucinha** (Rua Sergipe 811, Funcionários, tel. 31/3261-5930, www.donalucinha.com.br, noon–3pm, 7pm-11pm Mon.–Sat., noon–5pm Sun.) where for R$41 you have unlimited access to a mouthwatering buffet of close to 40 dishes that serve as a fine introduction to Mineiro cuisine.

In Ouro Preto, **Casa dos Contos Restaurante** (Rua Camilo de Brito 21, tel. 31/3551-5359, noon–midnight Sun.–Tues., noon–10pm Wed.–Sat.) also serves up mouthwatering Mineiro cuisine in the former slave quarters of an 18th-century mansion. While lunch is a per-kilo buffet, dinner is à la carte.

In Brasília, conveniently located off the Eixo Monumental, **Don'Durica** (CLS, Qd. 115, Bl C, Lj. 36, tel. 61/3346-8922, www.dondurica.com.br, 11:30am–3pm, 6pm-11pm Mon.-Fri., noon-3:30pm and 6pm-11pm Sat.) offers an amazing array of hot, cold, fresh, and appetizing dishes for a reasonable price in agreeable surroundings. Other locations exist in CLS and CLN.

In Curitiba, **Estrela da Terra** (Rua Jaime Reis 176, São Francisco, tel. 41/3222-5007, www.restauranteestreladaterra.com.br, 11:30am–2pm Tues.–Thurs., 11:30am–3:30pm Fri.–Sun.) is one of the few restaurants that serves typical Paranaense cuisine. Hearty dishes created by the state's earliest settlers, which reveal a marked indigenous influence, are laid out in a lavish and very affordable buffet (during the week, à la carte dishes are also available). Try Paraná's most famous dish, *barreado*.

In Floripa's Centro, a classic spot to eat and hang out is at the **Mercado Público** (Rua Conselheiro Mafra 255, 48/3225-8464) where you can fill up on fish and seafood while slugging back icy beers. **Box 32** (tel. 48/3244-5588, www.box32.com.br, 10am–8pm Mon.–Fri., 10am–3pm Sat.) is a Floripa institution that draws locals and tourists. The shrimp stuffed *pastéis* are particularly addictive.

One of the best spots for traditional *churrasco* in Porto Alegre is **Barranco** (Av.

Protásio Alves 1578, Petrópolis, tel. 51/3331-6172, www.churrascariabarranco.com. br, 11am–2am daily). In a given month, some 15,000 local carnivores devour 8,000 tons of prime cuts of beef, pork, and lamb. The best seats are those scattered beneath a shady canopy of jacarandas.

NORTHEAST
Accommodations

In Salvador, the low-key and attractive **Pousada Estrela do Mar** (Rua Afonso Celso 119, tel. 71/3264-4882, www.estreladomarsalvador.com, R$125–185 d) in Barra is only a block from the beach. The friendly Scottish owners have transformed two houses into 12 apartments (the upstairs ones are nicer), decorated in maritime shades of blue and white. Just off the Corredor da Vitória, **Casa da Vitória** (Rua Aloísio de Carvalho 95, tel. 71/3013-2016, www.casadavitoria.com, R$215–285) is owned by a brother-sister team who converted their handsome two-story family residence, on a quiet cul-de-sac, into a casual guesthouse that feels like home (albeit with a fabulous collection of contemporary Bahian artwork).

In Recife, **Hotel Jangadeiro** (Av. Boa Viagem 3114, tel. 81/3086-5050, www.jangadeirohotel.com.br, R$195–275 d) is one of Boa Viagem's nicest affordable beachfront options. The large comfy guest rooms all have full or at least partial sea views.

In Fortaleza, **Hotel Marina Praia** (Rua Paula Barros 44, tel. 85/3242-7734, www. hotelmarinapraia.com.br, R$100–130 d) is a cozy, small-scale hotel located in a residential building in Meireles surrounded by a pretty little garden. Simple air-conditioned rooms are bright with good lighting and hardwood floors. Staff is friendly.

Dining

In Salvador a practical, affordable, not to mention pleasant, option for lunch or dinner is the fresh and varied per kilo buffet at the Teatro Castro Alves's café **Teatro do TCA** (Rua Leovigildo Figueiras 18, tel. 71/3328-5818, 11:30am–3pm daily, 5pm–11pm performance nights), overlooking Campo Grande. Local and visiting musicians, dancers, and thespians performing at Salvador's premiere theater eat here, making it a great place for people watching. Salvador's favorite fast food is the *acarajé*, a crunchy deep-fried bean fritter stuffed with dried shrimp and traditional fillings such as *vatapá* and *caruru*. Deep fried in palm oil by Baianas, you'll find them throughout the city's beaches and streets, but the most famous are Dinha and Regina in Rio Vermelho's Largo de Santana, which are open daily in the afternoons and evenings.

In Recife, the tiny beach neighborhood of Pina, wedged between Boa Viagem and Centro, concentrates a wide assortment of restaurants and bars and really comes to life at night. **Pra Vocês** (Av. Herculano Bandeira 115, tel. 81/3326-3168, 11am–midnight Sun.–Thurs., 11am–2am Fri.–Sat.) is one of the more traditional seafood restaurants in the city. The varied menu ranges from simple fare such as fried *agulinhas* (sardine-sized swordfish) to lobster thermidor.

In Fortaleza, **Colher de Pau** (Rua Frederico Borges 206, tel. 85/3267-6176, 11am–midnight Sun.–Thurs., 11am–1am Fri.–Sat.) is a classic address for regional home-cooked dishes such as *arroz-de-carneiro* (a local version of lamb risotto) and *peixada* (fish stew) as well as the most tender *carne de sol* in town. Outdoor tables shaded by leafy trees are also very pleasant. Live music is performed nightly.

DAILY LIFE

MAKING THE MOVE

Making a move is always a stressful experience. Making a move to another country, in another hemisphere, with a different language and culture, different laws and ways of doing things can be even more so. Brazil is a notoriously bureaucratic country where often the most simple procedure is transformed into a process more complexly baroque than the famed architecture of its colonial churches. Expect things to take a lot of time and to not always make sense. Count on there being a discrepancy between what you're told over the phone and what you're told in person (and from person to person). Be prepared to be stonewalled—or for things to be made miraculously easy. Arm yourself with every official document under the sun (even ones that aren't specifically asked for) and a good book for potential waiting periods. It helps to be patient—and to be charming—but also to be firm if you sense you're being given the runaround (which can happen). It also helps to have Brazilian friends or contacts to help you navigate the often murky waters.

Immigration and Visas

Whether you're traveling to Brazil for a short or long period of time, the basic requirements include a passport valid for at least six months from the date of your arrival and a visa. To find out all the necessary requirements (which change from time to time) and to apply for a visa, check the website of the Brazilian consulate closest to you.

Application forms for all visas can be filled out online (https://scedv.serpro.gov.br) and printed out. Regardless of the type of visa for which you're applying, you'll need to schedule an appointment at the site of the Brazilian consulate closest to you. Do this as soon as possible since time slots can get booked up. Along with providing recent color passport-sized photos, you must pay a visa fee (ranging from US$140–240 depending on the type of visa) by purchasing a U.S. Postal Service money order payable to the Consulate General of Brazil.

Visa applications must be done in person by scheduling an appointment online for *each* visa applicant and then showing up at the nearest consulate with the necessary documents and payment. Expect processing for tourist visas to take around five working days. Other visas take longer. For some visas (including tourist visas), authorized family members or third parties that live in the consulate's jurisdiction can apply for you (although there is an extra $20 fee).

Common Types of Visas

TOURIST VISA

Brazil operates on the basis of reciprocity, which means that citizens of countries, such as Canada and the United States, that demand tourist visas from Brazilian citizens, must apply for tourist visas to visit Brazil. Basic tourist visas allow you to stay in Brazil for 90 days. Many travel agents specializing in Brazil as well as visa agencies can also process your visa for you (which involves an extra US$20 fee).

Aside from the standard requirements listed above, if you're applying for a tourist visa, you must provide a copy of your round-trip itinerary or e-ticket confirmation.

If you're traveling with a child under 18, a copy of his or her birth certificate is necessary. Children not traveling with both parents or guardians require a letter of consent from the parent not traveling, and those between 3 months and 6 years of age must provide a certificate of vaccination against polio or a doctor's note explaining that the child can't be inoculated.

Brazilian tourist visas are valid for multiple entries within the period of time shown on your visa stamp. If you want to stay longer than the initial 90 days, you can apply for an extension for another 90 days once you're in Brazil. This can be done by visiting the closest branch of the Polícia Federal; a list of offices can be found online at the Polícia Federal site: www.dpf.gov.br. Online, you can schedule an appointment for your extension and fill out the necessary form, the **Guia de Recolhimento da União** (www.dpf.gov.br). Print it out and bring it with you along with your passport, airline ticket, credit card (as proof of financial means), and the embarkation/debarkation card all foreigners receive upon arriving in Brazil. The Guia includes the visa extension fee (R$102

Documents always need to be authenticated at a *cartório*.

in 2012), which is payable at any Banco do Brasil where you will receive a receipt that you must provide along with your documents at the Polícia Federal office.

Keep in mind that visitors can only spend a total of 6 months within a 12-month period in Brazil on a tourist visa. No matter how you divide up your time, once you've fulfilled your 180-day limit, you have to leave the country. It is an offense to stay in Brazil beyond the duration of the visa. If you do so, you'll have to pay a fine based on the number of days you overstay (up to a maximum limit).

BUSINESS VISA

If you're traveling to Brazil for a business meeting, to close a deal, to explore investment, relocation, or outsourcing opportunities, or to engage in filming or media coverage, you should consider applying for a business visa. Note that business visas do *not* give you the right to work or earn income in Brazil or to acquire a business (including rural land). On your application form, you'll have to specify what activities you plan to carry out in Brazil.

Aside from the standard visa requirements listed above, you'll need to provide a letter on your company's letterhead, signed by management, explaining your job, the purpose of your trip, who will pay your expenses, and how long you plan to stay in Brazil. If you're self-employed, you'll need to provide a bank statement showing you have enough funds to finance your stay. You'll also need a letter from your business contact in Brazil (in Portuguese) stating the reason for, and duration of, your visit and the activities you'll be engaged in.

A useful source for those interested in investing or doing business in Brazil is BrasilGlobalNet (www.brasilglobalnet.gov.br). Operated by the Ministério das Relações Exteriores (Ministry of External Relations), this network offers a wide range of information on various aspects of doing business in Brazil, ranging from Brazilian regulations and trade agreements to investment opportunities and trade fairs.

WORK VISA

If you're going to be doing any kind of work at all in Brazil—either paid or volunteer, with or without a contract—or you are participating in any type of training, internship, or residency program, you need to have a work visa.

In order to obtain a work visa, an application has to be sent to the local Ministério do Trabalho e Emprego (Ministry of Labor and Employment) by the Brazilian company—or the foreign company's affiliate based in Brazil—that wishes to employ you. Different visas are available depending on your situation and the work you plan to do.

Permanent visas (valid five years) are available for company administrators and for those who plan to invest in a Brazilian business as well as scientists, professors, and researchers. Temporary visas are available for skilled workers who can prove that no Brazilian citizen can perform their duties. Valid for two years, they can be renewed for another two years. Such visas are often issued to people hired by Brazil-based affiliates of foreign companies, but they are also available to similarly qualified individuals who want to work as independent contractors on specific projects (usually for Brazilian companies).

To find out about requirements relative to your specific activity, consult the online procedure guide published by the Ministry of Labor (www.mte.gov.br).

Once the Ministry of Labor has approved your application—deliberation could take a month, provided you have *all* your documents in order—it is sent to the Ministry of External Affairs, which will authorize the consulate to begin processing the visa itself. Aside from filling out the online application form, you need proof of residency in the consulate's jurisdiction for more than one year and a certificate from your city police department showing you have no criminal record.

Applicants who don't have a work contract or who aren't employees of a business based in Brazil—for example, those doing volunteer work—need to provide further documentation, including proof of health insurance that is valid in Brazil and a letter of invitation from the Brazilian organization where you'll be working or volunteering that attests to its legitimacy and outlines your duties.

The bureaucracy involved in obtaining a work visa is notorious. In response to the scarcity of qualified labor in Brazil and the recent flux of foreigners seeking to fill positions, efforts have been made to speed up and streamline the process, but it's still a fairly long and drawn-out affair. When applying, you basically have to prove why no Brazilian can do the job that you are being hired to do. This is much easier if you're an engineer, scientist, tech expert, or are angling for a job in the booming oil, mining, or IT industries.

In many cases, the company that is hiring or transferring you will have immigration lawyers or specialists on hand that will deal with the visa process for you as well as for your family. A work visa allows spouses and dependents to legally reside in Brazil, but does not allow them to work. In order for a spouse to work in Brazil, he or she would need to get his or her own work visa or become a permanent resident of Brazil.

STUDENT VISA

If you're planning to study in Brazil, you'll need a student visa. Aside from the standard visa requirements listed above, you'll need to provide an official letter from the Brazilian university or educational institution where you'll be enrolled that includes details of the program and any grants that you will be receiving. Students without grants must provide a notarized letter proving that your parents have the means to support you during your studies. If you're under 18, you'll need a letter of consent from both parents that allows the consulate to approve your visa. If you're over 18, you must provide a certificate from your city police department that you have no criminal record as well as proof that you've been residing in the consulate's jurisdiction for more than a year. Also necessary is proof of valid health insurance that covers you in Brazil.

SCIENTIFIC RESEARCH VISA

A scientific research visa is a temporary visa for foreigners who are experts in a field of knowledge and who are coming to Brazil to give a presentation or engage in teaching, research, or training activities. If you're doing graduate or postgraduate work, you might also apply for this visa. Apart from the standard visa documents listed above, you'll need to provide a letter of invitation from the Brazilian institution that is sponsoring you and a copy of the government decree (*portaria*) issued by the Ministério da Ciência e Tecnologia (Ministry of Science and Technology) (for projects that involve scientific and technological cooperation). If you plan on staying longer than 90 days, you'll need to provide proof of a research grant as well.

RETIREMENT VISA

If you're 50 years of age or older, you can apply for a retirement visa on condition that you can prove that you have an official monthly pension (social security or private) equivalent to R$6,000 for one person, and an additional R$2,000 per additional dependent, which can cover up to three immediate family members (i.e., you, a spouse, and a child). As proof, you'll need a notarized letter from the institution that pays your pension and a notarized declaration from your bank branch that will be responsible for transferring your funds to Brazil.

Other documents you will need are a letter stating why you want to move to Brazil; an authenticated copy of your passport (notarized by a notary public and authenticated at the consulate); certified copies of your birth certificate and if married, marriage certificate; a recent identification record issued by the FBI (www.fbi.gov) showing you have no criminal record, legalized by the Consulate General of Brazil in Washington D.C. (www.consbrasdc.org); and proof that you've been living in the jurisdiction of your consulate for more than 12 months.

Permanent Residency

Foreigners with either temporary or permanent visas can apply to be permanent residents of Brazil based on the following conditions:

- Marriage (or stable union) with a Brazilian citizen
- Having a child with a Brazilian citizen
- Retirement
- Family reunion
- As a high-level scientist or researcher
- As an administrator, director, or manager of a Brazilian company (or Brazilian affiliate of a foreign company)
- As an investor in a Brazilian company or start-up

In general, the most common—and easiest—ways of acquiring permanent residency are by marrying a Brazilian and by investing in a Brazilian company or starting a business.

MARRIAGE TO A BRAZILIAN NATIONAL

If you're married to a Brazilian citizen, you can begin the process of applying for permanent residency at your local Brazilian consulate—or travel to Brazil on a tourist visa and begin the procedure in Brazil at the Serviço de Estrangeiros section of your local Polícia Federal office. In either case, aside from a valid passport and documents from both spouses, you'll need to supply copies of the marriage certificate and statements from witnesses along with proof that you have no criminal record. All documents will need to be notarized, but if you undergo the process in Brazil, you'll need to have them all officially translated as well (which can add up).

Many recommend beginning the process outside of Brazil since it seems to go more quickly; the difference can be a matter of a few or many months (the time it takes for the Ministério da Justiça (Ministry of Justice) in Brasília to sift through all the paperwork and grant permission). In general though, expect to wait anywhere from seven months to a year before you obtain your Permanent Residency Card, or Carteira de Identidade de Estrangeiro (CIE); the actual card—valid for nine years—will be given to you at your local Polícia Federal office, upon providing a photo and a permanent Brazilian address, paying a processing fee, and being fingerprinted.

If you get married to a Brazilian within Brazil, the moment you begin the application process for permanent residency, you'll be able to stay in the country indefinitely (pending the outcome of the Ministry of Justice's decision). Make sure in advance that you have *all* your non-Brazilian documents in order (some can only be authenticated by the Brazilian consulate in your home country); if not, you'll have to fly home to do so. Among the Brazilian documents you'll need to supply are a declaration that your Brazilian spouse will support you (accompanied by proof of his or her income) because until you receive your permanent residency, you won't be allowed to legally work in Brazil. Also be prepared for at least one surprise visit from the Polícia Federal to make sure that your marriage is legit and not just one of convenience.

Although Brazil has not legalized gay marriage, it has legalized *uniões estaveis* (stable unions) whereby couples—both heterosexual and homosexual—who have been living together have the same rights as married couples, provided they can prove that they have been cohabitating (usually for a minimum of three years). Under this law, unmarried foreigners—whether straight or gay—can be sponsored by their Brazilian partners and obtain permanent residency. Under the same provision, once in Brazil, the foreign partner also has the rights to share the Brazilian partner's health insurance, welfare, and other benefits.

INVESTMENT

If you have the funds, another common way of gaining residency is by investing in a new or preexisting Brazilian company or in your own start-up business. A start-up business can include the purchase of real estate or rural land—provided that it involves a productive activity that is creating jobs (i.e., buying a house that will function as a restaurant or *pousada* or purchasing land that will be used for farming). Presently, the minimum investment required is R$150,000.

People who apply for permanent residency based on investment start out by applying for a permanent resident visa at their local Brazilian consulate, but they must also have a lawyer or a Brazilian partner (with a power of attorney) who begins the proceedings in Brazil through the Ministry of Labor. The key to acquiring this visa is submitting a business plan that itemizes how much you plan to invest, which economic sector and Brazilian region you will operate in, and how many Brazilian jobs will be created. After opening a corporation in your name (in the position of owner), you open a corporate bank account that is registered with the Banco do Brasil upon the transfer of R$150,000. The bank will then issue a certificate that will accompany your visa application as it is judged, approved, and issued in Brazil and then sent to your local Brazilian consulate so that your passport can be stamped with the investor's visa.

Upon arrival in Brazil, you have 30 days to appear at your local Polícia Federal office to register and receive your CIE, which is valid for three years. At the end of this time, in order to have your CIE extended, you'll have to submit to a review to prove that you are actually carrying out the activity you promised in your initial business plan and providing jobs. The investor's visa allows you to bring your spouse and dependents with you to reside in Brazil. When you receive your permanent residency status, your family members receive permanent residency as well.

APPLYING FOR RESIDENCY

Applying for residency can be a complex process, particularly if you don't speak Portuguese and if you don't have any Brazilians around who know the ropes and can guide you. Even those who have mastered the language and have a solid Brazilian support system might want to consider using an immigration lawyer who is up to date on all the necessary requirements, can shuffle the paperwork for you, and may even have access to inside tracks. Although not essential, having a good *advogado* can often save you a lot of time, money, hassle, and tearing out of hair.

Most people outside of Brazil who are seeking permanent residency start the process of applying for a permanent visa through the Brazilian consulate closest to them. Once you receive your visa, you have 90 days to appear in Brazil and complete the process at the Polícia Federal office in the city where you plan to reside. No matter what kind of visa you hold, you must be living in Brazil to obtain residency.

Upon submitting your residency application, you'll receive a protocol number that serves as proof of temporary residency status. Even if your original visa expires, this document allows you to legally reside in Brazil while your application is being processed. To check on the status of your application—which could take anywhere from seven months to two years—you can log on to the Ministry of Justice website (http://portal.mj.gov.br) using your name and protocol number.

During this time, you can apply for a **Carteira de Trabalho,** or work permit, which is valid until your residency is approved. A Carteira de Trabalho allows you to legally work or set up your own business or both.

Once your demand has been processed, the outcome (if approved) will be published in the *Diário Oficial da União* (Official Journal of the Union), a government journal that is published daily and is available for purchase at most newsstands as well as online. You then have 90 days to return to the Polícia Federal, armed with a printed copy of your application's approval in the *Diário* so that you can receive your CIE. A laminated plastic card larger than a credit card, your CIE will feature your photo, thumb print, and **Registro Nacional de Estrangeiro** (RNE), an identity number for foreign residents that you'll need any time you're required to present official ID.

With the exception of residency permits accorded to those with investment visas, residency is permanent; all you need to do is renew your CIE card at your local Polícia Federal office when it expires (once every nine years). However, if you stay outside of the country for more than two years, you automatically lose your residency status and will have to reapply.

Moving with Children

Getting kids excited about a move to Brazil shouldn't be that difficult; the country is one of the most exciting places on the planet with adventure in its DNA. Large Brazilian cities offer endless opportunities and diversions for children of all ages, but no matter where you live, the ease with which kids can access beaches, waterfalls, mountains, rainforests, and other incredible outdoor destinations assures contact with nature and unforgettable experiences (not to mention endless vacation possibilities).

DAILY LIFE

LANGUAGE ISSUES

A big issue for kids moving to Brazil is language. Arriving in a foreign country and not being able to communicate or be understood can be very frustrating and even scary. For this reason, it's a good idea for kids to learn as much Portuguese as possible before the move. Very few Brazilians speak English with any fluency. If you end up in a large city, of course, like many expats (especially those moving for short-term durations), you'll probably—at least initially—want to enroll your kids in private American, British, or international schools where the main language of education will be English, but Portuguese lessons will also be offered. Your kids will quickly be able to make friends and fit in culturally and linguistically with other expat children from North America and around the world as well as Brazilian children intent on learning English.

International schools have many benefits, foremost of which are the quality of the education and the fact that curricula are based on those in North America or Britain, ensuring kids on short-term stays do not get behind in their studies. Drawbacks, however, include the high fees and the fact that most are only located in big cities and your kids may end up interacting with a very select social group (i.e., expats and children of wealthy Brazilians). That said, there are many other ways your children can have uniquely Brazilian experiences and learn new skills while also coming into contact with Brazilian kids from different walks of life and perfecting their Portuguese. Many cities and towns, for example, have capoeira academies and soccer and volleyball teams for boys and girls of all ages. Teens can benefit from an even greater range of activities including more adventurous ones such as hiking, climbing, and surfing.

FITTING IN

Once kids have gotten over the language barrier, they usually find it very easy to meet people and fit in. Brazilians of all ages are a notoriously open, tolerant, and welcoming bunch, quick to embrace and accept foreigners into the fold without making a big issue of their foreignness. This goes double for kids; in fact, you might end up meeting a lot of friends through your children.

In Brazil's kid-friendly culture, not only do children interact amongst themselves with ease, but adults and children also interact with much greater frequency and naturalness. Adult strangers (albeit usually other parents with kids) stopping to talk to your kids might initially unsettle some Northern Hemisphere parents who were raised on the "don't talk to strangers" adage, but it's quite normal. A big advantage of this tendency is that your kids will likely end up being highly socialized.

Kids of all ages will find themselves going to more *festas* than they ever imagined. Aside from *festas populares* (yes, in big cities and small towns, in particular, even tiny tots take part in Carnaval festivities), there are tons of birthday parties (major extravaganzas featuring clowns, trampolines, live music, and sweet and savory delicacies) and, for teens, all sorts of parties featuring music and dancing. Moreover, children are often included in family and even adult *festas* (in Brazilian culture, celebrations and commemorations trump regular bedtime schedules). Although the official drinking age is 18, Brazilians in general are less hung up (for better) and more lax (for worse) about drinking alcohol.

BABIES AND TODDLERS

Brazilians uniformly adore newborns and toddlers. Indeed, foreigners are often struck by the number of strangers who insist upon cooing to, greeting, and mussing the hair of their offspring. By extension, babies and toddlers are welcome in many venues that would be strictly adult in the Northern Hemisphere, such as restaurants and even bars. You'll also find that public breastfeeding is fairly common.

In terms of baby clothing, accessories, toys, etc., you'll find pretty much everything you need, especially in large cities, although you can count on prices being higher than those in North America (diapers, for example, are a small fortune).

Most Brazilians make their own baby food (pureed fruits and vegetables for example) or have their *babás* (nannies) or *empregadas* (housekeepers) do so. Indeed, most middle- and upper-class Brazilians hire part-time or full-time nannies to help out (or even raise) their children. This can make bringing up baby a lot easier, especially since wages are much more affordable in Brazil (though they are steadily rising). There's no shortage of *babás* in the workforce, although you will have difficulty finding employees that speak English. Of course, this could actually be an advantage in that it gives expat parents an opportunity to practice or perfect their Portuguese while exposing youngsters to the language. Don't worry that your child's language development will be slowed by hearing two languages: Although some children in bilingual environments take longer to begin speaking, studies show that eventually young children sort out two (or three) languages and quickly juggle them with great proficiency.

SAFETY CONCERNS

A big issue—for kids and their parents—is security. Without being paranoid or overprotective, it's quite simply not as safe for school-age kids and even teens to wander around a lot of places on their own as they would in North America or Europe. Most middle-class Brazilian kids in big cities end up spending more time at each other's apartments or on supervised play dates, not to mention playing or hanging out in enclosed playground and social areas. This is sensible—although it needn't be taken to extremes (i.e., you don't want your child to feel as if he or she is living in a goldfish bowl). Sometimes, you have to make an effort to get kids to beaches or parks where they can interact more freely with other children. Of course, if you're living in a small town or rural area, your kids will be able to run much more wildly and interact more easily with Brazilians, and especially with Brazilian children, from all walks of life.

It's important to train your kids to take added precautions (not stray from the beaten path, not to wear flashy items of clothing, to be careful with money and other valuables, to stick with other kids or teens, to inform adults of their whereabouts) while not leaving them feeling nervous or anxious. Some expats—like many wealthier Brazilians—live out their lives in gated communities, shopping centers, and wealthy enclaves where the rest of Brazil is kept at bay, but doing this means you'll risk missing out on the best of Brazil and miss teaching your kids invaluable lessons with respect to complex socioeconomic realities.

Moving with Pets

If you plan on moving to Brazil for a significant amount of time—or permanently—you might want to consider bringing your pet along with you. Keep in mind, however, that depending on the species, age, health, and personality of your cat or dog, life in Brazil could have a major—and not necessarily beneficial—effect on your pet's well-being.

TRAVELING WITH CATS AND DOGS TO BRAZIL

A certain amount of bureaucracy is involved in taking a cat or dog to Brazil, some of which must unavoidably be done at the last minute. In order to minimize stress for both yourself and your pet, it's best to prepare as much as possible in advance.

Check with your closest Brazilian consulate to verify the latest updated requirements for traveling with pets. Also check out different airlines' policies in terms of pet travel; these can vary somewhat. For your pet's comfort, book a flight with the most direct route possible. Keep in mind that long flights can be traumatic for animals. It's a good idea to have your pet take short trips in a carrier in advance.

Brazil doesn't demand that cats and dogs be outfitted with ISO pet microchips prior to travel (a simple procedure that can be carried out at your local vet); however, you may want to do so for safety purposes. What is necessary is that cats and dogs over three months of age receive a rabies shot, administered more than 1 month and less than 12 months before travel. They'll also need to be accompanied by a valid rabies vaccination certificate, issued by a USDA-licensed vet, and endorsed by the USDA or CFIA if entering Brazil from either the United States or Canada, as well as an International Health Certificate issued by the same vet, attesting that your pet is in good health. The latter must be issued within 10 days before your departure to Brazil. In addition, you'll need to bring all other information regarding your pet—name, weight, breed, sex, etc.—to the USDA to be stamped.

Before flying, check with the airline about pet carrier requirements as well as special check-in procedures and where and how you will retrieve your pet in Brazil. Make sure your animal's carrier is large enough for it to turn around in and is stocked with a water dispenser, training pad, favorite blanket, and toys.

This upscale pet shop features a beauty salon.

DAILY LIFE FOR PETS

Pets are popular in Brazil though not to the same extent as in North America which has a significant pet culture. Due to a combination of heat and dense urban centers where (small) apartment living is the norm, you rarely encounter large and long-haired breeds of dogs. In working class and poorer neighborhoods as well as rural areas, you'll encounter a lot of (stray) mutts.

Wealthy Brazilians go gaga over small pure breeds, but especially poodles; in the upscale neighborhoods of Rio, São Paulo, Salvador, and other big cities, it's very common to see owners—or their hired help—taking poodles for daily outings, decked out in all manner of ribbons, bows, doggie tees, and even little shoes. Hiring dog walkers in Brazil is inexpensive; more challenging is finding places where dogs can actually walk considering the scant distribution of parks compared to North American cities. Meanwhile, in both rural and wealthy urban areas, houses often come equipped with ferocious sounding dobermans and other guard dogs (inevitably signaled by a big *Cuidado Cão Bravo* [Careful Angry Dog] sign).

Although you'll come across apartments with No Pet clauses, Brazilians tend to be more easygoing in terms of allowing tenants to own pets (particularly cats). If you have cats, be prepared to safety proof your apartment by outfitting windows and balconies with netting (window screens are rare). Make sure you provide your pet with filtered water and be on the lookout for ticks.

Finding basic offerings of dry food for dogs and cats at small stores and markets throughout Brazil is always easy. Larger supermarket chains will have wider offerings in terms of food as well as other products and accessories; however, expect selection to be lower and prices to be considerably higher than in North America. In wealthy neighborhoods of large cities, especially Rio and São Paulo, you'll find a glut of specialized pet stores not to mention pet salons, spas, and high-quality vets. Vets in Brazil are very qualified and their services are reasonably priced in comparison with North American counterparts (some even do house calls), but you'll be hard-pressed to find vets that speak English outside of certain enclaves in Rio and São Paulo.

What to Take

Deciding what to take or not to take with you to Brazil depends on a lot of factors. The main one, however, is the amount of time you plan to stay. In general for short-term moves, the less you take, the better—unless you have a company that's picking up the costs—because once you get into shipping costs, you're going to start getting into serious expenditures.

On the flip side, a combination of high import taxes combined with a very high Brazilian *real* means that prices for most nonessential goods in Brazil—electronics, cosmetics and health care products, housewares, furniture, clothing—range from expensive to astronomical when compared to those in North America. Moreover, many items which in North America are seen as basic and are thus priced—everything from box-spring mattresses and high thread count sheets to Tylenol and high-SPF sunscreen—are viewed as luxuries or status symbols in Brazil and priced accordingly. If you're lucky enough to have a company paying for your move, you might want to bring as much as you can. Otherwise, focus on small but essential items that you can pick up cheaply in North America but will cost a fortune in Brazil. And then be prepared to adapt to local goods and improvised solutions upon your arrival.

ELECTRONICS

Electronics in Brazil—everything from flat-screen TVs, laptops, and digital cameras to cell phones and tablets—have become a lot more popular in recent years, as well as popularly priced. That said, they are generally still two-to-three times as expensive as in North America, so bring as much as you can from home.

HEALTH CARE AND COSMETICS

Brazil has a cutting-edge pharmaceutical sector, and you'll find that most medication, both over-the-counter and prescription, is reasonably priced, especially if you opt for the generic versions. At both pharmacies and stores selling natural products you can also find an amazing array of natural and herbal remedies, some of which are typically Brazilian ones based on indigenous traditions. If you take prescription medicine, you'll likely find the equivalent in Brazil (usually less expensive), although sold under another name; however, it's always best to research the differences before you leave home.

In terms of basics, nothing beats the likes of Duane Reade, Target, and Shopper's Drug Mart with their jumbo-sized packaging at cut-rate prices. For this reason, stock up on your favorite analgesics (a bottle of 100 Tylenol in the United States will cost the same as a dozen in Brazil) and items such as multipurpose vitamins and mosquito repellent. Above all bring tons and tons of high-SPF sunscreen; despite the fact that Brazil is world champion in terms of skin cancer, sunscreen is marketed as if it's imported Chanel perfume and costs just as much. Speaking of Chanel, also bring along your favorite high-quality brand-name moisturizers and facial cleansers, which are also exorbitantly priced. That said, Brazil has some terrific homegrown natural beauty product lines that take advantage of the healing, beautifying, and (supposedly) aphrodisiac properties of many native (particularly Amazonian) plants and fruits.

Sunscreen is astronomically priced in Brazil.

Specifically, look for bath and beauty products for both men and women made by Natura and O Boticário.

HOUSEWARES AND FURNITURE

Brazil has lots of domestically made housewares that you can purchase quite cheaply. The issue then comes down to a question of quality, performance, and sometimes aesthetics. For example, if you're fine using flatware with plastic handles whose fork tines get bent out of shape when squeezing lime juice, crushing your garlic and pepper corns in a traditional wooden mortar, drying your freshly showered self with YMCA-worthy towels, and sleeping on flimsy sheets stamped with bright colors, then you're set. However, if you're addicted to 300-thread-count sheets in neutral colors, plush towels, pepper grinders, garlic presses, and other kitchen tools of various degrees of so-phistication, consider bringing some or all of them from home since the prices of such items, targeted to the rich and nouveau rich, once again, are extravagant.

Good quality furniture is also hard to come by in Brazil unless you plan on spending a lot of money. Once again, there's no shortage of inexpensive, functional options, but if quality, comfort, and design are important to you, you'll be challenged unless you (or the company who sponsors you) possess a large budget.

Of course, with a little imagination, a local mindset, and a willingness to sleuth around, you can find an amazing array of quality, functional, and insanely beautiful solutions to a good many of your household needs. However, it means going off the beaten track of shopping malls, chain stores, and chic boutiques and eschewing imports and their imitations for artisanal products fashioned by local craftsmen and *donas de*

HOME CRAVINGS

It seems too churlish to mention foods Brazil doesn't have when it has such an abundance of fruit, fish, and other delicacies unfound and unheard of beyond its borders. The truth is, if you're in a big city, you can pretty much get your hands on everything your nostalgic taste buds desire—for a hefty price—by heading to a fancy delicatessen, which will always have a section relegated to imports. Truly, the only cravings that are likely to go unsatiated are for delicacies such as really good dark chocolate (rare and insanely expensive), licorice (red and black), and salt-and-vinegar potato chips, all of which I always stock up on.

casa (housewives). Brazil has a fantastically rich regional *artesenato* tradition, particularly in the states of the Northeast and North as well as Minas Gerais.

Examples include handwoven hammocks, ceramic vessels, enameled cups and dishes, intricately hand-embroidered towels and linens, mats and carpets of palm and other natural fibers, and hand-carved wooden tools and utensils. Aside from traveling to these regions, you can increasingly find such objects in markets and specialized *artesanato* stores in Rio and São Paulo. Meanwhile, stake out markets and *brechós* (second-hand stores) as well as antique stores for interesting furniture and decorative object finds. Know that it's often worthwhile to hire a local (but recommended) tailor, upholsterer, carpenter, woodworker, furniture-maker, etc. to make the customized curtains, sofa coverings, cabinets, desks, and shelving units of your dreams (not to mention of your design). This was the solution I hit upon when furnishing my first apartment in Salvador.

CLOTHING

Brazil has a reputable textile and leather industry and one of the world's most happening fashion industries. Brazilian beachwear, casual wear, and jeans—not to mention ever trusty Havaiana flip-flops—are innovative, high quality, and globally coveted. The only problem is that, spurred on by the valorization of the Brazilian *real,* clothes shopping in Brazil is no longer the bargain it used to be. In fact, if you're comparing items in terms of price and quality, you'll get more bang for your buck stocking up in the States or even Canada.

In terms of price and selection, North America really has the upper hand in terms of cold-weather clothes, formal wear, sports gear and apparel, plus-sized clothes, and babies' and kids' clothes (which in Brazil tend to be excessively Technicolor). Women with ample breasts might find it challenging to find clothing that fits them since Brazilian women tend to be ampler in the derriere than in the chest.

Shipping Options

Shipping possessions to Brazil from North America is very expensive (with the exception of books, which can be sent quite cheaply by mail; expect them to take several months to arrive), but it might be worth it in the event that: (1) you're employed by a company that agrees to pay for the shipping costs, or (2) you're making a long-term or permanent move. Although bringing things from home can provide great comfort and familiarity, keep in mind that living spaces (usually apartments) are often smaller than those in North America and often have different configurations, which might make fitting all your furniture (king-sized beds, for example) a challenge. Also factor in the potential havoc that humidity, heat, intense sunshine, and termites may have on your belongings.

When choosing a shipping company, try to get one with good references. Most will come to your house and give you a quote based on the amount you want to ship. The most common and least expensive option is surface shipping, which will usually take anywhere between 30 and 90 days. It's worthwhile to choose a shipping company (either Brazilian or North American) that has a branch both in your city of origin and in Brazil to facilitate logistics on both ends. Also helpful are shippers that come to your house and pack up all your belongings before shipping them off to Brazil where, after clearing customs, they will be delivered to your home and unpacked.

Customs is a notoriously sticky point when it comes to shipping. Often, possessions are held upon arrival in Brazil pending outstanding paperwork or payments (including the odd bribe). A brutal detail is the fact that import duties on your possessions will amount to 60 percent of their value. The only way of skirting this cost is if you're married to or partnered with a Brazilian who by law is entitled to return to Brazil and bring all his or her home possessions without paying duty on them.

HOUSING CONSIDERATIONS

Regardless of whether you plan to rent or buy a home, the issue of housing is a complex one for those planning a move to Brazil. This is because many factors that wouldn't necessarily come into play in North America, or would be minor considerations, are major issues in Brazil.

Security, for instance, is a massive issue. For this reason, some expats—like many middle- to upper-class Brazilians—opt to live in closed condominium complexes, not just in urban and suburban centers, but even in smaller towns and coastal areas. Electric fences, 24-hour guards, security cameras, alarm systems, and indoor garages, not to mention windows with bars (*grades*) so that thieves can't scale walls and break into houses or apartments, are all amenities that Brazilians consider when renting or buying a home. Unfortunately, you'll need to consider some or all of them as well.

On a more macro scale, when choosing a potential neighborhood to live in, you'll need to do some research into possible dangers and safety issues. Even the most up-scale urban neighborhoods fall prey to crime; after all, thieves know very well that that's where all the spoils are located. Without becoming paranoid, it's important to be

aware of vulnerable areas. In many cases, safety issues will narrow down your choice of housing options considerably.

Another major consideration is the elements. While a bonus of living in tropical Brazil is the abundance of natural light that ensures you'll never suffer from SAD (Seasonal Affective Disorder), you have to keep in mind that the closer you are to the Equator, the more brutal the effects of the sun's rays. Lots of direct sun exposure can wreak havoc on objects and furniture, bleaching colors, fading photos and book jackets, and weakening fabrics. Depending on what time of day the sun hits, it can also turn your home into a miniature furnace. For this reason, many apartments, particularly in the Northeast, advertise themselves as *nascente* (rising) and *poente* (setting); these terms refer to the periods when the sun will cast its light and heat within your space. In general *nascente* apartments are cooler (since the rising sun is weaker), but if your bedroom is *nascente*, you'll need to invest in serious black-out curtains. *Poente* means you may be treated to a magnificent sunset (if the horizon is unobstructed), but in the hours leading up to this spectacle, rooms facing the sun will heat up like ovens.

On the other hand, some direct sunlight is useful to combat humidity and moisture and to ensure freshly washed clothes get dry (driers are rare in Brazil). In tropical regions of Brazil, particularly along the coastline, it can get very humid, especially during the rainy season. As a result, you'll find yourself battling enemies such as mold, mildew, and rust, which will attack everything from clothes and shoes to your favorite photographs. Living near the ocean complicates things even further because you'll be subject to *maresia*. A common term in coastal areas, *maresia* refers to the oxidization caused by sea (*mar*) water that leads to gradual corrosion of all metallic objects. Over time, it can wreak havoc on computers, sound systems, and other types of electrical equipment and appliances.

Renting vs. Buying

Only a few years ago, back when the exchange rate was very favorable for North Americans and Europeans and before Brazil's economic boom kicked in, buying real estate in Brazil was an amazingly good deal and buying land was incredibly cheap. Those days, however, are gone.

In 2011, the Brazilian *real* was considered the most overvalued currency on the planet (it has since fallen somewhat; from R$1.6:US$1 in 2011 to R$2:US$1 in early 2013). However, a combination of political and economic stability, rising incomes and purchasing power, an emerging middle class eager to buy, and the unprecedented availability of credit have all resulted in a booming construction segment and skyrocketing real estate markets throughout Brazil. Between February 2011 and 2012, the average asking price for apartments in Brazil increased by 24.8 percent according to the FIP ZAP Index of dwelling price offers. During the same time period rents in São Paulo and Rio rose by 12.6 percent and 20.2 percent, respectively.

The upshot is that both purchasing prices and rents for new and used apartments are both much more expensive than they were five years ago. That said, buying prices have actually soared higher than rents; between 2008 and 2012, average real estate prices in Brazil jumped by 129.5 percent while average rents only rose by 68.4 percent.

Although, in 2012, Brazil's economic slow down has seen prices soften a little, experts feel that values will not only continue to rise but to overheat. Some even predict the creation of a housing bubble that, at some point in the future, could burst. As such, these days most specialists concur that it makes more economic sense to rent than to buy.

Home Hunting

There are various ways of finding properties to rent and buy in Brazil. Local newspapers have *Classificados* sections that list real estate for rent and for sale, both in print and online. Also worth checking out are national classified sites, two of the largest being Zap Imóveis (www.zap.com.br/imoveis) and Classificados Brasil (www.classificados-brasil.com). Expat websites such as InterNations (www.internations.org), Gringoes.com (www.gringoes.com), and The Rio Times (www.riotimesonline.com) all have real estate classified sections in addition to online forums in which expats sometimes announce properties for rent or sale.

If you have a very clear idea of what neighborhood(s) you want to live in, it's often worthwhile to drive or walk around and take note of apartments or properties with *Alugue* (Rent) or *Vende* (Sale) signs posted in the windows. Signs always include telephone numbers belonging to the owner/seller or real estate agent. Often building *porteiros* (doormen) are great sources. They usually not only know if an apartment is available—or soon will be—in their building, but also are aware of vacancies along a particular street, or neighborhood, as well. In beach and rural areas, it's always useful

© MICHAEL SOMMERS

Art Deco buildings are common in Copacabana.

COMMON HOUSING TERMS

alugar para temporada: to rent short-term or seasonally

aluguel: rent

andar: floor (or story in a building, e.g., o quinto andar or the fifth floor)

área de serviço/dependência: service area

armário: closet

banheira: bathtub

banheiro: bathroom

chuveiro: shower

cobertura: penthouse

condomínio fechado: closed condominium complex

cozinha americana: open kitchen

edifício/imóvel: building

elevador de serviço: service elevator

elevador social: (regular) elevator (i.e., not for the help)

estacionamento: parking

fatura (de luz): (electricity) bill

hipoteca: mortgage

imobiliário: real estate agency

linha branca: literally, "white line," meaning appliances such as refrigerators, stoves, washing machines

mobiliado: furnished

nascente: receives early morning (rising) sun

quartos: rooms

parcelar: to pay in (monthly) installments

pé direito: the distance between the floor and the ceiling (a pé direito alto refers to an apartment or house with high ceilings)

persianas: shutters

playground: main common recreation area, generally on the ground floor or garden of an apartment building, where tenants hold parties and kids play

piso: floor

poente: receives late afternoon (setting) sun

porteiro: door attendant

sala: living room

síndico do prédio: building superintendent

sub-solo: below ground

taco de madeira: parquet wood floors

taxa de condomínio: apartment maintenance tax (includes common building costs such as water, salaries of building staff, security, amenities)

térreo: ground floor

varanda: balcony

vista: view

zelador: building maintenance person

to hit up locals that receive lots of traffic: Bar, restaurant, and hotel owners and staff often have information about available properties.

Probably the most common way to rent or buy an apartment or house is to go through a real estate agency, the vast majority of which have online presences featuring listings and photographs. It's worth comparison shopping online before actually meeting with one (or several) agents who can take you to visit properties that match your criteria. In Rio and São Paulo, in particular, you'll find agencies that specialize in expat clients and their particular needs. They feature bilingual websites and agents that often speak English. In most other cities and regions, however, agencies operate exclusively in Portuguese.

Renting Property

Unless they have considerable savings piled away or want to buy property in order to start a business, most foreigners moving to Brazil—especially if they're only staying for a definite period—opt to rent an apartment.

SHORT-TERM RENTALS

If you're coming to Brazil for a very short time (i.e., six months or less), you might want to consider staying in an *apart-hotel* or renting a furnished apartment. This is easily done year-round in cities such as Rio and São Paulo, but less so throughout the rest of the country. The exception is summertime, when many locals rent out apartments to holiday-goers, often at inflated prices (which quickly become stratospheric during New Year's, Carnaval, and any other major regional *festa*). In Rio, especially, there are many real estate agencies that specialize in temporary rentals for foreigners such as Homes in Rio (www.homesinrio.com) and RioApartments.com (www.rioapartments.com).

In other places, you'll have to rely on local newspapers, websites, or signs plastered on houses and buildings announcing *Aluga para Temporada*. Keep in mind, however, that short-term rentals, while cheaper than hotels, are usually fairly pricey because tenants are inevitably gringos (and supposedly wealthy). Although it's possible to find more affordable options, expect the "furnishings" in less expensive choices to be somewhat spartan or of inferior quality.

Another good short-term option is to check out sites such as Airbnb (www.airbnb.com.br), which is increasingly popular throughout Brazil (many expats rent out rooms or apartments through the site). This can be ideal for students as well as newcomers who want to get their bearings while looking for a long-term rental. A big bonus of sharing a home is making friends and contacts with locals in your chosen city and getting the chance to practice your Portuguese.

LONG-TERM RENTALS

In Brazil the standard contract term for long-term rentals is 30 months. This is especially the case if you're renting through an agency. Renting directly from the owner, one always has more leeway to negotiate and 12-month contracts are frequent as well. In any event, all contracts include a clause that allows a tenant to move out after the first 12 months provided you give the agency or owner advance notice of 60–90 days (this will be stipulated in the contract). Should you move out prior to the first 12 months, you'll still be responsible for the 60–90 days of rent. If your employer transfers you, you must give 30 days' written notice. If you do stay for the full term, once the 30-month contract has expired, it can be automatically extended under the same terms if both parties are in agreement.

Rental contracts (*contratos de locação*) lay out all the terms and conditions of your rental and are prepared by the real estate agency or directly by the owner. If your Portuguese is shaky, you'll definitely want someone fluent whom you trust (preferably a Brazilian) to go over the fine print before you sign it.

Agencies usually demand a substantial amount of paperwork. A salaried or self-employed person (*pessoa física*) will need to provide the following documents:

APART-HOTÉIS

In big cities, especially Rio and São Paulo, you'll find many *apart-hotéis*, also known as flats. Located in high-rises, they are usually frequented by business travelers who want a sense of "home away from home." Cheaper than hotels of the same caliber, *apart-hotéis* usually have a living room and a kitchen where you can make your own meals. Amenities include garages and 24-hour security, plus often a pool, fitness room, restaurant or bar, laundry service, maid service, and even room service.

- An authenticated copy of your RNE and CPF (if you're a couple, both partners will need to supply copies)
- Proof that your income is three times the monthly rent or your three most recent bank statements (if self-employed)
- Personal income tax declaration for the current year (Imposto de Renda das Pessoas Físicas [IRPF])

If you have permanent resident status but no proof of income or no recent history of living in Brazil, you can sometimes substitute these documents with a *título de capitalização* (capitalization title) the amount of which is equivalent to six months' rent. This money is deposited in a bank where it acts as security for the owner in the event of nonpayment. The sum can earn interest and is returned in full at the end of the contract if all clauses have been met.

Apart from documents, you'll need to provide a deposit (*depósito*) upon signing. This is usually the equivalent of between one and three months' rent. This too is used as security against damage to the property or unpaid rent and is returned at the end of the contract following a *vistória*, a visit during which the state of the apartment and its furnishings is verified to make sure it complies with the original detailed inventory laid out in the contract. Usually, the owner is responsible for painting the apartment before the tenant moves in, and the tenant is responsible for repainting upon moving out. The owner is also responsible for making sure the apartment is in good condition and that all amenities are working; if you have issues, bring them up *before* you sign the contract or they will never get resolved.

Regardless of whether you're renting through an agency or directly with an owner, you'll need to provide at least one guarantor (and sometimes two) known as *fiadores*. A *fiador* must be a Brazilian citizen or permanent resident of Brazil. He or she must own property in the same city in which you plan to live and will have to demonstrate proof of a monthly income that is at least twice the value of your rent. Aside from signing the rental contract, *fiadores* (along with their spouses) will need to provide authenticated copies of their RGs (identity documents) and CPFs, proof of payment of their most recent income tax, and the deed (*escritura*) that proves ownership of their property. If you provide a *título de capitalização*, you can dispense with *fiadores*.

In the event you rent directly from an owner instead of an agency, the terms of the contract may be more flexible and negotiable. This is particularly the case in terms of the rent, which may remain stationary throughout the duration of your contract. No such luck if you rent from an agency. In this case, it's standard for your rent to be raised every year based on legislation that applies an index known as the IGP-M

(General Market Price Index). Depending on economic factors, the increase could be between 5 and 10 percent.

Buying Property

Brazil is one of the easier countries for foreigners who are seeking to buy property. You don't need to be a permanent resident; all you need is a CPF and a passport. The only restrictions are that you must be a permanent resident (with a permanent Brazilian address) if you're buying property in rural areas and there are limitations on purchasing property within a certain distance from the coast (which is owned by the government in Brazil).

As with rentals, there are two ways to purchase property in Brazil; directly from the owner and through a real estate agency. Unless your Portuguese is impeccable and you know Brazil—and the seller—very well, it's extremely advisable that foreigners take the second route. This isn't only because the amount of paperwork involved is quite complicated, but also because irregularities and scams are not at all uncommon. Going through a real estate agent will cost you more: If the seller lists the property with an agent, you'll split the commission costs, but if you use an agent to help you close a private sale (*venda particular*), you'll be responsible for them all. However, the advantages in terms of speed and security are definitely worth the cost.

In the event you're buying a newly constructed house or apartment, you'll have no choice but to use an agent. It can be an advantage to purchase a property *na planta* (in the planning or building stages) because the asking price—which can be paid in monthly installments over the course of construction—can be quite a bit lower than the value once the building is completed. In the event you're purchasing rural or coastal real estate, or a historical house or building, it's also a good idea to rely on a property lawyer, specifically one who speaks English and has experience in dealing with expats. It's not uncommon for older land and property deeds in Brazil to have long, sketchy, and convoluted histories of ownership.

a street sign announcing an apartment for sale

Buyers can usually negotiate asking prices with owners, especially if owners are in a hurry to unload their property because they're in need of fast cash. Moreover, you can usually get a significant reduction if you're prepared to pay the entire sum—or a significant chunk—up front, which is known as *pagar à vista*. All sorts of installment options can then be worked out; such as paying 50 percent immediately and then subsequent installments over a period of months. Unless they're permanent residents with bank accounts and fixed incomes, foreigners aren't allowed to take out mortgages from Brazilian banks such as the Caixa Econômica Federal. However, given the fact that Brazilian interest rates are so high, chances are you wouldn't want to go this route anyway.

In Brazil, it's the responsibility of the owner/seller to provide you with a number of certified documents that prove that the property being sold is completely free of debt and obligation. By law, all property must be registered at a Cartório de Registro de Imóveis (real estate registry office), which will have records of all registered transactions related to the property as well as a physical description. Access to the information is public, and it can even be consulted online. However, it's a good idea for foreigners to rely on brokers, lawyers, or both to analyze the fine print and make sure everything is legit. Among the things you should watch out for are these issues:

- That the owner/seller actually owns the property
- That the house or building was built legally with specifications that were approved by the city
- That no imminent land dispossessions are pending
- That all third-party or government debts in relation to the property have been acquitted (i.e., taxes, fees, or condominium maintenance charges)

Once you're assured that everything is in order, you'll have to provide a down payment, known as a *sinal,* which is usually between 10 and 20 percent of the property's total value. Payment of the *sinal* is accompanied by the signing of a precontract receipt, which lays out the conditions for the final sale and ensures that your deposit will be returned should either party decide to back out.

The final step involves both buyer and seller signing the public deed of sale and purchase in front of a notary officer. This definitive contract should include the price and all payment details as well as timelines and delivery deadlines if the property is under construction. As the new owner, you'll have to register the property with the Cartório de Registro de Imóveis, and the seller will be responsible for transferring the title to your name. At this point, the buyer and seller also have to pay all fees and charges. The buyer is usually responsible for transfer-related costs such as municipal and state taxes and *cartório* registration and authentication fees. Expect transference fees to cost around 5 percent of the property's value, although they can vary depending on the state you're in and the type of property you're purchasing.

BUILDING AND RESTORING

Although the price of land in many urban and coastal areas in Brazil has skyrocketed in recent years, the farther inland you go—or off the beaten path—the cheaper costs become for land and property. If you're prepared to sacrifice beach access, proximity to big cities, and amenities, and you're willing to invest in a four-wheel drive and tackle secondary and dirt roads, you can still pick up land, or property, for very little in parts of Minas Gerais, the Central-West, and the Northeast of Brazil.

Prospective builders should be aware that, in recent years, the cost of both materials (especially wood) and labor has risen. This means that once you have your cheap land or inexpensive but dilapidated abode, you'll have to invest a considerable sum on construction or renovation, not to mention have the hassle of dealing with logistics and finding qualified labor (whom you'll then have to supervise). The other concern regarding the purchase of land or property in a beach or rural region is that, if you're not living there full time, you'll have to invest in maintenance. Usually, this means hiring a local person who lives nearby to take care of your house and property or else contracting a *caseiro* (houseman), who often comes equipped with a family, to live on your land and take care of it. For reasons of security and upkeep, it's pretty much impossible to leave a rural or beach property unattended for any significant amount of time.

Many foreigners who come to Brazil are attracted by colonial towns or historic city quarters that often feature stunning old architecture in various states of disarray. In major cities, the old central neighborhoods have long been eschewed by middle- and upper-class Brazilians in favor of swanky residential neighborhoods or spanking new suburbs. This means that there are quite a number of old buildings that boast central locations and great atmospheres, though they aren't always zoned for residential purposes. Moreover, they're not always quiet (by day) or safe (by night). Nonetheless, if you have a pioneering spirit, you might want to consider investing in an old house or building. The tendency is that these historic neighborhoods will begin to gentrify. Keep in mind, once again, that even if you buy an old house, loft, or building for a bargain price, you'll spend a fortune in materials and labor when it comes to renovating. Additionally, Brazil has very rigid rules when it comes to making changes in historical buildings. Often you can't alter any external part of the building at all. If you are considering investing in a historical property, the first thing you should do is check with the local branch of IPHAN, the Instituto de Patrimônio Histórico e Artístico Nacional (National Historic and Artistic Heritage Institute). Here you can find out if any unauthorized modifications to the building were made in the past and what kind of restrictions would affect any external and internal remodeling projects you might have.

Property Taxes

Regardless of whether you rent or own your property in Brazil, you'll have to pay a property tax known as Imposto sobre Propriedade Predial e Territorial Urbana (IPTU). This tax varies based on the location and size of your property, but it's usually around 0.6 percent of the assessed value. Although it can be paid in a lump sum at the beginning of the year (at a discount), most people pay their IPTU in 10 monthly installments throughout the year. If you're renting an apartment, the IPTU will either be included in your rent invoice, or you'll receive a booklet containing payment slips for the entire year that you use to pay at any ATM or lottery house.

EMPREGADAS

In Brazil, it's very common among the middle and upper classes to have an *empregada*. In fact, it's almost unheard of *not* to have one. *Empregada* translates into "housekeeper," but in truth an *empregada's* duties vary enormously. While many only clean and take care of the house, others take on cooking and nanny or babysitting duties as well.

Traditionally, many upper-class Brazilians had live-in *empregadas* who worked for them 24/7 and lived in tiny rooms known as *dependências*. You'll find *dependências* in almost all old apartment buildings and houses, as well as more upscale new ones, adjacent to the *areas de serviço* (service areas). Many of these live-in *empregadas* barely had lives of their own and rarely got to see their own biological kids. They spent so much time raising their employers' children that many wealthy Brazilians developed stronger emotional ties to their *babas* (nannies) than to their biological parents.

These days, live-in *empregadas* are less common, but many households still have day workers that come daily throughout the week. These *empregadas* receive a fixed salary. Legally, they should be declared and receive a *carteira assinada*, which allows them to collect unemployment insurance, social security, and worker's compensation (monthly charges are usually both paid by the employer and deducted by the *empregada*) as well as to receive paid vacation time and a 13th month's salary (a month's payment at year-end).

Meanwhile, an increasing number of Brazilians opt to have a *diarista* that only comes in one or two *dias* (days) a week. This phenomenon is due to smaller families and smaller apartments, along with the fact that poorer, less educated Brazilian women whose only means of livelihood was being an *empregada*, are now more educated, more qualified, and capable of earning a living in myriad ways. As a re-

sult, the supply of *empregadas* has diminished while demand has grown. In fact, São Paulo is experiencing an *empregada* shortage, which has resulted in both salaries and day rates rising to unheard of levels.

At the same time, in other parts of the country, particularly in the Northeast, the *patroa-empregada* relationship continues to be one that ranges from paternalistic to exploitative, but mingles a lot of personal with the professional. In some cases, foreigners will be torn between shock at witnessing how "the help" is treated and equal shock at seeing how "the help" submits to such treatment. Needless to say a lot of socioeconomic and racial subtext is at play, and you'll have to factor some of this in when it comes to hiring and forging a relationship with your own *empregada*.

© MICHAEL SOMMERS

Shops sell uniforms for domestic empregadas.

Household Expenses

With the exception of telephone, internet, and cable TV (covered in the *Communications* chapter), housing expenses in Brazil are generally less expensive than in North America.

CONDOMINIUM FEES

Regardless of whether you're an owner or a renter, if you live in an apartment building you'll have to pay a condominium fee, which includes all common area charges as well as building maintenance, security, cleaning, repairs, and staff salaries. In most cases (but not always in the case of new buildings), the condo fee will also include the cost of water in all apartments as well as the building (which is somewhat unfair if you're single and paying the same amount as the family of five down the hall). Condo fees vary wildly depending on the number of residents in a given building and the number of services, amenities, and employees. In general, fees are paid directly to the building super, or *síndico,* upon receiving the monthly bill.

ELECTRICITY AND GAS

Electricity costs are fairly moderate in Brazil, but it depends on your use of electrical appliances. For instance, if you blast multiple air conditioners and take long hot showers, costs can quickly add up. Different states throughout Brazil have their own electricity companies. In general, getting connected or disconnected and paying bills is easy, aided by the fact that companies have 1-800 numbers and websites.

In Brazil, the majority of stoves are gas, which is supplied by hooking up the stove to a gas cylinder known as a *butijão.* The standard kitchen *butijão* is 13 kilograms and can be purchased by calling local gas suppliers that ensure very fast delivery (usually within 30 minutes). A *butijão* costs around R$40 and lasts for several months. Some people make it a habit of keeping a spare handy since the gas always seems to run out when you're in the middle of cooking dinner for eight on a Sunday (when few companies deliver).

butijãos of gas for cooking

LANGUAGE AND EDUCATION

These days, most people are aware of the fact that Brazil is the only country in Latin America whose official language is Portuguese, *not* Spanish. Indeed, with 236 million speakers around the globe, Portuguese is today the sixth most spoken language in the world (and the third in the Western Hemisphere).

If you come to Brazil speaking Spanish, you'll definitely have an advantage in terms of understanding both written and spoken Portuguese. However, it's likely that Brazilians will have a fair amount of difficulty understanding *you*. Ultimately, Spanish can be a hindrance as well as a help; while the two Latin-based languages share many similarities, they also have many differences that will trip you up.

Brazilian Portuguese

Those who come to Brazil with a knowledge of Portuguese from Portugal will have a much easier time in terms of communication but will also run into trouble. The differences between Portuguese from Brazil vs. Portuguese from Portugal are perhaps more acute than those between American and British English, particularly when it comes to the spoken version. Vowel and consonant sounds in Portuguese from Portugal are often distorted beyond easy recognition (even many Brazilians have difficulty understanding the Portuguese spoken by their linguistic forefathers). In contrast, Brazilian Portuguese is pretty much pronounced as it is written (a blessing for those trying to master it as a second language). Portuguese grammar and most of the spelling is the same in both nations, but usage and expressions can vary (for instance, in Brazil a train is a *trem* while in Portugal it's a *comboio*).

During its five centuries in the New World, Brazilian Portuguese has incorporated hundreds of words from other idioms. In the first century of Brazil's colonial history, many newcomers adopted expressions and even spoke indigenous languages quite fluently. To this day, many place names (Ipanema, Paraíba) and names of animals (*tucano* [toucan]), plants (*mandioca* [manioc]), and fruits (*abacaxi* [pineapple]) are of Tupi-Guarani origin. With the proliferation of sugar cane plantations followed by the gold and diamond rushes of the 18th century, millions of Africans were brought to Brazil as slaves. They too left an important linguistic legacy. Many expressions related to specific Brazilian foods (*moqueca, quindim*), music (*samba, maxixe*), and religion (*macumba, orixá*)—many of Yoruba or Ewe origin—have entered the vernacular as have terms such as *cafuné* (caress) and *moleque* (brat).

In more recent times, words from other European languages entered the vernacular, specifically French and English. Terms such as metrô (subway), *abajur* (lamp), *chique* (chic) all hail from French. Meanwhile, the global influence of English in spheres such as business (commodities, layout, marketing, freelance) and technology (app, Internet, email, modem), not to mention pop culture (skinhead, junkie, vibe), has seen a growing number of English expressions infiltrate contemporary Brazilian Portuguese. The tricky thing is recognizing these homegrown idioms in their Brazilian guises: When pronounced by Brazilians, terms such as "nerd"—pronounced "nairdjee"—will often leave you scratching your head and scouring through your Portuguese dictionary in vain.

Considering the size of the country, Brazilian Portuguese is surprisingly uniform. It helps that no matter where you are, the dominant media (initially radio and today television) beamed across the land features standardized accents and vocabulary of the Southeast. Nevertheless, regionalisms abound in terms of idiomatic expressions, slang, and accents. Some of the most pronounced (and colorful) regional "dialects" are Carioca (from the city of Rio de Janeiro), Baiano (Bahia), Mineiro (central and northern Minas Gerais), Gaúcho (Rio Grande do Sul), and Caipira (interior of São Paulo, northern Paraná, southern Minas Gerais, Goiás, parts of Mato Grosso, and Mato Grosso de Sul). Although initially you might not be attuned to the differences, Brazilians themselves derive great mirth from imitating and gently making fun of each other's accents and expressions.

DAILY LIFE

Learning the Language

Although most Brazilians are taught English at school (even public schools theoretically offer English and/or Spanish), the quality of the teaching is often so mediocre that it's hard to get more out of them than "Hi...how are you?...The book is on the table." Outside of specialized milieus such as financial, design, tech, and some academic spheres, not to mention a few sophisticated tourist enclaves, it's pretty rare that you will meet Brazilians that can carry off a fluent conversation in English, although this is beginning to change, especially in big cities such as Rio and São Paulo.

Nonetheless it's impossible to stress how important it is to learn as much Portuguese as you can as early as you can (i.e., before even setting foot in Brazil). There are many obvious reasons for this, such as dealing with bureaucracies where *nobody* will speak English. Ultimately, however, Brazil is a country where a certain level of unpredictability (and even chaos) exists, and lapses in efficiency are as common as *enrolação* (a term whose figurative meaning, to stonewall, procrastinate, or even deceive, comes from the verb enrolar, meaning literally "to roll").The only way to do battle with such tendencies is by dominating the language; otherwise you'll be at a complete loss and end up feeling frustrated and victimized by situations that have the potential of slipping out of your control.

While all Brazilians have to deal with such issues, it's potentially worse if you're a gringo. Though Brazilians overall are terribly welcoming to foreigners and will often take great pains to assist you, there are situations in which your gringo-ness brands you as a pushover or an easy mark. Even if your appearance screams "I'm not Brazilian," if

English words crop up in many commercial contexts.

you're able to communicate like a local (despite the accent and grammatical slip ups), you'll be treated like one. In the end, mastering Portuguese is essential to your ability to survive, let alone thrive, in Brazil.

Being able to express yourself in Portuguese and understand others is also essential to your enjoyment of Brazil and Brazilians. I'll never forget the first time I traveled to Bahia and didn't speak Portuguese. The sensation of being an outsider and missing out on what appeared to be the most lively, captivating conversations on the planet was more frustrating than any similar experiences I'd had in other foreign countries. Brazil has a strong oral culture, and Brazilians in general have a pronounced gift of gab. Socializing is very communal and when people get together an enormous amount of storytelling, anecdote sharing, and fofocando (gossip) goes on. Much of it is extraordinarily entertaining, especially when peppered with colorful slang, sprinkled with idiomatic expressions, and delivered with frequent theatrical flair.

One of the most difficult sensations expats confront in Brazil is the degree of marginalization—and sense of powerlessness—they experience when they don't dominate the language. Though some find comfort in the company of other English-speaking expats, those who rely exclusively upon expats often (consciously or unconsciously) find themselves living in an artificial bubble that exists within Brazil but never really merges with it. It's safe to say that you'll never feel at home, fit in, begin to understand, or fully enjoy Brazil without some Portuguese under your belt.

LEARNING PORTUGUESE BEFORE YOU COME

If you have enough lead time, it makes sense to start ingesting Portuguese before you leave home. The Brazilian consulate closest to you is a good place to find information about classes for adults and children taught both at language schools and by private Brazilian tutors. The bonus of having a private professor is that your teacher can customize lessons to meet your personal needs (a specific area of study, a particular professional milieu, oral vs. written communication, etc.). Your instructor can also offer useful advice about many aspects of living in Brazil.

Outside of major urban centers, it can be tricky to find qualified teachers of Brazilian Portuguese. Fortunately, because interest in Brazil has grown, there's also an increasingly wide selection of educational materials available. Living Language's *Complete Portuguese: The Basics* is an easy-to-follow beginner's method that includes a book, dictionary, and CDs. Recommended for more in-depth study is the U.S. Foreign Service Institute's Brazilian Portuguese courses, whose texts (in PDF format) and audio files (in MP3) can now be downloaded for free. Also free is Tá Falado, a series of podcasts (covering grammar and pronunciation) accompanied by PDF transcripts and a discussion blog. Developed by the University of Texas at Austin (whose Brazil Center is one of North America's premier Brazilian studies programs), it's geared towards English speakers who already have Spanish under their belts.

Other language systems popular with expats include Mango Languages (www.mangolanguages.com), which focuses on practical conversational skills (with a dose of culture thrown in) and Pimsleur (www.pimsleurmethod.com), which relies upon an innovative recall method to drum vocab and grammar into your head (while making the repetition more entertaining than tedious). Another great way of immersing yourself in the language, not to mention the culture, of Brazil is to get your hands on

LACK OF ENGLISH SPEAKERS

If you come to Brazil with the intent of immersing yourself immediately and completely in Portuguese, you're in luck. However, if you arrive thinking that you'll be able to get around by speaking English, think again.

According to EF, a global English education company, in 2011, Brazil was one of the bottom-ranked countries in terms of English proficiency (coming in 31st out of 42 countries). And in a 2012 survey compiled by the GlobalEnglish Corporation that measures English fluency in the workplace, Brazil once again received a dismal score. According to a 2011 Catho survey only 11 percent of Brazilian job candidates can communicate well in English and only 3.4 percent are fluent.

Apart from the increasing demands of a global economy, a big game changer could be Brazil's obligations as host of international events such as the 2014 World Cup and 2016 Olympics. As these high profile events draw near, the pressure is on for Brazilians—particularly those in transportation, hospitality, and tourism sectors—to beef up their foreign language skills, especially English. In the private sector, language schools are mushrooming to keep up with a demand that's expected to increase by 30-40 percent between 2012 and 2016. Even governments are getting in on the act. In 2011, Rio's state department of transit (DETRAN) launched a series of free courses for taxi drivers to be taught basic English. Imagine having your cabbie understand when you plead with him to, "Please drive more slowly."

some Brazilian films and music. Just walking or driving around with a nonstop dose of samba, bossa, or MPB seeping into your brain is a great way to absorb the words and rhythms of Brazil.

LEARNING PORTUGUESE IN BRAZIL

Once you arrive in Brazil, things will automatically become both more easy and more difficult in terms of Portuguese. On the upside, you won't have to seek out speakers of Portuguese; you'll be surrounded by them and will be putting whatever skills you have into immediate practice. As a rule, Brazilians are incredibly encouraging of foreigners who are making the effort to learn their language—and also very patient with errors (although they're often too gracious to correct you).

On the downside, plunging into Portuguese all at once can be an overwhelming experience. In real life—as opposed to the controlled atmosphere of the classroom—Brazilians have a habit of talking very quickly (especially in Rio) and, when in groups (which is often), talking simultaneously (i.e., carrying on and following multiple and overlapping conversations). Depending on the context in which you find yourself, you'll also have to struggle with some colorful, but hard to fathom, slang and idiomatic expressions. Another challenge is ambient noise. Apart from the aforementioned tendency toward multiple conversations, in many social instances you'll also have to try to speak and comprehend while an (inevitably loud) musical soundtrack is blaring in the background.

If you come to Brazil as the employee of a foreign company, your corporation might already have a deal in place with a language school or private tutors through which you (and your family) can receive Portuguese lessons. If not, you might benefit from some intensive courses in Portuguese as a second language. Language centers that offer

DIMINUTIVES

Brazilians have a great fondness for using the *diminutivo* (diminutive), which accounts for the flood of *"inhos"* and *"zinhos"* attached to most words. Although the diminutive's true function is to indicate smallness in size—a *cafezinho* is an espresso-sized coffee, a *casinha* is a modest-sized house—in Brazil, the diminutive is also used as a sign of affection between friends and family members. Since Brazilians are very affectionate, these are used more often than are standard names. Men named Carlos are often called Carlinhos and women named Ana become Aninha. A *filho* (son) is a *filhinho* and a *mãe* (mother) is *mãezinha*, a *namorado* (boyfriend) is a *namoradinho*, and even a beloved *cachorro* (dog) is often a *cachorrinho*.

Moreover, Brazilians possess a great talent for recounting everything form *historinhas* (stories) to *fofoquinhas* (gossip), and in the recounting the diminutive is often used for emphasis. It can also be used to downplay an event—a *joguinho* is a *jogo* (game) without importance—or to placate someone (asking a client to wait just a *minutinho* for service is somehow less onerous than having to wait an entire *minuto*). There are, however, some instances in which a diminutive might refer to something quite different. A *camisinha* is not a small *camisa* (shirt), but a condom. An *abóbora* is a pumpkin, while an *abobrinha* is a zucchini.

DAILY LIFE

such courses for foreigners are mostly only in major cities where such a demand exists. Recommended schools that specialize in teaching Portuguese to foreigners include Fast Forward (www.fastforward.com.br) in São Paulo, Diálogo (www.dialogo-brazilstudy.com) in Salvador, and Conselho Cultural das Nações (www.conselhocultural.com) in Brasília. In Rio, the Instituto Brasil Estados Unidos, or IBEU (www.ibeu.org.br), offers intensive Portuguese immersion programs for business as well as introductory language and culture classes. Much more affordable is the Casa do Caminho Language Center (www.casadocaminho-languagecentre.org), which also offers intensive group classes at all levels for R$14 to R$25 an hour. An added bonus is that profits go to the Casa do Caminho orphanages. In most cases, you can choose between small group and one-on-one classes.

Some Brazilian universities also offer Portuguese courses for foreigners that are more reasonably priced than private language schools. Examples include the Portuguese for Foreigners courses offered by the University of Brasília (UnB) and both the Pontifical Catholic Universities of Rio (PUC-Rio) and São Paulo (PUC-SP). In general, however, these courses last anywhere from a half to full semester in length.

Universities and language schools—along with consulates, expat blogs, and forums—are also good sources for finding private Portuguese teachers. One-on-one lessons have many advantages. A good private teacher can customize material to your needs and proficiency level and can focus a lot more on conversation. In terms of practicality and logistics, most private teachers are also prepared to meet you at your house, office, or any other locale (usually for a higher fee). Although rates vary, they usually start at around R$40 an hour.

Education

Despite vast progress in the past 10 years, education levels in Brazil are still quite low. Indeed, lack of education is considered one of the major obstacles preventing the country from unleashing its full potential as an economic powerhouse; in terms of education, Brazil lags behind the three other BRIC countries, Russia, India, and China.

Traditionally, a major problem has been that many Brazilians haven't had access to school or incentive to study. In 2003 President Lula—the former and still intensely beloved president who grew up in the poor Interior of Pernambuco and famously dropped out of school in the fourth grade to work—launched the much lauded Bolsa Família program (BFP); it has made important strides in providing poor Brazilians with access to basic public education. Under the BFP, the federal government pays 14 million poor Brazilian families (with monthly incomes of R$140 or less) between R$32 and R$320 (depending on family income, the number of children, and their ages) to send the children to school.

The Bolsa Família program, along with other incentives, has had a significant impact. Still, the larger problem is less about access to education than to *quality* education. In the decade between 2000 and 2010, compared to their global peers, Brazilian students routinely received some of the lowest scores on international exams measuring basic math, reading, and science skills (lagging significantly behind other Latin American students from Uruguay, Chile, and Mexico, for example). In 2006, Brazilian 15-year-olds tied for 49th place among students from 56 countries who took the Program of International Student Assessment reading exam. In the math and science tests, they performed even more poorly. Such figures can be understood when one takes into account the fact that 28 percent of Brazilian children have to repeat first grade (one of the highest rates in the world). Meanwhile, in 2010, the number of Brazilians who graduated from middle school was still only 47 percent.

Although only 10 percent of the Brazilian population is completely illiterate, a whopping 68 percent is functionally illiterate, meaning they can't write more than simple words or basic phrases and can't read or comprehend the majority of longer more complex texts. Each year, millions of students graduate from high school and are unable to write an essay or solve basic math problems. As such, even though more Brazilians than ever before are pursuing postsecondary education, it's less than surprising that 32 percent of university undergrads are functionally illiterate. To date, only 10 percent of Brazilians possess a college or university degree.

PRESCHOOL

Education in Brazil begins with *educação infantil,* which is optional and varies significantly from very basic daycare facilities (usually public) to private preschools with activities and lessons that focus on the development of cognitive, motor, and social skills. In Rio, and especially São Paulo, not to mention a handful of other cities, you can even find private bilingual (English/Portuguese) preschools, or bilingual elementary schools that include preschool classes. A popular choice among expats, with over 50 preschools and elementary schools throughout the country is Maple Bear Canadian School (www.maplebear.com.br), which employs Canadian teaching philosophies and methodologies. For information about bilingual education and schools throughout Brazil, Educação Bilingue no Brasil (www.educacaobilingue.com) is a useful source.

ELEMENTARY AND HIGH SCHOOL

The Brazilian equivalent of North American elementary school is divided into two stages known as Ensino Fundamental I and II. Ensino Fundamental I is the equivalent of grades 1 through 5 and focuses on core subjects taught by a single teacher. Ensino Fundamental II covers the years from grades 6 through 9 and offers more subjects (i.e., history, geography, science, physical education, English), each of which is taught by a specialized teacher. In Brazil, the nine years of Ensino Fundamental is mandatory for all Brazilians.

The Brazilian equivalent of high school, or secondary school, Ensino Médio covers the final three years prior to graduation (grades 10 through 12) and prepares students for higher education. A variation on Ensino Médio is Ensino Técnico, which prepares students directly for the job market. In addition to covering the regular high school curriculum, *escolas técnicas* (technical schools) offer professional training in specialized fields such as business, management, hospitality, health, and industrial control and processes. Federally funded, these schools are considered among the best schools in Brazil.

In Brazil, there is a vast difference between public schools and private schools. Although public schools are partially funded by the federal government, both primary and secondary schools are also funded—and operated by—either the municipal or state education secretaries. The problem is that wealthier states and cities (generally in the South and Southeast) have more money to invest in education, not to mention more educated citizens who demand better infrastructure and resources. That said, despite variations, public education throughout Brazil is generally renowned for having low standards plus problems that range from lack of basic materials and infrastructure, poorly qualified teachers, and overcrowded classrooms to serious discipline and security issues (particularly acute in poor inner city regions).

Because the situation has become critical in recent decades, the Brazilian middle class (and even members of the working class who can afford it) have yanked their children out of the public system in favor of private schools. The oldest—and often most reputable—private schools in Brazil are Catholic schools founded by various religious orders. Established decades, and even centuries, ago, many of these schools were where children of local elites went to receive a sound academic education, accompanied by lessons in religion. However, in

a preschool in Salvador

© MICHAEL SOMMERS

recent decades there has been a mushrooming of secular private schools. Large cities, in particular, have seen a small proliferation of alternative, bilingual, and even international schools.

Brazilian private schools range widely in terms of quality (and reputation, which isn't always synonymous with quality) as well as price. In general, though, you get what you pay for. Monthly fees may cost anywhere from R$90 to R$900, although top-ranked and prestigious schools in Rio, São Paulo, and Brasília range from between R$1,000 and R$2,500. Brazilian private schools are generally quite happy to accept foreign children.

The majority of international schools are American or British and employ highly qualified (generally foreign-recruited) English-language staff. They offer U.S.- or U.K.-based curricula (usually mixed with some Brazilian content) with the aim of preparing students who want to attend university in North America or Europe (through the completion of an International Baccalaureate Program [IBP]), as well as in Brazil. Monthly tuition fees range from pricey to exorbitant, but an average range is R$2,500–5,000. Indeed, in 2011, Brazil's international schools were ranked as the seventh most expensive on the planet (with top honors going to São Paulo's American International School, where a year's tuition can set one back US$40,000). However, the more expensive schools usually boast excellent teachers (drawn by high salaries), more diverse courses and extracurricular activities, and sophisticated infrastructure ranging from libraries and media centers to deluxe gyms and swimming pools.

Among the many advantages of an international school is that it makes transitioning much easier on kids since they'll be studying and socializing with peers from North America, as well as from all over the world (including Brazilians). On the flip side, however, a disadvantage may be that children (and, by extension, parents) end up operating in a privileged foreign microcosm that may inhibit integration into Brazilian society at large and interaction with Brazilians from all walks of life.

Expats with kids who travel to Brazil for a short time and don't want to interrupt their children's education by subjecting them to the trials of a different curriculum and language often opt to send their children to international schools (or bilingual schools in the event they can't afford the former). In the case of employees who are transferred to Brazil or come to work for foreign affiliates, companies usually offer to pay children's tuitions at international schools as part of the employee's package. Be aware that depending upon the school and your child's age, both international and top-ranked Brazilian private schools may have waiting lists.

HIGHER EDUCATION

If private trumps public when it comes to primary and secondary education, the opposite holds true when it comes to Brazilian universities. In general, state and (especially) federally funded universities have superior reputations and are much more coveted than private universities and colleges. Indeed, in a 2012 ranking of the best universities in Latin America (carried out by the British Quacquarelli Symonds Institute), three Brazilian universities, the Universidade de São Paulo (USP), the Universidade Estadual de Campinas (UNICAMP), and the Universidade Federal do Rio de Janeiro (UFRJ), were among the top 10, with USP finishing first out of 250 universities.

As a result of federal funding that prioritizes higher education (while neglecting

SCHOOL DAYS

Brazilian schools at all levels follow a two-semester calendar. The first semester starts at the end of summer (usually early to mid-February) and extends until late June. The second semester lasts from the end of July to mid-December. In between, students, teachers, and professors are treated to two sets of holidays: a long summer vacation that stretches from Christmas to February and a shorter winter break in July. Specific dates vary according to regions and whether the school is public or private. International schools sometimes follow different calendars.

Traditionally Brazilian students have had the option of studying either in the morning (7am-noon) or afternoon (1pm-6pm). However, an increasing number of both public and private schools throughout the country are switching to full-day programs known as *escola a tempo integral*.

Ensino Fundamental and Médio), public universities are, in general, better than private institutions. Because they aren't run as profit-seeking businesses, capital is invested in professors and research, not to mention study centers and equipment. As a result, some of the best courses, as well as cutting-edge R&D, in areas such as science, medicine, and engineering can all be found in public universities.

Ironically, even though public universities are free of charge in Brazil, they are almost inaccessible to poor Brazilians. This is because entrance is based on merit. To nab one of the set number of available *vagas* (vacancies), which vary depending on the program applied for, students must pass an entrance exam known as the *vestibular* during their final year of studies (students who graduate from public schools can alternately take a standard knowledge exam known as the ENEM [Exame Nacional do Ensino Médio], which is accepted by all public universities and some private ones). Competition is so fierce for these *vagas* that many students also enroll in pré-vestibular courses, known as *cursinhos*. These schools often try to cram three (and even more) years of high school into one year of intensive course work. Pré-vestibular courses are widespread in large and medium-sized cities. Many grow into franchises and indulge in heavy marketing campaigns promoting their (usually quite qualified) staff members as if they were rock stars.

Of course, those who have the best chance of scoring highest on *vestibulares* are middle-class and wealthy Brazilian students who spent years attending expensive private schools. Meanwhile, poorer students who graduate from public schools and want to pursue higher learning are often forced to attend one of the exploding number of private universities that have been cropping up throughout the country. Although a few are very good (notably the traditional Catholic universities [PUCs], whose campuses in São Paulo and Rio rank among Latin America's top universities) and others are strong in specific areas of study, still others are mediocre or even worse. Profit oriented, many are operated like assembly lines whose goal is to take students' money and award them with a diploma, regardless of their performance (one basically "earns" the diploma by paying for it through high monthly fees). Once again, depending on the institution in question, its location, its staff and amenities, and the program being undertaken, monthly tuition can range from R$400 to R$4,000.

One upside of private universities is that they offer courses more geared toward the

© MICHAEL SOMMERS

"Faculty of Law" at the Federal University of Bahia

job market whereas public universities are more narrowly focused on academics and research, although this is starting to change. What is also changing is public school students' improved access to higher education. This has been done through ProUni, a government program that offers partial and full scholarships to low-income public school students who want to attend private universities, and by implementation of racial quotas that reserve a certain percentage of public university *vagas* for Afro-Brazilian and indigenous students. Despite the fact that only around 2 percent of Afro-Brazilians possess a university degree, the quota system is extremely controversial. Critics claim it categorizes the population based on race as opposed to socioeconomic factors (which amounts to the same things since the poorest Brazilians are inevitably black).

STUDY ABROAD

The majority of foreigners who study in Brazilian universities do so as part of year-abroad or semester-abroad programs organized through their home universities, many of which have academic partnerships with federal and state Brazilian universities. There are myriad advantages to such programs starting with the facts that you'll receive academic credit for your studies and that your home university will be able to facilitate everything from visas and paperwork to your living arrangements in Brazil. Moreover, those dependent on financial aid will be able to continue receiving loans or scholarships (in some cases, you can apply for supplementary aid to offset the costs of travel and living abroad). Once in Brazil, you'll have the advantage of a support group of other students and staff to ease the adjustment of parachuting into a new country, culture, and language. Some study-abroad programs also supplement academic offerings with cultural and travel programs.

The majority of foreigners who study in Brazil do so because they are interested in specific issues related to Brazilian history, society, or culture, i.e., they are "Brazilianists." Many are enrolled in Latin American Studies or Brazilian Studies programs with major areas of concentration that include Afro-Brazilian studies, Anthropology, Architecture, Geosciences, Government, Brazilian Literature, Music, and Public Policy. Particularly hot topics these days include issues related to race, public security, and biofuels. In view of Brazil's vast, rich, and unique natural ecosystems, the country also attracts many natural scientists and environmentalists, particularly to the Amazon region. Many come to do postgraduate work or to participate in scientific research projects carried out by universities or scientific institutes.

Among the U.S. and Canadian universities that have their own Brazilian studies programs are the University of Texas at Austin; University of California, Los Angeles (UCLA); Harvard University; Brown University; Georgetown University; University of Illinois at Urbana-Champaign; University of Pittsburgh; University of Washington; and Université du Québec à Montréal (UQAM). A great resource is the bilingual site belonging to the Brazilian Studies Association (BRASA): www.brasa.org.

DAILY LIFE

HEALTH

Prior to moving to Brazil, it's natural that foreigners might worry about potential health issues considering the country's tropical climate and considerable degree of poverty. In truth, however, as an expat you'll likely be living among the First World version of Brazil as opposed to the Third World version, i.e., chances are you won't be living without electricity and indoor plumbing in an urban favela or rural backwater. In fact, you might find health conditions—and health care—to be superior to those you were used to in North America.

Unless you're in the Amazon, where outbreaks of yellow fever and, to a lesser extent, malaria are legitimate concerns, the only disease you're more likely to be exposed to in Brazil than in North America is dengue fever. Otherwise, you might find you actually get sick a lot less in Brazil. Exposure to fresh air and sunshine (within limits) and easy access to nature, combined with healthy living and eating, will ultimately have a beneficial effect upon your overall health.

Although certain precautions must always be taken (not drinking tap water, refrigerating food shortly after cooking so that it doesn't go bad), in most cases the hot climate means that Brazilians automatically take more precautions with hygiene because of how easily food can spoil or be exposed to insects. Barring poor decision making on your part, you're as likely to come down with a case of diarrhea or food poisoning

© MICHAEL SOMMERS

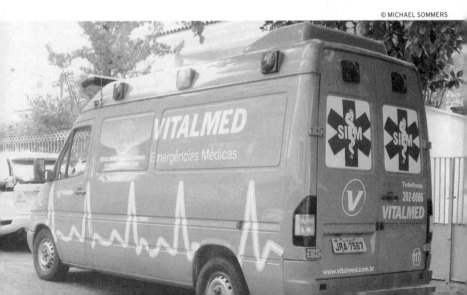

in New York City as you are in São Paulo. You're definitely likely to come down with fewer colds and cases of flu—although chances of acquiring heat rashes and intestinal worms are higher. Should you have an accident or experience a serious illness, rest assured that Brazil's major cities boast some world-class hospitals, clinics, and medical specialists, not to mention an innovative pharmaceutical industry and an interesting array of natural, homeopathic, and alternative treatments.

Safety, however, is a whole other issue and one that will inevitably require expats, particularly those who settle in large urban centers, to take far more precautions than they do in North America. However, it's important not to get overwhelmed by statistics and sensationalism. Although robberies are commonplace, if you're not living in a favela controlled by drug traffickers and rival gangs, you're far less likely to be exposed to the types of violent crimes that are routinely talked about in the media.

Public vs. Private Care

In theory, Brazil has an admirable universal public health care system. Exceptional among Latin American countries, the Unified Health System, or Sistema Único de Saúde (SUS), which is enshrined in the 1988 Constitution, is available to all Brazilians and foreign residents for free. In practice, however, funding, which is shared by the federal and state governments, is often inadequate and varies wildly from place to place. To wit, there is a big difference between medical care in São Paulo and Rio (where public hospitals often rival private clinics) and that available in rural areas and cities in the poorer North and Northeast states. Moreover, the fact that roughly 75 percent of the Brazilian population relies upon the overtaxed and underfunded public system often results in a shortage of staff, equipment, and facilities, not to mention long waits in the emergency room and even longer waits if you need to see a specialist.

The state of many Brazilian public hospitals can be frightening to someone used to North American hospitals. There is a saying among Brazilians that a sick person who goes into a public hospital often gets worse instead of getting cured. Though doctors and nurses are often qualified, facilities can be basic or even precarious. Moreover, the sight of sick and suffering people lining up on the sidewalk as early as 2am and then waiting for hours in the hot sun to get medical attention is tragic.

For this reason, almost all middle- and

© MICHAEL SOMMERS

Hospital Português is considered one of the top private hospitals in Salvador.

IVO PITANGUY

If Brazil is the plastic surgery capital of the world, then Ivo Pitanguy is the celebrity surgeon who put it on the map. Pitanguy, whose father was a surgeon, began his pioneering techniques in reconstructive surgery by working on wounded World War II soldiers and, later, on burn victims. When he opened his own private clinic in Rio de Janeiro, he set the stage for what would be one of Brazil's most renowned industries. With cutting-edge technology and affordable prices—not to mention an idyllic location for recuperation—Rio, always a city where appearances mattered immensely, became a mecca for celebrities around Brazil and the rest of the world who were in search of a little nip or tuck. Recently, the city has become a prime destination for "cosmetic vacationers"—a new breed of tourists who combine going under the scalpel with postoperative trips to beaches and mountain retreats.

upper-class Brazilians—and expats—rely upon Brazil's efficient and generally top-of-the-line private segment. In fact, in many areas—plastic surgery is a classic example—Brazil draws medical tourists from throughout the world who are lured by the highly qualified surgeons and excellent inpatient provisions of hospitals and clinics in Rio and São Paulo.

However, over the last few years, private medical costs in Brazil—once a bargain—have skyrocketed. Since 2009, despite protests from patients and health insurers, private hospitals that operate along the lines of North American and European standards have raised prices by 20 to 30 percent. In some cases, private health care costs are on par with those in the United States. As such, if you don't want to rely on the public system, it's imperative that you invest in a decent health coverage plan.

HEALTH INSURANCE

Prior to coming to Brazil, it's a good idea to purchase international health insurance or travel insurance that will cover your first few months in the country and give you time to shop around among the various national coverage plans. In some cases, health insurance is actually a compulsory requirement if you're to obtain certain types of visas, such as some work and student visas. Even with this insurance, should you need to visit a private hospital or clinic, you'll usually need to pay a hefty deposit upon being admitted. This can be done in cash or with a credit card. Prior to leaving North America, your health insurance company should provide you with a card that will guarantee you're reimbursed for all charges.

Most Brazilian health insurance plans offer comprehensive coverage and often include access to specialists, such as acupuncturists, nutritionists, and even aestheticians. In general, the bigger the insurance company, the more—not to mention the better—hospitals, clinics, and specialists you'll have access to. If you want dental insurance, this will cost extra, but it's worth it since dental work costs a small fortune in Brazil. Like medical care, private dental care in Brazil is good in the large cities; in fact, certain top Rio and São Paulo dentists have developed a thriving medical tourism trade.

Costs for insurance plans vary depending on the company, your location, and the degree of coverage you desire, not to mention your age. When you sign your original contract read the fine print, which usually outlines the various increases that the company is entitled to charge; expect annual increases along with small or sizable spikes every time you enter a new age bracket. If you're in your early 40s, expect to pay between R$400 and R$500 a month for a comprehensive plan. Plans that are popular with expats include Unimed, which is the biggest health plan operator in Brazil, and Pacific Prime.

Popular in the Southeast and South, HMOs (health maintenance organizations) are another alternative that combine insurance and health care under one umbrella. Similar to HMOs in the United States, they offer access to a network of hospitals, laboratories, and health care providers for fees that are often 25 to 40 percent less expensive than those charged by large insurance companies. Unlike HMOs in the United States, in Brazil there are no co-pays, deductibles, or gatekeeper physicians. In fact, in Brazil you can often call a specialist and make an appointment without a referral from a general practitioner (GP).

Expats who come to Brazil as employees of large companies will usually receive insurance plans as part of their employee packages. In many cases, this can be an incredible benefit because it gives you free access to medical treatment and services that would be completely out of your range in the United States. For example, with the high quality of prenatal and postnatal care in Brazil, many expats actually plan to be pregnant or give birth in Brazil.

Pharmacies and Prescriptions

Pharmacies are everywhere in Brazil. Most are open until 10pm. In most central neighborhoods, you'll always find one that stays open 24 hours and on Sundays. All *farmácias* have at least one licensed pharmacist trained to deal with minor medical problems and emergencies, which could save you a trip to a clinic or hospital; the only problem is that it's very unlikely that the pharmacist will speak any English. You'll be able to find good medicine for whatever ails you (an upset stomach, diarrhea, a headache, rashes, a cold, or a cough), even though you probably won't recognize the names. For this reason, it's a good idea to bring from home any prescription medication you're taking so that the pharmacist can find the Brazilian equivalent.

Most medications in Brazil are inexpensive and, in many cases, you have the option of buying a lower cost generic version as part of a government initiative to provide greater access of medications to poorer Brazilians. Officially you need a prescription for a wide range of drugs, including antibiotics, but in practice, you can often find pharmacies willing to *dar um jeito* and provide you with

© MICHAEL SOMMERS

a popular pharmacy chain

medication over the counter (although with stricter 2011 legislation, this is increasingly difficult to find). Keep in mind that basics, ranging from multivitamins to Tylenol, often cost considerably more in Brazil, so it's worthwhile to stock up in North America.

Preventive Measures

Before your trip, check your country's travel health recommendations for Brazil. You'll find up-to-date information and travel advisories on these websites: www.phac-aspc. gc.ca (Canada) and www.cdc.gov (United States).

The **MDtravelhealth.com** website (www.mdtravelhealth.com) has complete travel health information, updated daily for both physicians and travelers, and the World Health Organization (www.who.int) publishes a useful tome entitled *International Travel and Health;* updated annually, it can be downloaded for free from the website.

VACCINATIONS

Brazil requires only one vaccination: for **yellow fever** if you are visiting the Amazon region (or arriving from certain countries)—it's an essential for that region, but otherwise only recommended. Be sure to bring an International Certificate of Vaccination yellow booklet because Brazilian authorities will sometimes ask for proof of vaccination for travelers going to and from the Amazon. If you've been in any other South American country (except Chile and Argentina), as well as some African ones, 90 days prior to coming to Brazil, then you will also need proof of yellow fever vaccination. Other recommended vaccines include **hepatitis A, hepatitis B, typhoid,** and **rabies** (many domestic animals in Brazil aren't vaccinated against rabies).

HEALTH PRECAUTIONS

Tropical heat and humidity favor the growth of bacteria and cause food and organic matter in general to spoil and rot very quickly. As a result, hygiene standards in Brazil are quite high. Nevertheless, it's wise to take certain precautions to avoid upset stomachs or diarrhea.

Be attentive to the conditions of any food you purchase on the street. Fruits with peels (bananas, mangoes, papayas) are safer than fruits without, which should be carefully washed. Similarly, boiled vegetables are safer than raw ones, unless you know they've been well washed, and veggies that have been sitting around in mayonnaise should be avoided. At home, many Brazilians not only wash vegetables, but often leave *folhas* (leafy greens) such as lettuce soaking in water with alcohol vinegar or even a tiny bit of bleach to kill off any microbes or insects. You should also be careful with seafood such as shrimp. If something looks poorly cooked, or smells or tastes slightly off, spit it out and stop eating.

Brazilian tap water is supposedly safe to drink in large cities, but few people actually do (in part because of the heavy chlorine taste). Most Brazilians drink filtered water or mineral water, either *natural* or *com gas* (carbonated), and you should too (although brushing your teeth or rinsing fruit with tap water is perfectly fine). Mineral water is inexpensive and available everywhere. Many Brazilians have water dispensers onto which they load large 20-liter water bottles, which can be delivered upon request. Others have filters that attach to their kitchen faucets. Ice is usually made from filtered water. However, if you're in an out-of-the-way place that seems a bit suspicious, you might want to order your drink without it (*sem gelo*). Also make a habit out of drinking from cans with a straw, which will invariably be offered to you. If drinking beer from a can, make sure you wipe the top off with a napkin or even your shirt.

Diseases and Illnesses

DIARRHEA

To avoid diarrhea, be careful about the source of the water you drink and the food you eat. Even so, you might get diarrhea simply from being exposed to different types of bacteria. In the event you do get sick, aside from taking medication, drink lots of fluids. Particularly good for diarrhea and upset stomachs are *água de coco* (fresh coconut water) and *suco de lima,* a juice made from a citrus fruit that is a cross between an orange and a lime. If your diarrhea is serious after 2–3 days, you should go to a pharmacy and ask for an antibiotic and an antidiarrheal drug. If you see blood and have a fever, chills, or strong abdominal pains, seek medical treatment.

DENGUE

Dengue fever is a viral infection that, like many tropical diseases (including malaria and yellow fever) is transmitted by mosquitoes. Dengue isn't caused by just any old mosquito but by a genus known as *Aedes* that breed in stagnant water, usually in densely populated urban areas with improper drainage. Plant containers and

DAILY LIFE

© MICHAEL SOMMERS

Public campaigns to prevent dengue are common throughout Brazil.

© MICHAEL SOMMERS

Try to avoid going to the beach during peak sun hours.

abandoned rubber tires are particularly common breeding grounds. Dengue mosquitoes usually attack during the daytime and are most common during hot, humid rainy periods. In recent years, Rio de Janeiro has had large dengue epidemics during its rainy summer months. Although rarely fatal, dengue is like having a really debilitating case of flu. Symptoms include fever, aching muscles, headaches, nausea, weakness, vomiting, and a rash. In general, the worst symptoms last 5–7 days, but full recuperation can take longer. Diagnosis is made by a blood test. There is no vaccine for dengue, nor is there treatment aside from rest, plenty of liquids, and acetaminophen (Tylenol). Do not take aspirin. Only severe cases require hospitalization. The best thing you can do to avoid infection is to take precautions to avoid getting bitten in the first place.

HIV/AIDS AND OTHER STDS

Brazil has one of the highest numbers of people living with HIV infection. According to statistics, more than 35 percent of infected people are women. Despite Brazil having one of the world's most highly respected and effective HIV/AIDS policies—aside from creating low-cost generic drugs, the Brazilian government's fight against HIV/AIDS involves free medication and medical follow-up for all patients for life—it doesn't help prevent people from getting HIV in the first place. Condoms, known as *camisinhas* (literally "little shirts"), are widespread (you'll find them in all pharmacies and many supermarkets), and there is not so much a stigma as a resistance to using them. As a result, you really have to be careful about HIV and STDs. Whether you're with a man or a woman, always insist on using a condom.

SUN EXPOSURE

When you arrive in Brazil from the cold and gray northern hemisphere, expose your-self to the sun gradually. The tropical sun, particularly during the summer months, can cause a lot of damage. Brazilians have a high rate of skin cancer; many don't use sunscreen because of its exorbitant cost. Using a strong sunscreen (bring it from home) that filters out UVA and UVB rays is essential. You should use at least an SPF 30. Even so, if you're foolish enough to stay in the sun between the deadliest hours of 11am–2pm, you will still get burned. On many beaches, you can rent a parasol or head to a thatched *barraca* for shade come high noon. Children and those with fair, sensitive skin should use a much higher SPF. A hat is always essential, whether you're on the beach or practicing any outdoor sport, and you'll practically be blinded without a pair of sunglasses with a protective filter. Remember to drink lots of liquids all the time, even if you're not thirsty. Beer and caipirinhas might be refreshing, but alcohol actu-ally dehydrates. An ideal replenishing drink is *água de coco*.

Safety

CRIME

The subject of crime and security in Brazil is an extremely important and complex one. Violent crime, holdups, robberies, and drug warfare in major cities dominate the Brazilian news media, often in a sensationalist manner, and have a major social impact. An increasing number of middle-class Brazilians are moving to closed condominium complexes with electric fences and 24-hour security. Wealthy Brazilians are the lead-ing buyers of security systems and bulletproof cars in the world. Meanwhile, poorer Brazilians who reside in peripheral neighborhoods or favelas live in fear of bus hold-ups, stray bullets, and drug traffickers. If you come into contact with Brazilians, read the papers, or watch TV, you will definitely hear such stories, and while the tone may be alarmist or melodramatic, the occurrences themselves are real. There's no need for paranoia, but don't let yourself be complacent.

Major cities are the most problematic in terms of crime, but around important tour-ist sites, such as Rio and Salvador, there has been an effort to have police on patrol, which has increased safety in the most touristy areas. Nonetheless, always have your wits about you. In smaller towns and rural areas, you will definitely feel more relaxed. Crime is much lower, and you can let your guard down somewhat (although don't be lulled into complete carelessness).

Theft

Having lived in Brazil for over 14 years, I don't know *anybody* who has never been robbed. I myself have been robbed more than once. Aside from having my home bro-ken into (someone scaled my building and climbed in through the window), on the other occasions I have to admit that I was in the wrong place at the wrong time: on a deserted, if central, street at night (7pm), and then in the middle of a multitude of drunk and celebrating people at a popular street festival when someone succeeded in sliding a hand into my pocket and making off with the contents.

SAFETY TIPS

- Unless you're on a very busy or major street in a good neighborhood, you'd be wise not to walk around at night in a city you don't know. While downtown business areas of major cities such as Rio, São Paulo, Salvador, and Recife may hum with energy by day, at night and on weekends, especially Sunday, they turn into ghost towns and should be avoided.

- If you're going to be amid a crowd (an outdoor performance, a parade, Carnaval) leave all valuables and original documents at home. Carry a small change purse around your neck or a money belt.

- While public transportation is safe enough during the day, at night take a taxi, even if it's just a few blocks to your destination. If you're driving, be careful where you park. Particularly at night, you don't want to be on a dark or isolated side street.

- At a stoplight, keep your windows rolled up because if you're stuck in traffic, you can easily be held up. At night, in many major cities, drivers slow down at stoplights but don't actually stop their cars (a practice sanctioned by law).

- Never walk around with a lot of cash in a purse or pocket. Do, however, keep a few small bills that you can easily access. Fumbling around for money in public, on a bus, or at a market, leaves you exposed to robbery.

- Don't take valuables to the beach. Bring enough cash for drinks or snacks, and that's it. Keep all your possessions with you (in a neat pile or a cheap local beach bag) within your line of vision. If you're on your own and want to go swimming, ask someone to watch your stuff. This is very common on Brazilian beaches.

- If you're going to be taking money out at an ATM, make sure nobody is watching you. Even though ATMs are open until 10pm, the best time to take out money is during the day in a busy area. Be careful on Sundays, when commercial areas are very quiet.

- Don't let people you don't know into your building if they are lingering outside the door and claim to be waiting for a neighbor, or if they buzz the interphone.

If you are robbed, in most cases it will consist of a *furto* (small theft), when your pockets are picked or someone grabs your bag and takes off. However, armed *assaltos* (holdups) do occur with increasing frequency. In the event that you are held up by someone, do not resist. Quickly and calmly hand over whatever the thief wants. It's a no-brainer between your money, watch, jewelry, cell phone, and car or your life. Accidents happen when people get very upset or try to resist, making the robber nervous and prone to act impulsively.

In the South and Southeast, it's easier to blend in physically with the local population, but if you are of fair European stock, then in the North and Northeast you will often stand out simply because of your physical type. Gringos are uniformly considered easy targets for theft, not only because they are all thought to be rich, but also because they are often careless. One thing to do is try to camouflage yourself: Get a bit of a tan, don't talk loudly in English, and try to dress like the locals (casually but smartly).

Without being neurotic, always try to be aware of where you are and what's going on around you. Trust your instincts. If a bar, street, or neighborhood feels sketchy, make a fast exit. If you feel like someone is watching you or following you, speed up your pace, cross the street, or enter a shop or public building. Be aware of possible scams, such as being approached by so-called officials at airports who want you to go with them after you've come out of the arrivals section. Another notorious *golpe* (scam) is "Boa Noite Cinderela" ("Good Night, Cinderella"), which involves someone slipping a drug into your drink and, while you're knocked out, robbing you blind. This trick usually befalls unsuspecting romantics who hook up with a potential conquest in a bar. If you find yourself in this situation, don't leave your drink unguarded (such as by going to the restroom).

Police

The North American or European concept of police as (for the most part) a symbol of law and order doesn't hold true in Brazil. When trouble occurs, most Brazilians avoid the police. Because police officers are grossly underpaid and subject to corruption and violence, it is sometimes difficult to distinguish them from the bandits and drug traffickers they are supposedly battling. This is, of course, a generalization, and there are many exceptions to the rule.

In Brazil, there are various types of police. The most efficient (and well paid, and thus, less corrupt) of the bunch are the **Polícia Federal,** who deal with all matters concerning passports, visas, and immigration. They have offices at all international airports, as well as at frontier posts and in state capitals, and are generally helpful. The **Polícia Militar** are a holdover from the era of military dictatorship. They dress in soldier-like khaki uniforms accessorized with tough lace-up boots and berets (even in the tropical heat). You'll often see them supposedly keeping the peace on street corners. Although they can be rough with Brazilian indolents, they leave foreigners alone. The plainclothes **Polícia Civil** deal with solving crimes. If you're robbed and you want to report the crime, in many places you'll need to go to the nearest *delegacia,* or station. Be prepared if you want an official report: You'll need to wait in line, and nobody will speak English. Unless you really need a report for insurance purposes, you might want to just let it go.

No matter where you are in the country, if you are the victim of a crime or want to report one, dial **190** (the equivalent of 911) to reach the police.

EMPLOYMENT

Historically, Brazil suffered from that common affliction of developing countries known as a "brain drain." Brazilians seeking employment outside the country far exceeded the number of foreigners immigrating to Brazil. However, in the last few years, the situation has reversed itself entirely. In 2011, for the first time in decades, not only were Brazilians returning to their homeland en masse from their economically depressed adopted homelands in Europe and the United States, but the record number of Americans and Europeans seeking refuge from their respective crises in Brazil's thriving economy was greater than the number of Brazilians leaving the country.

One of the rare countries to emerge unscathed from the global recession, Brazil's economy—which in 2011 became the world's sixth largest—continues to grow as does its vast domestic market. Aside from 40 million new middle-class consumers spending up a storm, it's estimated that the country is spawning close to 20 millionaires every day (which explains why the national market for luxury goods grew by more than 30 percent in 2011). The country is a hot spot in terms of financial services, telecommunications, health care, alternative energy, biotechnology, pharmaceuticals, aerospace, manufacturing, agribusiness, and tourism. With recent offshore oil discoveries, its booming oil and gas sector is poised to be the biggest in the Americas. Its burgeoning IT and software segment, the seventh largest in terms of spending, is already bigger

© MICHAEL SOMMERS

than India's. Moreover, in preparation for the 2014 World Cup and 2016 Olympics, major investments are being made in large-scale public works and infrastructure projects as well as massive hydroelectric dams that will help meet the country's rapidly growing energy needs.

The fact that Brazil is sorely lacking in skilled professionals in many of these areas means that both Brazilian and multinational companies are scrambling like never before to hire qualified foreigners, particularly technicians, engineers, and high-level experienced managers. In fact, the opportunities are so great—and so well paid—that an increasing number of foreigners don't just view moving to Brazil as a career stepping stone, but as a (lucrative) end in itself. According to a 2011 survey carried out by the Minas-based Dasein Executive Search firm, the average salary of a CEO in São Paulo is $620,000 compared to $574,000 in New York and $550,000 in London.

To quickly fill the growing number of vacancies, the Brazilian government is already looking at ways to streamline the notoriously bureaucratic visa and immigration process to accommodate the professionals it desperately needs to prevent its economy from stalling. Such legislation is expected to be passed in 2013 or 2014, which will make it easier for both Brazilian and international firms based in Brazil to hire skilled foreign workers. As it is, between 2010 and 2011, the number of work visas issued to foreign professionals rose by 32 percent. However, according to official estimates, Brazil desperately needs between one-half to one million qualified professionals in key growth areas such as oil, mining, and IT.

The Job Hunt

Working expats in Brazil can be divided into two categories: those who come to Brazil with a job already and those who come hoping to find one once they arrive. Regardless of how you gain employment, in order to obtain a work visa issued by the Brazilian Ministry of Labor you (and the company that decides to invest in you; a costly process) will have to prove that your skills are unique to the extent that no Brazilian applicant is capable of performing your job. Detailed information about obtaining a work visa is included in the *Making the Move* chapter.

Expats who are either transferred from a home company to Brazil or hired from abroad and arrive in Brazil with a job waiting for them can count on receiving high salaries along with multiple perks including housing allowances, health care, school tuition for children, and even cars with drivers. In most cases, the company that employs you will have lawyers who can deal with all red tape related to visas, immigration, moving, and other sundry bureaucracy, which facilitates life enormously. Initial work permits are temporary (usually two years) but can be extended for another two years.

Expats hoping to find work *after* they move to Brazil will be up against a number of serious challenges. One problem is you can't get a work visa without a job and you can't legally work in Brazil without first being a permanent resident. The chances of a Brazilian company hiring you and going through the process of getting you a work permit are very low considering the red tape and costs involved. Even if you are a permanent resident, while transferred employees of multinationals can get away with limited Portuguese, it's very unlikely you'll be considered for a job without a strong command of Brazil's lingua franca. Moreover, unless you have very specialized skills, don't count on it being easy to find a job in your field, let alone at the salary you're used to making back home. Know that foreign certifications and academic titles aren't automatically accepted in Brazil. You will either have to go through the lengthy process of having them recognized or completing the necessary requalification in Brazil. "*Não é o que você sabe, é quem você conhece.*" In English, "It isn't what you know; it's who you know," says it all. Brazil has its share of employment agencies, headhunters, online ads, and job boards. However, personal contacts, word-of-mouth, and networking are far more influential in a country where the professional and the personal are so tightly bound and so many businesses are family owned.

If you really want to risk coming to Brazil jobless, try to do some legwork (if possible before you leave home). Research Brazilian companies and multinational or North American companies with branches in Brazil that operate in the fields that interest you and try to make contact with them (i.e., through the HR manager). Also hit up any expat or Brazilian friends or contacts to see if anybody knows anybody in your field and can offer you insider tips or contacts. In Brazil, introductions from mutual acquaintances carry a lot of weight. Having someone contact Brazilian friends or colleagues before you go to Brazil, or traveling with a letter of introduction can help open doors. Expat clubs and online forums are good places to network. Chambers of commerce and consulates sometimes have listings of multinationals located in Brazil, with details and contact information.

Apart from networking there is the more traditional route of recruitment agencies, headhunters, and websites. Recommended recruiters include Fesa (www.fesa.com.br), one of Brazil's oldest and largest executive recruiting firms, Abrahams Executive Search (www.abrahams.com.br), and Dasein (www.dasein.com.br).

Top employment websites in Brazil (in Portuguese only) include Catho (www.catho.com.br), Manager (www.manager.com.br), Empregos.com.br (www.empregos.com.br), and Curriculum.com (www.curriculum.com.br). You can also try the Brazilian versions of Olx (www.olx.com.br) and craigslist (www.craigslist.org). For a site that specializes in jobs at Brazilian start-ups, log on to Mais Startup (www.maisstartup.com.br).

A big misconception held by foreigners who come to Brazil is that they can make a living teaching English. This was true once upon a time, back in the days when gringos and language schools were scarce. However, these days it's almost impossible to make ends meet because the cost of living in Brazil is so high and most language schools pay a pittance (between R$10–20 an hour). Increasingly, you also need a TESL diploma. Although you can make more money giving private lessons, it takes a while to build up a clientele, and even then, you often have to deal with cancellations and dropouts.

Self-Employment

An alternative to finding a formal, full-time job in Brazil is to go the self-employed route, either by working as a freelancer (with clients in Brazil—or North America—or both) or by starting your own business. To start your own business in Brazil, or to invest in a new or preexisting company, involves applying for—and being granted—an Investment Visa, which you can read more about in the *Making the Move* chapter.

Good sources of information for investors and entrepreneurs alike are Rio Negócios (www.rio-negocios.com) and Investe São Paulo (www.investe.sp.gov.br), business development agencies that focus on helping foreign businesspeople find investment and start-up opportunities in Rio and São Paulo. The national equivalent, BrasilGlobalNet (www.brasilglobalnet.gov.br) provides a breakdown of trade and investment opportunities available in all the Brazilian states.

STARTING A BUSINESS

Despite an attractive economy and expanding consumer markets (both physical and virtual), as well as untapped potential and lack of competition in many areas, starting a business in Brazil is not for the faint of heart. According to the IBGE (Brazilian Institute of Geography and Statistics), 4 out of 10 new companies close their doors after their first two years in business. And according to the World Bank's 2012 *Doing Business* report, which examines issues such as the ease of starting a business, dealing with construction permits, registering property, and paying taxes, Brazil is still one of the worst counties in the world for a foreigner to start a business, ranking 126th out of 183 countries.

Major obstacles include high tax rates and swollen bureaucracy. For instance, the World Bank report found that it takes an average of 13 procedures and 119 days of work just to start a business, which can involve getting approval from a dozen different government agencies and laying out R$2,000 just for shuffling paperwork. Construction permits alone involve an average of 17 procedures and 469 days before they are finally authorized. Navigating the thick tangle of rules and regulations is impossible without a lawyer, not to mention an accounting specialist. Complicating matters further is the fact that such baroque bureaucracy lends itself easily to corruption. Using bribes as a means to speed up the issuing of a document is quite common.

Many gringos dream of operating their own beach *pousadas*.

DAILY LIFE

THE "BRAZIL COST"

The notorious "Brazil Cost" refers to the (escalating) operational costs of doing business in Brazil, which in turn makes Brazilian goods and services so expensive. Currently, the "Brazil Cost" is a major obstacle in the country's fulfillment of its great competitive potential and underscores the Brazilian government's urgent challenge to come up with structural reforms that encourage entrepreneurship, create new jobs, and stimulate private investment. Contributing to the "Brazil Cost" are some of these leading factors:

- Byzantine layers of bureaucracy
- Corruption
- High taxes and complex tax regulations
- Expensive labor costs
- Woefully underdeveloped infrastructure, which increases transportation costs
- High interest rates
- High crime (which translates into high security expenses)

Another consideration is finding the right business partner. In many cases, it's almost impossible to start a business in Brazil without an experienced Brazilian partner who speaks the language, understands the culture (specifically when it comes to dealing with employees), and can navigate the stormy seas of bureaucracy. Such an associate has to be someone you can trust (there are legion stories of naïve gringos who were fleeced or scammed by Brazilian partners) and someone who shares your goals and a certain mindset (Brazilians in business tend to be more prone to improvising than planning and focusing on the short term as opposed to the long term). If you decide to fly solo—a possibility in cases such as opening a *pousada*, for example—you'll definitely need to rely on an experienced Brazilian lawyer and business consultant.

A lot of expat businesspeople also have problems when it comes to dealing with employees. Brazilians have a tradition of changing jobs frequently, especially these days with the shortage of professionals and specialized workers. This stems from a tradition in which a successful career is more about money than loyalty to a company or brand. In many cases, notions such as taking initiative, motivation, teamwork, and "the customer is king" are fairly alien to Brazilian employees. Meanwhile, lateness and absenteeism are common.

Such attitudes are understandable when one considers the way many employers have traditionally treated—and continue to treat—workers in Brazil. Many are exploited, woefully underpaid, and obliged to work under very difficult conditions (i.e., construction workers with no protective gear whatsoever who are exposed to hazardous situations and toxic substances; maids who work seven days a week and receive far less than minimum wage). Because of the many abuses against workers, labor laws in Brazil are heavily skewed toward protecting employees. While positive in theory, in practice this can create complications: Even when employees give just cause to be fired, it's often very difficult to dismiss them. Moreover, employees can (and do) often sue employers for wrongful termination. In fact, Brazil has one of the highest number of labor claims in the world.

Business Culture

Probably the biggest difference between North American and Brazilian business culture is the extent to which personal and professional are intertwined in Brazil. Great emphasis is placed not just on your qualifications, but also on the personal impression you make. Meeting face-to-face—whether for an interview or to seal a deal—is essential and much more important than trading emails or talking on the phone. Even in person, a business meeting may be productive, but going out and socializing after the meeting is likely to prove even more so.

Although networks and relationships are important everywhere, they are the key to success in Brazilian business. Keep in mind that, even in business, Brazilians don't just want to meet you, they want to know you. Some North Americans are puzzled by what they view as unnecessary socializing in the midst of a business meeting or during a phone conversation. However, for Brazilians such socializing is an integral part of business negotiations, and they view North Americans' narrow focus on brass tacks without engaging in social niceties as aggressive or even rude.

Another cultural difference to be aware of stems from Brazilians' tendency to avoid confrontation and favor nuance over directness. This means that instead of Brazilians outright saying "no," you're often likely to get various degrees of "yes," most of which aren't actually full-out affirmatives. So another reason why face-to-face encounters (not to mention Portuguese fluency) are so essential is that they allow you to factor body language, facial expressions, and tone into any given exchange.

In terms of greetings, even in business, Brazilians tend to be warm and not overly formal. When you first meet, one usually shakes hands. However, afterward, the ritual one- or two-cheek kisses will be shared as a greeting between two women or a woman and a man. While men stick to handshakes, friendly pats on the shoulder or arm are not uncommon.

Meanwhile, one aspect in which Brazil is more formal than North America is the way people address each other in the workplace. Unless you're invited to do so, being on a first-name basis is not customary in meetings or between employees and their higher-ups. This is because socioeconomic status, age, and position carry a lot more weight in Brazil. As such, it's common to hear people addressing business associates or superiors as "*o Senhor*" or "*a Senhora*" (for example, "*A Senhora quer uma água?*" for "Would you like some water?"). Big bosses and high-ranking male execs are often called "*doutor*," which is more a sign of respect than reflective of whether or not they have a PhD. It's also common when addressing an associate or employee (particularly one who is older) to use a person's first name preceded by the pronoun *Seu* for men and *Dona* for women (for instance, "Bom dia, Seu Pedro"), at least until they tell you otherwise. However, in the case of ongoing relations with close colleagues of the same age group (particularly younger people), first names are generally used.

As for clothing, keep in mind that even in informal situations, appearance is very important to Brazilians (far from being a cardinal sin, vanity is viewed as a positive trait). Recommended business attire for women include a fashionable business suit or a dress, or a skirt and blouse, paired with a jacket or cardigan. Skirt and dress hemlines are usually knee length or above the knee. Fabrics such as cotton, rayon, and linen are good choices for beating the heat. Lightweight wool and tweed are recommended for cool winters in São Paulo and the South. Men should invest in a stylish suit with a European design or tailoring accessorized with a silk tie, good leather shoes, and a belt.

Labor Laws and Workers' Rights

Brazil has fairly rigid and complex labor laws that protect workers' rights—at least in theory. Sometimes they are not followed to the letter of the law, and other times they are not followed at all.

CONTRACTS AND WAGES

Although managers, executives, and other midlevel and high-level professionals sign individual work contracts, most Brazilians, in lieu of contracts, have an employee record book known as the Carteira de Trabalho e Previdência Social. The CTPS serves as an employee's Social Insurance Identity Card and contains all relevant information about every job an employee has held in her or his lifetime (official position and function, salary and raises, vacation time, etc.). Should you need one, you can apply for a CTPS at the Ministry of Labor once you have your CIE.

When starting out a new job, a probation period of up to 90 days is permitted. Temporary work contracts (Contrato de Trabalho por Prazo Determinado) can have limits of up to two years (otherwise, by law, they are unlimited). Once a temporary contract has been extended more than once, it must be transformed into an unlimited contract. Part-time contracts (Contratos de Trabalho de Tempo Parcial) are limited to 25 weekly hours without overtime.

Brazilians are eligible to work full time beginning at age 14, although between the ages of 14 and 18, various protective regulations apply. As of 2013, the minimum monthly wage in Brazil is R$675. Approximately a third of all Brazilians earn this minimum wage.

BENEFITS AND SOCIAL SECURITY

All employees in Brazil have the right to an annual bonus (a *décimo teceiro salário*) or "13th salary." The equivalent of a month's salary, it is usually paid in two installments in November and December (just in time for end-of-year holidays). Overtime is paid with a premium of 50 percent, except for Sundays and public holidays (100 percent) and at night (20 percent). Legally, the full-time workweek is between 40 and 44 hours depending on whether an employee works five or six days. By law, Brazilians have the right to 30 paid vacation days a year, which can be taken all at once or in two parts. Additionally, Brazil has 11 national holidays, along with myriad local and regional ones.

Previdência Social (Social Security) covers illness, disabilities, maternity, unemployment pensions, and death. Depending on how much they earn, employees contribute between 8 and 11 percent of their monthly salary to the INSS (Instituto Nacional do Seguro Social), which is met by 20 percent from employers. This amount is automatically deducted from your monthly paycheck. If you're self-employed, then during the first three years you're in business, you contribute 10 percent, and then 20 percent, calculated upon a base salary. In order to make payments and receive benefits, you'll

BETTER LATE THAN NEVER

The notion of time in Brazil is different than in North America. In Brazil, time tends to be much more liquid, elastic, and vague, which means that North Americans used to promptness and punctuality will be tempted to tear their hair out. For this reason, whenever you're scheduling or attending a meeting, or any other event, *expect* that colleagues will arrive late or that the conference won't start on time. Always carry a book or an iPod or some work to distract yourself from keeping track of the ticking clock. It isn't that Brazilians are procrastinators, disorganized, or oblivious to how precious your time is. It's quite simply that life in Brazil doesn't run that smoothly and, as such, schedules—like everything else in Brazil—are flexible.

need to register with Previdência Social by phone (135) or online (www.previdencia-social.gov.br). You'll be given a registration number and a payment code that will calculate the amount of your contribution. To make your monthly payments, you'll need to buy a Guia de Previdência Social (available at most newspaper stands). Payments can be made at branches of Caixa Econômica Federal and Banco do Brasil as well as at lottery *casas* and through online banking.

In Brazil, you're eligible for unemployment benefits after having worked continuously for a minimum of six months. The contribution to unemployment insurance, known as the Fundo de Garantia por Tempo de Serviço (FGTS), is 8 percent of an employee's monthly salary and is paid by private employers to the government. This fund is kept in an account at the Caixa Econômica Federal and can only be accessed when the employee is fired from a job. Legally, the minimum amount of time for an employee or employer to give notice of termination is 30 days. If a serious reason for dismissal (which can be justified by labor laws) exists, no notice is necessary. However, if an employer fires an employee without just reason, the employer will have to pay a penalty.

Employees are eligible for sickness or disability benefits after having contributed to Previdência Social for a minimum of 12 months. Benefits vary depending on whether the basis is temporary, long term, or a permanent disability. In the case of sickness or injury that keeps you away from work for more than 15 days, you're eligible for benefits equivalent to 91 percent of your monthly salary. Permanent disability benefits equal 100 percent of your monthly salary, with an increase of 25 percent if you need a caretaker.

Pregnant women are entitled to 180 days of paid maternity leave, which they can begin to take advantage of from the eighth month of their pregnancy. Men are allowed five days of paternity leave. To date, men over 65 and women over 60 are eligible for pension benefits. Pension payments start out as 70 percent of a worker's average monthly salary and increase by 1 percent every year up to a maximum of 100 percent. As the population ages, Brazil's pension system is becoming increasingly unsustainable, even though a majority of Brazilians earn pitifully low salaries.

EXPAT PROFILE: OWNING A *POUSADA* IN PARADISE

Charles, 57, moved from New York to Bahia in 1979. After living in Salvador for years, he moved to Ilha de Boipeba, an island off the southern coast of Bahia, where in 2001 he opened the Pousada Santa Clara guest-house and restaurant (www.santaclaraboi-peba.com) with his brother Mark. Here he talks about his experience.

WHY HE CAME

In 1979, I was completing a graduate program at the University of Vermont, and I became fascinated with Brazilian culture... music, film, literature. I was crazy about anything Brazilian without having been to Brazil. So I came to Salvador where Afro-Brazilian culture and music were so strong and immediately fell in love with the city. Carnaval was 1,000 times better than I thought it would be. The city was much smaller then, and I met great people and decided to stay. Everything just clicked. I didn't know what I was doing, but Salvador was the right place to be.

HOW HE CAME

I came as a backpacker with a tourist visa. Very few foreigners were here and the officials never checked papers. In the early '80s, there was an amnesty program and through that I got permanent residency. Back then, it was very easy.

MAKING A LIVING IN SALVADOR

When I first came I got a job teaching English. At the time, there weren't a lot of English schools or teachers. It was hard to find natives who taught English, so it was really easy to survive and get students. Not like today, with many more foreigners.

After a while, teaching English wasn't satisfying me. I realized I knew a lot about Bahian culture, and I thought it was important to share it with foreigners—so I started working as a tour guide. This allowed me to learn even more about Bahia since to be a guide I had to get credentials from the Bahian tourist board. Back then Brazil was a cheap destination, and there were a lot of tour guides and a lot of work. Today, there are fewer tour guides and fewer tours. More people speak foreign languages, and travel agencies are becoming extinct since tourists can get information on the Internet. These days you can't make a living unless you're really good and have lots of contacts.

DECIDING TO OPEN A *POUSADA* ON BOIPEBA

Salvador was growing fast and becoming more globalized, and less charming. More and more I found that I loved being out of the city where I could get in touch with Bahian culture. My brother Mark used to visit me here, and we decided to buy beach land. Boipeba was the place we liked the most. We found affordable land with a crumbling *pousada*. At that time I wasn't planning on leaving my tour guide career. I made decent money. So my brother worked on Santa Clara while I funded it. After a few years the business got too big; I decided I had to be in Boipeba. Gradually I spent less time in Salvador, did less guide work, and moved here for good.

CULTURAL DIFFERENCES

When we purchased the property, our lawyer told us that technically the land belonged to the state—and technically they could take it away, but they probably wouldn't. That would put a lot of foreigners off, but in Brazil, there's always something that's not 100 percent. If you want land, you have to do it. You have to be a person who can go along with the gray areas all the time. It's the same with taxes and staff. Culturally, it's so different here. Things get done with a smile and a twist. Unless you have a lot of money to pay people off, you're screwed. Otherwise you have to rely on resources other than financial, like the famous Brazilian *dar um jeito*.

RUNNING A *POUSADA*

When we bought it, the *pousada* was a small place and we didn't have a lot of money. We thought we'd receive friends, maybe rent some rooms, and Mark, who's a good cook, would cook for people. We stumbled in the beginning. We didn't really know what we were doing. My brother is a perfectionist and he made it really nice. But we were thinking of this as a way of life.

© MICHAEL SOMMERS

one of Boipeba's idyllic beaches

Opening a beach pousada is a great fantasy and people should follow their dreams. If your only goal is financial though, it's not going to work. I've seen many foreigners come to the Northeast, and they come looking to make money, not because they love Brazil. So in a sense, they're doomed to failure. I see it happening over and over. It can work if you're good and you have something to offer. Otherwise, you'll go out of business. We were the first that tried to do something different than a traditional beach *pousada*. What made us special is the fact that my brother is a great cook. Nobody else has this.

There are still opportunities along the Northeast coast, but many are overpriced. You can still find cheap land and even a cheap house, but maintenance is a lot here. Humidity and salt destroy things. Wood gets eaten away. There's a constant pressure to maintain things. Have some experience. Don't go into it cold. And have some funds to fall back on because something always comes up.

The best thing about owning a *pousada* is that you meet interesting and wonderful people. You constantly learn things and have interesting conversations about the world. That keeps me going in a small place like Boipeba. The worst thing is something always needs fixing. So there's always a little stress. No electricity, no Internet, no water, no phone lines. Such problems crop up on a day-to-day basis and you have to roll with the punches.

LIVING IN BOIPEBA

I'm a big-city person from New York City. I'm very urban. It took some time to make my life in such a small rural community. But I started enjoying it after a while. The best things are the sense of community, of knowing people and knowing about their lives, and being involved on a local level. This is a beautiful place with clean beaches, fresh food, no pollution, a great quality of life. On the downside, sometimes you want something else that only a city offers. And logistics are a big problem. You're so far from First World things such as health care—that's a big issue.

A WORD OF ADVICE FOR OTHER EXPATS

I see a lot of foreigners who come to places like Boipeba to open a business and they fail. They don't get it. They don't know Brazil, the people, the laws, the customs. Without this knowledge, a business venture is almost impossible. You have to know the country well to survive it. You also have to have a connection with Brazil. You can't be on the outside, you have to be on the inside...part of a couple, a family, or a community. That's why I like living in Boipeba. I do things to make the community better. For example I'm on the municipal environmental council. Foreigners who are outside the community just aren't happy because they aren't integrated. You have to work hard to be integrated, but ultimately how much time can you spend just looking at the beach?

DAILY LIFE

FINANCE

Expats who moved to Brazil as recently as 2005 can still recall a heyday of very easy living when the U.S. dollar was king (a single greenback traded for four *reais*) and prices across the board were extremely affordable. One could live it up for ridiculously low rents in massive apartments, dine out at the chicest restaurants in town without your credit card breaking a sweat, and take frugal vacations that involved traveling around the country by plane and checking into posh *pousadas*.

Then the global economic crisis kicked in, the Brazilian economy took off, the dollar sunk, the *real* rose, and inflation kicked in, forcing prices up, particularly housing prices, which exploded as a record number of Brazilians suddenly had access to credit (not to mention credit cards). At the same time, as the number of imported products increased, so did the taxes levied upon them, in part to protect Brazilian manufacturing industries, which were suddenly struggling to compete in the global market due to the valorized *real*.

Even though the U.S. dollar has bounced back somewhat since late 2011, if your source of income is U.S. based, and you earn your living in U.S. dollars, you'll find your money often doesn't go as far in Brazil as in the U.S. If you earn Brazilian wages—generally inferior to those you'd make in North America—you'll find it very difficult to get by. Of course, those working in the upper echelons of Brazilian companies or

for multinationals in Brazil can still make out very well living in Brazil, especially if expenses such as education costs, health insurance, and living allowances are provided by the employer. Even so, you'll chafe at high prices that are often quite a bit more inflated than those in North America as well as high corporate and personal income taxes and interest rates (great if you're an investor, but crippling if you're a borrower).

Cost of Living

Economic growth in Brazil slowed in 2011 and 2012 (the country's GDP expanded only 2.7 in 2011 compared to a whopping 7.5 percent in 2010), the *real* lost value, and the nationwide housing market slumped (slightly), but the cost of living in Brazil still remains higher than North America's. According to Mercer's Cost of Living Survey (which measures the comparative cost of living for expatriates in 214 major world cities based on the costs of more than 200 items, including housing, transportation, food, clothing, household goods, and entertainment), in 2012 Brazil's biggest cities (Rio, São Paulo, and Brasília) were the most expensive in the Americas. Outside of the Southeast and major cities, daily life is somewhat cheaper (particularly in terms of housing): Life in São Paulo, for example, is considerably more expensive than life in Salvador or Curitiba. However, in some cases smaller consumer markets can actually drive prices up because of the lack of access to certain goods and services as well as an absence of competition.

Despite rising salaries, Brazilian purchasing power has actually declined in recent times. Although life in Rio and São Paulo is more expensive than life in New York City, according to a 2011 UBS survey, average salaries are 66 percent less in Rio and 61 percent less in São Paulo than those in New York. Meanwhile, high inflation rates (in the first six months of 2012, monthly rates hovered between 5 and 6 percent compared to rates of around 1.5 percent in the United States), coupled with rising costs for Brazilian businesses in terms of logistics, transportation, rents, and employee salaries have caused prices across the board to continue to increase.

For a more detailed breakdown of the expenses involved in moving to and living in Brazil, consult the chapters on *Prime Living Locations* to get a better sense of expenses in different cities and regions of the country. Meanwhile, the other *Daily Life* chapters provide specifics in terms of costs related to housing, health care, communications, travel, transportation, etc.

BALANCING YOUR BUDGET

Regardless of how much—or how little—money you make in Brazil, there are lots of ways to stretch your *real*. First of all, know that the majority of housewares, luxury goods, cosmetics, clothing, shoes, electronics, technology, and books are all far cheaper in North America than in Brazil. Every single expat under the tropical sun will tell you stories of how they can't wait to make their annual pilgrimage to the United States in order to stock up on sunscreen, kids' clothes, cameras, tablets, kitchen gadgets, iPhones, designer sheets, Tylenol, antiaging creams, Ray Bans, multivitamins, sneakers, second-hand books, and so on.

Unless you're filthy rich, avoid upscale neighborhoods where rich Brazilians are

DAILY LIFE

© MICHAEL SOMMERS

In Brazil, many basic American foodstuffs are priced as luxury items.

crazy enough to fork out scads for outrageously overpriced meals, drinks, goods, and services that would cost half as much back in North America. Keep in mind that although prices have gone up in Brazil, a vast portion of Brazilians are *not* upper-middle class and *don't* spend R$10 for an espresso, R$120 on dinner, and R$60 to get into a nightclub. Seek out local haunts in alternative middle-class and working-class neighborhoods as well as *bairros populares* where you can get delicious home-cooked meals for under R$10 and big icy beers for R$4. Free music performances are inherent throughout Brazil; many of them are sponsored by state and city cultural secretaries as well as banks and utility companies. All state-run museums are free (others have free days or nights) and Brazil's biggest cities have a terrific number of top-notch cultural centers where offerings are also *livre* (free) or very affordable.

When it comes to grocery shopping, think local and fresh. Imported goods—ranging from peanut butter to Pringles potato chips—as well as pre-prepared foods, target the upper classes and are priced accordingly. In terms of food preparation, research local and regional recipes and reinvent your own favorite dishes in order to take advantage of the amazing bounty of regional fruit and vegetables. Substitute mangos for pears, cashews for walnuts, and collard greens for spinach. Invest in a *panela de pressão* (pressure cooker) and start soaking and cooking up cheap and healthy grains such as *feijão*.

AVERAGE PRICES IN BRAZIL

- Toyota Corolla: R$65,000
- Men's Armani suit: R$3,900
- King-sized sheet set (600 thread count): R$2,300
- Apple iPad 2 3G 16 GB: R$2,100
- 40-inch flat screen TV: R$1,500
- Refrigerator: R$1,000
- Gas stove: R$300
- Levi's jeans: R$160
- Paperback book: R$60
- Disposable Pampers diapers (package of 16): R$22
- Decent bottle of red wine: R$20
- Movie ticket: R$18
- Big Mac, fries, and drink: R$17
- 1 kilo ground beef: R$12
- Dozen eggs: R$4
- Can of Coca-Cola: R$1.70

Brazilian Big Macs are among the world's most expensive.

Banking

CURRENCY

Brazil's currency is the *real* (pronounced "ray-ALL;" the plural, *reais*, is pronounced "ray-EYES"). One *real* (R$1) can be divided into 100 *centavos*. You'll come across bills in denominations of 2, 5, 10, 20, 50, and 100 *reais*. Bills are easy to distinguish because each is a different color. Coins are trickier since some have several versions, but you'll find coins worth 5, 10, 25, and 50 *centavos* as well as R$1. Because they were virtually worthless, there are no longer any one-*centavo* coins. If you're purchasing something, the total will be rounded up or down (e.g., if the total comes to R$4.37, the cashier will expect R$4.35; if it comes to R$1.38, you'll get no change for R$1.40). In January 2013, the exchange rate was R$2.07:US$1.

EXCHANGING MONEY

Unless you're a client of a Brazilian bank with your own account, United States dollars can be exchanged either at a limited number of banks—usually large, centrally located branches or ones situated in airports or tourist areas—or at a *casa de câmbio* (exchange house). In general, rates aren't very advantageous; it's better to make a withdrawal using an ATM card. Regular banking hours are 10am–4pm Monday–Friday. There are very few places where dollars—or U.S. dollar travelers checks—are accepted. Meanwhile,

Change *(troca)* is also known as *moeda*.

as the 2014 World Cup and 2016 Olympics draw near, be on the lookout in areas with high tourist traffic for special ATMs that will allow you to feed the machine foreign bills and receive *reais* in exchange.

ATMS

The best way to deal with money concerns in Brazil is to bring an international Visa or MasterCard (or both to give you more options) and withdraw cash from bank machines. Not only is this the most secure method, but you'll get the best exchange rate (although you will pay a foreign transaction fee). Most major branches of Banco do Brasil and Bradesco have at least one ATM that accepts Visa cards while Bradesco, HSBC, and Citibank accept MasterCard/Cirrus. Meanwhile, red Banco 24 Horas ATMs accept all cards, all of the time. In all cases, you need to have a four-digit PIN number. Many ATMs have an option in English. More and more ATMs in all major and reasonably sized cities accept international cards. If you're going to a small town or somewhere off the beaten track, it's best to stock up on cash beforehand, although credit cards will be accepted by most hotels and larger restaurants.

For city ATMs, your best bets are banks in downtown commercial areas, spots with lots of tourist activity, airports, bus terminals, and shopping centers. For security reasons, bank ATMs are open 6am–10pm daily. Most have a withdrawal limit of R$1,000 (although Bradesco's is R$800). To check out locations online in advance, consult the sites for Visa (www.visa.com) and MasterCard/Cirrus (www.mastercard.com). During big holidays, such as New Year's, Carnaval, and any long weekend, it's wise to stock up on cash in advance because sometimes the machines run dry.

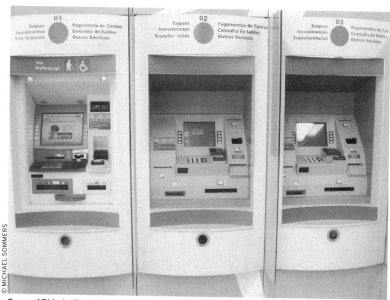

Some ATMs in Brazil feature palm scanners for identification.

CREDIT AND DEBIT CARDS

Most Brazilian hotels, restaurants, and stores accept international credit cards. Using a card not only alleviates carrying around big wads of cash but also offers the most advantageous exchange rate. The only thing it won't get you is the discounts (usually 5–10 percent) that you can ask for (and usually get) if you pay for accommodations or shopping items in cash (*em dinheiro*). Visa and MasterCard are the most widely accepted cards (once again, bring both to increase your payment possibilities), although some places will take American Express and Diners Club. In light of frequent credit card fraud, don't let your card out of your sight.

Increasingly most Brazilians with bank accounts use credit and debit cards instead of cash. Indeed, in recent years the percentage of Brazilians who have obtained credit cards (and maxed them out) has skyrocketed. In 2011 alone, nine million Brazilians got credit cards for the first time and quickly proceeded to go into debt. By mid-2012, almost 50 percent of Brazilians who earned R$4,800 or less per month were spending half of their salaries paying off their credit card debts. Many credit cards allow users to register for programs that earn points toward significant savings on everything from airline tickets to electronics. Just make sure you pay your credit card bills on time because interest charges are frighteningly high. In May 2012, some credit card companies were charging interest rates of 32.9 percent a month—and up to 200 percent a year!

MONEY WIRES

Should you have an emergency and require a money wire but don't have a Brazilian bank account, Banco do Brasil has a partnership with Western Union. A person can send you money from North America via Western Union (www.westernunion.com) to

© MICHAEL SOMMERS

The Caixa is the largest federally owned financial institution in Latin America.

any Banco do Brasil branch. Once you've specified the city you're in, all you need to do (aside from standing in a long line) is show up with your passport and the wire transaction code and get your cash.

If you have a Brazilian bank account, you can have dollars wired directly from a bank in the United States to your Brazilian bank account (you'll need to provide Swift number plus bank branch and account numbers). This is usually fairly quick (several business days) although the sum is limited to R$10,000, from which a small processing fee will be deducted.

OPENING A BANK ACCOUNT

Depending on whom you ask, opening a bank account as a foreigner in Brazil can be either an easy or a complicated experience. Often it varies depending on your status, as well as the bank and branch in question, and whom you have the fortune (or misfortune) to be dealing with on any given day. Of the five biggest Brazilian banks, two are public (Caixa Econômica Federal and Banco do Brasil) and three are private (Bradesco, Banco Santander, and Itaú). In major cities, HSBC and Citibank also have a large presence.

To open an account, you need to be a permanent or temporary resident (i.e., with a work visa valid for over 12 months) and to provide your RNE (or RNE approval form) along with your CPF and proof of address (such as a utility bill in your name). With these documents, you can open a savings account (*conta de poupança*). You'll be given a debit card with which you can withdraw, deposit, transfer funds, pay bills, and make debit purchases.

If you want to open a checking account (*conta corrente*) or a salary payment account (*conta salário*), you'll usually have to provide proof of earnings or income. If you relocate to Brazil for a job, often the company that hired you can help you open these accounts. A *conta corrente* allows you to write checks (almost nonexistent these days) and to apply for a credit card. For certain financial transactions in Brazil, including some investments, you must have a *conta corrente*. In addition to the aforementioned documents, in some cases the bank may ask to verify personal and employer references.

The Brazilian banking system is amazingly efficient as long as you don't actually have to go to the branch to do business, which will inevitably involve waiting in a long line and involve some sort of bureaucracy. All banks have sophisticated automated banking systems. You can easily make transfers and pay all your bills (rent, health insurance, phone, television, electricity, etc.) online, by phone, or by scanning bar codes at the ATM. You can also set it up so that all your bills are deducted via direct deposit.

CHORAR: THE BRAZILIAN ART OF BARGAINING

In Brazil, bargaining is more than just haggling for a good price. It is a lively social ritual, and once you get the hang of it, you will likely enjoy yourself so much that subsequent trips to the impersonal aisles of supermarkets and department stores will seem downright dull. The best way to bargain with someone is to *"chorar"* or *"cry."* This doesn't mean you have to literally burst into tears (although this technique actually works wonders), but you do have to haggle down the cost of an object based on some operatic tale of woe that will convince the seller that you have suffered immensely and are thus deserving of a discount. For instance, when you arrive at an airport and are confronted with inflated prices a cab driver is charging for a ride into town, you do the following: complain about how many delays you faced, lament that your luggage was lost, curse the fact that security tore through your bags, etc. Based on your acting chops, you'll be able to knock 5 to 10 percent off the fare. While a greater command of Portuguese makes for highly effective *"chorando,"* exaggerated facial gestures, hand-wringing, and sign language can do wonders. Although the person you're bargaining with will do his or her share of "crying" too, once you get your discount, you'll find that you're actually both satisfied—due to the sheer satisfaction of having had a good "cry."

Unsurprisingly, all this convenience comes with a price. Most banks charge a monthly fee for basic services although depending on the package of services you choose and your minimum account balance, you can often get some of these waived.

Taxes

All foreign residents in Brazil are subject to personal income tax known as *imposto de renda das pessoas físicas* (IRPF). This income tax is collected by the federal government's Receita Federal do Brazil, the Brazilian equivalent of the IRS. For tax purposes, you're considered a resident if you hold a permanent visa or a temporary work visa, or if you spent more than 183 days in the country within a 12-month period. In principle, all income you earn in Brazil is subject to taxation and every April you'll have to file taxes with the Receita Federal using your CPF. This is fairly easy to do online (easier than filing taxes in the United States) by accessing the Receita Federal's website (www.receita.fazenda.gov.br). However, as an expat, things will probably be more complicated, and it's recommended you use an accountant.

BRAZILIAN INCOME TAX

Brazilian income tax is calculated according to a progressive scale based on how much you earn in a given year. In 2011, Brazilians who earned less than R$18,000 (roughly US$9,000)—the lowest tax bracket—were exempt from paying taxes. Those who made R$45,000 (roughly US$22,500) or more—the highest tax bracket—had to pay 27.5 percent of their income to the Receita Federal.

Aside from income earned from salaried and nonsalaried jobs, pensions, rental and rural activities, and wages, other forms of paid remuneration including bonds, commissions, and prizes are also subjected to income tax. If you work for a Brazilian company, taxes are usually deducted directly from your salary every month by your employer. However, tax payments on other income (excluding investments) must be made monthly at a commercial bank.

Capital gains are usually subjected to tax at a rate of 15 percent while gains from the sale of securities on a public stock exchange are taxed at 20 percent. Nonresidents have to pay 15 percent on capital gains relating to property in Brazil. There are no inheritance or wealth taxes in Brazil, nor are there any regional or state income taxes.

Keep in mind that in Brazil residents are required to pay tax on their worldwide income. Although Brazil has signed agreements with some countries to avoid double taxation (which means that taxes paid in one country can be offset by those paid in another), it currently has no agreement in place with the United States.

U.S. INCOME TAX

If you live in Brazil, but you are a citizen or permanent resident of the United States, you're obligated to file taxes with the IRS every year. Aside from the regular income tax return, you may also have to file a return based on your foreign bank assets (Form TD F 90.22.1 [Report of Foreign Bank and Financial Accounts]). To avoid double taxation, you can take advantage of the foreign earned income exclusion, which allows you to exclude up to US$93,000 of foreign earned income from your U.S. taxes. There is also the foreign tax credit, which allows you to offset taxes paid in Brazil with your U.S. taxes, and the foreign housing exclusion, which you can use to deduct certain household expenses. It's a good idea to find a qualified accountant who is familiar with these and other strategies and can help to reduce or even eliminate your U.S. tax payments. Remember that even if you don't think you owe any U.S. income taxes, you'll probably still have to file a return.

Investing

In recent years, foreign investors have been flocking to Brazil, lured by the combination of a booming economy, stable financial market, liberal investment climate, and multiple growth opportunities, not to mention the strong *real* and some of the highest interest rates on the planet. Unlike the majority of other Western nations, the global economic crisis of 2008 hardly made a dent in the economy. In fact, in 2010 GDP grew by 7.5 percent, the highest rate in 25 years.

Recently, however, things have begun to slow down. In 2011 Brazil's GDP grew by only 3 percent; the second-worst performance since 2004 and the worst in Latin America. The *real* has weakened—between the beginning of 2011 and August 2012, it has lost 20 percent of its value against the U.S. dollar. Steadily diminishing interest rates and tighter financial conditions have accompanied a fall in commodities and a housing bubble that many experts feel is bound to burst sooner or later. As a result, the potential for asset appreciation is considerably lower than it used to be. The upshot is that, increasingly, you must be very selective when it comes to making good investments in Brazil.

THE STOCK MARKET

Brazil possesses one of the most world's most sophisticated stock exchanges called BM&F Bovespa. It was created in 2008 from the merger of the Brazilian Mercantile & Futures Exchange (BM&F) and the São Paulo Stock Exchange (Bovespa), which has been around since 1890. The newly integrated BM&F Bovespa offers all sort of trading options including stocks, futures, commodities, ETFs, options, forwards, and corporate and government bonds. Some 450 companies are listed on Bovespa. All trading in equity and equity derivatives take place on an order-driven electronic trading platform known as the Megabolsa. The country's second-largest stock exchange, the Rio de Janeiro Stock Exchange (BVRJ), trades in government bonds and currencies. In terms of the most consistently important investment sectors in Brazil, the strongest have always been—and continue to be—oil, gas, minerals, and alternative energy.

HOW TO INVEST

Resident and nonresident foreigners can invest in most of the same financial and capital market instruments as Brazilians without any restrictions. However, nonresidents will need to hire a local representative to deal with regulatory and tax related issues. All investors need to register with the Brazilian Central Bank (all funds coming in and out of Brazil go through the Central Bank), the stock market regulator, CVM, and the Receita Federal. To place orders on the stock exchange, you'll need to choose a brokerage firm that is a member of BM&F Bovespa. Most Brazilian financial institutions provide many umbrella services through which you can register and invest.

Brazil's banking system includes both commercial and investment banks as well as some that provide both commercial and investment services, including consumer financing and fund management. Although Brazil's interest rates are steadily decreasing—from a record high of 23 percent in 2003 to a record low of 8.5 percent in May 2012—they are still considerably higher than those in North America. Even after factoring in income tax deductions, funds and other similar investment products still constitute a safe way to earn interest on any savings you might have. In mid-2012, most financial experts were advising investors to keep their money in funds and steer clear from investing in overly expensive real estate, for example.

DAILY LIFE

COMMUNICATIONS

In recent years, the Brazilian telecommunications sector has undergone a small revolution as it transitions from one of inefficient, expensive, publicly owned monopolies to a burgeoning, increasingly competitive private industry that's growing in leaps and bounds in order to keep up with soaring demand for services. While Brazilian telecommunications technology is very sophisticated, lagging investment in infrastructure means that coverage, speed, and service are vastly different in the South and Southeast vs. the Northeast and North as well as wealthy vs. poor neighborhoods and urban vs. rural areas. Another problem is that operators and providers are not always very efficient when it comes to consumer service.

In general, obtaining a phone line, cable TV, or Internet access is a smooth and easy process. However, when problems crop up, fixing them can be a major headache that involves multiple protocol numbers, hours of being placed on hold while being transferred from one robotic assistant to another (when you're not completely cut off) and days waiting for a technician to fix the actual problem. Before choosing an Internet or phone plan (with the possibility of cable TV), ask around to see what coverage and service are like in your particular city or even neighborhood and to get a sense of other people's experiences with various operators and providers.

Telephone Service

Brazilian phone service is quite efficient, if not exactly cheap. Local calls from both fixed and mobile phones are charged by the minute. Calls within Brazil have become less expensive in recent years with the privatization of the phone industry. However, international calls are pretty astronomical. Unless it's essential, you're better off emailing or using Skype with loved ones at home. If you make an international call from a hotel, it will be even more exorbitant (it will be much cheaper if you ask people back home to call you).

Brazil has several telephone companies, or *operadoras,* and whenever you make a long-distance call outside of your area code (known as a DDD), you'll have to precede the phone number with a two-digit number belonging to one of the *operadoras.* Embratur (21) is the biggest one, with national and international coverage. Other *operadoras* are Intelig (23) and Oi (31). When calling a number in Brazil, dial 0, followed by the *operadora* code, then the DDD, and the number. An example of a call to Rio (whose area code is 21) would be 0/21-21-3333-3333. An example of an international call to Canada or the United States (whose country code is 1) would be 00/21-1-416-921-7777). It is also possible to make a collect call (*uma chamada a cobrar*) from Brazil via the Embratel operator. To do so, call 0800/703-2111.

Cell phones are immensely popular throughout Brazil and their use has far surpassed more expensive fixed lines. Calling to or from a cell phone, however, is more expensive than calling from a fixed phone. If you're calling long distance, charges are steep.

You'll find cell phone coverage in most places throughout Brazil. Your own cell phone should work in Brazil *if* it is compatible with international triband GSM standards and is *unlocked* (meaning you can remove and insert local SIM cards). Although smartphones and iPhones are all the rage and highly coveted (by consumers and thieves) in Brazil, they are much cheaper in North America than in Brazil. (When the iPhone 4S went on sale in December 2011 at the price of R$2,000, it was the most expensively priced phone of its kind on the planet; 60 percent more expensive than in the United States.)

CELL PHONES

At the beginning of 2012, over 236 million cell phones were in operation in Brazil—that translates into more than one phone for every man, woman, and child in the country. In 2011 alone, the number of cell phones in use increased

© MICHAEL SOMMERS

Phone booths *(orelhãos)* are scattered throughout Brazilian streets.

ORELHÕES

Throughout Brazil, you will see dome-shaped phone booths known as *orelhões* (big ears). With the popularity of cell phones, you'll now find them abandoned (and often not working). To use an *orelhão*, you'll need to purchase a phone card, *cartão telefônica*, sold at most news kiosks. They usually come in 40 and 60 units (*unidades*). A quick local call will use up one or two units. A short long-distance call will quickly use up an entire card.

© MICHAEL SOMMERS

An *orelhão* in Maceió, Alagoas, is shaped like a *pinha* fruit.

by 19.5 percent. The vast majority (81 percent) of these are prepaid *pré-pago* phones. Users purchase credits with a specific operator when they charge their SIM card or *chip* (pronounced cheepee). A SIM card can be charged basically everywhere, including supermarkets, shopping centers, and even some newspaper kiosks. Depending on the operator, you can add R$1 to R$100 in terms of credit. Getting a *pré-pago* phone line and number is fairly easy, usually requiring no more than a CPF, RNE, and proof of residence (although often a CPF is sufficient).

Brazil currently has four major service providers: Vivo, with 30 percent of the market, TIM with 26 percent, Claro with 25 percent, and Oi with 19 percent. Competition among the four is fierce, which is great for consumers since promotions abound. In general, it's much cheaper—and sometimes even free—to call other cell phones that use the same provider. For this reason, Brazilians often invest in SIM cards for all four companies, which they rotate depending upon whom they might be calling (some phones possess slots for two or even four SIM cards, which allow users alternate providers using the same device). Some people even invest in multiple phones, each one with a different provider or calling plan.

If you use your phone a lot, for fast Internet and texting as well as for calls, it's advantageous to get a monthly *pós-pago* phone plan with one of the providers. Various rates are available depending on your phone use, i.e., the amount of time you talk, the number of texts you send, the Internet capacity you need. It pays to comparison shop between the four operators to see which plan—or promotion—best addresses your personal needs. A typical iPhone or smartphone monthly plan that includes

100 minutes of phone time, 50 text messages, and 2 MB of data transfer will cost in the vicinity of R$150–200 a month depending on the operator and the promotions available.

Regardless of which plan and provider you choose, in order to get your own mobile phone line, aside from your RNE and CPF, you'll also need to provide copies of your rental lease or property contract, proof of payment of monthly property taxes known as IPTU, and a recent income or pension statement. All four operators have stores in major cities (addresses, along with information about plans and promotions, are available on their websites), often on large commercial streets and in shopping centers. After doing your online homework, visit the store closest to you where you can present your documents and fill out the forms required for you to obtain your mobile phone line. If later, you decide to change operators, you can do so without changing your phone number.

LANDLINES

It wasn't so long ago in Brazil that landlines were reserved for the moneyed while the masses lined up at pay phones. This is because originally when you requested to have a phone line installed in Brazil, you then owned it for life (unless you sold it privately, often at a heavy profit due to the high demand). Later, as private operators multiplied and prices fell, landlines could be installed for next to nothing (although without the perks of ownership). However, monthly "rental" fees combined with the cost of calls per minute has always made landlines somewhat of an expense. With the popularization of cell phones and smartphones and increasingly cheap mobile plans and promotions—not to mention the widespread use of VoIP solutions such as Skype—many Brazilians are forsaking landlines altogether.

Because of this trend, fixed phone operators are actually lowering prices by offering promotional plans that bundle fixed phone lines and cell phones with broadband or Wi-Fi and cable TV service. Plans vary in price according to the number of free minutes you want per month (fixed calls between landlines are usually free). For example, if you choose a plan with 120 free minutes a month, calls can be divided between your landline and mobile lines and can include long-distance calls throughout Brazil. If you work at home or travel a lot or if you're a couple or a family (with more than one cell phone), these customized plans that bundle many features can be very advantageous in terms of price, not to mention convenience as you receive multiple services from one provider (and only have to pay one bill).

Currently the main phone line providers in Brazil are Oi and Claro, available nationally, and Vivo and CTBC, which are present in many Central-West, South, and Southeast states. However, depending on the state you're in, these providers work with authorized operators (TIM and GVT being two particularly large and popular ones) that also provide their own services and fixed phone, Internet, and cable TV packages while using the telecommunications networks of the main providers.

To get a landline in Brazil is usually quite quick and fairly uncomplicated. After comparison shopping among providers and plans, just call the operator and provide your name and address and CPF. After checking your credit, your line should be set up in a matter of days.

Internet Access

Brazilians are the fifth largest group of Internet users on the planet. Although it took some time to graduate from very slow and sketchy dial-up service to faster and faster broadband and wireless service, the country is quickly attempting to catch up.

The most frequent options for Internet access are via telephone operators who offer dial-up, broadband, and wireless service (including modems and routers). Increasingly, however, mobile phone and cable TV operators are getting in on the act, offering broadband and wireless as part of increasingly affordable bundled packages that include phone and cable TV service. Currently, the largest providers are Vivo, Oi, Net, Claro, and CTBC, which control around 80 percent of the market. However, there are close to 2,000 small-scale broadband service providers throughout the country, most of which offer wireless connections that don't require installed technology.

With the increased popularity of smartphones, Internet access via mobile phones has expanded enormously in large cities and among young Brazilians, especially since the cost (between R$0.30 and R$0.50 a day) is cheaper than paying for a monthly landline plan (starting at R$30). In 2011, 50 percent of Brazilian municipalities were already covered, although access varies widely. The mobile phone company with the broadest coverage by far is Vivo, followed by Claro, TIM, and Oi. Meanwhile, another popular solution consists of portable 3G mini modems, which plug into a laptop or tablet and allow you to access different speeds of Internet connectivity while working or on the go. In 2011, the Brazilian government unleashed a plan to invest R$11.7 billion in communications infrastructure and access. The goal is to have mobile phone

a Wi-Fi modem and program for home installation

BRAZILIANS AND SOCIAL MEDIA

It's hardly surprising that people as famously chatty and social as Brazilians have taken to social media with such enthusiasm. In 2011, the average Brazilian spent 26.7 hours a month online—only cybersurfers in the United States, United Kingdom, South Korea, and France racked up more hours—and 23 percent of this online time was spent on social media sites such as Facebook (today Brazilians—48 million of whom have Facebook accounts— are the second-largest nationality of Facebook users in the world after Americans). While Brazilian Facebook users represent 23 percent of the population as a whole, they represent a whopping 63 percent of all Internet users. Brazilians also have one of the world's highest Twitter participation rates. The fact that 95 percent visit blogs on a monthly basis makes Brazilians one of the world's most avid frequenters of the blogosphere.

coverage across 92 percent of the country and 4G mobile wireless networks in all major cities by 2015.

Outside of home and work areas, you'll find Wi-Fi access in most hotels and *pousadas* (usually for free) and airports (usually not for free). Lots of shopping centers have free Wi-Fi zones as do a growing number of cafés, bars, and bookstores. Such access has cut down significantly on the number of LAN houses (LAN stands for Local Area Network), Internet cafés that as recently as five years ago were mushrooming throughout the country. These days, LAN houses have dwindled and are more likely to be found in poorer neighborhoods and smaller towns where Brazilians have less access to personal computers and smartphones or where telecommunications companies have not felt it was worth their while (i.e., profitable) to invest in high speed fiber optics. Nonetheless, in 2011 close to 30 percent of Brazilians accessed Internet via LAN houses.

Postal Services

It's easy to identify post offices (*correios*) by their bright yellow-and-blue marquees. Every main city has a rather grandiose main Correios building as well as dozens of small post offices. Aside from those found in urban centers, airports and major shopping malls also usually have postal kiosks. With the introduction of the Internet, the once interminable lines are now gone. When sending a letter or parcel, you can send it *simples* (regular mail) or *registrada* (registered).

Sedex is the Correios version of Fedex and is quite efficient, covering both national and international destinations. The Correios sells cardboard boxes of various sizes as well as postcards and aerograms. For envelopes, you'll often have to go to a *papelaria* (stationery store). There are no adhesive envelopes in Brazil, but the Correios will always have a pot of glue and a brush, and you can proceed to make a big mess. Postage within Brazil is very affordable, but sending letters or packages abroad is inevitably expensive, especially once you start packing on the grams. On the bright side, intensely colorful Brazilian postage stamps (*selos*) are quite stunning. For information regarding post office addresses, prices (according to weight and destination), and all products and services offered, check out the very well-organized website: www.correios.com.br.

Media

NEWSPAPERS, MAGAZINES, AND BOOKS

Brazilian media offerings are fairly diverse, especially when one considers the fact that most of the media is controlled by a small handful of powerful, family-owned and -operated corporations with their own agendas. While close to 500 Brazilian newspapers are published daily across the country, the closest thing to a national paper is the São Paulo–based *Folha de São Paulo,* a mildly left-leaning paper popular with liberals and intellectuals. Sort of a Brazilian equivalent to *The New York Times,* it has its devotees as well as its detractors, but it is definitely an important journalistic reference. It is also a good source of arts and culture listings for São Paulo. The online version publishes an international edition in English along with blogs by foreign reporters based in São Paulo.

Also providing good coverage are the slightly more conservative, São Paulo–based *O Estado de São Paulo* and Rio-based *Jornal do Brasil.* You'll find both papers sold throughout the country. In Rio, *O Globo*—owned by the Globo media giant that also owns radio stations, a record company, and the famous Globo television network (the third-largest media conglomerate on the planet)—also puts out a popular daily paper that has good arts listings for the city of Rio. Otherwise, major cities throughout the country publish their own newspapers, although they are more provincial in character.

Brazil has magazines galore. The three weekly news magazines along the lines of *Time* and *Newsweek* are *Istoé, Época* (owned by Globo), and *Veja.* None of them are quite as hard-hitting and high-quality as they used to be in the pre-Internet age.

© MICHAEL SOMMERS

a post office *(correios)*

A newer alternative is the left-leaning weekly *CartaCapital,* which offers serious news analysis written by a small group of savvy journalists, intellectuals, and experts from diverse spheres. If you buy *Veja* in Rio or São Paulo, you'll receive a free *Time Out*–style city guide with the upcoming week's cultural and arts listings and events along with shopping news and restaurant reviews. *Veja Rio* (www.vejario.abril.com.br) and *Veja São Paulo* (www.vejasaopaulo.abril.com.br) can be found online, as can *Veja* guides to other cities, such as Brasília, Salvador, and Recife, all with reviews and listings (in Portuguese). There are also online versions of Time Out to both Rio (www.timeoutrio.com.br/rio de janeiro/en) and São Paulo (www.timeoutrio.com.br/sao-paulo/en) in both English and Portuguese.

If you're interested in Brazilian food

© MICHAEL SOMMERS

magazines for sale at a *banca de revista*

and restaurants, *Gula* is a great magazine. *Bravo* is an intelligent and attractive magazine devoted to the Brazilian and international art world while *Piauí*, specializing in literary journalism, was founded by documentary maker João Moreira Salles. *Trip* and *TPM* are two funky magazines aimed at hipster twenty-something females. Brazilian *Vogue* is fun for fashionistas. Meanwhile, those curious about travel might want to check out *Viagem e Turismo*, a gorgeously photographed monthly travel mag that always puts out interesting special editions on different Brazilian regions (it is published by Abril, which also publishes the *Quatro Rodas* maps and guides).

You can get your hands on major English-language papers, particularly *The International Herald Tribune*, and all sorts of international magazines (sometimes they are a month or two old) at airport bookstores and major *bancas de revistas* (newsstands) in Rio and São Paulo. Many bookstores in major cities also carry a wide selection of English-language press and books. These are harder to find in other cities, but the spread of mega bookstores such as Cultura, Siciliano, and Saraíva (all of which have online stores that ship throughout the country) means you can usually find English-language magazines and books in these *livrarias,* most of which are located in glitzier shopping malls. Because these items are imported, they will cost a lot more than you would pay for them back home.

TELEVISION AND RADIO

Wherever you wander in Brazil, even in the most modest and isolated outpost in the middle of nowhere, there will inevitably be a shack with a lit-up TV and someone watching it. Brazilian TV is a great unifier, and no matter how much the landscape, temperature, or accent changes, you'll see people watching the same soccer games, *novelas,* newscasts, reality shows, and live audience shows. For the most part, Brazilian TV is also pretty terrible.

The major networks beamed across the nation are SBT, Record, Bandeirantes, MTV (a Brazilian version of the American music network), Globo, and TV Educadora, a state-owned educational network that has a mix of high-brow round tables, films, and very good cultural programming (including great live music performances).

The all-powerful Globo is the leading network. Its nightly *novelas* (which air at 7pm, 8pm, and 9pm Mon.–Sat.) are the most watched of all nightly programs. These soap operas go all out in terms of sets, costumes, lighting, and production, and they star a roster of gorgeous (and usually pretty talented) actors, actresses, and models, all of whom are part of a permanent stable of stars, known as Globais, that hearkens

NOVELAS

Brazilian *novelas* are much more than soap operas. They comprise one of the country's biggest forms of popular entertainment and a major cultural touchstone. No matter where you are in Brazil–a simple adobe home in the northeastern Sertão or a luxury condo in Leblon or Jardins–between 6pm and 10 pm, you can rest assured than tens of millions of Brazilians are tuned in to the same sagas night after night. And even if they aren't within range of a TV, it's a given that, sooner or later, the topic of who slapped whom or slept with whom will come up in conversation. However, *novelas* aren't just about over-the-top melodrama. In recent years, they've been responsible for tackling major social issues ranging from AIDS, racism, and homosexuality to depression, Alzheimer's, domestic violence, and even cyber-porn addiction. Such topical storylines have been a catalyst for interesting discussions in the media and society at large–and have even had concrete repercussions in the real world.

back to the Hollywood studio system. When these Globais aren't participating in a *novela*, miniseries, or other Globo production, they make commercials and give the paparazzi and gossip columnists endless fodder. If you don't speak Portuguese, you will find *novelas* cheesy and melodramatic. If you do understand the language, you will still find them cheesy and melodramatic, but you'll easily get drawn into them and, perhaps, become addicted.

You don't need to understand much Portuguese to watch the broadcast of a live *jogo de futebol* (soccer game). The machine-gun fire of words rattled off by Brazilian sports commentators with jacked-up fervor and excitement will have you alternately biting your nails and cheering for joy, even if you've never been much of a soccer fan.

Cable TV has been around since the late '90s, but due to high rates, Brazil remains a country in which a very small proportion of the population has access to cable (roughly 20 percent of the population; 70 percent of whom are wealthy Brazilians). Currently, the two major cable companies are NET and SKY, whose basic monthly rates start at around R$40 and go upward from there. However, increasingly, telecommunications companies (namely Embratel, Telefônica, and Oi) are entering the scenes and offering packages that include cable TV along with phone and Internet services. Since 2007, Brazil has been transitioning from analog to HDTV (digital) TV; Brazilian TV is expected to have completely digital coverage by 2016.

With the spread of television and Internet, radio, once a dominant vehicle of information and entertainment, has waned in terms of importance and presence. However, Brazil being the musical powerhouse that it is, one need only turn on the radio to be treated to a mixture of golden oldies and latest hits sprinkled with imported global pop ditties. If you want to be exposed to Brazilian music in all its historic and regional richness, tune in to Radio Cultura, a national public radio station, based in São Paulo, that pays homage to Brazil's musical past and present with a variety of high-quality programs (available online and as podcasts as well).

TRAVEL AND TRANSPORTATION

In a country the size of Brazil, transportation is a big issue. In the more compact South and Southeast, distances are more manageable, infrastructure is generally better, and transportation options are more varied and frequent (although traffic—whether by car, bus, or plane—is usually denser). Once you get into the Central-West and Northeast, the crowds thin out somewhat, but distances swell and roads and highways (particularly in rural regions) can be in poor shape. As for the North, you're lucky if you can find roads amidst all the rivers, rainforest, and rain. To wit, most transportation between far-flung cities and towns of the Amazon is carried out by boat or by plane.

The economic boom of the 2000s has placed enormous strain on Brazil's transportation infrastructure. With more *reais* in their pockets and greater access to credit, the number of Brazilians hopping airplanes and buses and taking to roads and highways in brand new (financed) cars has exploded exponentially. Unfortunately, spending on infrastructure—most of which falls to inefficient, and often corrupt, state and municipal governments—has been woefully inadequate in terms of meeting demand. As a result, airports throughout the country are without the capacity for the growing number of flights and passengers, highways are clogged up with cars and trucks, and

TRANSPORTATION

residents of Brazilian cities spend hours every day stuck in traffic. The upshot is that you'll always want to carefully consider *when* you travel (i.e., never leave town on a Friday afternoon or return on a Sunday afternoon), *how* you travel (depending on the time of day, the Metró in Rio and São Paulo can be much speedier than travel above ground), and sometimes even whether it's worth traveling at all.

By Air

Because of Brazil's vast distances, flying is an ideal way to get from one region to another in record time. Brazil's airports are modern and well appointed with cafés, restaurants, bookstores, boutiques, banks, and Wi-Fi access (usually not free). So should your flight be delayed, you will not suffer by having to wait around for a couple of hours. The good news is that, in recent years, both routes (international and domestic) and airlines have increased while prices have generally fallen (until a few years ago, flying was considered an elite form of transportation). The bad news is that airports and airlines have been unable to keep pace with soaring demand. As a result, expect delays and even cancellations if flying during major holidays or peak hours.

The vast majority of international flights fly into São Paulo's Guarulhos or Rio's Tom Jobim international airports. From these two hubs there are numerous daily flights available to all the state capitals. Fares between destinations in the Southeast, South, Brasília, and the Northeast are quite reasonable, especially if booked in advance. Flights to cities in the Amazon, such as Manaus and Belém, can cost quite a bit more. With a lack of passable roads, the Amazon is a region where flying is a must (unless you want to spend days on a boat). Although there are many regional *aerotaxis*, it's safest to stick to the main domestic operators.

In recent years, numerous domestic airlines have started up. Currently, the major players are **TAM** (a member of the Star Alliance) and **GOL,** both of which also operate international flights. More recent upstarts giving both a run for their money include **Azul** and **Trip** (which merged together in late 2012) and **Avianca.**

The airlines offer various fares depending on when you fly and how far in advance you book. Great promotions (such as paying full fare one-way and receiving your return ticket for R$1 for certain routes) are often advertised online during off-season. Even if you don't purchase online (often the cheapest and easiest way), you can comparison shop and then take your findings to any local travel agent, who can then purchase the ticket for you (for a small service fee). For the best fares, it's worthwhile booking as far in advance as possible. Budget airlines pop up from time to time, so it's worth checking with travel agents for alternatives. Depending on the conditions of your ticket, you can usually change your flight or get a refund (within 24 hours), although you might need to pay a fee. Confirm with the airline or travel agency beforehand.

Barring delays during high traffic times, flying within Brazil is usually a less stressful experience than flying in Europe or North America. You can check in an hour before the flight's departure (although make sure you factor in traffic), and security checks are refreshingly hassle-free and not humiliating. The carriers themselves are top of the line: clean, comfortable, with gracious cabin staff, and in most cases (miracle of miracles!), free food and drink.

By Bus

LONG DISTANCE BUSES

With the exception of the Amazon, you can get absolutely anywhere you want to go by bus. Service between capitals and major cities within the states and along the coasts is usually very efficient and fairly inexpensive. Long-distance buses leave punctually (don't be late), and the comfortable vehicles themselves (often Mercedes-Benzes) are equipped with plush, fold-back seats, air conditioning, bathrooms, TVs, and coolers with free mineral water. Although bathrooms start out clean, by the end of the trip they are usually less so. When you buy your ticket, you can reserve your seat—choose one at the front or the middle of the bus (the bathroom is at the back). Air-conditioning can be extreme; make sure you have a sweater and long pants (or a towel or light blanket) or you'll freeze to death in the tropics.

On overnight journeys between major cities, you can opt for deluxe *leito* buses whose large, reclining seats will lull you to sleep. *Leitos* usually cost twice as much as a regular bus. Also more expensive are *executivo* buses, which usually make express stops as opposed to cheaper, locally or regionally operated *convencional* buses. Because they drop off and pick up passengers at any spot along the route (including in the middle of nowhere), they can take a long time to reach their final destination.

Buses are operated by hundreds of private companies (national, regional, and local), but prices are compatible between rivals. More and more companies have websites where you can check schedules and prices and even purchase tickets in advance. For interstate travel, especially during high-season or holiday periods, it's recommended you purchase your ticket in advance. Although major companies sell tickets through travel agents, often your best (and only) option is to purchase them at the *rodoviária* (bus terminal), where all companies have kiosks with schedules. When purchasing a ticket, specify that you want it *sem seguro* (without insurance), an added fee that bequeaths a small sum of money to your loved ones should you be involved in a fatal bus crash (not likely).

Traveling by bus in Brazil is safe, but do keep an eye on your belongings at all times. Luggage stowed beneath the bus is quite secure (it can only be retrieved with a baggage claim). Otherwise, keep valuables close by, particularly at night, and take them with you at rest stops. Except for *leitos,* most long-distance buses make stops every 2–3 hours. This gives you a chance to stretch your legs,

© MICHAEL SOMMERS

municipal bus in Salvador

grab some food or a drink, and use a clean bathroom. It's nonetheless advisable to bring some mineral water and a snack, such as biscuits (cookies), fruit, or nuts.

CITY BUSES

In Brazilian cities and towns, buses are the most popular and extensive form of public transportation. In major cities, you can count on them going everywhere, at least until around midnight (despite Rio and São Paulo bus service on main arteries continuing throughout the night, riding late at night is a calculated risk). By day, the biggest problems with buses are that they can get really packed, and (like cars) they get mired in rush-hour traffic (the worst of which is from 7am-9am and 5pm-7pm), although some cities have created bus-only lanes to ease the flow. Safety precautions are an issue because of pickpockets and occasional armed holdups. For this reason, try to limit your valuables (it's not a great idea to carry a laptop or big wads of cash) and always keep bags or other belongings closed and close to your chest, especially when it's crowded.

Final destinations are written on the front of the bus, and along the side are the main stops and the routes. Make sure you check this out since sometimes the *ida* (the way there) is not the same as the *volta* (the way back). If in doubt, ask other passengers or the *cobrador* (collector), who sits at the turnstiles (usually located at the back or middle of the bus) and collects the fare. Bus fares range from around R$2.50–3, although executive buses (usually smaller buses with air conditioning and plusher seats) cost a bit more. Make sure you have small bills (nothing more than R$10) or change; it's a good idea to separate your fare in advance.

Metrôs and Trains

A handful of Brazilian capitals—Rio, São Paulo, Brasília, Belo Horizonte, Recife, Porto Alegre—have Metrô (subway) systems (Fortaleza and Salvador keep promising to inaugurate theirs as well). Brazilian Metrôs are fast, clean, quite safe, and often (in theory) air-conditioned. The only problem is their size. Although São Paulo's and especially Rio's Metrô systems have been undergoing desperately needed expansions, to date they can only be counted on to get to points downtown and other key destinations. The other cities' Metrô systems are more suburban than urban and often replace, or link up with, suburban trains used to transport workers from the poorer suburbs and *periferias* into the city center (Rio, São Paulo, and many other capitals also have extensive suburban train networks). A big bonus to taking Metrôs and trains is bypassing surface traffic and gridlock. However, keep in mind that during rush hour, the crush of passengers can be downright alarming.

DAILY LIFE

Taxis

Taxis are an efficient way of getting around cities—or even to close-by, yet out-of-the-way beaches—and are cheaper than in North America or Europe. You can flag one down anywhere. City cabs are metered and have two rates, or *bandeiras*. Bandeira 2, which is more expensive than Bandeira 1, is in effect after 8pm and on Sundays and holidays, and sometimes during the "holiday" month of December. Sometimes, cab drivers will refer to a rate sheet: This happens when fares are raised but haven't yet been factored in to the meter. If you hit it off with a cab driver, ask for his or her card. Often a driver will give you special rates for trips to airports or other long journeys. In small towns and for longer trips in cities, you can often propose a set price instead of paying the metered fare. Many airports have taxi kiosks where you prepay your fare according to distance. Although the fare is more expensive, these cabs are generally more comfortable, and you won't have to worry about getting scammed.

VANS AND *MOTO-TÁXIS*

In rural areas, along beaches, and increasingly in major cities, vans—also known as *kombis* or *lotações,*—are an alternate and unofficial source of public transportation. The term *lotação* is the most apt of all—*lotar* means to fill up, and that's precisely what these vans tend to do, stuffing as many people as possible inside. Although fares are similar to those you'll pay on a bus, vans have the advantage of careening along at high speeds that will get you to your destination more quickly.

© MICHAEL SOMMERS

taxi stand in Rio

© MICHAEL SOMMERS

moto-táxi in Minas Gerais

In beach areas, particularly along the northeastern coasts, vans (also known as *táxis comuns* or just *comuns*) are much more frequent than local bus lines. Even if you don't understand Portuguese, riding in a van can be a fun, if cramped, experience.

In small and medium-sized towns throughout Brazil, you'll find *moto-táxis* to be much more common than vehicle taxis, not to mention considerably less expensive. Many people who don't have cars rely on them, and they're great for short distances, steep hills, and trips along dirt roads to secluded beaches or waterfalls. In large cities, *moto-táxis*—although not regulated—are also becoming popular in suburban areas where taxis are rare and, increasingly, in central neighborhoods where their ability to weave through stalled traffic is a major advantage.

DAILY LIFE

Driving

Driving in Brazil is not for the faint of heart. Brazilians have a love affair with speeding and are hardly sticklers for following the rules of the road. As the economy has improved in recent years, more and more people have purchased cars, which means traffic in major cities is increasingly congested, and not just in Rio and São Paulo, whose traffic jams are nightmarish. In the Northeast and the North in particular, the state of the roads can be dismal once you get out of the major cities, although main coastal highways are kept in good shape. Until recently, drunk driving was a major problem. However, in July 2008, Brazil's lamentable record for having one of the highest vehicle accident death tolls caused the government to enact the law of Zero Tolerance. This has resulted in police-organized blitzes around the country. Drivers are stopped arbitrarily and must take a Breathalyzer test. If even the slightest amount of alcohol is detected, you're looking at a R$955 fine and a suspension from driving for one year. In reality, however, these "blitzes" are only a partial deterrent; it's best to be on your guard when driving back from a long day at the beach (where it's a Brazilian tradition to knock back more than a few).

There are instances when a car is a definite plus in Brazil. If you want to visit natural attractions around big cities, a car gives you much more freedom to hit off-the-beaten-track destinations where buses don't go (if they do, it's likely they'll make 200 local stops or the one daily departure is at 5am). Also, for beach or waterfall hopping, cars can come in very handy since you can hit secluded coves and cascades not accessible by bus. Avoid traveling on big holiday weekends when traffic is guaranteed to

an ingenious tractor-driven "bus" in Bahia

be atrocious. Also avoid driving at night. Outside of major cities, roads are poorly lit and speed bumps and potholes are common. Another problem is the number of cargo trucks on highways, especially unpaved and two-lane routes. It's not uncommon for drivers on long hauls to be sleep deprived or amped up on amphetamines. In more isolated regions, there is also the risk of highway robbery.

If you have kids, a car is close to essential for reasons ranging from comfort and practicality to safety, not to mention the ease with which you can go on family outings and holidays. With or without children, cars also come in handy at night when public transportation options dwindle and security is more of an issue. That said, even night driving in major cities has its risks. It's best to stick to main streets and be careful of veering off into unknown neighborhoods. Also be careful when stopping at traffic lights to keep windows rolled up. Some cities, such as São Paulo, have even passed legislation for drivers to merely slow down at red lights, but they are not obliged to stop—on account of the risk of holdups and carjackings.

Coupled with the challenges of driving are the challenges of parking. Aside from shopping centers and other main commercial and recreational venues, parking lots are rare in Brazilian cities. The upshot is driving around and looking for a spot in the street. Whether or not you need help finding a space (and navigating your car into it), you'll usually have the assistance of an informal parking attendant known as a *flanelinha*. Aside from helping you back in and out, he'll promise to watch over your car as well. Regardless of whether he does or not, it's customary to "tip" him a couple of *reais* (this could be more depending on the city or neighborhood) since he makes his living this way. Many *flanelinhas* aggressively make you feel payment is obligatory and will demand a certain price; if very high or if you're only stopping for a short time,

a rare moment of light traffic in Rio de Janeiro

feel free to point this out. However, know that if you don't give something (upon your return; don't pay up front), you risk finding a scratch, or worse, on your car. Despite the fact that attendants also claim they'll "watch over" your car to prevent theft, never leave any valuables in your vehicle, even in the trunk.

DRIVER'S LICENSES

If you plan to drive in Brazil, it's a good idea to get an International Driving Permit (IDP) before leaving home. An IDP is more widely recognized than a foreign license, but the latter is valid for up to six months and can be used along with a valid photo ID (e.g., a passport). If you're staying in Brazil for a short time, you can use either of these two licenses to rent a car. Major international car rental chains such as Avis, Hertz, and Localiza can be found throughout all major cities and airports, although you might find small local agencies to be less expensive. Rates for unlimited mileage cost R$100–150 a day. Prices don't necessarily include insurance, so check beforehand.

After you've been in Brazil for six months (180 days), you'll have to apply for a Brazilian driver's license at the local Departamento Estadual de Transporte (Transit Department), known as **DETRAN.** To obtain a Brazilian license, or **Carteira Nacional de Habilitação** (CNH), you'll need to pass a medical (physical and psychological) examination at a DETRAN-authorized clinic and supply both original and authenticated copies of your national and/or international driver's license (accompanied by a certified translation), your temporary or permanent RNE and CPF, and proof of a Brazilian residence (e.g., a utility bill in your name or a bank statement). Applicants will have to pay for both medical exams as well as a processing fee (payable at a bank) that you then submit, with your documents, to DETRAN's section for foreign applicants. If

DAMN THAT TRAFFIC JAM

One of the biggest and most ubiquitous headaches of 21st-century urban Brazilian life is the *engarrafamento*, or traffic jam. Given the fact that an estimated 12,000 new cars hit Brazil's roads every day, it's not surprising that people are spending more and more of their daily lives stuck in *trânsito*. Although all major cities are bad, Brazil's traffic hell on earth is São Paulo, where an estimated 1,000 new cars are launched upon the roadways daily. The kilometric jams that clog the highways when weekends roll around are legendary and make for prime time television viewing. Less spectacular is the daily congestion that accounts for the fact that, in 2010 the average Paulistano spent 2 hours and 42 minutes stuck in traffic *every day*. Indeed, it's not uncommon to glimpse car captives shaving, applying makeup, watching DVDs, creating PowerPoint presentations, or eating and drinking the many offerings hawked by savvy *ambulantes* (street vendors) who have mined the city's gridlock into a business opportunity.

all is in order, you'll receive a receipt that will allow you to pick up your license, usually around a week later.

PURCHASING A CAR

As discussed above, there are many advantages to owning a car in Brazil. However, there are also some downsides to keep in mind.

Depending on where you live, your lifestyle, and your income, owning a car might not always make sense in terms of the cost benefit once you factor in maintenance, insurance, IPVA taxes (a yearly tax calculated upon the value of your vehicle—usually around 5 percent, but it varies from state to state), gas, and parking, not to mention depreciation on cars that cost between 30 and 50 percent more than they do in North America due to extraordinarily high taxes and import tariffs. There is also a certain stress factor that comes from dealing with insane urban traffic and dangerous and drunk drivers. Statistically speaking, the number of fatal automobile accidents in Brazil is triple that of Canada, Japan, and Sweden and the third highest in the world. In 2008, 22 percent of all deaths in Brazil were due to car accidents (mostly the result of drunken drivers and the rise of motorcycles on the roads).

To buy a car in Brazil is easy; usually all you need is a CPF. However, to register it with DETRAN, you'll also need your driver's license, temporary or permanent RNE, and proof of residence. The car's previous owner or dealer is required to provide you with a bill of sale as well as the title, which is then signed over to you. Both of these documents need to be authenticated at a *cartório*. It's a good idea to take a Brazilian friend or colleague with you to inspect the car—especially in the case of a private sale.

NEW VS. USED

In Brazil, there used to be a big difference, in terms of quality, between new cars and used cars (which were *extremely* used), but those days are gone. The truth is that purchasing a car has become the Great Brazilian Dream. As the economy has boomed, auto production has soared. Prices have fallen, purchasing power has risen, and credit options and payment plans have proliferated. Because of this—and the fact that a car is

FLEXIBILITY RULES

Shockingly for a country that is self-sufficient in terms of oil production, gas prices in Brazil are about 80 percent higher than those in the United States. Much of this huge discrepancy is due to government taxes. In Brazil, the total sum of government taxes and charges placed on fuel comprise 55 percent of the price of gas compared to 13 percent in the United States. As a result, when the global price of oil goes up, Brazilians see not only a rise in the price of fuel itself, but an increase in the taxes as well.

Of course, when the price of gas gets too high, Brazilians have an ace up their sleeves: ethanol. Since the 1973 oil crisis, in an inspired attempt to wean itself off fossil fuels, the Brazilian government has invested heavily in the use of alcohol from sugarcane as fuel for automobiles. Today the country is the world's largest producer of sugarcane ethanol, which is far less polluting and less costly than the ethanol derived from corn that is used in the United States. Moreover, Brazilians possess the largest fleet of flex-fuel vehicles—which run on both pure ethanol and any combination of ethanol and gas—on the planet.

Aside from being more sustainable and offering lower mileage than cars that run on pure gasoline, the advantage of flex-fuel cars are that consumers can choose the ratio of fuels based on fluctuating market prices. To date, more than 45 percent of Brazilian light vehicles are flex fuel as are over 93 percent of new cars that are purchased.

a status symbol, which until recently was mostly accessible only to members of Brazil's upper and middle classes—everyone and their mother now wants one, not just to get around, but as proof that they've made it. The more money they have, the more they're likely to spend—and to upgrade.

As a consequence, today there is a vast market of *semi-novos* (used cars), some of which are traded in after only one or two years of ownership. Buying a *semi-novo* is considerably cheaper than buying a new car, although the advantage of the latter is a manufacturer's guarantee. If you do opt for a *semi-novo,* it's recommended you go through a dealer. Not only will you receive a limited warranty, but you'll also be ensured of the vehicle's origin.

The problem with buying a used car privately is that, unless you know the seller well, you could end up getting (figuratively) taken for a ride. As such, before finalizing the purchase, ask the owner for the car's license plate number and registration number, and then go online to DETRAN's website and verify that the vehicle has no outstanding fines and that all IPVA taxes have been paid. If not, you'll have to pay them yourself before DETRAN will register the car. However, keep in mind that DETRAN won't know if the car was recently stolen or the owner recently committed an infraction; either scenario could be the source of a major headache.

CARROS POPULARES

Roughly half the cars sold in Brazil today are vehicles known as *carros populares* or economy cars. *Carros populares* emerged in the early 1990s during a period of considerable economic instability in Brazil. Compact and inexpensive, these cars made it possible for many middle- and lower-income Brazilians to invest in wheels of their own, while also providing a needed boost to Brazil's auto industry. *Carros populares* usually feature 1000cc engines and lack accessories such as airbags and ABS safety brakes.

BIKE IT OR NOT

Although in recent years, both Rio de Janeiro and São Paulo have made much to do about their new municipal *cyclovias*, in both cases these bike paths cater largely to recreational and weekend cyclists. Indeed, as a transportation option, you'll be hard-pressed to find bikes in general use in Brazil. The exceptions are small towns, as well as rural and coastal areas, particularly in the poor and flat regions of the North and Northeast. While you'd think bikes would be an ideal solution for circumnavigating urban gridlock, the state of most roads, coupled with the recklessness of most drivers, makes biking in cities downright dangerous. Since Brazil has no bike culture to speak of, neither drivers nor pedestrians possess a minimum of bike consciousness. Proof is in the number of serious accidents that cause bikers to tragically end up as roadkill.

Because they are less powerful and sturdy (not to mention less comfortable) than conventional cars—which in Brazil are considered *carros de luxo* (luxury cars)—you'll have to think about how you'll be using your car (i.e., some models won't withstand lots of long-distance driving and tough road conditions). In terms of price, new *carros populares* usually hover between R$20,000 and R$30,000 while so-called *carros de luxo* start at around R$60,000 and are depressingly more expensive than their North American and European counterparts.

Once you've purchased and registered your car, you'll also need insurance. Insurance is calculated on the car's market value so that the more expensive your car, the more expensive your monthly insurance payments. It's worth doing some online comparison shopping to see how much individual insurance companies charge for different brands and models. Rates can oscillate considerably because some models and makes are much more popular with auto thiefs (i.e., they're easier to resell), which jacks up the rates considerably. Also make sure what your insurance will cover. For instance, every summer the city of São Paulo experiences torrential rains that often flood streets and neighborhoods; most insurance companies won't cover any flood damage (you'll need to take out a separate policy).

PRIME LIVING LOCATIONS

OVERVIEW

Deciding where to live in Brazil is as complex as deciding whether you want to move to Brazil in the first place. Of course, if you're moving because you've already landed a job, enrolled in a specific study program, or fallen in love with a Brazilian, the decision of where to live will already have been made for you. However, in many other cases—if you're looking to start a business, immerse yourself in a particular culture, lead a certain type of lifestyle—you'll have the freedom of choosing which city or region of this vast country offers the most opportunities and best corresponds to your needs and desires.

Geographically, the four *Prime Living Locations* chapters cover four out of five of Brazil's territorial regions. The South, Southeast, Central-West, and Northeast are all explored to various degrees, but the largely remote, undeveloped, and scantily

© MICHAEL SOMMERS

populated North (much of which is embraced by the vast Amazonian rainforest) has been excluded.

The Southeast contains Brazil's three wealthiest and most populous states: Rio de Janeiro, São Paulo, and Minas Gerais, as well as its respective capitals of Rio, São Paulo, and Belo Horizonte. All of these cosmopolitan cities boast sizzling economies and cultural scenes, not to mention lots of opportunities for expats. Rio and São Paulo are so big and booming that each megacity easily merits its own chapter. In terms of size, importance, and sheer diversity, they are like city-states unto themselves.

Belo Horizonte and the surrounding state of Minas Gerais have been grouped together in the chapter that also covers the Central-West and South regions, both of which are thriving areas with high standards of living. The rapidly expanding economies of the Central-West state of Goiás and southern state of Paraná are particularly strong magnets for foreigners these days. While attention in passing is given to the regions as a whole, the main focus is upon the efficient, medium-sized cities such as the southern capitals of Curitiba, Florianópolis, and Porto Alegre where opportunities are growing and the living is easy. The Central-West's major city is the nation's capital, Brasília, which because of its importance, always attracts a steady stream of foreign diplomats, journalists, and professionals involved in international businesses, think tanks, and nongovernmental organizations (NGOs).

Traditionally the poorest region in Brazil, today the Northeast possesses the country's fastest growing economy. As the first Brazilian region to be colonized, the Northeast boasts one of the nation's most pungent histories and one of the most compelling and complex ensembles of regional and local cultures. Owing to its economic woes and relative marginalization from Brazil's political and economic centers of power in the Southeast, the Northeast has never drawn expats en masse. However, its climate, culture, and relaxed lifestyle have always succeeded in seducing a small, but significant, share of foreign dreamers and adventurers. This chapter's principal focus is the region's main cities of Salvador, Recife, and Fortaleza, all of which are economic and cultural hubs. However, the Northeast also boasts Brazil's longest and most beautiful coastline, which merits some attention with the possibilities it offers those seeking to start a tourism-related business in paradise—or merely drop out of civilization for a while (or forever).

Rio de Janeiro

A postcard-perfect symbol of Brazil itself, the aptly nicknamed *Cidade Maravilhosa* (Marvelous City) is a living legend and incontestably one of the world's great cities. The omnipresence of lushly carpeted mountains, sugary white sand beaches, and a 500-year mash-up of architectural styles also make it one of the world's most beautiful cities—and the most fun. Rio easily intoxicates foreigners with its beguiling mixture of extravagant nature and exuberant culture, its heady urban frenzy, and its laid-back beachy vibe, not to mention the charm and warmth (some say superficiality) of native Cariocas. Due to the tropical climate, much of life takes place outside, from sipping

Copacabana Beach, Rio

beer on the beach to sambaing the night away in a corner *boteco*. Rio has never gone out of fashion, but like Brazil itself, after being down and out for a couple of decades, it's finally back in business, spurred on by its upcoming hosting duties of the 2014 World Cup and the 2016 Olympics, as well as booming financial, commercial and cultural segments, all of which are driving the real estate market—and cost of living in general—sky high. With a pumped-up economy and beefed-up security, Rio may be safer than ever before, but it's also more expensive, more crowded, and more exhausting as well. Without turning its back on myriad traditions, the city is undergoing vast changes—most of which are for the better. These days, Rio is a city of unbridled optimism and opportunity, which is why more expats are settling here than ever before, lured by jobs (particularly in the offshore petroleum sector), research and study opportunities, and the desire to be in one of the most happening cities on the planet.

São Paulo

South America's largest city, São Paulo is the quintessential concrete jungle with skyscrapers filling in for trees, multilane traffic-clogged avenues substituting rivers, and instead of flying insects, the buzz of the world's largest fleet of helicopters. This isn't to say that São Paulo isn't a fascinating city—it is (although you really have to love big cities). Its population not only embraces migrants from all over Brazil, but the world as well. The resulting mix spills over into the city's rich cultural and culinary scenes, not to mention the dense urban, constantly mutating fabric of the city itself.

Centro, São Paulo

São Paulo is by far Brazil's most international city. It's also where all the money is. For these reasons it attracts so many expats, who are drawn less to the city itself than to the amazing career opportunities it offers in sectors as wide-ranging as financial, telecommunications, and IT to health and science (some of the hemisphere's top universities and hospitals are here). While professional salaries are generally high, you'll need them to afford living in a city that is currently one of the most expensive on the planet. That said, you can generally live quite well. São Paulo concentrates Brazil's largest middle class. Cultural, leisure, and recreational options are limitless as are services and amenities (although it might take you hours of weaving through traffic to take advantage of them; logistics are a nightmare here). Although foreigners rarely fall in love with São Paulo, this is a city of villages and pockets, of vast contrasts and unexpected surprises. Unlike other parts of Brazil, it's not likely to seduce you, but it just may grow on you.

Minas, Central-West, and South

Relatively few foreigners visit, let alone have heard of, Brazil's states of the Central-West and South. Even Minas Gerais, which has a much more prominent history, culture, and economy, isn't on the tip of most North American tongues. And yet, these lesser known regions have much to offer expats—including the fact that the lack of expat communities means less competition for the increasing number of positions available for foreign professionals in the thriving medium-sized cities of Belo

© MICHAEL SOMMERS

Niemeyer's Catedral Metropolitana, Brasília

Horizonte, Curitiba, Porto Alegre, and Goiânia. It also means it's much easier to assimilate and be welcomed into a less harried, more authentic style of regional Brazilian life, without all the crime, socioeconomic extremes, and sky-high prices of Rio de Janeiro and São Paulo. Altogether, Minas, the Central-West, and the South possess Brazil's highest standards of living. Their cities, relatively newer and boasting better urban planning, are smaller and more human in scale, making them more organized, efficient, and agreeable for expats who prize a certain quality of life. Although, with the exception of Florianópolis, none of the region's cities are blessed with beaches, all of them lie within close proximity to magnificent natural attractions that are largely unexplored or undeveloped. In fact, the ecotourism potential of these regions is enormous.

The Northeast

Along with the North, the vast Northeast region is easily the most exotic, alluring, and "different" part of Brazil from a North American viewpoint, not to mention the most perennially hot and sunny. The region is steeped in a rich history that dates back to Brazil's 16th-century origins and still lingers in places, particularly once you step out of the coastal capitals and head up and down the alluring shoreline and deep into the arid Interior. The various cultural manifestations of the Northeast are unique and utterly fascinating as indigenous and especially African traditions mingle with those of the Portuguese who settled the region. Despite rapidly expanding cities and quickly developing coastlines, that cultural influence is still felt in day-to-day life, which makes living in this region very special for foreigners who want to experience an alternate lifestyle in which culture still trumps consumerism and human interaction can be particularly warm. Living in the Northeast is not always easy, but it can be both relaxing and enriching—although it probably won't make you rich. Despite the economy of this historically backward region now growing at an unprecedented pace, formal opportunities for expats are still fairly scarce. If you want to live in the region's capitals of Salvador, Recife, or Fortaleza or along the spectacular coast that stretches up from Bahia to Maranhão, in most cases, you'll need to be a self-starter with a large reserve of patience and an ability

© MICHAEL SOMMERS

colonial Olinda, a UNESCO World Heritage Site in the Northeast

to adapt. Culturally, and in terms of socioeconomics (the extremes between rich and poor are still quite pronounced), the Northeast is perhaps the Brazilian region most likely to provide North Americans with the biggest shock.

RIO DE JANEIRO

One of the truly great cities of the world, Rio is also one of the most beautiful cities on the planet. Wedged between the cobalt blue of the Baía de Guanabara and dramatic mountains covered in native Atlantic forest, this tropical metropolis of 6 million (12 million in terms of metropolitan area) is the second-largest city in Brazil and the third largest in Latin America.

Founded by the Portuguese in 1502, Rio became the capital of Brazil in 1763 and then the capital of the Portuguese Empire in 1812, when the exiled Portuguese court arrived and transformed the city from a muddy backwater into a cosmopolitan world-class metropolis with wide avenues and glorious palaces that exist to this day. Rio took a hit when the capital moved to Brasília in 1960, and another when São Paulo consolidated itself as the nation's financial and economic powerhouse in the '70s and '80s. In recent years, the city suffered due to increasing urban violence and escalating drug wars.

However, in the last few years, Rio has come back with a vengeance and is now considered one of the world's "It" cities. Hosting the 2014 World Cup and 2016 Olympics—coupled with an economic boom and residents' mounting protests against lack of security—have spurred government officials to take on the drug traffickers and violence. Special UPPs (Police Pacification Units) are now occupying many of the city's marginalized favelas with the aim of keeping crime at bay and integrating favelas into

© MICHAEL SOMMERS

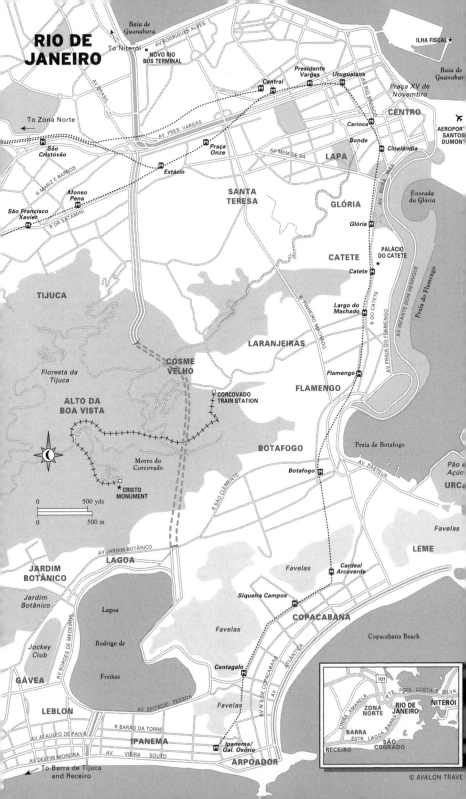

the rest of the urban fold. Meanwhile, the city is witnessing the revitalization of run-down neighborhoods (such as the port zone), the extension of the (woefully insufficient) Metrô line, and the mushrooming of start-up ventures along with a burgeoning IT sector. Rio also serves as headquarters for major oil, telecommunications, and media companies as well as a hot spot for Brazilian R & D companies.

Today, Rio continues to be a somewhat chaotic, but compelling, patchwork of rich and poor, jungle and skyscrapers, where 500 years of history mingle with contemporary innovation. If it can be an exhausting (and increasingly expensive) place to live, it can also be incredibly relaxing. Rio is not for the faint of heart; it's frequently funky (in all senses) and a little on the edge. Yet it's often charming, sometimes downright romantic, and never, ever boring.

The Lay of the Land

Rio sits on the western shores of the landlocked harbor created by the picturesque Baía de Guanabara, whose entrance is guarded by the iconic Pão de Açúcar (Sugarloaf). Extending 197 kilometers (111 miles) along a narrow strip of alluvial plains, the city is literally squeezed between the ocean and the foothills of the Serra do Mar mountain range, which is covered with native Atlantic forest (Mata Atlântica) as well as favelas.

CITY DIVISIONS

The oldest part of Rio—riddled with baroque churches and belle époque palaces and rife with '70s skyscrapers and new millennium traffic—is known as **Centro.** This downtown core lies on the western shore of the Baía de Guanabara. To the north, sprawl the industrial, working-class, and poor neighborhoods of the **Zona Norte (North Zone),** by far the largest portion of the city. To the south, the oldest **Zona Sul (South Zone)** middle-class neighborhoods of **Glória, Catete, Flamengo, Botafogo, Urca,** and **Laranjeiras** spill into the wealthier and famous beach neighborhoods of **Copacabana, Ipanema,** and **Leblon,** which, separated by mountains, sit along the open Atlantic. More mountains separate the Zona Sul from the much newer and more suburban and soulless "Miami-style" beach neighborhoods of **São Conrado, Barra da Tijuca,** and **Recreio,** which are the most upscale neighborhoods of the **Zona Oeste (West Zone).** Throughout Rio, expect to find favelas, or slums (there are close to 1,000 of them), which are inhabited by roughly 20 percent of the population. The most "famous" favelas such as **Rocinha** and **Vidigal** are renowned for their size as well as their juxtaposition (they literally sit cheek by jowl) to some of the richest neighborhoods in the city.

CLIMATE

Rio enjoys a tropical Atlantic climate with a mixture of intense sun and lots of rain (which explains the lushness). The main period of heavy rains usually extends from December to March. Coinciding with the summer months, the precipitation really ups the humidity factor. This is the period when Rio and the surrounding region experience the worst (and sometimes catastrophic) series of flooding and landslides.

Although summertime temperatures famously soar to heights of 40°C (104°F), such

© MICHAEL SOMMERS

a rainy day in Centro

peaks are infrequent (average temperatures are in the 30s C (80s F) and are offset by cooling sea breezes. In winter months (June–Sept.), comfortably sunny days in the low-to-mid 20s C (70s F) are interrupted by frequent cold fronts that bring rains, blustery winds, and cool temperatures in the high teens (60s F) from Antarctica. During the rest of the year, temperatures are quite moderate, ranging from 25–30°C (77–86°F).

CULTURE

Rio is a diverse, cosmopolitan melting pot. From colonial times up until the mid-20th century, the city drew many waves of Portuguese immigrants; most Cariocas boast some Portuguese ancestry. More than other places, the legacy is still felt, particularly in Cariocas' fondness for Portuguese culinary specialties like *bacalhau* (salted cod) and rich, eggy deserts such as *quimdim*.

Another pronounced influence derives from the fact that in the 19th century, Rio received more slaves (both from Africa and other parts of Brazil) than any other city in the New World. As a result, today around half the population identifies themselves as black or mixed race. This pronounced Afro-Brazilian legacy seeps into various aspects of the culture but is most apparent in the city's off-the-charts musicality (samba, pagoda, funk, rap, hip-hop) as well as religions such as Umbanda and Candomblé, which are adhered to (both casually and seriously) by a significant number of Cariocas.

More recently (in the mid- to late 20th century), Rio received truckloads of poor migrants from the Brazilian Northeast, who came south in search of work. Traditionally, many ended up in favelas and working menial jobs; to this day, there is a certain veiled discrimination against *nordestinos* (northeasterners). At the same time, their cuisine and music have infiltrated the city and added to its rich cultural tapestry.

© MICHAEL SOMMERS

Beach culture rules in Rio.

Regardless, no matter where you come from, it's easy to become folded into the embracing culture that is distinctly Carioca. An oft-quoted adage claims that in São Paulo people play to work whereas in Rio people work to play. Indeed, you'll rarely encounter a big city where so much emphasis is placed on enjoying life. Of course, it helps when you have some of the most beautiful beaches on the planet within walking distance. Rio has an incredibly sophisticated beach culture, which influences everything from clothing—it's ground zero for the world's *biquíni* (bikini) and *sunga* (swim trunks) fashions—and health (part of the reason the city is so packed with gyms and juice bars is so Cariocas can flaunt their buffed and bronzed bods) to socialization (neighborhood beaches are subdivided into microcosms, which attract everyone from surfers and yuppies with kids to leftist intellectuals and gay "bears").

The laid-back beach vibe spills over into the city at large. Cariocas are a decidedly relaxed and casual bunch. Justly celebrated for their warmth, hospitality, and extroverted charm, they're also known (for better and for worse) for their wiles—many in the rest of Brazil subscribe to the myth of the Carioca as a *malandro,* a trickster type who resorts to artifices to get what he or she wants, often by circumnavigating the rules or laws.

Daily Life

EXPAT RESOURCES

In recent years, Rio's expat community has swollen significantly, and it's certainly not difficult to meet people from back home as well as other foreigners. Traditional expat clubs that have been around for decades include the American Society of Rio de Janeiro, the British Commonwealth Society of Rio de Janeiro, and the St. Andrew's Society (whose base membership consists of Scots as well as lovers of Highland dancing and golf). The International Club Rio (InC) is a more diverse group, whose members hail from over 30 nations; InC organizes activities, excursions, and special-interest groups aimed at helping foreigners connect.

Another good place to meet expats is at church. Both Christ Church, the Anglican Church of Rio de Janeiro, in Botafogo, and the Union Church of Rio de Janeiro, an interdenominational church located in Barra, hold weekly services in English. They also organize social events as well as outreach volunteer projects.

Several online expat communities also have Rio groups that congregate in both virtual and real-life spheres. Meetup hosts the Expats and English Speakers of Rio de Janeiro (www.meetup.com), whose members include small business owners, investors, and entrepreneurs living in or doing business in Rio. They usually get together once a month to network and kick back at various bars and restaurants throughout the city. InterNations also has a Rio group (www.internations.org) of expats that post online and meet offline as well. Finally, there is a big expat blogging community in Rio; to access the latest posts and join the virtual fray, navigate through Destinations to the Rio page from www.expat-blog.com.

SCHOOLS

Sending kids to private English schools in Rio does not come cheaply. Monthly fees range from around R$3,000 for half-day preschool to R$5,000 for high school, and schools also charge staggeringly high one-time entrance fees. Most expats who are transferred to Rio for work purposes try to have school fees included as part of their compensation packages. The top two schools for English-speaking children are the Escola Americana do Rio de Janeiro (EARJ), which dates back to 1937, and the British School, founded in 1924. Be aware that there are sometimes waiting lists for admission.

The Escola Americana's main campus, offering preschool through grade 12, is located in the tony residential neighborhood of Gávea. However, it also has a campus in Barra that offers classes from nursery school to grade 3 and another campus—with less impressive facilities—in Macaé with classes from nursery school through grade 6.

The British School also has two campuses. The main Zona Sul campus consists of a nursery and primary school in Botafogo and secondary school in adjacent Urca. A second newer campus is located in Barra. When fully completed in 2015, it will be open to kids from 2 to 18 years of age who want a bilingual education.

Also in Barra is the more recently established Rio International School (RIS), a small international Christian school (member of the Network of International Christian Schools) offering courses from preschool through high school. Although RIS has an international staff and student body, the curriculum is American based.

EXPAT PROFILE: STATES OF THE UNION

Jim, 52, moved to Rio in 2008 from San Francisco with his husband, Luiz, and settled in Niterói. Jim blogs about his life in Brazil at qualidadedevida-jim.blogspot.com. He talks here about his experience.

WHY HE CAME

Shortly after I met Luiz in San Francisco, he said "You must buy your ticket to come to Brazil with me in December." I said "I don't know if I'm going to still like you in December." "Don't worry," he said. He was right. I fell in love with him and with Brazil. Over the next few years, we traveled to Brazil, for months at a time, visiting the entire country. When he decided he wanted to move back to Niterói to take care of his mother, I said, "Okay, let's go." I worked four more years to save money and get my pension, and then we moved.

THE MOVING PROCESS

Shipping is very expensive because of Brazilian duty taxes (foreigners are charged around 60 percent), but because Luiz is Brazilian, we could bring the contents of his home back to Brazil without paying duty on them. We brought everything important to us—art, some furniture, and our entire kitchen. It filled about one-third of a container and cost $3,000-4,000. We used a Brazilian company that came to our house in San Francisco and packed everything, shipped it, and delivered it to us in Niterói. A few things broke, but we filed a complaint and were reimbursed 100 percent. Everyone says that your possessions will be held at customs upon arrival in Brazil and that you have to pay a bribe to get them released. That never happened to us.

GETTING HERE

The Brazilian government passed a law recognizing stable unions. If you prove through documentation that you've been together for several years as a couple—regardless of sex—the Brazilian partner can sponsor the foreign partner to come live in Brazil. We started this process in San Francisco at the consulate and finished it in Rio with the help of an immigration lawyer (who gave us a discount on her R$2,000 fee because she was a lesbian). The whole process—which included writing an essay about our relationship—took 11 months to process in Brasília. After that, I received permanent residency.

LIVING IN NITERÓI

I love Rio, but it's in the middle of a housing bubble and rent is stupid. In Niterói, we live in a house by the ocean, which is beautiful and the quality of the water is better. It's calmer, quieter, safer, and cleaner here.

MAKING A LIVING

I'm an exception because we own our apartment and don't have to pay ridiculous Rio rents. And I'm happy to take buses. Because our monthly expenses are under R$1,500, I don't have to make a lot of money. I work about six hours a week teaching English privately to adult professionals (I charge R$45 an hour), and Luiz is a tour guide. However, unless you're on your own and prepared to live very cheaply, it's almost impossible to get by in Rio teaching English, particularly at private language schools, which pay R$15 an hour.

A WORD OF ADVICE

Bring way more money than you think you're going to need. Rio is expensive. Also Brazilian consumer goods are not only poorer quality than those in the United States, but cost two to three times as much. My motto: "If you can, bring it with you."

Aside from price, some expats complain that the schools described above—whose curriculum is almost entirely in English—are somewhat isolated enclaves (although wealthy Brazilian students attend them as well). Other alternatives are bilingual schools such as the Escola Bloom and the Maple Bear Canadian School; both are located in Barra and offer English-Portuguese education to younger children.

Universities

In terms of higher education, Rio has dozens of universities of varying quality, both public and private. The most reputed, not to mention the largest federal university in the country, is the Universidade Federal do Rio de Janeiro (UFRJ), whose diplomas are internationally recognized. It's especially known for its engineering, science, and technology programs as well as social, human, and biomedical sciences. UFRJ stands out for its research as well as for the many community projects it develops dedicated to improving the life of Cariocas. The university benefits from its ties with many cutting-edge Brazilian companies (including oil giant Petrobras, which has facilities on one of the four city campuses) as well as numerous partnerships with international universities and institutions. Those partnerships facilitate spending a year at UFRJ on a study abroad program.

Operated by the state of Rio de Janeiro, the Universidade Estadual do Rio de Janeiro (UERJ), whose sprawling campus is located close to Maracanã soccer stadium, is another reputed public university with options for international exchange students and visiting students in addition to regular diploma programs. Located in Gávea, the Pontífica Universidade Católica do Rio de Janeiro (PUC-Rio) is a Catholic university that is one of Rio's top private universities. Aside from partnerships with various international institutions, PUC offers Portuguese courses for foreigners, at five different levels, ranging from intensive six-week courses to four-month full-semester courses.

HEALTH AND SAFETY

Rio's private medical sector boasts some world-class facilities. One of the most popular with expats, the Clínica Galdino Campos in Copacabana, is a private clinic that has a tradition of treating foreigners. Open 24 hours, it has an English-speaking staff. Another top hospital in Copacabana is the Hospital Copa d'Or. Owned and operated by the internationally accredited Rede d'Or Group, it's recognized for its state-of-the-art surgical centers where complex operations are performed. Also highly recommended is the Casa de Saúde São José. Located in Humaitá, it has a special international-patient section with English speaking staff. The large hospital has departments in all areas of medicine as well as a 24-hour emergency service. If you plan on having a baby in Brazil, the CPDT, Centro Pré Natal de Diagnóstico e Tratamento, is a renowned facility. Located in Laranjeiras, it offers excellent service not to mention stunning close-up views of Corcovado for mothers and newborns.

LEISURE ACTIVITIES

Rio is one city where you'll never lack for things to do. Splendid beaches offer unlimited opportunities for baking and flaking out, as well as walking, running, cycling,

© MICHAEL SOMMERS

volleyball on Ipanema beach

beach yoga, soccer, volleyball, and surfing. Swathed in native Atlantic forest, riddled with hiking trails and refreshing waterfalls, the Parque de Tijuca is the largest urban park in the world. However, Rio also boasts refuges and recreational areas such as Lagoa Rodrigo de Freitas, Parque do Flamengo, the Jardim Botânico, Parque Lage, and myriad other spaces to relax and practice all manner of outdoor activities. That Cariocas are an extremely healthy—not to mention body-conscious bunch—is hardly surprising. The city certainly doesn't lack for gyms, fitness centers, Pilates studios, capoeira academies, or spas.

Those who seek nurture as well as nature will find it in spades. Rio possesses an impressive cultural life that mingles the best of international and national offerings with a fabulous array of homegrown talent in every art form. Dance, theater, visual arts, and cinema are all thriving in Rio. That the musical scene is one of the world's most vibrant is unsurprising considering that Rio was a cradle of both samba and bossa nova, not to mention many of their respective offshoots. The city boasts an immense array of musical events, from popular street *festas* (festivals) to erudite music recitals, favela funk *bailes* (dance parties) to stadium concerts, century-old *gafieiras* (dance halls) to hipster-filled nightclubs. Rio also has a great number of museums and cutting-edge cultural centers, often housed in beautiful, historical buildings, which host a compelling roster of events, most of them at very affordable prices or free. A bonus is that many offerings are geared toward children and families.

Cariocas love to eat, drink, and make merry and jubilantly do so everywhere from the simplest *barracas* (kiosks), and beloved neighborhood *botequins* (neighborhood bars) to juice bars, healthy per-kilo restaurants, cafés, bistros, and bakeries, not to mention an abundance of fine food restaurants offering creative homegrown and international cuisine. A number of fine food delicatessens and the beloved Zona Sul chain of supermarkets allow foodies to stock up on basically everything their taste buds might desire (and to satisfy the majority of their import cravings).

Those who count shopping as a leisure pursuit won't be disappointed by Rio's offerings. Like any Brazilian urban center worth its salt, the city boasts its share of shopping malls—in fact, it possesses some of the biggest and chicest in the country. However, Rio is also blessed by fashionable boutiques (especially in Ipanema) selling cutting-edge beach and casual wear, as well as outdoor markets, great antique stores (in Lapa and Copacabana's Shopping dos Antiquários), terrific bookstores, and the wonderfully souk-like atmosphere of Centro's cheap Saara district.

PRIME LIVING LOCATIONS

VOLUNTEERING

There's no shortage of volunteering activities in Rio. A good place start, especially if your Portuguese is shaky and you also want to meet some other expats, is by contacting the American Society of Rio de Janeiro, in Gávea. They have a long history of participating in community outreach projects and fundraising activities as well as providing help to U.S. and other foreign citizens in Rio who find themselves in dire straits.

Those with a better grasp of Portuguese might want to check out volunteer opportunities with Viva Rio, a renowned Rio-based nongovernmental organization (NGO) involved with multiple social projects which prioritize community outreach and education programs in favelas. Meanwhile, nature lovers should consider checking out the volunteer possibilities available among the orchids, gigantic lily pads, and carnivorous plants housed at Rio's Jardim Botânico.

Where to Live

In the last several years, the Rio real estate market has exploded like never before, driving buying and rental prices sky high. Apart from the booming economy, Rio's market has taken off as a result of investors attracted by the development surrounding the 2014 World Cup, the 2016 Olympic Games, and the potential of offshore oil drilling. The pacification of the Zona Sul favelas has driven up prices in once sketchy "frontier" areas near favelas, not to mention in the favelas themselves where locals are selling out to intrepid foreigners and locals who covet the relatively (temporarily?) safer areas, blessed with amazing views and locations. In the year 2011 alone, apartment rentals in Rio increased by an average of 21 percent while prices for real estate on a per-square-meter basis soared by an average of 35 percent (with the average square meter costing R$7,500).

BUYING PRICES

Unless you're independently wealthy or plan on winning a lottery, you'll probably gasp at the prices being charged for apartments in Rio de Janeiro. At the end of 2011, the average price of a new apartment in Rio was R$399,000. Based on size, the two most expensive neighborhoods in Rio (not to mention Brazil) were Ipanema and Leblon, where in 2011 new apartments cost R$35,660 and R$17,900 per square meter, respectively, which explains three-bedroom apartments priced at upward of R$2 million.

Other *bairros* are less astronomical, but still pricey. In early 2012, average prices in Copacabana and Botafogo hovered around R$1 million (with price per square meter nearing R$9,000) for a three-bedroom apartment. An average three bedroom in Barra da Tijuca went for between R$800,000 and R$900,000 while Recreio dos Bandeirantes was slightly more affordable at around R$650,000 to R$750,000 and about R$600,000 in Catete and Lapa.

Of course, there are alternative options. With the pacification of Rio's favelas, small numbers of intrepid expats—usually young, single adventurous ones—have been moving into these (temporarily) safer, but still somewhat risky, areas. In Rocinha, for instance, you can probably find a one- or two-bedroom apartment starting at around

R$25,000 or R$30,000. Property in less well-known and well-located favelas can be had for much cheaper.

RENTAL PRICES

Rental prices listed below are rough monthly averages based on April 2012 values. Within a given neighborhood, rents may vary considerably according to factors such as beach proximity, building amenities, and size. The one bedrooms listed below are all roughly between 30 and 60 square meters (100–200 square feet) while the three bedrooms measure between 90 and 120 square meters (300–400 square feet).

ZONA SUL

The Zona Sul is the most coveted area of Rio to live. Its neighborhoods are attractive, vibrant, and easy to get around by foot as well as bus and Metrô. These atmospheric neighborhoods possess decades' old botecos (bars), great restaurants, lots of culture, cinemas, terrific shopping, tree-lined secondary streets, mountain views, and of course, some of the most famous beaches on the planet.

Some of the most popular neighborhoods for expats are the beach neighborhoods of Ipanema, Leblon, and Copacabana, which also happen to be the most popular with foreign tourists as well. As such, while you'll encounter sky-high housing prices, you'll also find a good range of temporary, furnished flats and apartments—along with agencies that specialize in renting to foreigners (usually at jacked-up prices). A good online source for buying and renting (in Portuguese) is www.zap.com.br. Started by a Swedish expat, Agente Imóvel (www.agenteimovel.com.br) lists properties for rent and for sale in Rio (and other Brazilian hot spots) in both English and Portuguese. Meanwhile, Homes in Rio (www.homesinrio.com.br) caters to foreigners in search of short and long-term (generally upscale) rentals and sales in the Zona Sul beach neighborhoods.

Ipanema and Leblon

The most desirable—and expensive—slice of beachfront property in Rio is the area where the first chords of "A Garota de Ipanema" ("The Girl from Ipanema") were set down by quintessential Carioca poet-composers Vinícius de Moraes and Tom Jobim. The song that seduced the world continues to sum up the charm of what continues to be Rio's hippest and most happening beach *bairro*. Since the swinging '60s, Ipanema has been a magnet for cosmopolitan artists, musicians, and leftist intellectuals, along with a rich and trendy crowd—including a wealth of foreign tourists and residents— who consistently fall for the lovely neighborhood with its shady tree-lined streets, fashionable bistros, bars, and boutiques, and magnificent white sands.

Adjacent Leblon is slightly more sedate, tranquil, and residential (not to mention richer) than Ipanema. Like Ipanema, during the day much of life revolves around the beach. As a result, it carries off the impressive feat of being both quite chic and disarmingly casual.

Aside from their laid-back vibe and attractiveness, not to mention relative security (they tend to be well policed), Ipanema and Leblon have everything you could desire: access to every type of good and service imaginable all within walking distance.

Ipanema beach

Highlights include some great bookstores and cafés, outdoor food and flower markets, top-notch supermarkets, 24-hour juice bars galore, and a proximity to nature (aside from the beaches, both are bordered by the Lagoa Rodrigo de Freitas).

The main drawback is demand is so high that even if you can afford the astronomical rents that are charged (often for very small spaces), you'll still have trouble finding availability. Even so, this is traditionally where the largest number of expats have always chosen to reside. In both neighborhoods, expect a one bedroom to be R$2,000–4,000 per month while a three bedroom will cost anywhere between R$4,000 and R$7,000 per month, with oceanfront apartments averaging a cool R$11,000.

Gávea, Lagoa, and Jardim Botânico

Although less hip and happening, and more residential, than Ipanema and Leblon, Gávea, Lagoa, and Jardim Botânico are attractive, well-to-do neighborhoods that lure their share of expats. The upper portions climb up toward jungle-clad mountains crowned by the dramatic Pedra da Gávea and Corcovado (a nice trade-off for lack of beach access). The flatter expanses are riddled with bars and restaurants and segue into the Lagoa Rodrigo de Freitas, a placid lagoon whose emerald shores, replete with walking and cycling trails, sports facilities, and kiosk bars, comprise one of Rio's favorite open-air playgrounds. The lower portions of Gávea, known as Baixa Gávea, are more lively (Rio's Catholic university is located here) and have more commercial activity than tonier Jardim Botânico. Expect average rents for a one bedroom to hover between R$2,500 and R$3,000 per month with three bedrooms costing around R$4,000–6,000 and upward.

a view of residential high-rises surrounding Lagoa

Copacabana

While its glamour days are long gone, Copacabana still manages to live up to its legend as the world's most famous strip of white sand. In the '60s and '70s, a Copa address was so coveted that the long but narrow neighborhood (hemmed in by mountains) was the most densely populated urban area in the world. To this day, Copa in not unlike a tropical Manhattan: People fork out absurd amounts of money to live in one of the thousands of closet-sized apartments located in the ugly high-rises that have mushroomed in the streets behind the oceanfront.

While many of Rio's rich and fashionable have since moved on, Copa has become one of Rio's most eclectic, vibrant, and democratic neighborhoods—a place where street kids and millionaires, models and muscle men, doormen and nannies, whether from Northeast Brazil or the deepest, darkest American Midwest, all rub shoulders. By day, senior citizens swarm the beaches and the dozens of bakeries along the main drag of Avenida Nossa Senhora de Copacabana. By night the stretch of Avenida Atlântica toward Ipanema has classically been a hot spot for prostitutes. Pickpockets attracted by tourists, and the proximity of four major favelas covering the hills behind middle-class condos, have traditionally led to safety issues.

Nevertheless, Copacabana is full of unrivaled vibrancy and diversity. It's hard to resist the charm of the local restaurants and traditional *botecos* that coexist alongside the multitude of 24-hour juice bars and gyms—and the famous crescent beach is a world unto itself. There are amenities and services galore and the location is ideal.

Finding housing in Copa is less difficult than Ipanema and Leblon. There is a greater number, not to mention variety, of living spaces, which range from wonderful old apartments in fabulously streamlined art deco buildings to closet-sized *quitinetes* (studios) in nondescript high-rises. It goes without saying that rents get cheaper the farther back from the beach you go. You can probably swing a tiny one bedroom for around R$700, but a more decent-sized place will cost R$1,200–2,200. Expect to pay anywhere between R$3,000 and R$5,000 for a three bedroom.

Botafogo and Urca

In its late 19th-century heyday, the lovely white crescent beach of Botafogo was the equivalent of Ipanema. Although it remains visually alluring, nobody would dream of bathing in its polluted waters these days. Since the mid-20th century, the once grand neighborhood has lost some of its former sheen and succumbed to verticality in the form of modern high rises. However, its leafy side streets are tranquil and stuffed with cinemas, cultural centers, and decades-old restaurants and bars prized by Cariocas.

Squeezed onto a promontory facing Botafogo, and sheltering Pão de Açucar, the tiny residential enclave of Urca has resisted much of the urban mayhem characteristic of Rio's other beachside *bairros.* Neglected by tourists, unmarred by developers, and ignored by *assaltantes* (thieves), it is a bucolic, picturesque, and slightly secluded area, which actually possesses a fair number of houses.

In terms of housing, Botafogo offers the greatest number of options as well as the most amenities and easiest access to public transportation. Smaller and more tranquil, Urca is more isolated (although served by buses). Rents in Botafogo fall in the range R$1,000–2,200 for a one bedroom and R$3,200–4,500 for a three bedroom. Expect to pay more in Urca: R$1,800–2,800 for a one bedroom and R$3,500–5,000 for a three bedroom.

Flamengo, Laranjeiras, and Cosme Velho

There are many elegant Art Deco apartment buildings in Flamengo.

Stretching along the Baía de Guanabara from Centro to Botafogo is the sprawling and attractive *bairro* of Flamengo. In the 19th and early 20th centuries, it was one of Rio's most posh residential neighborhoods. To this day, many of the wide avenues and tree-lined side streets conserve an impressive array of gracious belle époque palaces and elegant art deco apartment buildings.

To the west of Flamengo is the equally enticing *bairro* of Laranjeiras, whose name attests to its rural origins when orchards of "orange trees" reigned. Placid and pretty, Laranjeiras is one of Rio's oldest and most charming neighborhoods, as is Cosme Velho, a somewhat more upscale residential neighborhood that winds its way up the hills to Corcovado. Far less trendy and touristy than the Zona Sul beach *bairros,* these neighborhoods offer appealing and colorful slices of traditional Carioca life. Apart from some classic bars and restaurants, the vast seaside Parque do Flamengo is one of Rio's most extensive and popular recreational spaces. Rents for one bedrooms average around R$1,500–2,500 while you can find three bedrooms in the vicinity of R$2,500–4,000. Laranjeiras and Cosme Velho tend to be a bit pricier while Flamengo has more options and more range in terms of prices.

Glória and Catete

In the mid-19th century, Glória and Catete were considered outskirts of Rio. Their proximity to Centro and the Baía de Guanabara lured Rio's burgeoning upper-middle classes and they remained fashionable until the mid-20th century. Since then, the area has lost much of its luster, but Catete in particular is a lively, traditional working-class area, with lots of local bars and small businesses, not to mention the placid Parque de Catete. Count on rent for a one bedroom being R$1,200–1,800 and for a three bedroom hovering around R$2,500–3,500.

CENTRAL
Centro and Lapa

Rio's historic downtown commercial district, Centro is pretty much devoted to business and, to date, offers few residential options (although this could change as the long-neglected port zone becomes revitalized). While clogged and chaotic by day, at night the place clears out and becomes a none-too-safe ghost town.

While adjacent Lapa is famed for its bohemian nightlife, it too offers slim residential pickings. If you're willing to rough it and get off on rich but dilapidated atmospheres, you might be able to unearth some digs. But be aware that Lapa is pretty sketchy in terms of safety. Apartments in these areas are mostly single-dwelling units, and it's rare that expats live in these areas. Expect a one bedroom in Centro to cost R$700–1,500 while trendier Lapa is also pricier at R$1,500–2,500.

Santa Teresa

Rising above Lapa and Catete is the charming bucolic hillside neighborhood of Santa Teresa. One of the city's oldest residential *bairros,* in the 19th century wealthy Cariocas built gracious villas along its narrow winding streets, with terraces overlooking the lush green mountains and blue waters of the Baía de Guanabara. The views are still alluring—as is the neighborhood, which is why after a long period of decline many artists began to move in, snatching up the dilapidated villas for a song and transforming them into ateliers. After an initial revival in the 1960s and '70s, a second revitalization began in 2005, resulting in the trickling in of foreign-owned boutique hotels and fashionable bistros as well as improved security (surrounded by favelas, "Santa" as it's referred to, has had a somewhat dodgy reputation, especially at night).

Thanks to the efforts of neighborhood artists, Santa Teresa has evolved into a vibrant community that has attracted a good number of expats with an artistic bent, not to mention the means and aspirations to acquire and renovate a good number of its most beautiful houses, driving up values. The great thing about living in Santa is that you feel so remote, as if you're living in a picturesque mountain town instead of a large, chaotic city. However, the downside of living in Santa is that it *is* remote. Barring a few bus lines and a problematic *bonde* (tram), there is no public transportation. The

An iconic yellow *bonde* (tram) transports passengers from Centro to Santa Teresa.

narrow, winding streets are easily clogged by traffic. Although you can see the city all around you, access to its amenities and services is a chore unless you're prepared to rack up a lot of money on taxi fare.

If you do succumb to its charms enough to tackle its complex logistics, know that a three bedroom will cost R\$2,500–4,500.

ZONA OESTE
Barra and Recreio

After Leblon, Rio's coastal road, Avenida Niemeyer, goes through a long tunnel that burrows beneath the Morro de Dois Irmãos, whose slopes are home to one of Rio's largest favelas, Vidigal. Although from a socioeconomic perspective the successive beach neighborhoods are considered extensions of the Zona Sul, geographically they are part of the Zona Oeste because they are situated west of Ipanema and Leblon. After the tiny but wealthy enclave of São Conrado, which directly faces Brazil's biggest—and most famous—favela, Rocinha, another long tunnel leads to the mega-developed, super-suburban *bairro* of Barra da Tijuca (known simply as Barra). Thirty years ago, this 16-kilometer (10-mile) stretch of coastline was little more than a long wild sweep of white sand. Now it is the playground and home to Rio's middle classes and *novo ricos* (nouveau riche), who alternate days spent on the beaches and at the many shopping malls with nights in its many bars, clubs, and shopping malls.

Getting around Barra without a car is nearly impossible, although buses careen up and down the main autobahn-like drag of Avenida das Américas and, to a lesser extent, along the parallel running Avenida Sernambetiba, which follows the ocean. Barra becomes less developed the farther west you travel and eventually turns into the 11-kilometer (7-mile) stretch of beach known as Recreio dos Bandeirantes, whose rough waves are a magnet for Rio's surfing crowd.

Due to geographical limitations, it's difficult to give full reign to Rio's searing hot real estate market within the confines of the Zona Sul. As a result, sprawling Barra is booming (adding fuel to the flames is the fact that Barra is the site of the 2016 Olympic Village). Availability combined with somewhat lower prices than those available in the Zona Sul has made Barra a hot spot for many expats, particularly those sponsored by companies. What its newer residences may lack in charm, they make up for in terms of larger spaces, increased amenities, and security, not to mention parking. Although you forfeit history, culture, and community (many residences are located in closed condominium complexes), you do have access to a great—and clean—beach. Moreover, culture shock is minimized; if it weren't for the fact that everyone speaks Portuguese, you could almost believe you're in Houston. Expect to pay R$1,200–2,000 for a one bedroom and R$2,500–4,500 for a three bedroom in Barra (due to its distance, rents in Recreio are somewhat cheaper).

ZONA NORTE

Although expats generally don't live in Rio's sprawling Zona Norte neighborhoods, millions of Cariocas do. The neighborhoods themselves vary in terms of socioeconomic level and in terms of safety. Although buses and suburban trains link these *bairros* to Centro, commuting is notoriously brutal. While not Rio's most attractive neighborhoods, some of the more traditional ones are chock full of authentic Carioca culture: All the city's samba schools hail from Zona Norte neighborhoods. Basically, though, the biggest reason you'd want to consider living in this area is that rents are much cheaper, with one-bedroom apartments averaging R$500–800 and three bedrooms hovering at R$1,000–1,500.

NITERÓI

Only 17 kilometers (10.5 miles) across Baía de Guanabara from Centro—accessible by ferry boat or by bus or car along the (often crowded) Rio-Niterói bridge—the pleasant, middle-class suburb-like city of Niterói offers a tranquil, cheaper, and generally safer alternative to living in Rio itself. Not only are Niterói's attractive beaches much cleaner and less crowded than Rio's, but they also offer stunning views of the *Cidade Maravilhosa* (Marvelous City) across the bay. Rents vary depending on location, but count on R$800–1,500 for a decent one bedroom and R$1,800–2,500 for three bedrooms.

Getting Around

Rio has an extensive and inexpensive public transportation system consisting of a limited but efficient and expanding Metrô and a far-reaching, if slightly more confusing, bus system. It's easy to get around the density of Centro and Zona Sul and much of the long but narrow beach neighborhoods of Copacabana, Ipanema, and Leblon on foot. For Barra and other farther-flung, much more sprawling, vehicle-friendly neighborhoods, you'll really want a car. At night, for safety reasons, it's always advisable to take a taxi if you're without your own wheels.

METRÔ

Rio's Metrô is clean, efficient, and safe (not to mention gloriously air-conditioned). The only problem is its size: Although plans are underway to extend Linha 1 to Barra, currently it only goes to Ipanema. Meanwhile, parts of the Zona Norte (Maracanã for instance) and Centro are well serviced. Metrôrio has streamlined things considerably by adding "surface Metrôs" and express buses that depart from Metrô stations. Tickets can be purchased in the stations (fare is R$3.20, which includes transfers) as can a prepaid R$10 Metrô card to which you can add as much credit as you want; not only is this cheaper than paying for individual fares, but you also avoid lines. The Metrô runs 5am–midnight Monday–Saturday, 7am–11pm Sunday. On weekends you can board the trains with bikes and surfboards.

EXPAT PROFILE: RELOCATION CHALLENGES

Sara, 30, moved to Rio in 2009 from Houston with her husband, Nate. The couple settled first in the town of Macaé ("The Petroleum Capital of Brazil") in Rio de Janeiro state, then in Barra. During this time, she had her first child. She talks here about her experience.

WHY THEY CAME

Nate works for an oil company and we knew we were going to be sent overseas. When they told us we were going to Brazil, we had a month to get ready! We were really excited; we had both wanted to live outside the United States, but we had no time to prepare. I bought a Rosetta Stone Portuguese language course and read some travel books, which sort of scared me because they focus a lot on dangers.

ON THE MOVING PROCESS

The company moved our entire apartment from Houston to our new house in Macaé. Only instead of taking two months for our things to arrive, it took eight! During that time, we lived at the Sheraton out of the two suitcases we brought with us. Although it feels like home to have your furniture here, smaller spaces and different layouts mean not all furniture fits well.

GETTING HERE

Because Nate's company needed him in Brazil right away, we came on tourist visas. It took two months for our work visas to be approved and longer to receive our CPFs. By Brazilian law, Nate couldn't be paid in Brazil without a CPF, so for six months we had to pay all our costs out of pocket before being reimbursed. This happens to a lot of people; we know a couple who went $60,000 into debt!

ON LIVING IN MACAÉ

Macaé is a very small town where Petrobras and all the oil companies are located. It has a huge expat community, but it's not a great city to live in. It's so populated by gringos that you don't get a taste of Brazil. Besides, prices are very high and service is very low. There are a lot of things you can't get. Nobody speaks English, so I had to really put myself out there to meet other expat women whose husbands all work for different oil companies. I was probably the youngest one there since most expats are couples just starting out or with kids who are grown.

LIVING IN BARRA

After two years, Nate was offered a promotion. I said I wouldn't stay in Macaé, so we went to Rio. Barra has a lot of oil company offices, and it's easier to work and live in the same neighborhood. Barra is not really Rio; it's more like Houston. You have to drive everywhere. I think the transition from the United States is easier.

MAKING A LIVING

I'm a nurse, and I thought I'd be able to work here, but you can't do it in Brazil. It's not just the language; nurses' roles are very different. It's very hard for expat wives to work here because you have to get your own work visa from a company that's willing to support you. Financially though, it makes sense for us to be here. Brazil is a real hot spot in terms of oil. We have great health insurance that covers everything; our baby was born here and the care was excellent. The company pays for our housing, car, and gas and provides a grocery allowance. With our savings, we'll be able to pay off our college loans and put down money on a house in the United States.

WORD OF ADVICE

Don't be an expat couple unless you have a very strong relationship with your partner. The communication has to be there. Many expat husbands work long hours and have a lot of difficulty adapting to the different way of doing business here. Meanwhile, many expat wives find themselves bored, lonely, and frustrated. Sadly, we had several expat friends who couldn't make it and divorced while they were in Brazil.

Metrô station in Rio's Botafogo neighborhood

BUS

Buses go everywhere in Rio. Except when they're mired in rush-hour traffic, they tend to go very, very fast, which depending on your thrill factor, can prove either exhilarating or hair-raising. The other drawback to Rio's municipal buses is that they're not the safest form of locomotion going because of pickpockets and occasional armed holdups, although daytime trips between points in the Centro, Zona Sul, and the western beaches of Barra and Recreio are usually fine. Do take care to have your change already counted out beforehand, and always keep bags or other belongings closed and close to your chest, especially when it's crowded. By day, buses run with great frequency. By night, you can risk taking buses between main stops in Flamengo, Botafogo, Copacabana, Ipanema, and Leblon, which are usually quite busy until around 9 or 10pm. Otherwise, stick to taxis.

Final destinations are written on the front of the bus, and along its side you will see the main stops along the routes. Make sure you check this out. From Centro, for example, there are buses whose final destination is Leblon that careen along the coast through Copacabana and Ipanema, while others go inland via Botafogo and Jardim Botânico. After paying your fare (R$2.50) to the *cobrador* (collector) at the back of the bus, make your way to the front, so you can make an easy exit when you get to your stop. If a bus stop is not clearly marked, look for a clump of people waiting. You can signal for a bus to stop by sticking out your arm.

TAXIS

Taxi service in Rio is reasonably priced, and for specific trips you can often bargain a fixed price with your driver. There are two kinds of taxis in Rio. Yellow cabs with blue stripes are the most common. They can be hailed in the street and are cheaper. Large white air-conditioned radio cabs are usually ordered by phone and are more expensive. Two reliable companies are **Central de Taxis** (tel. 21/2593-2598) and **Coopacarioca** (tel. 21/2518-1818). Most Carioca cab drivers are friendly and honest (although very few speak English).

DRIVING

Driving in Rio is not for the timid. It's not that Cariocas are poor drivers, but they tend to forget they're not at the Indy 500. Then there are the rush-hour traffic jams, which aren't only stressful, but also stiflingly hot with the tropical sun beating down. One-way streets, poorly marked turnoffs, and holdups—at stoplights and when you're parked—are further dissuading factors. However, depending on where you live, a car can range from extremely useful to essential. They come in especially handy at night and if you want to take trips to more far-flung beaches and mountains (which you will) on the outskirts or outside the city. If you have kids, a car is pretty much a must.

BIKING

Rio has 130 kilometers (80 miles) of bike paths. Those in search of a languorous outing can take to the paths that line the beaches (stretching from Flamengo to Leblon and then along Barra) and ring the Lagoa Rodrigo de Freitas. Meanwhile, hard-core jocks can take on the steep trails leading into the Floresta da Tijuca. Off the paths, things get hairier because you have to contend with dense and unpredictable vehicle and pedestrian traffic, neither of which has been trained to deal with, let alone consider, bikers. Meanwhile, following the example of other big cities, Rio operates a bike rental system, SAMBA, which to date boasts close to 60 bike terminals in the Zona Sul. To actually get your hands on a bike, you have to register at www.mobilicidade. com.br for Rio. Using a credit card, you can opt to rent for a day (R$10) or a month (R$20). Rides of up to 60 minutes are free, after which you're charged R$5 an hour. To register and activate bikes, you need to have a cell phone number.

SÃO PAULO

When most people think of São Paulo, they immediately conjure up the smog-horizoned, high-rise-infested megalopolis of 20 million (in the metropolitan area) and find the expression "concrete jungle" to be an understatement. Teeming with noise, activity, and a certain degree of urban chaos, São Paulo is bewildering for those unfamiliar or not enamored with cities its size—and alluring for those who are. Brazil's economic and cultural powerhouse is overflowing with banks and mega-corporations as well as an astounding number of world-class museums, cultural centers, theaters, concert halls, and cinemas. If you're looking for Brazil's quintessential tropical paradise, you won't find it here. However, you will encounter a unique and fascinating fusion of elements from all over the country—and the world.

Although São Paulo gives the impression of being a relatively new city, it was actually founded over 450 years ago. Few vestiges remain of São Paulo's early days as a Jesuit missionary settlement or as a thriving 19th-century trade center where coffee barons lived it up in grand style. In the early 20th century, São Paulo began to morph into a bustling and somewhat grand metropolis. British, German, and French companies flocked to invest in the city's infrastructure while immigrants from the rest of Europe, the Middle East, and Asia came in droves to work in the factories that sprang up in

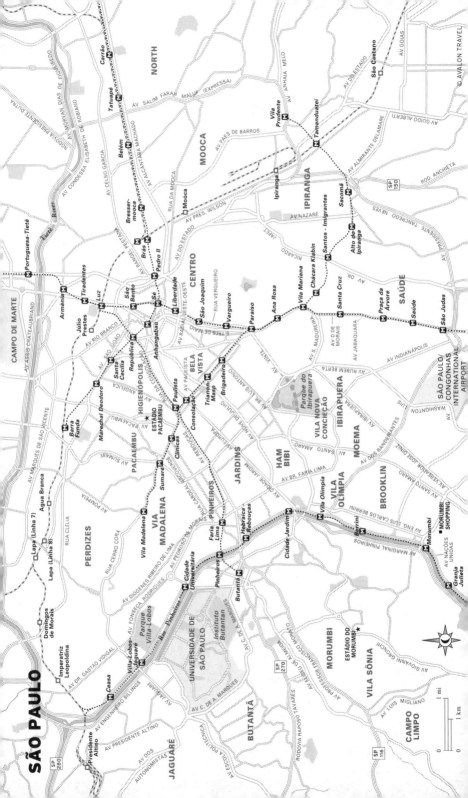

and around the city. As the population multiplied exponentially, commerce flourished and skyscrapers rose.

The nation's automobile industry started in São Paulo, and by the 1940s the country was experiencing its first traffic jams. To clear space for the six-lane *avenidas* and viaducts necessary to (attempt to) ease the eternal congestion of vehicles, buildings were knocked down with amazing speed—and, unfortunately, complete disdain for historical or architectural preservation. By the 1950s, São Paulo was the largest industrial center in Latin America. In the 1970s it had become the driving force of Brazil's "Economic Miracle," a period of exponential economic growth that attracted a vast new wave of immigrants from Brazil's poor northeastern states to the city and its suburban favelas.

Today "Sampa," as it's lovingly called by its residents, anchors the state of São Paulo, which boasts a population of 41 million and an economy that accounts for 34 percent of Brazil's GNP. São Paulo state concentrates much of the nation's industrial activities while its increasingly globalized capital reigns supreme as the most important commercial, financial, technological, and service center in Latin America.

However, despite its relative wealth and pockets of extremely sophisticated First World character, not to mention a large and continually expanding middle class, the same extreme social and economic inequalities that plague the rest of Brazil—as well as severe problems ranging from pollution to urban violence—are rampant here. While the working rich rely on the world's largest fleet of private helicopters to commute from posh suburbs to glittery office buildings, the less fortunate—and far more numerous—working poor spend hours snarled in lengthy traffic jams caused by the world's largest fleet of municipal buses, not to mention the cars. In 2011, the average Paulistano spent 2 hours and 42 minutes a day in traffic!

Just as varied as the city itself are its residents (known as Paulistanos). Aside from Portuguese, São Paulo boasts particularly large Italian, Japanese, and Lebanese communities. Working-class and "popular" *bairros* (neighborhoods) exist alongside heavily guarded, posh residential areas. Indeed, Sampa is all about highs and lows: If you're after foie gras, you'll find it, but you can just as easily enjoy a cheese-filled *pastel* washed down with sugarcane "juice" at a street market.

Although there's a neverending array of things to see and do, ultimately most foreigners who move to São Paulo do so because of the career opportunities it offers. The city is not just the economic and financial capital of Brazil, but of Latin America; São Paulo's thriving Bovespa is the largest stock exchange in Latin American and the third largest in the world (indeed, expats with financial know-how can make more money these days in Sampa than on Wall Street). Most major Brazilian corporations have their headquarters here, as do an increasing number of global multinationals—including banks, insurance, and health care companies, software and IT businesses, media and telecommunications companies, international law firms. All of them are looking to expand into Brazil, and many are offering expats two- to three-year work contracts and great relocation packages.

Earning power is an important consideration for those planning to move to São Paulo. According to the Mercer's 2012 Cost of Living Index (which measures the comparative cost of living for expats in 214 major international cities by comparing the cost of over 200 items, including housing, transport, food, clothing, household goods, and entertainment), between March 2011 and 2012, São Paulo was ranked as the 12th most expensive city in the world.

The Lay of the Land

São Paulo is located upon a plateau amidst the Serra do Mar mountain range in the southeastern part of São Paulo state. While most of the city's terrain is rolling, the Zona Norte (northern zone) is more elevated, as it fuses with the Serra da Cantareira mountain range, which is still covered with native Atlantic forest. Indeed, one of the bonuses of living in the city is the ease with which you (and millions of others) can easily (within two to three hours) get away to cool mountain retreats as well as some stunning beaches: The Atlantic Ocean is only 70 kilometers (33 miles) away.

Two major rivers run through São Paulo: the Tietê and its tributary, the Pinheiros. As a result of industrial waste and poor drainage, both are famously polluted, but a recently inaugurated cleanup project idealistically aims to return the Tietê to its pre-20th-century aquatic heyday when its banks were a major source of fresh water and recreation.

Known as Centro, São Paulo's bustling downtown core boasts few vestiges of its colonial past; its handful of baroque churches and 19th-century palaces are all the more striking for being hemmed in by a forest of skyscrapers. Surrounding Centro, the city's urban tapestry fans out into what were traditionally four geographical zones: Norte (North), Sul (South), Oeste (West), and Leste (East), but since 2008 these have been further subdivided into a total of nine zones. In addition to the five aforementioned regions, these include Noroeste (Northwest), Leste 2 (East 2), Sudeste (Southeast), and Centro-Sul (South Central). Within these geographic zones are 31 administrative subprefectures. Each of these is further divided into 91 districts, which may be further subdivided into *bairros* (neighborhoods) whose designations have been historically used by Paulistanos themselves (confusing matters even more is the fact that within some districts are *bairros* of the same name). Although more peripheral and less visible than those in Rio, São Paulo boasts more than 1,500 favelas—and the largest number of favela dwellers in the country: between 1.6 and 2 million people. Close to half of São Paulo's favelas are located in the Zona Sul.

CLIMATE

São Paulo has a subtropical climate, which is moderated by its elevation. As such, it enjoys distinctive seasons.

© MICHAEL SOMMERS

Avenida Paulista, São Paulo

Summers are usually not too hot (temperatures range from 17°C [63°F] to 32°C [90°F]) although the concrete combined with pollution can make temperatures seem higher and more uncomfortable. Built-up humidity is often punctuated by sometimes daily torrential thundershowers, which due to poor drainage systems, famously cause flooding throughout the city (with most devastating consequences in poorer neighborhoods). Winters are drier but see the same temperature fluctuations: from highs of 23°C (73°F) to lows of 11°C (52°F) and sometimes even lower at night. Transition seasons are more moderate. However, especially in recent years, São Paulo weather has been erratic and unpredictable. Within a few hours, temperatures and weather systems can change fairly drastically.

CULTURE

São Paulo's history and identity are inseparably linked to immigration. One of the most multicultural cities on the planet, the city was built by immigrants who arrived from all over Brazil and the world, lured by the endless opportunities available. As a result, Paulistanos are an incredibly diverse people who live, work, and mingle together in harmony, without the ethnic conflicts that affect some other major metropolises. For expats, it might offer a less "exotic" Brazilian living experience, but culturally, it's also easier to fit in and assimilate regardless of your background or lifestyle (the city has a large, diverse, and active gay and lesbian population).

Among the ethnic groups that have left their mark most deeply on the city are Italians (approximately 60 percent of the population boast at least one Italian ancestor), Portuguese, Spanish, Germans, Syrians, not to mention the largest Lebanese and Japanese populations outside of Lebanon and Japan.

PRIME LIVING LOCATIONS

© MICHAEL SOMMERS

Sampa is a thriving laboratory for contemporary Brazilian cuisine.

Many of the original downtown neighborhoods they settled continue as thriving ethnic communities. Bixiga, for example, also known as Little Italy, is cluttered with decades-old traditional trattorias and *pizzarias* (pizzerias) while the Japanese *bairro* of Liberdade is stuffed with emporiums selling Asian produce and hosts an open-air market where you can buy everything from medicinal herbs to bowls of stir-fried *yakissoba*, a mixture of noodles, meat, and vegetables that has become a Paulistano staple, second only to sushi.

The initial and largest waves of European and Asian immigration took place between the 1870s and the 1930s. In the following decades, poor migrants from the Brazilian Northeast boarded open-air trucks and traveled south to São Paulo in search of employment in the city's thriving industries and service sectors. As in Rio, many originally ended up in menial jobs; despite their contribution to the city's culture, there remains a certain lingering prejudice against *nordestinos* who are sometimes pejoratively referred to as *Baianos.*

São Paulo's cosmopolitanism is reflected in unparalleled eating opportunities as well as cultural offerings that rival those of New York and London. A vibrant arts scene, great museums, and an intense and varied nightlife ensure that Paulistanos—famed for their efficiency, organization, and work ethic (by Brazilian standards)—play harder than anyone else in Brazil.

Although Sampa's size can initially seem overwhelming, once you get to know the city, you realize that its neighborhoods function like a patchwork of villages stitched together. That said, like any international megacity, there is a certain hardness to the place; it can be an exhausting and sometimes harsh place to live, particularly if you don't have the money to lead a more comfortable life.

Daily Life

EXPAT RESOURCES

Given its large, if geographically dispersed, expat population, there are various ways of hooking up with other expats in São Paulo. Traditional social clubs that have been around for decades include the American Society of São Paulo, the British Commonwealth Council, and the Canadian International Society. The International Newcomers Society (INC) is a more diverse group, whose members hail from various countries but all of whom speak English. Aside from regularly scheduled and special social and networking events, many have social outreach programs that allow you to get involved in volunteering.

Another good place to meet expats is at church. Several churches hold English-language services in São Paulo. Among the most traditional are St. Paul's Anglican Church, in Chácara Santo Antônio, and Our Lady Help of Christians Catholic Church, in Chácara Flora.

Several online expat communities also have São Paulo groups that congregate in both virtual and real-life spheres. InterNations has various São Paulo groups that post online and meet offline as well (www.internations.org). Both the Expats São Paulo Facebook Page (www.facebook.com/expatsaopaulo) and Expat Blog's São Paulo Page (www.expat-blog.com) are also good sources for information and contacts.

SCHOOLS

São Paulo has a good dozen English-language and bilingual private schools for kids of all ages. Most of these private schools are located in upscale residential neighborhoods and the tuition reflects the locales. Monthly fees range from around R$3,000 for half-day preschool to R$5,000 for high school, and schools also charge staggeringly high one-time entrance fees of up to R$20,000. Most expats who are transferred to São Paulo for work purposes have school fees included as part of their compensation packages. Depending on the school and the age of your children, there are sometimes waiting lists for admission. Due to São Paulo's sprawl—and the omnipresent issue of traffic—it pays to consider schools that are as close as possible to where you're living.

Graded - The American School of São Paulo is the most sought-after English-language school for children from 2 to 18 years of age. Here, students can prepare for both U.S. and Brazilian high school diplomas as well as the International Baccalaureate (IB) diploma. In operation since 1920, in Morumbi, the school boasts a qualified staff and particularly diverse student body as well as lots of resources, including a cutting-edge arts center—great for stimulating kids' creativity—all of which come at a fairly hefty price.

Rivaling Graded in terms of popularity among expats is St. Paul's, which receives high marks for academic excellence and extracurricular activities, although it tends to attracts more Brits than Americans. Its curriculum combines elements from both the Brazilian and British National Core curricula and International Baccalaureate diploma program. The campus is located in the leafy Jardim Paulistano neighborhood.

Two other schools that receive high marks are the Chapel School and PACA (the Christian American School of São Paulo). Both are American international schools that are Catholic. Although student bodies are diverse, there is a religious component involved. Both schools are located in the Zona Sul: Chapel in Flora Chácara, situated within the upscale residential neighborhood of Santo Amaro, and PACA in Rio Bonito, which is only five minutes away from Sampa's famous Interlagos Formula 1 racetrack. Fees are considerably lower (within the R$1,000–2,000 range) at these schools. Curricula at both are designed to meet the needs of students preparing for American and Brazilian universities as well as the IB diploma (in the case of the Chapel School).

Fusing contemporary Canadian educational practices with a Brazilian curriculum, the bilingual Maple Bear Canadian School, which extends from preschool to the beginning of secondary school, has several locations in Alto de Pinheiros, Vila Nova Conceição (Moema), and Morumbi.

UNIVERSITIES

In terms of higher education, São Paulo is home to five of the top ten universities in the country: the Universidade de São Paulo (USP), Universidade Estadual de Campinas (Unicamp), Universidade Federal de São Paulo (UNIFESP), Universidade Estadual Paulista (UNESP), and Pontifícia Universidade Católica-São Paulo (PUC-SP).

Ranked as the number one university in Brazil and in Latin America in 2012 (in a survey of Latin American universities carried out by British consultancy firm Quacquarelli Symonds [www.topuniversities.com]), USP is internationally renowned for playing a leading role in diverse fields of research. Brazil's largest university, with campuses in seven cities throughout São Paulo state as well as the capital, this public university attracts some of the best students, and faculty from around the country and the world, particularly when it comes to its postgraduate programs. USP's scholarship is such that its students and faculty are responsible for close to 25 percent of all scientific papers produced in Brazil. The university also has a significant impact on Brazilian culture and society. USP operates four major museums along with orchestras and chorales. It also runs four hospital-schools that play a seminal role in the development of Brazil's public health policy.

Also popular with foreigners pursuing higher education in Brazil is UNICAMP, located in the well-to-do suburban-style town of Campinas, about an hour from downtown São Paulo. UNICAMP places considerable emphasis on being international, both in terms of its students and faculty. Unlike many Brazilian public universities, including USP, which were originally influenced by French systems of higher education, UNICAMP's model is more American (reflected by a considerable number of Americans on staff) in terms of course structure, methodology, and student-professor relationships. It's considered a leader in technology, health sciences, natural sciences, human sciences, and the arts.

Located in Pinheiros, PUC-SP is a private Catholic university with a very strong reputation, particularly in the humanities and arts. Like USP and UNICAMP, it also attracts its fair share of foreign students. Indeed all three universities boast multiple partnerships with international universities and higher learning institutions, which makes it easy for those who want to take advantage of study abroad programs.

HEALTH

As the largest health care center in Latin America, São Paulo boasts some of the best public and private hospitals and clinics in the country, not to mention the world. Two of the most distinguished private options are Hospital Albert Einstein, which has several units around town in addition to the main Morumbi branch, and Hospital Sírio Libanês, located just off Avenida Paulista, which is particularly renowned for its oncology center. Its emergency service possesses a special pediatric section. Popular with foreign expats, particularly Europeans, is the Hospital Alemão Oswaldo Cruz. Located in Paraíso, it was founded by German immigrants in 1897 and is known for complex surgeries performed by eminent physicians. Also founded in the 1890s by a group of American, British, and German immigrants, the Hospital Samaritano is a distinguished and centrally located modern facility in Higienópolis. All of the aforementioned hospitals have English-speaking staff. Specializing in maternity is the Hospital São Luiz, which boasts state-of-the-art obstetric centers at its Itaim Bibi and Anália Franco branches. Widely considered one of the best maternity hospitals in Brazil, its neonatal intensive care unit is a reference point in Latin America.

LEISURE ACTIVITIES

São Paulo boasts the most vibrant and varied cultural scene in Brazil. Surpassing even Rio (after all, Cariocas have the beach for entertainment), the city reunites the best of Brazil and a fantastic array of offerings from the rest of the world. Irrespective of whether they were born or migrated here, Paulistanos are notoriously innovative, and the city pulses with creative energy that spills over into all the arts.

The city has dozens of top-notch museums (the Museu de Arte São Paulo [MASP], the Pinacoteca do Estado, the Museu do Futebol) and a terrific number of cutting-edge

Paulistanos consider Parque Ibirapuera their "beach."

cultural centers patronized by major banks (Banco do Brasil, Itaú, Caixa Federal) as well as SESC (www.sesc.org.br), a private nonprofit organization dedicated to improving the lives of Brazilian workers, where most events are free, or dirt cheap. Large-screen cinemas abound (including one, the CineSESC, where you can sip caipirinhas while watching the film) and a plethora of theaters serve up both fringe productions and Brazilian versions of Broadway extravaganzas. The splendid turn-of-the-century Teatro Municipal is home to the highly reputed Orquestra Sinfônica Municipal and the city's classical ballet company, Balé da Cidade, while the Estação Júlio Prestes, a renovated train station, houses the Sala São Paulo, whose acoustics are considered among the best in the world.

Paulistanos love to eat out, and the city has an incredibly diverse restaurant scene with something for every palate and wallet. At the high end of the scale are world-class kitchens ruled by innovative chefs that traffic in both traditional and contemporary Brazilian cuisine while at the other end of the spectrum, numerous bakeries, cafés, and bars offer bites, snacks, and sandwiches. Due its diverse immigrant population, the city is rich in international cuisines, with special mention going to Middle Eastern, Japanese, and Italian offerings (many Italians claim that the pizza found in São Paulo is superior to that found in Italy).

For those fond of nightlife, Sampa boasts one of the hippest, most happening and varied scenes this hemisphere has ever seen with cafés, lounges, bars, and clubs that cater to every walk of life. Unlike other Brazilian cities, whose tropical climes create nocturnal options that take place outdoors, Sampa's indoor night spots invest heavily in décor, ambiance, and vibe.

Those seeking respite from the concrete jungle will find a few welcoming green oases in and around the city. The most famous and centrally located is Parque Ibirapuera (which Paulistanos refer to as their "beach"). Near the southern outskirts of the city, the Parque do Estado is a vast expanse of native Atlantic rainforest with walking trails and picnic areas as well as a botanical garden and a zoo.

With its inflated prices, São Paulo can no longer be considered the shopping paradise it once was. In a country that takes great pride in its *shoppings,* Sampa's are by far the biggest and glitziest, and a very far cry from suburban strip malls in the United States. Unlike many Brazilian cities, São Paulo also possesses a large selection of boutiques, particularly concentrated in Jardins (a Brazilian version of Rodeo Drive) and Vila Madalena (more funky alternative fare and lots of art). However, shopping in Sampa doesn't have to be synonymous with shelling out wads of cash. The city has its share of designer outlets, secondhand stores, and flea markets. Amazing bargains can be found in two areas of Centro—Rua 25 de Março (www.guiada25.com.br) and Bom Retiro (www.omelhordobomretiro.com.br)—which traffic in cheap goods and designer knockoffs.

VOLUNTEERING

If you're interested in getting involved with volunteering in São Paulo, a good place to start, especially if you also want to meet some other expats, is by contacting the American Society of São Paulo (www.americansociety.com.br), whose community outreach programs provide homes, security, and education to orphaned, neglected, and abused children from the city's poorest neighborhoods. The society's website has a list of children's nonprofit organizations that accept volunteers, along with phone numbers and email addresses for English-speaking contacts. Another good source for volunteering is the São Paulo Center for Volunteering (www.voluntariado.org.br), a nonprofit organization devoted to matching volunteers with over 1,200 social organizations operating in and around the city.

Where to Live

Like Rio, in recent years, São Paulo's real estate market has exploded. As a result, both those in the mood to rent or to buy should expect to pay more than they would in cities such as New York and London. In the year 2011 alone, housing prices in São Paulo rose by an average of 20 percent while rents rose by 14 percent. A good online source for buying and renting is www.zap.com.br. Real estate agents that have experience working with expats include Anglo Americana (www.angloamericana.com.br), Maber (www.maber.com.br), and VNC (www.vnc.com.br).

The neighborhoods listed below comprise only a handful of those that are most popular with expats and with middle- and upper-class Brazilians and which tend to be somewhat central. São Paulo is an enormous city with a great many living options (including ones that are cheaper, albeit not as conveniently located or safe).

BUYING PRICES

Although there are predictions that a housing bubble could occur, as of 2012 prices for real estate continued to rise in São Paulo. Demand continues to outstrip supply and prices are astronomical. For this reason, unless you're filthy rich, you'll probably want to rent as opposed to buy. At the end of 2011, the average price of a new apartment in São Paulo was R$350,000. Based on size, the two most expensive neighborhoods in São Paulo were Jardim Europa (Jardins) and Vila Nova Conceição (Moema), where in 2011 new apartments cost R$16,400 and R$15,600 per square meter, respectively, which explains three-bedroom apartments priced at upward of R$1.5 million.

Other *bairros* are less astronomical, but still pricey although there is considerable variation. In early 2012, the average price of a three-bedroom apartment in the Centro's Higienópolis was well over R$1 million while options in Santa Cecília ranged from R$700,000 to R$900,000 (with prices per square meter nearing R$6,800 and R$5,900, respectively). In funky Vila Madalena, an average three bedroom went for between R$800,000 and R$1 million.

RENTAL PRICES

Rental prices listed below are rough monthly averages based on July 2012 values. Within a given neighborhood, rents may vary considerably according to factors such as location within the *bairro*, views, and building amenities. The one bedrooms listed below are all roughly between 30 and 60 square meters (100–200 square feet) while the three bedrooms measure between 90 and 120 square meters (300–400 square feet).

CENTRAL SÃO PAULO

Central São Paulo comprises the city's historic heart and soul. Busy, dynamic, and endlessly interesting, Centro and surrounding areas are also fairly chaotic, although quiet, upscale residential pockets exist, such as Higienópolis and Jardins. However, if you want to be right in the swing of things, the central *bairros* are a great option. Public transport options combined with shorter distances mean you can easily do everything you want on foot. And there is so much to do: every imaginable type of bar, restaurant, club, theater, cinema, museum, and shopping option, not to mention some appealing, if sometimes dilapidated, older areas. If you have a fondness for architecture and history, these neighborhoods are the only ones where you'll be treated to some of the vestiges of centuries and decades gone by. Thankfully, both public and private entities are finally investing in Sampa's sadly neglected Centro, and this is making some of the lovely older buildings appealing.

Higienópolis and Pacaembu

The attractive residential *bairro* of Higienópolis developed during the late 1890s. Its elevated heights offered a "hygienic" alternative to the frequent floods and epidemics that put an increasing damper on life in the city's downtown. By 1900, Sampa's wealthiest families were flocking to Higienópolis in droves. The opulent mansions they built in the early 1900s gave way to seductively streamlined art deco and modernist apartment buildings of the '30s, '40s, and '50s. Although only a few of the houses remain, many of the apartment buildings are still standing; as a result, this is one of Sampa's most attractive and atmospheric neighborhoods and the apartments tend to be big, beautiful, and sprawling (although often bereft of parking).

Higienópolis remains one of São Paulo's most traditional and wealthiest residential *bairros*. It possesses a significant Jewish population, both secular and orthodox, which

Higienópolis is filled with beautiful Modernist apartment buildings.

accounts for the many kosher products available in the neighborhood's numerous delicatessens. There are quite a few pleasant little restaurants and cafés as well as small stores, some health clubs, Parque Buenos Aires, and the upscale Shopping Higienópolis.

Equally upscale and verdant, but more sprawling and exclusively residential, the adjacent *bairro* of Pacaembu came of age in the 1940s, when it became all the rage for Paulistano high society to live here. Its eponymous art deco soccer stadium still houses games as well as the Museu de Futebol.

Expect average rents for a one bedroom in Higienópolis to hover between R$1,800 and R$3,000 with three bedrooms costing around R$3,200–4,500 and upward.

Santa Cecília

Higienópolis's scrappier, more dilapidated, but also more lively sibling has lots of texture and rough bohemian charm, not to mention some great corner shops, restaurants, and *botecos*. This old neighborhood is seedy around the edges, with its share of homeless itinerants, and it suffers from its share of noise and pollution. On the upside, it boasts a great central location (with good access to bus and Metrô service) and more affordable rents. If you like a bit of urban grit, this is a good choice that is safer than other parts of Centro and is trending upward. Expect the cost to rent a one bedroom to be R$1,300–2,000 while a three bedroom will cost anywhere between R$3,000 and R$4,000.

Bela Vista

One of São Paulo's most traditional old residential neighborhoods, Bela Vista covers a large hilly area between Centro and Avenida Paulista. Socioeconomically, it runs the gamut from upper-middle class to working class. Closer to the Avenida, in the region known as Morro dos Ingleses, you'll find lots of swank high-rise apartments. These gradually grow smaller and simpler as you make your way down to Centro toward Bixiga, a.k.a. Little Italy, an area filled with decades-old pizzerias, cantinas, and pastry shops as well as lots of small apartment buildings and houses, in various states of upkeep (Bixiga has had its ups and downs). Rents vary, but range from R$1,000 to R$1,500 for a one bedroom to R$3,000–4,500 for a three bedroom (the latter tend to be in more upscale buildings).

Jardins

Modeled after the British garden suburbs of the early 20th century, Jardins (Gardens) is a wealthy and perennially fashionable neighborhood whose name conjures up lifestyles of Brazil's rich and famous (although expats love it too). Jardins actually embraces four separate "gardens": Jardim Paulista, Jardim Paulistano, Jardim América, and Jardim Europa.

Bordering Avenida Paulista, the exclusive high-rise condos of Jardim Paulista (part of the district known as Cerqueira César that spills over onto both sides of Avenida Paulista) sit ensconced amidst a sea of über-trendy restaurants, cafés, and upscale boutiques—concentrated along Rua Oscar Freire—selling the fashionable wares of leading Brazilian and international designers.

Leading down to Avenida Brigadeiro Faria Lima, on the edge of Pinheiros, Jardim Paulista turns into Jardim Paulistano, an area with still more trendy restaurants and bars. Meanwhile, Avenida Estados Unidos marks the beginning of Jardim América and Jardim Europa—two residential enclaves that are even more exclusive and wealthy, as evidenced by the opulent mansions that peek out from behind heavily guarded, thickly hedged, electrically fenced-in estates.

There are pros and cons to living in Jardins. On the upside, the location is very central, especially if you opt for an apartment in Jardim Paulista. Aside from proximity to Avenida Paulista, with tons of buses and the Metrô, Jardins has amenities galore and you can really walk everywhere. The fact that it is older than other upscale neighborhoods farther south means you can find lodgings in better built, larger, and more atmospheric buildings. Jardins also has a great neighborhood vibe, with tons of places where you can shop, idle, and hang out. However, living amidst McMansions and Gucci boutiques is not for everyone and you might grow weary of the excess of beefy

© MICHAEL SOMMERS

view of Jardins toward the Zona Sul

EXPAT PROFILE: FAMILY BENEFITS

Author of the blog Keeping Up with the Joneses *(http://popojonesandme.blogspot. com.br), Maike, her husband, Porter, and their two-and-a-half-year-old son moved to São Paulo in 2011 from Boston. Here Maike talks about their move.*

WHY THEY CAME

Porter was a doctor but wanted to follow a less traditional path in medicine, so he decided to do an MBA at Harvard. Upon earning his degree he met a doctor from São Paulo's Albert Einstein Hospital, one of the foremost hospitals in the world. After various phone interviews and flying down in 2010, he was hired in 2011 to be in charge of the hospital's international partnerships (the hospital's goal is to be fully bilingual). Coming out of school in the United States, there were very few career opportunities, and this was an influential position. Our family is young and we thought this was a good opportunity for Porter to advance quickly in his career. Many multinationals want people who have worked abroad; they want that commitment. For us, it was a huge leap of faith, but we did it.

THE MOVING PROCESS

I don't know a single expat who moved here without a relocation package because the moving costs are so high. The hospital hired a Brazilian relocation company that worked with the Brazilian Consulate to help with visa procedures. Fortunately, there is a consulate in Boston because we had to go there a lot. It's a complicated and expensive process with lots of paperwork and red tape. Our permanent visas took six months from start to finish.

BEING AN EXPAT SPOUSE

Although I had worked in politics in my home state of Utah, I had taken time off to raise our son. When we arrived in Brazil, I didn't think there would be opportunities for me. However, people at the hospital asked my husband if I taught English and that's how I ended up becoming a part-time language coach. São Paulo is a wealthy city, and people are willing to pay a lot to learn from natives with experience. I have a business background and that helps a lot because I work mostly with doctors who want to improve their English for professional purposes. Ironically, it's much more lucrative for me doing coaching here than working in politics in the States.

MAKING FRIENDS

When my husband was 19, he worked as a missionary in Brazil for two years in Curitiba, so he knew the language and culture and that helped a lot. We also knew two Brazilian couples from Harvard who had returned to São Paulo. Through them we made connections with other Brazilians. I know a lot of expats who socialize with each other and

---

security guards not to mention the R$35 martinis. Although you can find one bedrooms that start at R$1,500, the bulk of options will hover between R$2,000 and R$3,500, while most three bedrooms are in the R$3,000–4,500 range.

ZONA SUL

Stretching south from Jardins are newer, sprawling neighborhoods into which are packed some of the city's richest and poorest *bairros,* often cheek by jowl. In recent years, much of Sampa's businesses have moved into this area. Vila Olímpia, Itaim Bibi, Brooklin Novo, Morumbi, and Santo Amaro, in particular, concentrate the headquarters of major banks and multinationals. For this reason—and for the fact that many top Brazilian private and international schools can be found here—these *bairros* and other surrounding neighborhoods are very popular with expats, particularly families and those who relocate to São Paulo to work for major companies.

only speak English. But it really limits your contacts if you don't speak Portuguese. We made a commitment to not hang out only with people we knew before and to not speak just English. We've made friends from our condo complex and our son's school and swimming class—all of whom are Brazilian. In terms of expats, I met some friends through services at the Mormon church and the American Society of São Paulo.

LEARNING PORTUGUESE
I study with a tutor twice a week, but it's a slow process. I don't use it every day because I work in English and talk to my husband in English. A lot of expats never speak Portuguese. They come down on three-year contracts with multinationals and have the mind-set that they will just be here for a while.

SCHOOLS
The American expats I know send their kids to American schools, and we would have done so if our son was older. Because he's only two and a half, we thought this presented a great opportunity for him to be bilingual, so we sent him to a top-ranked Brazilian private school called Porto Seguro, recommended by Brazilian friends in Boston. It was a process to get him in, with a six-month waiting list, which is common. We're the only U.S. expats I know who send our son to a Brazilian school.

LIVING IN SÃO PAULO
We live in Morumbi, which is more of a suburb, with lots of high-rises, but also favelas. There are lots of schools here and lots of families. Everyone lives in largo condo complexes with many facilities—pools, gyms, playgrounds—because kids can't go outside the condo complexes and parks are hard to get to. I miss the convenience of the States; simple things like running errands involve more planning here. Traffic is frustrating. Do I really want to drive for an hour to get to the restaurant 6 kilometers [3.7 miles] away?

THE FUTURE
I think we'll be here for a least five years. It depends on the opportunities in terms of my husband's career. Eventually I'd like to go back to the States. When my son is older, I'd like to be somewhere more permanent. But right now things are open ended. We follow opportunities rather than insisting on living in a certain place.

A WORD OF ADVICE FOR OTHER EXPATS
It really helps if you have a close relationship with your family because there are going to be lonely moments when you feel isolated. If you move here alone, make friends; ultimately, what endears you to a place is people.

PRIME LIVING LOCATIONS

Ibirapuera, Vila Nova Conceição, and Moema
Parque Ibirapuera is São Paulo's equivalent of Central Park. Like the neighborhoods surrounding its New York alter ego, those bordering Ibirapuera—particularly Ibirapuera and Vila Nova Conceição—are the most coveted and expensive in São Paulo. Many of the country's highest paid bankers and executives who work in the environs of Avenida Faria Lima and Avenida Juscelino Kubitschek live in the region; millionaires are particularly fond of the vicinity surrounding Praça Pereira Coutinho, where the fashionable wares of leading Brazilian and international designers are sold.

Despite the lofty prices, the area is a favorite with expats who are lured by the relatively central location, tranquil tree-shaded streets, and proximity to the vast oasis of a park with its many museums, jogging and biking paths, and endless array of events and free concerts. A big advantage of these neighborhoods is that you don't need to own a car; instead you can rely upon a combination of walking and relatively short cab rides (public transport is poor). Both Ibirapuera and Vila Nova Conceição lie within the larger district of Moema, which also possesses more affordable, middle-class enclaves the farther one gets from the park. Well equipped with restaurants, bars, and commercial establishments, Moema is conveniently adjacent to Brazil's busiest domestic airport, Congonhas.

Depending on amenities, in Vila Nova Conceição, expect one-bedroom apartments to cost between R$2,000 and R$3,000 while three bedrooms will be R$4,000–6,000.

Itaim Bibi, Vila Olímpia, and Brooklin

Until the early 20th century, much of the area south of Jardins was occupied by rural estates. It wasn't until the 1970s, with the construction of Avenida Berrini and Avenida Kubitschek, that these neighborhoods began to develop vertically. However, their big boom came in the 1990s, when they began to usurp Avenida Paulista's role as São Paul's financial and business hub. Today, a vast majority of banks, multinationals, and high-tech companies (Google, Microsoft, Samsung, etc.) are all headquartered in and around Itaim Bibi (the name of both the *bairro* and the larger district that embraces it) as well as in Vila Olímpia and Brooklin; if you happen to have a job in these areas, living close by can be an advantage. At the same time, another major draw of Itaim and Vila Olímpia is that they are overflowing with trendy bars, restaurants, and nightclubs (some of them too trendy; many vastly overpriced). This, combined with the excess of soulless modern high-rises and serious noise and traffic congestion may explain why these neighborhoods are less popular with foreigners than young, ambitious, upwardly mobile Paulistanos.

Farther south, Brooklin has found more favor with foreigners who appreciate the green spaces and residential flavor of this old German neighborhood. Although well served by commercial amenities, much of the oldest residential part, known as Brooklin Velho, consists of middle- to upper-middle-class apartments and houses. Meanwhile, Brooklin Novo, which is bisected by Avenida Berrini, is home to luxury condos along with the offices of major multinationals, media companies, and consulates. Its futuristic skyline features some of the tallest—and most *Blade Runner*-esque—skyscrapers in Latin America. In 2008, the inauguration of the Ponte Octávio Frias de Oliveira, a cable-stayed bridge spanning the Pinheiros River, became one of Sampa's newest and most recognized landmarks and sealed Brooklin's similarity with its American namesake. Depending on amenities (which vary), expect to fork out an average of R$2,000–4,000 for a one bedroom and R$3,000–4,500 in Brooklin.

Morumbi

Although officially situated within the Zona Oeste, Morumbi is usually lumped together with other wealthy neighborhoods of the Zona Sul. Like many of them, Morumbi began life as farmland. In fact, the region originally consisted of one massive estate, the Fazenda de Morumbi, owned by an Englishman named John Rudge who brought the first tea plants from India to Brazil. It wasn't until the 1950s that the area began to be urbanized. Originally, it was wealthy Paulistanos who built mansions amidst the sinuous, tree-lined streets, but beginning in the 1980s the area became increasingly vertical, particularly around the main commercial artery of Avenida Giovanni Gronchi.

Today, Morumbi holds the dubious honor of being one of São Paulo's (and Brazil's) most flagrant examples of social inequality. The district is simultaneously home to some of Brazil's richest and poorest neighborhoods with opulent mansions and São Paulo's chicest mall, Shopping Cidade Jardim, within spitting distance of favelas such as Paraísopolis, the largest in the city. It also shelters the state government palace, São Paulo's top hospital (Hospital Albert Einstein), and the famous Morumbi soccer stadium.

Despite the distance from the center of town, predominantly residential Morumbi is popular with expats because of its proximity to many multinationals. Families in particular like its location near many top international schools and the abundance of green space; one of Sampa's most verdant *bairros,* the region boasts two large parks, Alfredo Volpi and Burle Marx. Aside from mansions of the rich and famous, most dwellings are located within vast condominium complexes filled with amenities (including more green spaces, as well as pools, gyms, playgrounds, barbecue areas) and boasting serious security. The living can be easy, but you might feel as if you're in a gilded cage, especially since this is one neighborhood where it's hard to get around—or get anywhere—by foot. In fact, a minimum of one car is a must. Not surprisingly, many expats—like their Brazilian counterparts—rely on drivers.

Rents for one bedrooms in Morumbi start as low as R$1,200, but average around R$1,500–2,500. Rent for a three bedroom is in the vicinity of R$2,000–4,000.

ZONA OESTE

Less wealthy than the neighborhoods of the Zona Sul, the Zona Oeste neighborhoods of Pinheiros, Perdizes, and Vila Madalena are also less traditionally popular with expats in search of housing. However, more eclectic and more affordable, they make for interesting alternatives, particularly because they allow you to experience living amidst a much more mixed cross section of Paulistanos. A bonus of these neighborhoods is that they're relatively well served by public transport (bus and Metrô) with easy access to Centro, Jardins, and the business districts of Itaim, Berrini, and Morumbi, which means you don't necessarily need a car to live here.

Pinheiros and Perdizes

Both a district and a *bairro,* Pinheiros dates back to São Paulo's beginnings when indigenous groups and Portuguese Jesuits settled along the banks of the Rio Pinheiros in the 1500s. Urbanization, however, only came on the heels of São Paulo's 19th-century coffee boom. Italian immigrants in the late 1800s were followed by Japanese immigrants in the early 1900s. During the 20th century, industries and businesses blossomed while the area morphed into one of the city's most traditional middle-class neighborhoods.

Little remains of Pinheiros's past. In fact, aesthetically it underwhelms with a notable absence of green space and an excess of nondescript commercial and residential high-rises, although some older smaller buildings and blocks of houses survive (the upscale hilltop region known as Alto dos Pinheiros boasts some very grand ones). On the upside, Pinheiros boasts some interesting boutiques, galleries, restaurants, and a vibrant nightlife scene. Unpretentious and unfashionable, it has a nice socioeconomic

EXPAT PROFILE: WHEN THINGS DON'T PAN OUT

Meredith, 35, moved to São Paulo from New York City in 2010, with her Brazilian partner, Dagmar. Here she talks about her experience.

WHY SHE CAME

Dagmar and I were both working for Bloomberg, a news company in New York. The economy was very turbulent in New York and there were a lot of layoffs at the company. But the CEO believed there was potential for business in Brazil, and Dagmar was transferred to develop it. We'd lived together for five years, so I asked to be transferred too.

HOW SHE CAME

Although there was no position for me (I was a manager for Internet projects; Dagmar was head of Brazilian TV), Bloomberg sponsored my permanent visa based on Brazil's recognition of us as a same-sex couple (*união estável*). The company knew this would be the easiest way for me to obtain a permanent visa and work card, and they paid for the lawyers. We had to do a lot of stuff here in Brazil, and it would have been easier if I had applied in New York (I would have saved myself a trip back home).

THE MOVING PROCESS

Our first three months in São Paulo—it took that long for our stuff to be shipped and to clear customs—we lived in the Hilton in Morumbi, which was close to Dagmar's work, but far away from everything else. It was expensive to get everywhere and you couldn't walk around. I was looking for apartments and spending a fortune on taxis. Dagmar had been to São Paulo before on business. We looked at a lot of maps and did a lot of research. It was exciting to think we could afford a larger space here than in New York. I looked at a few places and was surprised how small the newer apartments were. Older apartments were enormous, and we found a three bedroom in a great old building in Jardins, with eight floors and amenities we'd never have in New York, parking, a door attendant, and an elevator, which many old buildings don't have.

LEARNING PORTUGUESE

I took 40 private lessons at a school called Brazil Station in New York and learned the basics. I had been to Brazil around twelve times and living with a Brazilian led me to take an interest in Portuguese. Here, however, we speak English, so my Portuguese hasn't advanced as much, although I have a teacher that I found through Craigslist. I can now understand more and read well. I interviewed for a job in Portuguese and can speak to Dagmar's parents without embarrassment. We go out a lot with friends, but it's much easier one on one than in a group setting. I like Portuguese; I think it's a fun language. I like the sound. And I like the music a lot...axé, samba rock, old samba, bossa nova, some forró, baile funk, Brazilian reggae . . .

MAKING FRIENDS

Even when Dagmar was working in New York, she had a team here and she had Brazilian friends in New York. Once we

and immigrant mix. On the streets, you can meet and greet neighbors, buy fresh bread at the local bakery, and hang out in neighborhood bars. Although there aren't any favelas in the vicinity, be aware that some patches are sketchy, particularly the area surrounding the Marginal Pinheiros.

Home to one of the country's best private universities, PUC-São Paulo, neighboring Perdizes has a significant population of students and professors and a pleasant, youthful vibe that spills over into the surrounding area. It's a good place to live if you're studying abroad since it's also not too far from USP, whose sprawling campus is located in the vast neighboring district of Butantã (also worth checking out for affordable housing).

came here, we met new friends through old friends. If you know people here, it's very nice. But it can be very lonely if you can't keep yourself entertained. Everyone lives in a different place, and I know people who don't leave work until 8pm and then get stuck in traffic, so it's even harder to connect. Getting across town is impossible with traffic—a 15-minute drive could take 2 hours.

MAKING A LIVING

The most important thing is to learn Portuguese quickly and well. There's a big misconception that you can get away with just speaking English, but everyone speaks Portuguese. Brazilian companies here don't care if you speak English; only foreign companies demand English speakers. I've had access to a lot of people involved in media, communications, and broadcast systems, and English is not important.

I've had a lot of false starts. I DJ as a hobby, and I worked in some clubs here but got tired of just getting paid in cocktails. At one point I thought of opening up my own business, a lounge. But everyone said it would be expensive and problematic. Brazilians all told me that people would steal from me and that the bureaucracy is just too difficult. I also had some freelance gigs, but they didn't work out. One was to create a project for a Brazilian company to help set up a traffic system, but after months of work I was let go after submitting a proposal. I was excited about the possibility of getting a permanent job, but in the end, I was treated as if I were an intern.

LIVING IN SÃO PAULO

I'm still getting to know the city. I like to check out museums and parks. There are some hidden gems. I also like to be able to go to the coast. But right now, I'm a little bit down on São Paulo. It's overpriced, pretentious, very classist. It's also violent. There are a lot of robberies. You can't use your laptop in public. I've never seen anything bad, but I've heard lots of firsthand stories. I've never felt in danger, but I've seen things happen, and it doesn't matter who you are and where you live. Initially, I was attracted to the chaos, but then after living within chaos for two years, I'm tired of feeling guarded and unsafe.

LEAVING BRAZIL

Last year Dagmar got laid off. She received a compensation package and health insurance for both of us. Since then she's had a few offers, but nothing panned out. So now we are planning to go back to New York. I'd like to come back to Brazil at some point in my life, but I've already given it three years. We've discussed dividing our time between North and South America and we'll pursue it. I've met a lot of interesting and nice people here; I think Brazilians are more friendly and accommodating, which I appreciate. There are things I know I'll miss, but I think I'd regret passing up opportunities in New York now, even though my life there might be a little boring. I've changed a lot since coming here.

Vila Madalena

Within the district of Pinheiros, Vila Madalena is Sampa's bohemian *bairro* par excellence. Originally, the area was a blue-collar neighborhood where workers lived in small bungalows surrounded by gardens where they raised livestock and vegetables. In the 1970s, students and professors from nearby University of São Paulo (USP)—along with artists, musicians, and hippies—began to migrate to the "Vila" for affordable housing combined with a relaxed bucolic setting. Many have never left, which explains the lingering intellectual-artist vibe, not to mention the high number of vegetarian restaurants and yoga studios. It also accounts for street names

© MICHAEL SOMMERS

bohemian Vila Madalena

such as Rua da Harmonia (Harmony), Rua da Simpatia (Sympathy), and Rua do Girassol (Sunflower).

By day, Vila Madalena is a laid-back place to wander around. Rua Aspiculta and surrounding streets are lined with funky boutiques, secondhand stores, and numerous artists' ateliers. At night, the *bairro* buzzes with activity as its many restaurants, bars, and clubs fill up with a mixed and alternative crowd (ambient noise can be a downside). Today, Vila Madalena is not as affordable as it once was, but it's truly one of São Paulo's most unique and appealing neighborhoods, particularly because much of it still consists of bungalows and houses that provide a welcome contrast to the ubiquitious high-rises. Rents here are not as cheap as they once were, but you can get a one bedroom for R$1,500–2,500 and a three bedroom for R$3,000–4,000.

Getting Around

São Paulo has an extensive public transportation system consisting of a relatively limited but efficient Metrô and a far-reaching, if slightly more confusing, bus system. There is also no shortage of taxis, which come in especially handy at night.

METRÔ

São Paulo's Metrô system is clean, efficient, and safe. The only problem is its small size: Although its five principal lines are slowly being extended and others are under construction, the system is unable to meet the demands of so much traffic. However, you will find the Metrô convenient for zipping around Centro and going up and down Avenida Paulista as well as out to Pinheiros and Faria Lima and getting to bus stations and Guarulhos airport. Beware of the Metrô during rush hour, when crowds can be really daunting. Tickets are sold in the station, but for security reasons kiosks are only open 6am–10pm. Lines to purchase a ticket can also be pretty long, making purchasing multiples a good idea. If you plan to take a Metrô and bus (or vice versa), it is cheaper to buy a *bilhete de integração* at a Metrô station or on a bus, which allows you to transfer from one to the other. For updated prices and a map of lines, check out the Metrô's bilingual website. You can also visit www.vademetro.com.br to find out how to get to sights throughout the city by Metrô by typing in your destination.

© MICHAEL SOMMERS

Motoboys (many of them daredevils) are endemic in São Paulo.

BUSES

Buses go everywhere in São Paulo—except when they're stuck in rush-hour traffic. Despite a fleet of over 10,000 vehicles, buses can get very crowded. Moreover, figuring out which bus goes where is a bit confusing. Final destinations are marked on the front while major stops are listed along the side. After clambering aboard at the front of the bus, you pay the *cobrador* (collector) in the middle and go through the turnstile. The exit is at the rear. You can pay for your fare in cash. An alternative is to purchase an electronic ticket, known as a *bilhete único*. Sold and rechargeable at SPTransportes kiosks at bus terminals and at lottery agencies, these cards allow you to make four separate bus trips in three hours for a single fare. For information about itineraries, **Transporte Público de São Paulo** (www.sptrans.com.br) offers a free number to call (156). The website also lets you type in a starting point and final destination and then provides you with possible buses and routes to take.

TAXIS

Taxis are the best and safest way of navigating São Paulo by night. By day, they can be useful for getting to specific destinations off the Metrô or main bus lines, although like other vehicles, they can get stuck in traffic during rush hour. Moreover, considering São Paulo's immensity, if you start shuttling back and forth across the city, you will rack up a small fortune in cab fares. *Taxis comuns* are the least expensive taxis. You can either hail one in the street (unless it's raining) or find one at a *posto* (taxi stand). *Rádio taxis* are a bit larger and a bit more expensive. Major companies include **Coopertaxi** (tel. 11/3511-1919) and **Ligue Taxi** (tel. 11/3873-3030).

DRIVING

Although São Paulo is definitely a city where cars rule (a whopping 25 percent of the city's constructed area is given over to parking), you'll have to possess vast amounts of patience to drive here. Traffic is a nightmare, parking is a nightmare, and rainstorms create nightmarish flooding (streets are instantly inundated because of poor drainage). Add carjackings, the exhaust fumes of thousands of idling buses, and the hundreds of daredevil *motoboys* who weave in and out of traffic on scooters, and you'll really appreciate sidewalks. Drivers also have to keep in mind the *rodízio* (rotation) system; to ease traffic during rush hour (7am-10am and 5pm-8pm Mon.–Fri.), cars must stay off the roads during such times if their license plates end in certain numbers: Monday, 1 and 2; Tuesday, 3 and 4; Wednesday, 5 and 6; Thursday, 7 and 8; Friday, 9 and 0.

That said, depending on what neighborhood you're living in (i.e., basically everywhere outside of central São Paulo), you pretty much have to have a car (or two)—especially if you have children. Upsides of having a car are avoiding crowded public transportation, getting out and about at nights and on weekends, and enjoying the ease with which you can get away from São Paulo itself to explore the coast or mountains of São Paulo state, particularly small towns or isolated beaches that are hard to reach by bus.

BIKING

São Paulo has 110 kilometers (68 mi) of bike paths although most of them are located in recreational areas. Biking amidst the urban fray is pretty hazardous but being able to weave through traffic means you can often reach a destination more quickly on two wheels than on four. The Metrô possesses 17 *bicicletários* where you can park your bike for free and also borrow a bike. To do so, you'll need a CPF, proof of residence, and a credit card with a limit of R$350.

MINAS, CENTRAL-WEST, AND SOUTH

Minas Gerais and the states within the Central-West and South of Brazil constitute vast and distinctive regions and are often less well known by foreigners than Brazil's Southeast, Northeast, and North, which are much bigger tourist draws. Though geographically, historically, and culturally these regions share both marked similarities and differences, what broadly unites them all is that, aside from a few colonial outposts and mining towns, they were mostly settled and subsequently developed at a much later date than the cities and states along Brazil's Northeast and Southeast coasts. Collectively, these regions comprise some of Brazil's most robust and fastest-growing economies due to a mixture of industry, services, and agriculture coupled with well-organized, pleasant cities whose standards of living are among the highest in the country.

MINAS, CENTRAL-WEST, AND SOUTH

© AVALON TRAVEL

Minas Gerais

Locked within steep mountain ranges and with no coast of its own, Brazil's fourth-largest and second most populous state of Minas Gerais is a country unto itself. Considering its size and unique history, it's not surprising that Mineiros have a different style and rhythm, with distinctive accents, expressions, and *jeitos*, or ways of doing things. Mineiros are known for being taciturn and nonconfrontational as well as extremely hospitable. They're also famed lovers of cachaça, an unsurprising habit given that they produce the finest *pinga* in the country.

Minas first gained attention in the 1700s when Portuguese adventurers discovered that the lush mountains in the center of the state were abundantly stocked with precious stones, diamonds, and especially gold. The subsequent gold rush was one of the biggest ever recorded. Throughout the first half of the 18th century fortune hunters from all over the world descended en masse upon the hills of the *minas gerais* (general mines). Portugal's profligate royal family profited the most from the tremendous riches mined by African slaves and shipped off to Europe. However, some gold managed to remain in Brazil. In burgeoning mining towns such as Ouro Preto (Black Gold), it was used to build opulent mansions and stunning baroque churches whose richness is unparalleled in the New World.

Today, while firmly rooted in the present, these colonial mining towns—the most famous of which include Ouro Preto, Mariana, Sabará, São João del Rei, Tiradentes, Congonhas, and Diamantina—continue to have one foot in the past. Although some (Ouro Preto, Tiradentes, and Diamantina) have weathered the centuries more successfully and with more charm than others (Sabará, Congonhas, and São João del Rei), they all offer a wealth of artistic and cultural diversions as well as exposure to authentic Mineiro life. It is this exciting juxtaposition and overlapping of past and present, baroque and modern, that makes Minas Gerais so unique.

Indeed, 21st-century Minas Gerais is a forward-looking place. An economic powerhouse—the state's GDP is third after São Paulo and Rio, and its industry is second only to São Paulo—in 2010, the state economy expanded by 10.9 percent, exceeding even China's growth rate. To this day, mining continues to be a major economic force that lures Brazilians and expats alike (the world's second-largest mining company, Vale, is based in Minas). Other key industries include metallurgy, steel, auto manufacturing, and agribusiness (Minas is a major producer of meat, milk, and some of the finest coffee in the world). The state also has a thriving telecommunications, electronics, and technology sector: Located in the southern part of the state, the town of Santa Rita do Sapucaí is known as Brazil's Silicon Valley.

Most expats who come to Minas settle in its dynamic capital of Belo Horizonte, located in the center of the state. Brazil's third-largest city in terms of metropolitan area, the cosmopolitan capital of 2.6 million boasts one of the highest standards of living in Brazil. The city's economy is heavily based on the service sector. As a result of government and private investment, it's also becoming an internationally renowned IT and biotechnology center.

At first glance "BH" (pronounced BAY ah-GAH), with its scores of nondescript high-rises and industrial outskirts that reflect its economic clout, doesn't seem very

© MICHAEL SOMMERS

the *cidade histórica* of Diamantina

alluring. Officially inaugurated in 1897, it was one of Brazil's first planned cities and was built as a progressive new capital that could replace Ouro Preto, whose fortunes had dwindled after the gold rush. Despite a relative lack of history and charm, BH is nonetheless a compelling city with an impressively varied cultural and culinary scene and a famous bar scene (it has more *botecos* per capita than any other Brazilian city). Although colonial architecture is nonexistent, fans of modernism are in for a treat; in the 1940s and early 1950s, the city served as a three-dimensional drafting board for an ambitious young architect by the name of Oscar Niemeyer. His earliest and still surprisingly vanguard buildings can be seen in the city center as well as in the well-to-do neighborhood of Pampulha.

THE LAY OF THE LAND

Minas Gerais is considered part of the Brazilian Southeast, along with the states of São Paulo, Rio de Janeiro and Espírito Santo, with which it shares frontiers. The fact that it also shares borders with Bahia and Goiás to the north and Mato Grosso to the west explains the economic, geographic, and cultural diversity you'll encounter within the state. Southern Minas shares many traits with Rio and São Paulo, ranging from big mountains covered in lush tropical forest to big industries. The more isolated and arid, traditionally poorer, but culturally rich north has much in common with the Bahian Interior. Meanwhile western Minas—whose flatter lands are given over to agriculture, ranching, and the unique (and endangered) savannah-like ecosystem of the Cerrado—resembles its Central-West neighbors and counts Brasília as its largest urban influence.

Belo Horizonte is located within the center of the state, in a deep valley ringed by the majestic Serra do Espinhaço mountain range—which explains the name Belo

Horizonte (Beautiful Horizon). While the city has ample green space, including the vast and verdant Parque das Mangabeiras, it is also happily surrounded by some great getaway destinations, including caves with prehistoric paintings, national parks replete with canyons and waterfalls, and some of Minas' most impressive historical gold mining towns, known as the *cidades históricas:* Sabará (only 30 minutes away), Ouro Preto, and Mariana (2 hours), as well as Congonhas (1 hour away), which is the site of master baroque sculptor Aleijadinho's final, and arguably greatest, works.

Climate

Minas' climate varies somewhat according to region. Considered subtropical because of its altitude, it is considered to have four seasons although the most distinctive are the hot, humid summers when rainfall can be heavy (particularly in December and January) and the cooler, arid winters. The coolest months are June, July, and August when temperatures at night can go below 10°C (50°F), particularly in the mountainous regions, such as those where the *cidades históricas* are located. Although there's no central heating, in many rural Mineiro homes, the *fogão a lenha* (wood-burning stove) continues to play a seminal role as a supplier of heat as well as heart-warming sustenance.

Culture

Minas Gerais boasts one of the richest and distinctive regional cultures in Brazil. There is a considerable emphasis placed on family, religion, and traditional rural life (Mineiros love nothing more than congregating at their country houses and cooking up small storms over their wood-burning stoves). Catholicism exerts a considerable force, particularly in the *cidades históricas,* which are famed for religious *festas* such as Semana Santa and Corpus Christi. Minas also boasts one of Brazil's most distinctive and best-loved cuisines—*comida mineira*—with mouthwatering specialties ranging from *tutu à mineira,* a thick bean puree, to *frango ao molho pardo,* chicken cooked in a pungent sauce made from its own blood. Just as varied as its main courses are its famously creamy *queijos* (cheeses)—an important ingredient in the highly addictive *pães de queijo* (cheese buns), served everywhere with *cafezinho*—and infinite desserts and *doces* made from regional fruits. The state is also beloved for its more than 4,000 regionally produced cachaças, the best of which rival world-class rums.

Meanwhile, Belo Horizonte has earned itself a reputation as an innovative center in terms of the performing arts, particularly with respect to theater and dance. Aside from its 8,000 odd bars (many of which host musical performances), the city has a handful of top-notch cultural centers—including the Oscar Niemeyer–designed Palácio das Artes—and a blossoming ensemble of innovative new museums, many of which occupy palaces from the turn of the 20th century and flank the elegant central square of Praça da Liberdade.

WHERE TO LIVE

Most expats based in Minas make their home in Belo Horizonte. As in any large Brazilian city, rents vary significantly depending on the *bairro;* however, in the past 10 years, BH's booming real estate market has grown by 108 percent causing rents to double. Among the most pleasant and centrally-located neighborhoods for living are the upper-middle-class Centro-Sul *bairros* of Funcionários, Lourdes, and Santo

© MICHAEL SOMMERS

rounds of *queijo mineiro* for sale at Belo Horizonte's Mercado Municipal

Agostinho, which are highly coveted (with prices to match) because of their privileged location near Praça da Liberdade. Expect a two-bedroom apartment in Funcionários to run from R$2,000 to R$4,000. Other attractive, upscale *bairros* that are a little farther afield, but very tranquil and a little less pricey, include the Centro-Sul (South Central) *bairros* of Cidade Jardim and Santo Antônio and the Leste (East) *bairros* of Serra and São Lucas. Less swanky and more affordable, not to mention very close to Centro, are two appealing middle-class residential neighborhoods: Floresta and the bohemian *bairro* of Santa Tereza, with its funky collection of *botecos*. If you're looking for even better deals without sacrificing convenience, consider moving into one of the older apartment buildings in Centro or neighboring Barro Preto where it's possible to come across a three bedroom for R$1,200. Although it can get crowded and noisy, BH's Centro is fairly safe and very convenient, not to mention full of amenities and lots of vibrant urban energy. From here you can get around very easily by bus or on foot.

Life in other parts of Minas—including *cidades históricas* such as Ouro Preto and Diamantina—is considerably cheaper, although not always as cheap as you'd expect; because these are university towns, the high demand for student lodgings means that rents can be inflated. On the upside, you can find yourself living in atmospheric centuries-old houses with verandas, balconies, and sometimes even gardens. In these towns you can easily get around by foot (or taxi), although if you want to take advantage of surrounding natural attractions ranging from mountain trails and waterfalls to bucolic villages, you might want to invest in a car.

RESOURCES

Although in recent years BH has drawn a fair share of expats, there isn't an organized community per se. If you want to hook up with other foreigners based in BH, try getting in touch with Minas International (www.minasinternational.com), an NGO that connects English speakers living and doing business in Minas with each other. Another option is to log on to Expat Blog (www.expat-blog.com) and search under Networks in Belo Horizonte, which will yield a list of foreigners based in the city along with options for making contact with them.

If you move to Belo Horizonte with children, the top international school in town is the American School of Belo Horizonte (ASBH) (www.eabh.com.br), an international school with courses based on the U.S. curriculum, but featuring a multilingual environment where Portuguese is also emphasized. The school, which extends from preschool through grade 12, is located on a rambling campus in the leafy suburb of Buritis. In terms of bilingual schooling for preschool and elementary school, a popular option is the Canadian-based Maple Bear school (www.maple-bearbh.com.br), which has three locations in the city, including one in Centro. For immersion in Portuguese, a recommended option for young kids up to the age of 10 is the Escola da Serra (www.escoladaserra.com.br), a small and friendly Montessori-modeled school with an emphasis on the arts, which is located in the Centro-Sul neighborhood of Serra.

With respect to higher education, Minas is home to the prestigious Universidade Federal de Minas Gerais (UFMG). Brazil's largest federal university, UFMG is routinely considered one its best. It also ranks as one of the top 10 universities in Latin America, according to Quacquarelli Symonds (QS) World University Rankings. It's highly claimed for its innovation in terms of research. The number one Brazilian institution in terms of patents, in 2010 it registered 350 national and 110 international patents. The main campuses are located in BH's Pampulha and Saúde neighborhoods. With UFMG's multiple international partnerships, the university attracts its share of visiting students from abroad. Meanwhile, regional campuses of the federal university are spread throughout the state, including the culturally rich *cidades históricas* of Ouro Preto, Mariana, São João del Rei, and Diamantina, all of which are famed as vibrant student towns.

© MICHAEL SOMMERS

The Edifício Niemeyer, a Modernist apartment building, overlooks BH's Praça da Liberdade.

GETTING AROUND

Most flights arrive at **Tancredo Neves International Airport.** More popularly known as **Confins** (after the suburb where it is located), it is around 40 kilometers (25 mi) from the center of Belo Horizonte. Much closer is the older and smaller **Pampulha Airport,** which is around 15 kilometers (9 mi) from Centro. The main **Rodoviária** is right in the heart of the city at Praça Rio Branco. From here, buses arrive and depart to destinations throughout Minas Gerais and the rest of Brazil.

Because of its many one-way streets, driving a car in Belo Horizonte is tricky. Moreover, the rules of which street goes which way are always changing (even the taxi drivers have trouble keeping up). Like other major Brazilian cities, traffic can be sluggish, and during rush hour, it's a nightmare. The bus system is very well organized and service is good and extensive. From Centro and Savassi, it is easy to get anywhere you want to go quickly. There is a subway, but you'll likely never use it since it is more useful for workers getting in and out of the suburbs than for tourists.

Central-West

It was just over 50 years ago that Juscelino Kubitschek was elected Brazil's president, largely as a result of his wildly ambitious plans to construct a capital from scratch right in the middle of Brazil (i.e., in the middle of nowhere). To carry out this endeavor, he hired two young talents: architect Oscar Niemeyer and an urban planner named Lucio Costa. Construction began in 1957, and three years later, the world's most famous and controversial planned city was unveiled. Although the Royal Institute of British Architects referred to its gleaming space-age geometric palaces, monuments, and "sectors" as "The Moon's Backside," over the years Brasília's unearthly charms have seduced architecture buffs from around the globe.

Architecture aside, one of Brasília's raisons d'être was to facilitate the opening up of the vast and isolated interior of Brazil's Central-West, a region of elevated plains whose unique landscape, the Cerrado, conjures up the muted colors and scrubby foliage of East Africa's savannahs. Aside from Brasília, the Central-West encompasses the surrounding states of Goiás, Mato Grosso, and Mato Grosso do Sul.

Until well into the 20th century, the Central-West remained a sparsely populated wilderness whose urban outposts were quite isolated from the bustling capitals of coastal Brazil. The region's fortunes changed radically, however, with the building of Brasília. The inauguration of the futuristic capital served to connect this isolated interior with the rest of Brazil, ushering in a period of thriving agribusiness that has continued to this day. Currently Goiás, Mato Grosso, and Mato Grosso do Sul—anchored by their respective capitals of Goiânia, Cuiabá, and Campo Grande—are Brazil's fastest-growing regions and the leading national producers of lucrative cash crops such as sugarcane, soybeans, rice, cotton, and corn, as well as beef. Other growing sectors include biofuels and pharmaceuticals—Goiás in particular is becoming a major producer of generic drugs and its two major cities Goiânia, the state capital, and Anápolis, are modern boomtowns. Increasingly, high-tech farms vie for space with nature reserves, the largest of which, the immense Parque Nacional do Pantanal Matogrossense, has managed (for now) to protect many of the natural treasures enclosed within the watery borders of the Pantanal. Indeed, in the early 21st century, the biggest issue in the region is one of sustainable development: how to balance continued economic growth with preservation of the region's unique yet increasingly threatened ecosystems.

In the end, however, the majority of expats who move to the Central-West are drawn to the opportunities provided in the nation's capital of Brasília, most of which involve administrative or diplomatic posts, jobs with nongovernmental organizations (NGOs) and think tanks, and assignments for journalists and foreign correspondents covering the political scene.

THE LAY OF THE LAND

The Central-West is a vast area that covers approximately 19 percent of Brazil's territory. At the same time, it is Brazil's least populated region. Brasília (population 2.5 million) and Goiânia (1.3 million) are the only urban centers with populations of more than 800,000. Most of the region is covered by relatively flat elevated plains, *planaltos.*

Much of the north of the region, stretching from Brasília and much of Goiás across northern Mato Grosso, is part of the Planalto Central, a sweeping plateau comprised of crystalline rocks (the presence of which has drawn myriad New Age communities to the region). The northernmost and western stretches are covered by dense, lush Amazonian forest while most of the rest is characterized by the Cerrado ecosystem, which mingles grasslands, dry forests, and buriti palms. Much of the Cerrado (half of whose 10,000 native plant species exist nowhere else on the planet) is under siege from big agribusiness, but fortunately a few large patches are preserved in national parks. Sweeping across southern Goiás and into Mato Grosso do Sul, the Planalto Meridional is a much more fertile plain. It's nutrient-filled *terra roxa* (red soil) is ideal for agriculture.

Straddling the center of Mato Grosso and Mato Grosso do Sul, the Planalto Pantanal constitutes the largest wetland on the planet. Every year, the area is flooded by the Paraguay River and its tributaries. Aside from traditional cattle farms, it's impossible for humans to encroach upon this rich ecosystem where caiman far outnumber homo sapiens, and frogs, birds, fish, butterflies, not to mention capybaras, sea otters, giant anteaters, and jaguars, all live in abundance, largely unfazed by human presence. As a result, the Pantanal has become one of Brazil's, and the world's, most fantastic ecotourist attractions.

Brasília is located within the Distrito Federal (Federal District)—similar to the District of Columbia in the United States—which lies in the eastern part of Goiás, within spitting distance of Minas' western frontier. Despite the fact that this region is growing faster than any other in Brazil, geographically it continues to be the middle of nowhere. Roads linking major cities are actually in decent shape, but distances are enormous. Brasília is easily reached by plane from all other cities; flights to the more remote cities of Mato Grosso and Mato Grosso do Sul (Cuiabá, Campo Grande, and Corumbá) are rarely direct.

Climate

Most of the Central-West enjoys a tropical climate, which means it's pretty warm year-round (Cuiabá owns the dubious claim to fame of being the most sweltering of all Brazilian capitals). Summers (Oct.–Mar.) are rainy and extremely humid with

EXPAT PROFILE: LIFE IN A SPACE-AGE CAPITAL

Jesse, a 42-year-old ethnomusicologist and musician, originally from Chicago, has been living off and on in Brasília since 1999–and permanently since 2009.

WHY HE CAME

In 1999, I was wrapping up a Masters at University of Wisconsin in Madison in ethnomusicology, and I met two visiting professors from the University of Brasília. We became friends and they invited me down to Brazil for 18 months to work on a project. When I went back to the United States to do my PhD, I decided to change my focus and started thinking of doing work in Brazil. I won a Fulbright Hays grant and came back to do research in Brasília in 2003. During this time, I did my research and had a girlfriend and played in various bands. I had a life set up.

After I defended my doctoral thesis in the United States in 2006, I spent a lot of time looking for a job to no avail. Then the economic crisis hit. I was living at my mother's, and the only career options were starting positions. So I decided to come back to Brazil because I loved living here. It was late 2009, and there were more opportunities here than in the United States. My goal was to do a postdoctorate degree so that I could stay in the country while I figured something out.

Then in the summer of 2010, the Brazilian Studies Association (BRASA) asked me to organize a panel about music in the city—the subject of my thesis—for an international conference. When I presented my paper, the executive director of the Fulbright Commission came up to me. He remembered me from 2004 (he recognized my mohawk) and asked me if I wanted to stay in Brazil. When I said "Yes," he said: "Jesse, I think I have a job for you." And that's how I came to work at the Fulbright Commission, coordinating educational partnerships and exchanges between Brazil and the United States.

HOW HE CAME

I had to solicit a work visa, but it wasn't difficult. I needed to pull the paperwork together, and there were all the hoops to go through. I knew it was just a matter of patience. I think the whole process took five months.

LIVING IN BRASÍLIA

I live in the Asa Sul, near the bridge, which is close to my work. It's really nice to live here. Very green and peaceful. Brasília is an easy place to live if you're in the Plano Piloto. What's hard is that there are no collective spaces; no places to run into people such as public squares or beaches. Because of the lack of social spaces, it's easy to feel lonely. The only places where people can meet up are places of consumption such as bars and shopping malls.

MAKING A LIVING

There are different kinds of opportunities all throughout Brazil if you speak English. Although there's not a lot of industry in Brasília, there are many opportunities because of all the government administration. You can end up translating government documents or getting hired to teach English in the Senate. You can be a guide or work embassy events.

temperatures easily hitting 38°C (100°F). Winters (Apr.–Sept.) are more comfortable (22°C [75°F])—but very dry. In Brasília, the dryness can become quite unbearable, and even the locals complain of parched throats and nosebleeds. Areas with higher altitudes experience cooler temperatures—particularly at night—during the winter months.

Culture

Although it shares some cultural similarities with Minas Gerais, the Central-West is a much newer place that lacks Minas' profound history and deep roots. The large bulk of the population consists of migrants from other parts of Brazil who, in the case of Brasília, built the city from scratch and then stuck around. They were followed

When I lived here between 1999 and 2007, life was very affordable. I had a grant and the exchange rate was favorable. I also did a lot of odd jobs. I taught English and did translations. I did voice-overs for radio spots. Now life is so expensive, and it's very difficult to make ends meet. I have a decent salary, but I have to watch my pennies. Brasília is one of the most expensive cities in the world; it's certainly much more expensive than Chicago where I used to live.

MEETING PEOPLE

Expats here are scattered all over the city, but there are not many Americans I know of. When I first came here I lived with other foreigners—a guy from Macedonia and a guy from Senegal. I didn't speak a word of Portuguese and that was a big barrier. But over time I started meeting Brazilians through the university and my research work interviewing people as well as through my interests. I joined a lot of bands: a hip hop band, a punk band, and an Irish band. I also met a lot of people through my girlfriend and her friends. Fortunately my social network here stretches back 13 years. Anywhere you have a lot of friends you're going to feel good.

STUDYING IN BRAZIL

I never actually studied at a Brazilian university, but I work in educational exchanges. Most foreign students come as grantees. If you're a junior in college, you're going to have fun anywhere in Brazil, but it's most interesting if you can do some research related to culture. I'd recommend going to

an interesting cultural milieu in the North, Northeast, or Central-West and staying away from the big cities such as Rio and São Paulo. The students that have the most unusual experiences are the ones who go to midsized places where they don't meet as many foreigners and can connect with local families and communities.

A WORD OF ADVICE FOR OTHER EXPATS

I love how affectionate Brazilians are, but if you're not part of an "in" group, then you're an outsider. Families are important here. I'm lucky because I always had a *família emprestada* (borrowed family)—either the families of my friends or girlfriends—who would invite me to eat lunch or spend Christmas. If you're not part of the home, you're out on the street. You're excluded and that's rough. You need to create groups and affiliations. It's hard for an expat without connections. Unlike places like Germany and France, for example, this isn't an easy place you can relocate to just like that.

Have stuff you can do that will interest other people, so you can make friends more easily. I'm a musician, so I can create moments of interaction. I also cook and often invite friends over and ask them to bring friends over. Bring baseballs and Frisbees—sports you can play that involve other people. Brasília can be really isolating. You need reasons to stay outside; otherwise you'll end up drifting back inside.

by subsequent generations of migrants lured by cheap and fertile land and booming new cities offering opportunities for a new life. Indeed, the Central-West has a bit of a frontier feel to it, a sensation that increases the farther West you go and encounter untamed landscapes, immense farms, and cattle ranches that feel ripped from a Wild West movie. Despite the growth of its urban areas, the Central-West is defined by *cultura caipira,* a rural culture of the Interior that manifests itself in a strong connection to the land. It's no coincidence that *música sertaneja,* a style of Brazilian music similar to American country and western is wildly popular; it provides an ideal soundtrack to the Central-West.

Both playing to and breaking with its surroundings, Brasília straddles a lot of

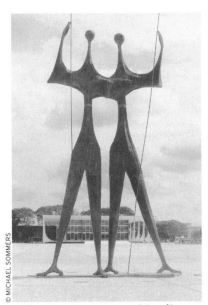

© MICHAEL SOMMERS

Os Candangos is a symbol of Brasília.

PRIME LIVING LOCATIONS

contrasts. The space-age city sprawled in the middle of a dusty plain manages the feat of being both cosmopolitan and provincial. Within the Plano Piloto, where government business is carried out and international restaurants, swank shopping malls, cultural centers, concert halls, and movie theaters are numerous, it's easy to remember you're in an important global capital. At the same time, the city is neither glam nor pretentious. On weekends, when all the country's pols head back to their home states, a small-town emptiness reigns. Meanwhile, beyond the Plano Piloto's carefully drawn lines sprawl satellite cities filled with poor favelas that belie Brasília's original utopian concept.

Despite the popular perception of Brasília as an arid city where concrete, glass, and asphalt rule, a surprising number of parks make the capital one of the greenest cities in Brazil. Within the city confines are the Parque da Cidade and the immense artificial lake of Lago Paranoá, surrounded by walking trails and sporting clubs. Moreover, within close proximity to the city are natural splendors such as the Parque Nacional de Brasília, the Salto de Itiquira, whose spectactular 170-meter-high (560-ft) waterfall is the equivalent of a 56-story building, and the charming colonial gold mining town of Pirenópolis.

WHERE TO LIVE

Like Brasília's middle and upper classes, almost all expats who move to Brazil wind up living within the modernist confines of Lucio Costa and Oscar Niemeyer's original Plano Piloto. Many choose to live in the apartments located in the Asa Sul, but those located in the Asa Norte are also recommended by Brasilienses (residents of Brasília). Aside from being close to the city center, these areas have good amenities within close proximity, are considered quite safe, and are aesthetically pleasing. Other popular choices are the upscale neighborhoods of Sudoeste and Octagonal, both of which lie close to the Parque da Cidade. If you like the idea of living in a house (or mansion), the swank Lago Sul and Lago Norte sectors—which boast the second-largest number of swimming pools per resident in the world—may appeal. Covering the hills above Lago Paranoá, these *bairros* are attractive and tranquil. Connected to the center of town via three bridges (including the landmark Ponte Juscelino Kubitschek), they are also a bit remote.

Keep in mind that Brasília is one of the most expensive real estate markets in the country. The fact that the Plano Piloto is considered a UNESCO World Heritage site means that its architectural unity is sacrosanct, meaning no new construction can be carried out within its confines. The consequence of high demand and limited supply for coveted apartments is inflated prices. Expect to pay around R$1,200 for a one bedroom and between R$1,800 and R$3,000 for a decent three bedroom.

RESOURCES

Brasília has a sizable foreign expat community. InterNations (www.internations.org) has an online community for Brasília expats with message boards, forums, and contact numbers for members as well as info about monthly gatherings. Several U.S. expats based in Brasília author blogs that describe their lives in the city; for links to them, log on to www.expat-blog.com.

Expats usually send their children to international schools. As old as Brasília itself, the American School in Brasília (www.eabdf.br) follows an English-language, U.S.-based curriculum—with the addition of Portuguese and Brazilian studies—from preschool through grade 12. Its sprawling, well-appointed campus is in Asa Sul, overlooking Lago Paranoá. Also fairly reputed, but smaller and less expensive, is the Brasília International School (www.bischool.com.br). A member of the International Network of Christian Schools (NICS), it follows a North American–based curriculum and attracts an international mix of students from prekindergarten to grade 12. It is located in the Indústrias Gráficas Sector.

There are also some good bilingual schools to choose from. Affinity Arts (www.affinityarts.com.br) is an innovative preschool founded by educators and musicians whose early child development program emphasizes creativity. Catering to preschool and elementary school children, the Canadian-based Maple Bear School (www.maplebear.com.br) has a location in the Indústrias Gráficas Sector. Another bilingual option whose curriculum extends all the way to grade 12 is the School of the Nations (www.schoolofthenations.com.br), located in Lago Sul. Founded by North American educators of the Bahá'í world faith, it promotes the teachings of unity through diversity and, as such, attracts an eclectic student body of both Brazilians and foreigners. Opened in 2011, the Swiss International School (www.swissinternationalschool.com.br) is the first SIS to open outside of Europe. Presently, its English-Portuguese curriculum exists only at the preschool level, but by 2017 the school, based in Asa Sul, hopes to offer primary and secondary school courses as well.

In terms of higher education, the federally operated Universidade de Brasília (UnB) is not only considered the top university in the Central-West, but one of the best in Brazil. Particularly strong areas include anthropology, economy, molecular biology, and geology.

GETTING AROUND

Most travelers arrive in Brasília by air. There is no shortage of flights from most state capitals, including numerous flights from Rio and São Paulo. The **Aeroporto Internacional de Brasília–Presidente Juscelino Kubitschek** is located 10 kilometers (6 miles) west of the Eixo Monumental. The other Central-West capitals of Goiânia, Cuiabá, and Campo Grande also have airports with direct flights to Brasília and São Paulo and connections to other Brazilian cities.

In Brasília, buses from all corners of Brazil arrive and depart at the long-distance **Rodoferroviária** at the western edge of the Eixo Monumental. Aside from destinations in neighboring Goiás, traveling anywhere else involves an exhaustingly

A DECODER GUIDE TO BRASÍLIA

Brasília's division into axes, sectors, blocks, and buildings may seem incredibly logical, but translating the coded abbreviations into an address that makes sense can be as confusing as traveling to a country where only Cyrillic script is used. The following are some of the acronyms that will come in most handy.

SETORES
The following refer to the *setores* (sectors) that line both sides of the Eixo Monumental.

- **Asa Norte/Sul**–The two *asas* (wings), Norte (North) and Sul (South), curving off of the Eixo Monumental and running parallel to the Eixo Rodoviário. The "N" and "S" indicate on which side of the Eixo Monumental an address is.

- **SBN/SBS** (Setor Bancário Norte/Sul)–banking sectors

- **SCN/SCS** (Setor Comercial Norte/Sul)–commercial office areas (adjacent to the shopping centers)

- **SDN/SDS** (Setor de Diversões Norte/Sul)–the two shopping centers (Conjunto Nacional and CONIC) on either side of the Rodoviária

- **SEN/SES** (Setor de Embaixadas Norte/Sul)–the two embassy sectors (east of the bank sectors)

- **SHN/SHS** (Setor Hoteleiro Norte/Sul)–the two hotel sectors (west of the Rodoviária)

ABBREVIATIONS
Abbreviations in the main residential areas are as follows:

- **SQN/SQS** (Superquadras Norte/Sul)–the individual *superquadras* in the main residential wings of Asa Norte and Asa Sul

- **SHIN/SHIS** (Setor de Habitações Individuais Norte/Sul)–residential zones around the northern and southern banks of Lago Paranoá

- **CLN/CLS** or **SCLN/SCLS** (Setor Comércio Local Norte/Sul)–the commercial blocks (stores, bars, restaurants) set amid the residential *superquadras*

DECODING A RESIDENTIAL ADDRESS
Decoding a residential address can be tricky. We've decoded the following address below as an example.

- SQN 204

- Bl. B-303
  SQN refers to *superquadra* north, No. 204, Building B, Apartment 303. The *superquadra* number provides the location: The first digit (2) is the position east or west of the Eixo Rodoviário (odd numbers are to the west, even numbers are to the east, increasing the farther away you get from the center). The last two digits (04) are the position north or south of the Eixo Monumental. So in the case of 204, you know that the *superquadra* you're looking for is four blocks north of the Eixo Monumental and one block west of the Eixo Rodoviário. If none of this makes sense, simply write out the address on a piece of paper and let a cab driver take care of the decoding for you.

long haul. Brasília's sole Metrô line is a cheap and useful way to get from the Rodoferroviária (from the Shopping station) to the central Rodoviária (Central station) and vice versa.

At first, Brasília, with its many Eixos and sectors, seems like an urban planner's trick to confuse a foreigner. However, once you get the hang of the sectors (which could take a while), you will see how orderly it all is. Roads are numbered instead of named. Digits represent positions and distances north or south of the Eixo Monumental and east or west of the Eixo Rodoviário. Each sector has its own acronym. The central Rodoviária de Brasília—the main urban bus station—is also the city's nucleus. The Eixo Rodoviário crosses over the Rodoviária while the Eixo Monumental passes around it.

Brasília is a sprawling city custom made for automobiles, so forget about wandering around town unless you're in a strolling zone (such as a park). In truth, it's pretty much impossible to imagine living here without four wheels of your own. The public transport system is one of Brazil's less inspiring. The most convenient buses run along the major axes of the Eixo Rodoviário and the Eixo Monumental, all of them stopping at the central Rodoviária, located at the crossroads of the two. Taxis are usually easy to hail, and if you can't make sense of Brasília's sometimes confusing system of *setores* and *quadras,* your cab driver can.

Originally, Brasília's thoroughfares were designed to make traffic lights unnecessary through the use of roundabouts at intersections. Although some traffic lights do exist, roundabouts rule—if you're driving, remember that the car that's already in the roundabout has the right of way. Otherwise, driving here is smoother than in other large Brazilian cities, although increasingly, traffic is just as bad.

The South

Brazil's Sul, or South, consists of three states—Paraná, Santa Catarina, and Rio Grande do Sul—which stretch south from São Paulo toward Brazil's frontier with Uruguay and Argentina. This region is not what most foreigners have in mind when they think of Brazil. The climate and vegetation are more Mediterranean than tropical, and the population—descendants of German, Italian, Polish, and Ukrainian immigrants—is distinctly European (which accounts for so many natural blonds).

Compared with much of the rest of coastal Brazil, the South's history is fairly recent. Officially, from 1500 onward, Portugal controlled the Atlantic coastline and interior all the way south to the Rio de la Plata. However, for centuries the area remained largely unsettled by Portuguese colonists. Aside from the presence of Azorean fishing communities along the coasts of Paraná and Santa Catarina, the most significant presence during the 17th and early to mid-18th centuries was that of Jesuit missionaries. Bent on converting the local Guarani native people, they established various missionary communities in the interior, particularly near the border with neighboring Argentina and Uruguay. By the time the Portuguese crown expelled the Jesuits from Brazil in 1767, much of the grassy highland plains of Rio Grande do Sul (the famous Pampas) had been given over to vast ranches owned by cattle barons of Spanish origin who employed Gaúchos—cowboys of mixed Spanish, Portuguese, and Indian descent—to care for their herds.

Large-scale settlement and development of the South as a whole didn't occur until the mid-19th century, when European immigrants arrived en masse, lured by the promise of fertile land, a temperate climate, and the commercial opportunities provided by burgeoning towns. Armed with advanced farming techniques and industrial know-how, these newcomers quickly transformed the South into a thriving region reputed for its dynamic economy, progressive politics, and clean and efficient cities. Currently, the South boasts the nation's lowest indexes of poverty and crime combined with its highest levels of education.

The wealthiest of all Brazil's states, Paraná is both an agricultural and industrial powerhouse whose prosperity is based on state-of-the-art agribusinesses and highly modern industries. Its capital, Curitiba, is a thriving, ecofriendly city of 1.8 million that has become a model for other urban centers throughout Latin America. Aside from its safety and general air of well being, it provides an interesting example of enlightened urban planning. Due to the work of city mayor (and later state governor) Jaime Lerner, a visionary architect who first came to power in the 1970s, Curitiba was an environmentalist's dream long before Al Gore came along. Concerned with the traffic pollution that was already afflicting large Latin American cities, Lerner inaugurated a modern, inexpensive, and extensive municipal bus system and turned much of the small but carefully preserved historic center into an agreeable pedestrian district. Recycling and antipollution programs were adopted, and vast tracts of land were transformed into public green spaces amid new high-rises. Literally, an emerald city, Curitiba possesses more than 30 municipal parks and wooded areas with plenty of walking and biking trails.

The smallest of Brazil's southern states, Santa Catarina is famed for its beautiful coastline, which draws sun- and surf-seeking visitors from neighboring Argentina and Uruguay as well as Paulistanos and even Cariocas. Some of the best beaches in the South surround the pretty island capital of Florianópolis (affectionate nicknamed "Floripa"), a vibrant, youthful, and prosperous city on the Ilha de Santa Catarina, whose 42 beaches range from highly developed to practically deserted. Santa Catarina boasts one of the narrowest disparities between rich and poor in Brazil, and Florianópolis boasts a quality of life that seduces harried middle-class Brazilians fed up with the stress and crime of cities such as Rio and São Paulo.

Bordering Argentina and Uruguay, Brazil's southernmost state of Rio Grande do Sul is also one of Brazil's most distinctive regions, with a climate, culture, and regional identity all its own. The fierce independence and distinctiveness of the modern-day Gaúcho dates back to the region's beginnings as a Wild West frontier zone between the Spanish and Portuguese colonial empires. As early as the 18th century, cowboys, traveling solo or in small bands, earned their livelihoods driving immense herds of cattle across the Pampas. These "Gaúchos"—a pejorative term of indigenous origin— became the stuff of legend, as emblematic of Rio Grande do Sul as cowboys in Texas.

The term *Gaúcho* became synonymous with all residents of Rio Grande do Sul during the Guerra dos Farrapos, a failed war of independence that pitted Rio Grande do Sul's freethinking rebels against imperial forces. Lasting from 1835 to 1845, this series of battles constituted the longest war ever fought in the Americas. During this period, Rio Grande do Sul became an autonomous republic, and its citizens defiantly adopted the "Gaúcho" moniker that was used as an insult by monarchists in Rio. After the war, the courageous Gaúcho became a symbol of the state and a popular hero that came to be idealized in local literature, music, and art and kept alive in the collective consciousness.

Stretched out along the eastern shore of the Rio Guaíba, the prosperous capital of Porto Alegre resembles a somewhat generic European or North American city. With a population of 1.5 million, it is the largest and most economically important of Brazil's southern capitals. Moreover, as the host of events such as the controversial World Social Forum—which has provided a counterpoint to the First World elitism of the World

Economic Forum—and the distinguished Bienal de Artes do Mercosul, Porto Alegre has proved itself to be a progressive and cosmopolitan place with a reputed gastronomic scene (particularly if you're a card-carrying carnivore) and a dynamic cultural life for a Brazilian city its size.

THE LAY OF THE LAND

The South is Brazil's most compact region. Occupying close to 7 percent of Brazil's territory, it is smaller than the state of Minas Gerais. Yet its population is also three times that of the Central-West. The only cities with populations exceeding 1 million, Curitiba and Porto Alegre constitute the region's most important urban centers. Despite being known for its many small and highly productive farms, 80 percent of the South's population is urban.

Most of the South is dominated by the Planalto Meridional (Southern Highlands) and the Planalto Atlântico (Atlantic Highlands). This series of plateaus were originally covered by a mixture of Mata Atlântica (native Atlantic forest) and coniferous araucaria highland forests (araucarias are also known as Paraná pines). As a result of intensive agriculture, only patches of both still remain. At their loftiest, these highlands morph into spectacular mountain ranges known as the Serra do Mar (Paraná and northern Santa Catarina) and the Serra Geral (southern Santa Catarina and Rio Grande do Sul). Meanwhile, over 60 percent of Rio Grande do Sul is covered by the grassy highlands known as the Pampas. Aside from Santa Catarina's strikingly scenic coastline, the South's most compelling natural attraction is the Iguaçu Falls, which straddle Paraná's frontier with Argentina and Paraguay.

Climate

The South is the only region of Brazil to boast a subtropical climate with four distinctive seasons. While summers can be hot, winters are quite chilly (especially with the winds that come up from the Argentine way), with temperatures plunging to 5–10°C (40–50°F) in coastal regions and to the freezing point in the interior. In the higher reaches of the Serra Geral, it's not uncommon to glimpse snow. Unlike other parts of Brazil that experience distinctive rainy and dry seasons, with the exception of parts of Paraná, rainfall in the South is fairly regular year-round.

Culture

The South possesses a distinctly European culture whose strongest traditions are a legacy of the main groups—particularly German and Italian, and to a lesser extent Polish, Ukrainian and Azorean—that colonized and settled the region. Consequently, you'll encounter Brazil's finest and most extensive wine-making region—Rio Grande do Sul's Vale do Vinhedo—as well as myriad restaurants serving sauerkraut, eisbein, and borscht. In the Azorean fishing villages along coastal Santa Catarina, lace making is alive and well as is the cultivation of mussels, oysters, and shrimp. Gaúcho culture remains an integral part of Rio Grande do Sul's identity, and its influence is felt in everything from literature and traditional dances to culinary legacies such as eating *churrasco*—the wandering cowboy's staple of slow-cooked charcoal-grilled cuts of beef seasoned with rock salt—and drinking bitter *erva maté*.

While Floripa flaunts a sophisticated beach culture, both Curitiba and especially

Porto Alegre have fairly sophisticated urban cultural offerings, particularly considering their size. Partially, this is a result of their lack of beaches and endless summers, but it's also due to the relatively high income levels and education of their populations. Both cities have eclectic dining, café, and bar scenes as well as important theaters (Curitiba's Teatro Guaíra and Porto Alegre's Teatro São Pedro). Porto Alegre also has an impressive number of cultural centers that are hosting interesting exhibits and events.

RESOURCES

Curitiba, Porto Alegre, and Floripianópolis all have relatively small expat communities. In Curitiba, the closest thing to an official expat group is the Curitiba Expat Meetup Group (www.meetup.com). Founded in 2012, it hosts monthly get-togethers in the city where expats can network and get to know each other. Expat Blog (www.expat-blog.com) also has an expat group of some two dozen international members based in Curitiba.

Expats who want to send their children to international schools where the main language of instruction is English have options in both Curitiba and Porto Alegre. Located in the *bairro* of Felicidade, the International School of Curitiba (www.iscbrazil.com) has been in existence since 1959. An independent nonprofit college prep school offering classes from preschool through grade 12, it is the only international school in Paraná that allows students to work toward American, Brazilian, and International Baccalaureate (IB) diplomas. In Porto Alegre's upscale Petrópolis neighborhood, the Pan American School of Porto Alegre (www.panamerican.com.br) is the city's only English-language school to teach an international curriculum ranging from preschool through high school.

Curitiba has a branch of the Canadian-based Maple Bear bilingual school (www.maplebear.com.br) that offers preschool and elementary school classes. In Florianópolis, the recently opened American School of Florianópolis (www.amesflorianopolis.com.br) is the city's first bilingual school with locations in Centro and Jurerê.

When it comes to higher education, the Universidade Federal do Rio Grande do Sul (UFRGS), based in Porto Alegre, is one of Brazil's largest and most reputed federal universities. Two former Brazilian presidents (Getúlio Vargas and João Goulart) as well as current president Dilma Roussef are alumni.

WHERE TO LIVE

Curitiba's most coveted neighborhoods are traditional upscale *bairros* such as Batel, Água Verde and Portão, which possess clean tree-lined streets, have tons of services and amenities, and are within close proximity to Centro. In fact, despite being primarily residential, well-to-do, yet bustling, Batel is known as the *"segundo centro"* because of its plethora of stores, gourmet cafés and restaurants, hotels, and chic shopping centers. Rents here, however, are among the highest in the city (expect a one bedroom to cost R$1,000–1,800). Despite traffic, noise, and the fact that it clears out at night, it is possible—not to mention cheaper—to find inexpensive digs in Centro itself; small apartments here are popular with local 20-somethings. Another well-located and less expensive area is Alto da XV, a traditional hilltop *bairro* in the Centro-Leste with panoramic city views that has a strong European immigrant presence and where a one-bedroom apartment costs R$600–900.

In Florianópolis, people who have jobs in the city or who want to be close to services and amenities opt to live in Centro (where there are some charming old buildings) or in surrounding neighborhoods of Beira Mar, an upscale seaside *bairro* of high-rise condos, and adjacent Agronômica, and Trindade. Much more appealing are the island's beaches. While those on the North Coast boast the warmest and calmest waters, they are also the most built up, with numerous generic hotels, condos, and restaurants. Facing the open Atlantic, the East Coast beaches are the island's longest and most dramatic, which is why they attract a younger more alternative crowd of surfers and singles (both straight and gay). The South Coast beaches are the most wildly beautiful and least developed, but also the most difficult in terms of access. Facing the continent, the West Coast beaches north and south of the city shelter the simple whitewashed houses of the island's oldest Azorean fishing colonies, such as Ribeirão and Santo Antônio. Drawbacks to beach living are that, come summer, the beaches are mobbed by tourists—which means inflated prices, noise, and traffic jams galore—while in winter, it can be cold and a little isolating (especially when it rains). With its strategic location in the middle of the island; its abundance of restaurants, bars, and amenities; and the sheer charm factor, living in and around the Lagoa da Conceição, with its cosmopolitan mix of residents and visitors is a good option for expats. Expect a one-bedroom apartment in Centro to cost between R$500 and R$700 while you can get a small beach house for between R$900 and R$1,400.

Porto Alegre is one of Brazil's greenest cities, with an estimated 1.5 million trees (i.e., one per resident). Among the most verdant, not to mention popular, neighborhoods is the centrally located, upscale Moinhos de Ventos, with its chic boutiques and restaurants and famously leafy streets anchored by the Parque Moinhos de Ventos. Here you can expect a three-bedroom apartment to cost between R$2,000 and R$3,000. Also appealing are surrounding neighborhoods such as Bela Vista, Mont'Serrat, and Três Figueiras, the latter considered to be the wealthiest residential *bairros* in the entire South. Equally central and more affordable, the lively *bairro* of Bom Fim is a traditional working-class neighborhood with a strong Jewish presence, where you'll be able to find a one bedroom in the vicinity of R$600–800. Busy during the week and bucolic on weekends (it borders the city's beloved Parque da Farroupilha), it has an alternative, bohemian vibe and draws lots of artists, students, and intellectuals. Farther afield in the Zona Sul district, Ipanema is a well-to-do neighborhood along the banks of Lago Guaíba whose name reflects its origins as a beachside summer retreat filled with vacation homes. Today, many houses still remain and its lakeshore boardwalk and bike paths are major draws.

GETTING AROUND
Curitiba and Porto Alegre, and to a lesser extent Florianópolis, are easily reached from all other Brazilian cities by air. Numerous daily bus connections link them to each other as well as to Rio de Janeiro and São Paulo.

Curitiba
Curitiba's modern **Aeroporto Internacional Afonso Pena** is 21 kilometers (13 miles) east of the city center. The main bus station and train station are one and the same, hence the hybrid moniker of **Rodoferroviária.**

EXPAT PROFILE: ENTREPRENEURIAL ADVENTURES

Chris, 36, moved to Florianópolis from San Francisco in 2008. From time to time he blogs about his life at Floripa Living (http:// floripaliving.blogspot.com.br). Here he talks about living in Brazil.

WHY HE CAME

I had a buddy who came to Florianópolis for a week's vacation in 2007. When he came back to San Francisco he said, "You have to go. It's unbelievable." So I came in November of 2007 for a week and totally loved it. Floripa is really unique with tons of beautiful places and unbelievable beaches. I went back to San Francisco and thought: "Brazil's blowing up. I want to buy something there." So I started looking for houses online. I had an American friend who ran a tourist company for foreigners in Florianópolis; by chance, I discovered he had just built two houses, and I bought one of them. At the time I was working at Merrill Lynch. I'd been working in finance for nine years, and I thought it would be an interesting time in my life to do something different. I didn't know much about Brazil, but things were getting scary in the United States. So I said: "Screw it, I'm going to move down there." On January 2, 2008, I walked into the office and announced I was moving to Brazil. I moved in March and arrived with no expectations. I originally planned to spend between six months and a year to see if I liked it. Almost five years later I'm still down here.

HOW HE CAME

I have the investor visa and it wasn't that difficult to get. I went through a lawyer—you have to use a local lawyer—who does 95 percent of the work, but you have to provide a ton of documents. Since I got my visa in 2008, it's become more difficult. When I applied I just had to bring down R$50,000. Now you have to invest R$150,000 and employ 10 people. It's a lot more difficult.

LEARNING PORTUGUESE

When I first came I took three months of private classes three times a week at a private language school. I also had a girlfriend who didn't speak English. Speaking Portuguese is totally essential here, especially if you own a business because owners have to be social and interact with customers. This is much more important in Brazil than in the United States, and it's essential in Florianópolis because it's a small city and people want to know you.

MEETING PEOPLE

I jumped right into the social scene and it was easier to integrate than I thought. Floripa has a big social scene, but it's a small place, and there aren't a lot of options. So you start seeing the same people, and it's a quick process to integrate yourself. There aren't a lot of expats in Floripa, but in the summer tons of people travel through.

LIVING IN FLORIPA

It's said that Floripa has the best quality of life in Brazil and I'd have to agree. It's very safe here and a huge plus is living surrounded by beaches and nature. It's really, really special. I live near a beautiful beach, Praia Mole, and I'm always going to the beach, surfing, hiking. Unlike California where you have houses on the beach, here there's nothing. The nature is so well protected. People who come to Floripa for the first time are always blown away, and I know how they feel.

I have people who reach out to me all the time for advice on how to live here. And I always end up telling them that it's a great place to enjoy, but incredibly difficult to make money. Business is very seasonal, and there aren't a lot of opportunities unless you create your own business. And outside of the summer, it's a very small market.

MAKING A LIVING

At first, I had no foresight into what I wanted to do. I spent six months just learning the language, meeting people, and having fun. Then I became friends with the owner of a sushi lounge that was in a unique spot in Centro. The owner—a Brazilian who had lived for 10 years in the States—was looking for a partner, and I had a concept. So we renovated and opened Tatsui in December 2008.

Meanwhile, on my first trip to Floripa I was struck by the fact that there was no Mexican food here. I grew up around California, Arizona, and Colorado where Mexican food was a staple. It seemed as if Brazil would be a great market for it because Brazilians love rice, beans, healthy food, etc. So after a year with Tatsui, I opened up Cactus Mexican Food with an American partner at a shopping mall here in Floripa. Since then, we've opened three other franchises in Florianópolis and Porto Alegre and have plans to expand into São Paulo.

RUNNING A BUSINESS

There are so many difficulties. It's a long, long road and you really have to take your time and know how Brazilians work. It took me three to four years to get a grip on everything. It helped a lot that at Tatsui my partner was Brazilian. That was essential since she could deal with HR stuff and paperwork and deal directly with employees. Employees are difficult to motivate and keep under control. So many steal or deal drugs out of the store. And when you encounter a problem, you can't do anything about it. For instance, a former employee broke into the store and stole stuff, and we couldn't get him arrested. Employees have all the rights. And don't get me started on the bureaucracy.

Be smart. Be patient. Be aware that you're in someone else's world, but as I tell my partner, we don't have to accept everything. We can bring some of our values and try to make a change. For instance, I tried to run Cactus as a Brazilian company, and it didn't really work. We had employees that didn't show up or showed up late. Their mother was sick, or they missed the bus. At first we accepted that it was okay to do this or that. But now we don't. Now we're trying to run Cactus as an American company. We're more strict, but we also show a lot of respect. We train and motivate our staff. We give bonuses based on sales and customer service. It's complicated, but it makes employees feel like part of the company. At first they didn't get it, but they're getting it now.

WORD OF ADVICE FOR OTHER EXPATS

Keep an open mind. Tread carefully. Be prepared. Be friendly. Things are so different here. At first everything's great, but the more time you spend here, the more the little things can start to frustrate you. The bad drivers. The waiting in line. Culturally, it can be difficult to adapt, but the more you settle in, the more you need to do so in order to sustain a life.

THE FUTURE

I leave it open. My goal is to eventually spend six months here and six months in California if I can get Cactus going with a team I can rely on so that I can work remotely. Right now that's impossible because I'm still really involved with every decision. Spending half my time here would be ideal. It's a beautiful place, but it can get small.

Getting around town is easy. Although you can easily walk in and around Centro, the city's municipal bus system is an urban planner's dream. From the two central municipal bus terminals at Praça Tiradentes and Praça Rui Barbosa, you can get a bus to anywhere in the city or the suburbs and to nearby towns (the destination is clearly marked on the front). Taxis are also easy to flag down. In Curitiba, traffic is lighter than in other major Brazilian cities, and roads within the city and throughout the surrounding state are some of Brazil's best.

Florianópolis
Floripa's **Aeroporto Internacional Hercílio Luz** is 12 kilometers (8 miles) south of the city center. Buses from around the state and the country arrive at the modern **Terminal Rodoviário Rita Maria** located between the Hercílio Luz and Colombo Machado Sales bridges.

Although bus service around the island is extensive, buses themselves are infrequent, and service can be slow. If you're living on the island, a car is essential. Bear in mind that traffic is terrible in the summer.

Porto Alegre
Porto Alegre's ultramodern **Aeroporto Internacional Salgado Filho** is only 8 kilometers (5 miles) northeast of the city center. Meanwhile, buses from around the state and the country arrive at the rather forlorn **Estação Rodoviária de Porto Alegre.**

Although getting around central Porto Alegre is easily done on foot, the city also has an extensive municipal bus service as well as a one-line **Metrô**, which despite being quite limited, is a convenient option for travel to or from the airport, Rodoviária, and the Mercado Público. Roads in Porto Alegre and throughout Rio Grande do Sul are well maintained.

THE NORTHEAST

The Northeast is the hottest, sunniest, most culturally rich and economically poor of Brazil's regions. Occupying roughly 30 percent of Brazilian territory, it shelters a population of 53 million, the majority of whom live in its coastal capitals, port cities that date back to the country's 16th-century colonial beginnings.

Indeed, the Northeast constitutes the cradle of Brazil. It was here that, in 1500, a fleet of Portuguese explorers led by navigator Pedro Alvares Cabral accidentally landed on the shores of southern Bahia after being blown off course on their way to India. Through their contact with the native Tupi, the Portuguese were introduced to a glossy hard wood known as *pau brasil* (brazilwood). The red dye it yielded proved to be all the rage in Europe. However, in a few short decades the supply had been exhausted. It was then that the Portuguese discovered the Northeast's rolling coastal hills were ideal for the cultivation of sugarcane, and they quickly set to work wiping out native populations and converting the occupied land into vast plantations. To sustain the expansion of the sugarcane economy, in the 1550s, Portugal began importing vast numbers of slaves from its African colonies to Brazil.

The production of sugar became the number-one source of revenues for the Portuguese crown. It also led to the creation of a colonial elite who poured their wealth into building extravagant churches and ornate mansions to adorn the thriving

© MICHAEL SOMMERS

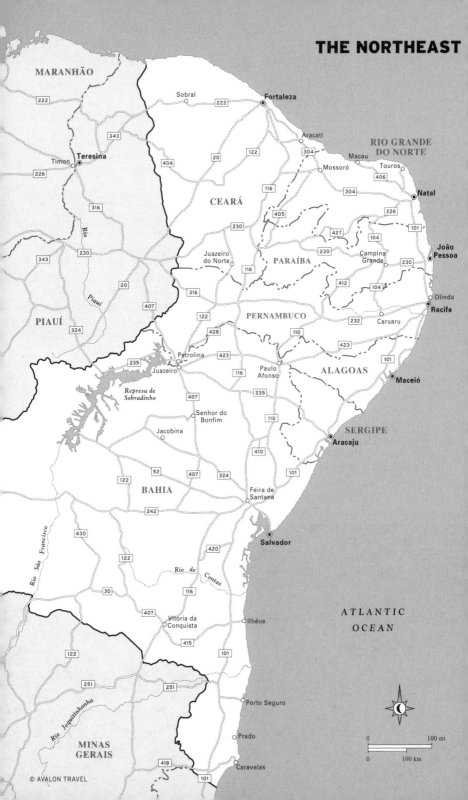

cities of Salvador—Brazil's first capital—Olinda and Recife. Sugar would also lay the foundations for the organization of Brazil's economy—as an exporter of monocultures (sugar, coffee, rubber, etc.), each of which would experience a boom-and-bust cycle—as well as Brazilian society. Plantation life—with the slaves in the *senzala* and the white aristocrats in mansions known as *casas grandes*—would come to permeate Brazilian society. Its legacy of a dual society that pits rich versus poor and black versus white exists to this day.

While on one hand, plantation owners were cruel and racist toward slaves, they had no compunction about fornicating with them. Masters who didn't have a black mistress or legions of illegitimate *mulato* offspring were the exception, not the rule. The consequence of this confusing behavior was the extreme interracial mixing of Brazil's population. In modern times, this has given rise to the myth of Brazil's racial harmony, but it also set the standard for a hidden but deeply rooted racism and glaring inequality that still pervades Brazilian society and manifests itself in subtle but shocking ways. These contradictions are most strongly present in the Northeast, which has Brazil's most racially mixed population—and the most gaping socioeconomic (not to mention racial) disparities.

The Northeast's decline began when the nation's capital moved from Salvador to Rio in 1763 and it was sealed when the abolition of slavery in 1888 brought its plantation-based economy to a dramatic halt. During much of the 20th century, the Northeast languished, and much of its population struggled with poverty. Aside from serious droughts in the Interior, agriculture (still dominated by sugarcane) remained in the hands of large landowners who relied upon unproductive methods. Industry, when it finally arrived, never diversified. As the Southeast became industrialized on a massive scale, truckloads of poor *nordestino* migrants piled aboard open trucks known as *pau de araras* and headed south in search of jobs in the large cities of Rio and São Paulo, where they were often treated with disdain. This southward migration only halted in the 2000s. As a result of both Brazil's economic boom and new government policies and programs created by Worker Party President Luiz Inácio (Lula) da Silva, who was himself a poor migrant from the interior of Pernambuco, the Northeast began to experience unprecedented development and economic growth.

Today, the Northeast has the fastest growing economy in Brazil, and it boasts the third-largest GDP after the Southeast and South. The historically wide gap between rich and poor has closed significantly—between 2004 and 2009, average wages increased by 28 percent and workers experienced a larger rise in salaries than anywhere else in Brazil. With more disposable income than ever before, the Northeast is now the fastest growing consumer market in Brazil, and business, not to mention the housing market, is booming within its largest cities and along its increasingly developed coast. The region's potential has brought a slew of investors, both national and foreign, to the region. However, myriad problems—ranging from poor infrastructure and local government corruption to lack of qualified labor—are major challenges. Despite much progress, the major Northeast cities are going through considerable growing pains due to a lack of urban planning. And despite the newfound (but poorly distributed) wealth, the Northeast still possesses Brazil's highest poverty rates; the socioeconomic extremes are quite glaring.

Most expats who come to the Northeast are drawn to the three biggest states with the three largest economies (Bahia, Pernambuco, and Ceará), whose respective capitals of Salvador, Recife, and Fortaleza—all with populations of over 1.5 million—are expanding at breakneck pace. However, aside from the burgeoning offshore oil segment (in Bahia, Sergipe, and Pernambuco), there are fewer formal opportunities than in Southeast Brazil. A lot of expats who come to the Northeast do so for purposes of study, or to immerse themselves in elements of a singularly rich culture (musical, artistic, artisanal, culinary), or simply because they fall in love with this unique and beautiful region (or a Brazilian who lives here).

Indeed, many are lured by the stunningly beautiful coastline—Brazil's longest at 3,300 kilometers (2,000 miles)—which shelters some of the most paradisiacal tropical beaches on the planet and which, with the idyllic climate, can be enjoyed year-round. The coast is the main reason the Northeast is the prime tourist destination for Brazilians; a 2009 study found that the two states most preferred by Brazilian tourists were Bahia (21 percent) and Pernambuco (12 percent). But international travelers are also lured to the Northeast. If you travel up and down the coast, regardless of whether you stop in a major city, a full-fledged resort town, a rustic fishing village, or a secluded beach, you'll inevitably (and enviously) encounter a fair number of inspired gringos of all ages who, fed up with the trappings of civilization, followed their dreams and decided to open up a *pousada* in paradise.

THE LAY OF THE LAND

The Northeast embraces nine Brazilian states. Stretching from south to north, they are Bahia, Sergipe, Alagoas, Pernambuco, Paraíba, Rio Grande do Norte, Ceará, Piauí, and Maranhão. All of them have Atlantic coastlines, most of which are exceptionally alluring. Bahia's 930-kilometer (580-mile) coastline is the longest while almost entirely landlocked Piauí possesses only 60 kilometers (37 miles) of beaches.

Geographically, the Northeast is divided into four major zones. The Mata Atlântica zone stretches from southern Bahia to Rio Grande do Norte and is somewhat of a misnomer because only around 5 percent remains of the native Atlantic rainforest that once covered the entire coastline. Nevertheless, this coastal stretch, home to the oldest and largest urban centers, remains lusher, more temperate, and more humid—it also receives more rain—than the vast dry interior known as the Sertão.

Hot, arid, and traditionally very poor, the scantly populated and largely rural Sertão covers the majority of the Northeast interior and, in Rio Grande do Norte and Ceará, edges right up to the coast. Scarce rains—and frequently devastating droughts—account for the singular vegetation of scrub, cacti, and thorn trees, known as *caatinga*. Between the coast and the Sertão is a transitional zone known as the Agreste. Meanwhile, parts of Piauí and much of Maranhão are known as the Meio-Norte because, like Brazil's Norte, this zone shares the intense rainfall and humidity of the adjacent Amazonian region.

CLIMATE

Temperatures along the Northeast coast are consistently tropical with lots of sun to go around, although rains can be intense April–July between the states of Bahia and Pernambuco (farther north the sun dominates most of the year). Throughout the year, temperatures hover between 25–30°C (77–86°F) although in the summer they

© MICHAEL SOMMERS

Água de coco sold in the street beats the heat.

can hit 35°C (95°F). The sun is especially hot during this time, but Atlantic breezes keep things refreshing. In winter, the thermometer can drop to 20°C (68°F). If you're venturing into the Sertão, which enjoys a semiarid climate, days can be furnace-like in summer while nights can cool down, hitting lows of around 10°C (50°F) in June–July.

RESOURCES

Although you'll run across foreigners living throughout the Northeast, expats tend to be pretty fragmented and most of them work hard to blend in and live their lives among locals. Not even the three main cities of Salvador, Recife, and Fortaleza have organized expat communities, either in person or in virtual online worlds. Your best chance of getting to know other North American expats in Salvador and Recife is to get in touch with the local U.S. Consulate branches or international schools, which have both staff and students from the United States.

Both Salvador and Recife have American international schools. Salvador's Pan American School of Bahia (www.escolapanamericana.com) follows a North American school calendar and offers bilingual education that extends from early childhood education through high school. Upon graduation, students receive two diplomas, enabling them to pursue higher education at both U.S. and Brazilian universities. The school, with a large campus, is located in the fairly far-flung neighborhood of Piatã. In operation for more than 50 years, the American School of Recife (www.ear.com.br) is Recife's main bilingual school with a U.S.-based curriculum that covers preschool through high school. Its campus—which includes a spanking new sports complex—is located in Boa Viagem.

Both cities as well as Fortaleza also have branches of the Canadian-based Maple Bear School (www.maplebear.com.br), which offers bilingual preschool and elementary school education. Recife's branch is located in the *bairro* of Aflitos, Fortaleza's in José Alencar, and Salvador's (which just opened in 2012) is in the coastal neighborhood of Jardim de Armação.

PRIME LIVING LOCATIONS

Salvador and Bahia

The largest state in the Northeast (and the sixth largest in Brazil), Bahia boasts the Northeast's largest economy and population. However, Bahia looms especially large in the collective imagination, throughout Brazil and abroad, because of its unique history and highly influential culture. Bahia isn't just the birthplace of Brazil, but the birthplace of samba, capoeira, and lambada, of Dorival Caymmi, João Gilberto, Caetano Veloso, and Gilberto Gil, of an inimitable brand of carefree, sensual, musical, slow-paced, fun-loving way of life. While the myths surrounding Bahia are inflated, there is enough heady reality to seduce Brazilians from all over the country and gringos from all over the world.

Bahia was named after the Baía de Todos os Santos (Bay of All Saints), the largest bay in Brazil (and the second largest in the world), into which navigator Amerigo Vespucci sailed on All Saints Day in 1501. It was decided that the strategic, and bewitchingly beautiful, bay would be an ideal site for a settlement that could serve as a capital for Portugal's new Brazilian colony. With its elegant *praças* (squares) and richly adorned baroque churches, São Salvador da Bahia de Todos os Santos soon became the sparkling jewel in the Portuguese imperial crown while the region around the bay, known as the Recôncavo, became a major producer of sugarcane.

For close to three centuries, Salvador boasted the biggest and most bustling port in the South Atlantic. During this time, Bahia became the biggest importer of African slaves in the New World, most of whom were brought over to work the sugar plantations. Aside from a lasting legacy of social and economic inequality, the arrival of the African diaspora in Bahia also created a fantastically rich culture that permeated every aspect of society, including religion, music, cuisine, and language. To this day, Salvador has Brazil's strongest African heritage, with around 85 percent of the population proudly declaring themselves descendants of African ancestry.

In 1763, Brazil's capital was transferred from Salvador to Rio de Janeiro. During the 19th century, its baroque grandeur fading fast, Salvador fell into a certain abandon, although it never lost its provincial charms and unique traditions. It wasn't until the 1980s and 1990s that oil, industry, and later tourism gave Bahia a new lease on life, accompanied by rapid modernization and increased favelas (in the last 30 years the population has quintupled). Today, while many of the treasures of its past are being carefully preserved (though others are shockingly neglected), Salvador is striving to assert its identity as an increasingly modern city of close to three million without losing its traditional *jeito baiano* (Bahian way).

Bahia's myriad natural and cultural attractions are a major draw, not only for tourists, but also for expats looking to retire or start a tourist-related business. Apart from the baroque riches of its capital, the state is blessed with the longest coastline in Brazil. Stretching north from Salvador, the beaches of the Estrada de Coco and Linha Verde mingle rustic fishing villages and coconut plantations with increasingly developed condo complexes and resorts such as Praia do Forte. Heading south, you can spend days or even weeks migrating from one long unspoiled strip of sand to the next. Ilhéus, the historical "cocoa capital," and the ultradeveloped Porto Seguro, a famed party capital, are surrounded by numerous white-sand beaches. Increasingly trendy but still

© MICHAEL SOMMERS

Salvador's colonial center

Robinson Crusoe–worthy are destinations such as Ilha de Boipeba, Barra Grande, Itacaré, and Trancoso. However, for all-out isolation, the area surrounding Caraíva and Corumbau in the far south of the state are still relatively secluded and off the beaten path. Meanwhile, six hours due west into the otherwise arid interior, lies the Chapada Diamantina (Diamond Plateau), a vast and ancient geological region filled with canyons and caverns and crisscrossed by rivers and waterfalls, whose spectacular natural beauty—anchored by charming colonial diamond mining towns of Lençois, Mucugê, and Capão—has made it the number one ecotourism destination in Brazil.

CULTURE

In Salvador and surrounding Bahia, life flows to a different rhythm. Time is more liquid. Although Salvador is a city of three million, its notoriously good-humored residents are a famously unstressed bunch who work hard but also have the fine art of relaxation down to a T. Of course, Salvador itself is very conducive to languor. Its balmy climate, sea breezes, and enticing beaches are constant companions. Music too is everywhere—from the chants of the beach vendors hawking popsicles and grilled shrimp to the twang of the one-string *berimbaus,* a bow-shaped instrument of African origin that accompanies spinning *capoeiristas* as they practice their graceful combination of dance and martial art.

African elements seep into every facet of Bahian culture: from the language and music to the popular Candomblé religion and the famous *moquecas* (a fragrant stew of fish or seafood), shrimp *bobós,* and spicy *acarajés* (crunchy deep-fried bean fritters) that have made Salvador a culinary capital. Fused together with Catholic elements, these traditional culinary treats show up in the dozens of popular *festas* that invade

LAND OF SAINTS AND *ORIXÁS*

Officially, Brazil is the planet's largest Roman Catholic nation. But despite the abundance of magnificent churches and the number of people wearing religious medallions, when it comes to spiritual matters, the country is a lot more heterogeneous than it might seem. And nowhere is this religious mixture more pronounced than in Salvador. When the hundreds of thousands of African slaves who were shipped across the Atlantic arrived in Bahia, they came armed with the divinities of their homeland. After Portuguese slave masters banned any practices that strayed from Catholicism, many of the slaves slyly pretended to adopt Christian dogmas and rituals, but in reality, their adherence was often only superficial. Instead, they merged Catholic symbols with age-old beliefs preserved from their religious heritages. The result was the syncretic Afro-Brazilian religion known as Candomblé.

As Candomblé developed, the *orixás*–traditional African divinities representing various natural forces–became associated with Catholic saints: Oxalá, the Creator, was associated with Jesus Christ; Iemenjá, queen of the seas, was identified as Nossa Senhora da Conceição (Our Lady of Conception); the great warrior and blacksmith, Ogum, was linked to both Santo Antônio and São Jorge; and Iansã, goddess of fire and thunderbolts, was associated with Santa Bárbara. This clever strategy ensured Candomblé's survival for more than four centuries. Nonetheless, during this time it was often brutally repressed, not only by clerical authorities but by the ruling elite as well as government and police officials. In fact, until quite recently, there was a lingering prejudice against worshippers, who were known derogatorily as *macumbeiros* (practitioners of *macumba*, or witchcraft).

Candomblé is still very much alive in Salvador. Indeed, its influences and references are woven into the tapestry of daily life. *Terreiros*–the sacred *casas* (houses) and surrounding areas where rituals and celebrations take place–are all over the city, and in many cases the public can attend ceremonies and celebrations presided over by *mães* and *pais de santos* (venerated Candomblé priests and priestesses). Among the most famous and traditional *terreiros* are Gantois, Ilê Axê Opô Afonja, and Casa Branca.

the streets in the summer, exuberant celebrations that are equally sacred and profane and which culminate in the world's biggest—and longest—outdoor party, Carnaval. Aside from the yearly axé music hits that take Carnaval by storm and then captivate the rest of Bahia and Brazil, Salvador is a musical hotbed where everything from rock and reggae to samba and soul can be listened and danced to, often at open-air shows, festivals, and impromptu street parties. Soteropolitanos (as the capital's inhabitants are known) are never hard-pressed to find an excuse for a party and are always commemorating something.

WHERE TO LIVE

While there's no expat community in Salvador, foreigners tend to be attracted to the city's older, more central, and most atmospheric neighborhoods that straddle the open Atlantic and the placid Bay of All Saints. In between the increasing number of new apartment buildings, there are a lot of charming old ones as well. Living in these areas means you can get around by foot—and bus—with ease. Bonuses include access to the beach and to many cultural venues and activities. A downside is that the municipal government (and many wealthy Bahians) has forsaken these areas for newer, wealthier suburbs stretching north along the coast, which means a certain degree of dilapidation and urban crime.

The middle-class beach neighborhood of Barra is a draw for foreigners because of its idyllic location between the picturesque Porto da Barra and Farol da Barra beaches, coupled with numerous amenities, bars, and restaurants. Barra has a laid-back beach-culture vibe and a certain degree of cosmopolitanism due to it being a major tourist draw. In the summer, though, it can get mobbed and noisy (especially during Carnaval), and it can also be a little seedy around the edges. North along the *orla* (coast), the middle-class beach neighborhoods of Ondina, Rio Vermelho, and Pituba are also popular. Rio Vermelho is headquarters for Salvador's throbbing bohemian nightlife scene; traditionally a lot of artists and intellectuals have lived here. Bland Pituba is a favored neighborhood of Salvador's somewhat square upper-middle class.

Inland from Barra, stretching up toward Campo Grande, lie the old wealthy residential neighborhoods of Graça, Canela, and the Corredor da Vitória. Graça and Canela are less chic than they used to be, but pleasant and central. Corredor da Vitória is literally a long sweeping corridor lined with a tunnel of mango trees and luxury high-rises overlooking the Bay of All Saints. The neighborhoods of Centro surrounding Campo Grande—Garcia, Barris, and Dois de Julho—are more *popular* but very vibrant. Dois de Julho, in particular, has an alternative vibe that mingles with the *bairro's* traditional street life and, unfortunately, some sketchy criminal elements.

Foreigners never fail to be impressed by the architectural splendor of Salvador's colonial district, the Pelourinho—some go so far as to open hotels and restaurants in this UNESCO World Heritage Site. However, the combination of tourists and the people who prey on them has made the area somewhat unsafe and less than desirable to live in. Not as old, but equally picturesque, and more authentic and tranquil is the adjacent working-class neighborhood of Santo Antônio. Its century-old houses overlooking the bay have seduced quite a few foreigners who, before prices began to soar, bought up many of the crumbling mansions for a song and transformed some into enticing *pousadas*.

Rents in all of the aforementioned *bairros* tend not to vary that significantly. Differences in price have more to do with an apartment's size, the building, and its amenities than the actual neighborhood. Expect a one bedroom to cost between R$500 and R$800 and a three bedroom to range from R$1,000 to R$1,800. Note however that summertime (between New Year's and Carnaval) is often a difficult period to rent since many owners take advantage of the influx of summer tourists to rent their apartments for short durations at inflated prices.

In terms of the rest of Bahia, those seeking to live on a beautiful beach have limitless opportunities. The coastline north of Salvador, stretching up to Bahia's frontier with Sergipe, has recently become one the most booming coastal real estate areas in all of Brazil. Between Salvador and Imbassaí, areas that 10 years ago were small fishing villages are now being overrun by middle- and upper-class condominium complexes. However, the area—particularly as you travel north and into the interior—still has interesting and affordable properties for sale. South of Salvador, expats are fond of secluded, but increasingly hip, hot spots such as Ilha de Boipeba, Barra Grande, and Itacaré. Meanwhile, stretching south from Porto Seguro, the alluring colonial towns cum beach resorts of Arraial de Ajuda and Trancoso also draw foreigners, many of whom are seduced into investing in everything from hostels to chic boutique hotels. Property costs in all of these areas, however, have increased substantially. Those who prefer mountains and waterfalls to sand and sea might consider purchasing land or an old colonial house in and around the diamond mining towns of the Chapada Diamantina, where prices are still significantly more affordable than the coast.

GETTING AROUND

Most international travelers arrive in Salvador by air at **Aeroporto Deputado Luís Eduardo Magalhães (Dois de Julho),** located some 30 kilometers (19 miles) from the city center. Both Porto Seguro and Ilhéus also have airports that receive flights from major Brazilian cities such as Salvador, Rio, and São Paulo.

Salvador's bus station, **Rodoviária Central** is across the street from the bustling Shopping Iguatemi. From here you can catch buses to destinations throughout Bahia and Brazil. Bus service throughout Bahia is quite extensive.

Municipal buses in Salvador are plentiful and go practically everywhere. The main municipal bus station in Centro is Lapa, but many buses also pass through Campo Grande en route to the rest of the city. At night, bus service dwindles and it's often safer to take a cab or to drive.

Having a car in Salvador isn't essential, particularly if you live in the dense, easily walkable older and more central neighborhoods. However, if you're living in newer farther flung areas, a car can be a major advantage even though you'll have to deal with the stress of increasingly bad traffic congestion. Driving in Salvador can be a challenge. It isn't that Soteropolitanos are poor drivers, but they have a penchant for not adhering to rules of the road. Meanwhile, for exploring the surrounding region, especially the beautiful north coast, which boasts an excellent (privatized) highway, having a car is a big bonus.

Recife and Pernambuco

Like Bahia, Pernambuco is another economic, demographic, and cultural powerhouse of the Northeast. With a rich history all its own, it boasts some of Brazil's most unique and fascinating cultural events and traditions, particularly in the realms of art and music. Despite a wide chasm between rich and poor, it possesses one of the Northeast's fastest growing economies, based in its capital of Recife.

Founded by the Dutch in the 1500s, Recife is known as Brazil's Amsterdam because its historical center is dissected by a series of canals flowing into the sea. The similarities, however, end there. Recife is humid, somewhat chaotic, and quite poor with a reputation for urban violence. Yet it is also a subtly alluring place with numerous historical buildings, Brazil's longest urban beach of Boa Viagem, and a distinctive cultural scene. Across the bay from Recife sits Pernambuco's original capital, Olinda, a UNESCO World Heritage Site whose gleaming baroque churches, cobblestoned streets, and lovely squares make it one of the most splendid examples of colonial architecture in the Americas. No mere ode to the glorious past, Olinda is home to a thriving artist community, whose numerous ateliers, galleries, and boutiques seduce tourists. Tourism is also big business along the southern coast of Pernambuco, particularly

© MICHAEL SOMMERS

Recife's Centro

around the resort of Porto de Galinhas and into the neighboring state of Alagoas, both of which are blessed with some of Brazil's dreamiest beaches.

Traveling inland from Recife, the landscape gives way to the dry, rugged desert-like Sertão, known for its blazing blue skies, red earth, thorn trees, and cattle. Many towns of the Pernambucano interior are reputed for their traditional crafts such as ceramics and woodcut as well as their *festas populares*. The most famous of them, Caruaru, boasts one of the largest and most colorful outdoor markets plus one of the most legendary *Festas Juninas* in Brazil.

Pernambuco was one of the first regions to be colonized by the Portuguese, who founded Olinda in the 1530s. The gently rolling hills of the coastline proved ideal for the cultivation of sugarcane. After the quick subjugation of the local native people and importation of shiploads of slaves from Africa, the region was soon covered in vast plantations that transformed Pernambuco and Alagoas into one of the biggest producers of cane in the world. Then in 1630, Dutch troops invaded. After laying siege to Olinda, they built a new capital on the marshy islands crisscrossed by rivers, 6 kilometers (4 miles) to the south, where the excellent natural harbor protected by offshore reefs (*arrecifes* in Portuguese) eventually lent the city its name. By the time the Portuguese took back control of Recife in 1654, it had grown into a thriving port.

Like Bahia, Pernambuco fell into decline in the 19th century with the demise of the sugar trade and the abolition of slavery. While to this day, sugarcane fields still dominate (and Pernambucano *cachaça* is some of the finest in the country), Recife has grown into an important industrial and commercial center. Aside from a booming construction sector (it has the dubious distinction of possessing more high-rises than any other Brazilian capital aside from São Paulo and Rio), Recife has a mushrooming

IT sector, headquartered at Porto Digital, the largest technological park in Brazil. On the city's outskirts, the Suape Industrial Complex is one of Brazil's largest and most modern ports as well as a major logistics and industrial hub. In recent years, it has drawn major national and international investment; the more than 100 companies headquartered at Suape are the source of various expat jobs.

CULTURE

While Pernambuco is fairly small in terms of size, in terms of cultural and historical importance, it is a giant. Aside from possessing an impressive array of colonial architecture, Recife and Olinda can lay claim to some of the richest artistic and musical traditions in Brazil. Aside from forró, which is ubiquitous throughout the Northeast, Pernambuco is responsible for the birth of rhythms such as *frevo, maracatu,* and *mangue beat.* Recife, in particular, boasts one of the most singular and creative music scenes in Brazil, which fuels a varied nightlife as well as many shows, performances, and popular *festas.* Traditions and new tendencies culminate in the exuberant, highly colorful street Carnavals of both Recife and Olinda, which attract revelers from all over the world.

Mirroring the eclectic influences of Pernambucano culture is the local cuisine, an intoxicating mixture of indigenous, African, and European (mainly Portuguese and Spanish) influences. Along the coast, dishes such as *peixada* and *moqueca* feature fish and seafood in stews that are seasoned with cilantro, lime, and coconut milk. From the rugged interior come robust dishes such as *carne-de-sol* (sun-dried beef) and *bode assado* (roasted goat) cooked with *macaxeira* (manioc) and beans. And then there are the desserts: simple but inspired creations such as tangy *coalho* cheese dripping with *mel de engenho* (sugarcane molasses) and *cartola,* a fried banana topped with creamy Sertanejo cheese and a dusting of sugar and cinnamon.

WHERE TO LIVE

Foreigners who live in Recife tend to stick to the vast Zona Sul middle-upper-class beachside neighborhoods of Boa Viagem and adjacent Pina, with their gleaming new high-rises, amenities galore, and direct access to Brazil's longest urban beach. However, Boa Viagem is certainly nowhere near as interesting as Rio's Copacabana, to which it is often compared. It lacks Copa's texture and mixture of people; indeed, Boa Viagem's sprawl, coupled with the number of shopping centers and skyscrapers, give it more in common with Barra de Tijuca (with which it shares a major traffic problem due to the number of cars). The fact that this is Recife's most upscale *bairro* means it's also its most expensive.

Less popular with foreigners are the older middle- and upper-class Zona Norte residential neighborhoods that include Casa Forte, Aflitos, Espinheiros, and Graças. Many of these *bairros* were originally plantations that date back to Recife's 16th- and 17th-century sugarcane heyday. Until recently, they still possessed many old mansions and houses, although the booming real estate market has caused many to be torn down and replaced by increasingly tall high-rises. However, many old squares and tree-lined streets have remained, particularly in Casa Forte. Advantages of these neighborhoods are that they are less touristy, more tranquil, and suffer from less crime than Boa Viagem. In recent years, however, rents have escalated. Expect rent for a three-bedroom apartment in any of these neighborhoods to range from R$1,500 to R$3,000.

colonial Olinda with Recife in the background

© MICHAEL SOMMERS

Another appealing option is moving into a colonial house in Recife's sister city of Olinda. Because few people actually work in Olinda, rent is lower than one would expect. In terms of its friendly, small-town vibe and immense charm—not to mention the omnipresence of striking baroque churches—Olinda is incomparable, although aside from some enticing restaurants and bars, amenities are somewhat lacking.

GETTING AROUND

Recife's **Aeroporto Internacional dos Guararapes** is at the far end of Boa Viagem, about 12 kilometers (7.5 miles) south of the city center. Meanwhile buses from all over Brazil arrive at the **Terminal Integrado de Passageiros (TIP),** which is pretty far—14 kilometers (8.5 miles)—from the center. Fortunately, the Metrô links the bus station with Recife's local bus station, **Estação Central,** at the Recife station.

Driving around Recife is somewhat tricky since there are many one-way streets and bridges. The urban layout is rather haphazard, and it is hard to identify streets in the center. As in Salvador, a car can be very handy the farther out you live from the more compact central neighborhoods. You'll especially appreciate one in order to make strategic getaways up and down the coast of Pernambuco and into neighboring states of Paraíba and Alagoas.

Recife's municipal bus system is complicated, and routes change frequently. By day, taking buses between Santo Antônio and Boa Viagem, and from both of these neighborhoods to Olinda, is fairly straightforward. The gradually expanding Metrô is useful for getting to and from the bus station and the airport, but that's about it. If you don't have a car, taxis are a great idea, especially at night. You can flag them down easily in the street.

EXPAT PROFILE: LEARNING OPPORTUNITIES

Michael Jerome Wolff spent a year between 2011 and 2012 living between Rio de Janeiro and Recife and doing research for his PhD in political science. During this time, he published The Rio-Recife Blog (http://photowolff.tumblr. com), a photojournalism blog where he chronicled his research into the complex worlds of police, drugs, and crime in the favelas of both cities. Here he discusses his experience.

WHY HE CAME
It all started when I went to Mexico and got robbed by the police and that made me furious with police corruption. That episode led me to Brazil, which is known for police violence. I first came here in 2008. Most recently, I received a grant from BRASA (Brazil Studies Association) and arrived in August 2011 to spend a year doing research in the favelas of Rio and Recife.

HOW HE CAME
I've come to Brazil on three different visas: a tourist visa, student visa, and work visa (I was a researcher paid by a foundation). The work visa was the most complicated because of the type of work I was doing. My demand was rejected several times, and I had to get letters written by U.S. and Brazilian members of congress. Ultimately, each consulate has a lot of discretion.

THE MOVING PROCESS
All I brought for a year was a large suitcase and a duffel bag with my computer, camera, books, and clothes. I rented places that were already furnished. The only thing I bought was a car.

LEARNING PORTUGUESE
I started picking up Portuguese when I first came in 2008 and was meeting a lot of people. In 2011, I spent a month in Rio studying Portuguese intensively. Ultimately, I found it more helpful just to read and write and talk to people a lot.

MEETING PEOPLE
The expat group in Recife is relatively small and mostly Europeans. I'm a pretty personable, outgoing guy, but I found it easier to meet people in Rio. Rio is much more international and more accommodating. The population is more used to foreigners, and there's a whole lot more going on. There's also a lot more money. The class structure

Fortaleza and Ceará

One of the largest, traditionally poorest, and most arid of the northeastern states, Ceará has a distinctive identity of its own, not to mention more than 600 kilometers (370 miles) of some of the most stunning coast in Brazil. Its vibrant, bustling, modern capital of Fortaleza is the second-largest city in the Northeast and a major tourist hub, not to mention one of the region's biggest economic and cultural centers.

Fortaleza was founded in 1600 by the Portuguese, who showed little interest in the area until the Dutch arrived on the scene in 1637 and constructed a formidable five-pointed fortress overlooking the sea. For a long time, Fortaleza's geographic isolation, coupled with frequent droughts and Indian attacks, kept it from developing into anything more than a colonial outpost. It was only in the 1820s, when Brazilian ports opened up to international commerce, that Fortaleza became a major shipping center from which cotton and beef raised in Ceará's backlands were transported to Europe.

However, during much of the 19th and 20th century, Ceará struggled with misery, primarily due to the harsh conditions in the drought-ridden Sertão. Waves of poor migrants from the interior flooded Fortaleza. Often unable to find work in the capital, is more disparate in Recife, and that doesn't facilitate social interaction.

FINDING AN APARTMENT

I found a couple around my age, in their mid-30s, an English guy and a Brazilian girl. Actually they found me on a website called Easy Roommate, where I had posted a profile. I ended up renting a room from them in a neighborhood called Casa Forte, a pleasant middle-class neighborhood with lots of trees. I was paying R$1,000 for a room, which included all my food. Recife rents are expensive in middle-class neighborhoods, but they're still really cheap in lower-class neighborhoods (in Rio, there is much more middle ground). Although rent in Recife is expensive, the rest of life is much more affordable.

LIVING IN RECIFE

Recife's a sweet place, a lot less touristy and a lot calmer than Rio, which is sometimes like a giant party. The people are really nice, and for the most part, accommodating. The weather is phenomenal. And there are always interesting cultural activities, like *maracatu* dancing, going on. On the downside there are security issues, and traffic and public transportation are terrible. Even with a car, you'll spend hours a day in traffic because of poor planning and no investment in roads.

ADVICE FOR OTHER EXPATS

The distance between upper-middle class and poor Brazilians is huge. In North America, we come from a middle-class society, and it's a shock to be confronted with these social contrasts. It's very easy to get comfortable with one (socioeconomic) group and completely alienate yourself from the other. The best thing to do is mix and mingle with all Brazilians as much as possible, which isn't easy. Make sure you don't always go out to the same part of town. Go downtown (where a lot of middle-class Brazilians won't go). Explore different neighborhoods. It's easy to set up English classes in favelas. NGOs are starved for money and teachers—this will give you intimate contact with the poor side of Brazil. The biggest misconceptions foreigners have about favelas are the same ones held by middle-class Brazilians: that if you go in, you won't come out alive. It's really changing though.

many continued on to Rio and São Paulo. Only recently have the city and coastal areas flourished as a result of new industries, a thriving service and commercial sector, and a booming tourist trade, coupled with enlightened state governments which have made significant headway in diminishing poverty through efficient education and health programs.

Today, Fortaleza has the third-biggest economy of the Northeast capitals after Salvador and Recife. However, unlike those other cities, practically nothing remains of Fortaleza's colonial past. In fact, the city's signature skyline is crammed with multistory office and apartment buildings, not to mention a multitude of tourist hotels. Fortaleza's saving graces are the urban beaches around which much of its social life revolves, where sweeping sands and clean blue waters are accompanied by sophisticated *megabarracas* where you can surf the web (or the waves), get a massage or a manicure, and feast on fresh crab.

Yet while Fortaleza's beaches are attractive, the shores stretching north and south from the city offer some of the most fabulous beaches in all of Brazil. The truth is that the tropical beaches in other parts of Brazil are likely to have look-alikes in the Caribbean, Thailand, or Polynesia, but nowhere else will you encounter the striking

© MICHAEL SOMMERS

Many of Ceará's beaches boast dramatic red cliffs.

blend of crumbling red cliffs, gleaming white sand, and intensely blue waters that are particular to Ceará.

CULTURE

In Ceará, the culture of the Sertão is omnipresent, even in Fortaleza. There is no shortage of places where you can listen and dance to live *forró,* which Cearenses claim is more popular here than anywhere else in the Northeast (no mean feat). And the local cuisine is dominated by Sertanejo dishes ranging from *carne de sol* (sun-dried beef) and *arroz-de-carneiro* (a local version of a lamb risotto) to *baião-de-dois* (the *dois* in question are beans and rice, bound together with melted *coalho* cheese). That said, along the coast you'll also encounter lots of fish and seafood, and since Fortaleza is Brazil's lobster capital, this crustacean is cheaper and more abundant here than in any other part of the country.

WHERE TO LIVE

Most foreigners who choose to move to Fortaleza are naturally attracted to the beach. The centrally located, upscale beach *bairro* of Meireles is a favorite in that it lacks some of the noise and seediness of Iracema and the rampant, overdevelopment of posh Mucuripe. The glittery high-rises that line the main ocean boulevard of Meireles' Avenida Beira Mar are reminiscent of Copacabana, as is the shady boardwalk favored by joggers, walkers, and bikers. Going inland, the well-to-do neighborhood of Aldeota is also highly prized. Its tree-lined avenues mingle residential and commercial buildings. Aside from a number of upscale shopping centers, it shelters some of Fortaleza's finest restaurants and hottest bars. The convenient location of these *bairros* allows for

EXPAT PROFILE: IDYLLIC RETIREMENT

James, 61, moved from Vancouver to Fortaleza in 2009 to be with his Cearense partner. He is the author of Flavors of Brazil (http://flavorsofbrazil.blogspot.com.br), a blog that offers a culinary tour of Brazil and discussion of regional dishes and local foods. Here he talks about what led him here and why he stayed.

WHY HE CAME

In the early '80s I quit my job to spend six months backpacking around South America. I started in Brazil and never got any farther. I made friends in Fortaleza and always came back. Then I met my partner and decided to move here. So like many who come here, my reasons were personal.

HOW HE CAME

I have a retirement visa which I received very quickly. The process was quite straightforward. I just had to go to the Brazilian Consulate in Vancouver and within 60 days I received my visa.

MAKING A LIVING

I had a business in Vancouver and I sold it. I also taught ESL in Canada and I had a TESL diploma. So now I teach English at the Receita Federal (Federal Customs), and I also give private lessons at home (for R$40 an hour). However, it would be hard to make a living teaching ESL. I do it to supplement my main retirement income, including my Canada Pension Plan.

MEETING PEOPLE

I socialize with a mix of expats and Brazilians, but probably 80 percent of my friends are Brazilians. There's not much of an expat community here. The foreigners who are here are almost entirely Europeans and most have Brazilian partners.

LEARNING PORTUGUESE

I taught myself as a tourist. I already spoke French and Spanish. But I also spent four weeks at a private language school here.

LIVING IN FORTALEZA

I'm happy I ended up here. I'm a big beach fan. Everywhere in Brazil you have beautiful beaches, but you can't beat Ceará, which has 400 miles of them. Fortaleza also has the best climate in the country. It never goes above 30 degrees during the day and never below 24 at night. Although the sun can be very strong—we're only a couple of degrees south of the equator—I live in Meireles, only three blocks from the beach, and there are always trade winds. The other thing I like most about living here is the people. Cearenses are great, fun-loving people. They love to have a good time and are not heavy in any sense.

The only thing I miss is that the city is lacking in cultural life. For instance, there's only one art house cinema. Ultimately, you end up socializing a lot at house parties, weekends on the beaches, or bars with live music. There's a good selection of casual nightlife.

A WORD OF ADVICE FOR OTHER EXPATS

Learn as much Portuguese as you can beforehand. If you come here thinking you're going to learn it on the go, you'll have a rough time.

PRIME LIVING LOCATIONS

easy access to beaches and Centro both on foot and via public transportation, meaning that you can get away with living in these neighborhoods without a car. In Aldeota, expect to pay around R$600–1,000 to rent a one bedroom and R$1,200–2,000 for a three bedroom.

Beyond Fortaleza itself, many foreigners are drawn to Ceará's superb beaches. Only 160 kilometers (100 miles) east of the city, the poetically named Canoa Quebrada (Broken Canoe) is one of the state's most popular getaways. A former fishing village that became a 1970s hippie haven and is now (sadly) transitioning from hip to hysterically mobbed, Canoa Quebrada possesses a youthful yet cosmopolitan vibe that draws an international crew of sun and sand worshippers, some of whom decide to stay permanently. The coastline running west of Fortaleza toward Maranhão is less developed and more deserted (for now) as you get some distance from the capital. The star attraction is Jericoacoara, a primitive paradise set amid magnificent dunes that is routinely celebrated by international *travelistas* as one of the planet's most perfect beaches (and for this reason isn't quite as primitive as it used to be although a saving grace is that "Jeri" lies within an environmentally protected zone). Despite (and because of) its remoteness (320 km [200 mi] from Fortaleza), Jeri has attracted a good many expats who, unable to face returning to civilization, have remained and opened charming yet simple *pousadas* and restaurants.

GETTING AROUND

Flights from most major Brazilian cities arrive at **Aeroporto Internacional Pinto Martins.** Long-distance buses arrive at the **Rodoviária João Tomé.** Fortaleza's airport and *rodoviária* are both in the southern suburb of Fátima. Transportation to Centro or the beaches is easy.

A modern, grid-planned city, Fortaleza itself is easy to navigate by car although like other big Brazilian cities, traffic can be a major hassle. As always, having a car gives you a lot of extra mobility, especially for quick trips to the more remote (and seductive) destinations up and down the coast. If you don't have a car, taxis are cheap, easy to find, and recommended for getting around at night. As for public transportation, bus service within the city and to nearby beach towns is quite good. Buses that circulate between Centro and the closer urban beaches include those marked "Grande Circular" and "Mucuripe." Moreover after 13 years of stalling, in June 2012, the city at long last inaugurated the first line of its subway system, Metrofor.

RESOURCES

Embassies and Consulates

IN BRAZIL
U.S. EMBASSY IN BRASÍLIA
SES - Av. das Nações, Quadra 801, Lote 03,
Brasília, DF, 70403-900
tel. 61/3312-7000
http://brazil.usembassy.gov

U.S. CONSULATE IN RIO DE JANEIRO
Av. Presidente Wilson 147, Centro
Rio de Janeiro, RJ, 20030-020
tel. 21/3823-2000
http://riodejaneiro.usconsulate.gov

U.S. CONSULATE IN SÃO PAULO
Rua Henri Dunant 500, Chácara Santo
Antônio
São Paulo, SP, 04709-100
tel. 11/5186-7000
http://saopaulo.usconsulate.gov

U.S. CONSULATE IN RECIFE
Rua Gonçalves Maia 163, Boa Vista
Recife, PE, 50070-060
tel. 81/3416-3050
http://recife.usconsulate.gov

CANADIAN EMBASSY IN BRASÍLIA
SES, Av. das Nações, Quadra 803, Lote 16
Brasilia, DF, 70410-900
tel. 61/3424-5400
www.canadainternational.gc.ca

CANADIAN CONSULATE IN RIO DE JANEIRO
Av. Atlântica 1130, 5 andar, Atlântica Business
Center, Copacabana
Rio de Janeiro, RJ, 22021-000
tel. 21/2543-3004
www.canadainternational.gc.ca

CANADIAN CONSULATE IN SÃO PAULO
Av das Nações Unidas 12901, 16 andar,
Brooklin
São Paulo, SP, 04578-000
tel. 11/5509-4321
www.canadainternational.gc.ca

IN THE UNITED STATES
BRAZILIAN EMBASSY IN WASHINGTON, D.C.
3006 Massachusetts Avenue NW
Washington, D.C. 20008-3634
tel. 202/238-2823
http://washington.itamaraty.gov.br/en-us

BRAZILIAN CONSULATE IN CHICAGO
401 North Michigan Avenue, Suite 1850
Chicago, IL 60611
tel: 312/464-0244
http://chicago.itamaraty.gov.br

BRAZILIAN CONSULATE IN HOUSTON
Park Tower North, 1233 West Loop South,
Suite 1150
Houston, TX 77027
tel: 713/961-3063
http:/houston.itamaraty.gov.br

BRAZILIAN CONSULATE IN MIAMI
80 SW 8th St., Suite 2600
Miami, FL 33130
tel: 305/285-6200
http://miami.itamaraty.gov.br

BRAZILIAN CONSULATE IN NEW YORK
1185 Avenue of the Americas (Sixth Avenue),
21st Floor
New York, NY 10036
Tel: 917/777-7777
http://novayork.itamaraty.gov.br

BRAZILIAN CONSULATE IN SAN FRANCISCO
300 Montgomery Street, Suite 900
San Francisco, CA 94104
tel: 415/981-8170
http://saofrancisco.itamaraty.gov.br

IN CANADA
BRAZILIAN EMBASSY IN OTTAWA
450 Wilbrod Street
Ottawa, ON, K1N 6M8
tel. 613/237-1090
http://ottawa.itamaraty.gov.br

BRAZILIAN CONSULATE IN TORONTO
77 Bloor Street West, Suites 1109 and 1105
Toronto, ON, M5S 1M2
tel: 416/922-2503
http://toronto.itamaraty.gov.br

BRAZILIAN CONSULATE IN VANCOUVER
2020-666 Burrard Street
Vancouver, BC, V6C 2X8
tel: 604/696-5311
www.vancouver.itamaraty.gov.br

Planning Your Fact-Finding Trip

TRAVEL RESOURCES
BACC TRAVEL
tel. 800/222-2746
www.bacctravel.com
Based in New York City, BACC offers discount fares from the United States to Brazil.

BRAZIL NUTS
tel. 800/553-9959
www.brazilnuts.com
Based in Naples, Florida, this travel agency has informed staff who can book flights and hotels.

D-AIRFARE
www.dairfare.com
Blog specializing in air travel to and from Brazil. The companion site, www.accommodationinbrazil.info, specializes in finding inexpensive accommodation.

GLOBOTUR
tel. 800/998-5521
www.globotur.com
Based in Houston, this Brazilian-run agency consistently comes up with great fares for travelers in the United States and Canada.

HIDDEN POUSADAS BRAZIL
www.hiddenpousadasbrazil.com
This site and its more budget-oriented sister site, www.pousadahotelbrazil.com, offer reviews as well as bookings of alluring and off-beat *pousadas* throughout Brazil.

VISIT BRAZIL
www.visitbrasil.com
The official site of Embratur, the Brazilian ministry of tourism.

RESOURCES

Making the Move

VISA SERVICES

Contact the Brazilian consulate's visa section in your jurisdiction for information about applying for all types of visas. Online application forms are available at https://scedv.serpro.gov.br

PASSPORT VISAS EXPRESS
tel. 888/596-6028
www.passportvisasexpress.com
This online visa expediting service is a recommended alternative for getting a tourist visa.

IMMIGRATION
FEDERAL POLICE (POLÍCIA FEDERAL)
www.dpf.gov.br
The site has information about all services for *estrangeiros* (foreigners) including extending visas and acquiring a CIE, along with addresses for *delegacias* throughout Brazil.

PF DELEGACIA IN RIO DE JANEIRO
Av. Rodrigues Alves 1, 3 andar, Centro
Rio de Janeiro, RJ, 20081-250
tel. 21/2203-4000

PF DELEGACIA IN SÃO PAULO
Rua Hugo D'Antola 95, Lapa de Baixo
São Paulo, SP, 05038-090
tel. 11/3538-5000

BRAZILIAN MINISTRIES
MINISTRY OF FOREIGN AFFAIRS (MINISTÉRIO DE RELAÇÕES EXTERIORES)
Palácio Itamaraty, Esplanada dos Ministérios, Bloco H
Brasília, DF, 70170-900
www.itamaraty.gov.br

MINISTRY OF JUSTICE (MINISTÉRIO DE JUSTIÇA)
Esplanada dos Ministérios, Bloco T, Edifício Sede
Brasília, DF, 70064-900
tel. 61/2025-3232 (Departamento dos Estrangeiros)
http://portal.mj.gov.br

MINISTRY OF LABOR AND EMPLOYMENT (MINISTÉRIO DO TRABALHO E EMPREGO)
Esplanada dos Ministérios, Bloco F
Brasília, DF, 70059-900
tel. 61/2031-6000
http://portal.mte.gov.br
For information in English about work visas, access www.mte.gov.br/trab_estrang_ing/Procedure_Guide.pdf

MINISTRY OF SCIENCE, TECHNOLOGY, AND INNOVATION (MINISTÉRIO DA CIÊNCIA, TECNOLOGIA, E INOVAÇÃO)
Esplanada dos Ministérios, Bloco E
Brasília, DF, 70067-900
tel. 61/2033-7500
www.mct.gov.br

MOVERS AND SHIPPERS
CONFIANÇA MOVING AND SHIPPING
www.confiancamoving.com

FASTWAY MOVING
www.fastwaymoving.com

HOUSING CONSIDERATIONS
Nationwide Online Real Estate Classifieds
CLASSIFICADOS BRASIL
www.classificados-brasil.com

ZAP IMÓVEIS
www.zap.com.br/imoveis

Language and Education

PORTUGUESE COURSES FOR FOREIGNERS

CASA DO CAMINHO LANGUAGE CENTER

Rua Farme de Amoedo, 135, Ipanema
Rio de Janeiro, RJ, 22420-020
tel. 21/2267-6652
www.casadocaminho-languagecentre.org

CONSELHO CULTURAL DAS NAÇÕES

SEPN 513, Bloco A, Sala 303, Ed. Bittar I
Brasilia, DF, 70760-521
tel. 61/3340-8977
www.conselhocultural.com

DIÁLOGO

Rua Dr João Pondé 240, Barra
Salvador, BA, 40140-810
tel. 71/3264-0053
www.dialogo-brazilstudy.com

FAST FORWARD

Alameda Lorena 684, Casa 4,
Jardim Paulista
São Paulo, SP, 01424-000
tel. 11/3051-7112
www.fastforward.com.br

INSTITUTO BRASIL ESTADOS UNIDOS (IBEU)

Copacabana Branch
Av. Nossa Senhora de Copacabana 690,
5 andar, Copacabana
Rio de Janeiro, RJ, 20050-001
tel. 21/2548-8430
www.ibeu.org.br/brazilian-portuguese

PONTIFÍCIA UNIVERSIDADE CATÓLICA DO RIO DE JANEIRO (PUC-RIO)

Curso de Português para Estrangeiros
Departamento de Letras
Rua Marquês de São Vicente 225, Casa XV,
Gávea
Rio de Janeiro, RJ, 22451-900
tel. 0800/970-9556
www.cce.puc-rio.br/letras/portugues.htm

PONTIFÍCIA UNIVERSIDADE CATÓLICA DE SÃO PAULO (PUC-SÃO PAULO)

Brazilian Portuguese Language and
Culture Course
Divisão de Cooperação Internacional
Rua Monte Alegre 984, Prédio Sede, Sala
T-39, Perdizes
São Paulo, SP, 05014-901
tel. 11/3670-8012
www.pucsp.br/arii/eng.html

UNIVERSIDADE DE BRASÍLIA (UNB)

Peppfol—Programa de Ensino e Pesquisa em
Português para Falantes de Outras Línguas
Prédio Multiuso 1, Bloco C, Sala 28/4
Campus Universitário Darcy Ribeiro,
Asa Norte
Brasília, DF, 70910-900
tel. 61/3107-5835
www.let.unb.br/peppfol

BILINGUAL EDUCATION
EDUCAÇÃO BILINGUE NO BRASIL

www.educacaobilingue.com
A useful source of information about bilingual education and schools throughout Brazil.

MAPLE BEAR CANADIAN SCHOOL
www.maplebear.com.br
With more than 50 schools around the country, Maple Bear's preschool and elementary school curricula are based upon Canadian teaching methodologies.

Health

HEALTH INFORMATION
MINISTRY OF HEALTH (MINISTÉRIO DE SAÚDE)
Esplanada dos Ministérios, Bloco G
Brasilia,DF, 70058-900
tel. 136 (SUS)
www.saude.gov.br

MD TRAVEL HEALTH
www.mdtravelhealth.com

PUBLIC HEALTH AGENCY OF CANADA: BRAZIL INFORMATION
www.phac-aspc.gc.ca

U.S. CENTERS FOR DISEASE CONTROL AND PREVENTION: BRAZIL INFORMATION
www.nc.cdc.gov

WORLD HEALTH ORGANIZATION (ORGANIZAÇÃO MUNDIAL DE SAÚDE)
SEN, Lote 19
Brasília, DF, 70800-400
tel. 61/3251-9595
www.who.int

HEALTH INSURANCE
PACIFIC PRIME
www.pacificprime.com

UNIMED
www.unimed.com.br

EMERGENCY PHONE NUMBERS
- Ambulance: 192
- Fire: 193
- Police: 190

Employment

RECRUITING FIRMS
ABRAHAMS EXECUTIVE SEARCH
www.abrahams.com.br

DASEIN
www.dasein.com.br

FESA
www.fesa.com.br

EMPLOYMENT WEBSITES
Brazilian Sites (in Portuguese)
CATHO
www.catho.com.br

CURRICULUM.COM
www.curriculum.com.br

EMPREGOS.COM
www.empregos.com.br

MAIS STARTUP
www.maisstartupcom.br

MANAGER
www.manager.com.br

International Sites (with Brazilian versions)
CRAIGSLIST
www.craigslist.org

OLX
www.olx.com.br

BUSINESS DEVELOPMENT AGENCIES FOR INVESTORS AND ENTREPRENEURS
AMCHAM-BRASIL
www.amcham.com.br

BRASILGLOBALNET
www.brasilglobalnet.gov.br

INVESTE SÃO PAULO
www.investe.sp.gov.br

RIO NEGÓCIOS
www.rio-negocios.com

SOCIAL SECURITY
PREVIDÊNCIA SOCIAL
www.previdencia.gov.br

Finance

BANKS
BANCO DO BRASIL
www.bb.com.br

BANCO SANTANDER
www.santander.com.br

BRADESCO
www.bradesco.com.br

CAIXA ECONÔMICA FEDERAL
www.caixa.gov.br

CITIBANK
www.citibank.com.br

HSBC
www.hsbc.com.br

ITAÚ
www.itau.com.br

TAXES
CANADA REVENUE AGENCY
www.cra-arc.gc.ca

FEDERAL REVENUE OF BRAZIL (RECEITA FEDERAL)
www.receita.fazenda.gov.br

U.S. INTERNAL REVENUE SERVICE
www.irs.gov

INVESTMENTS
BM&F BOVESPA (SÃO PAULO STOCK EXCHANGE)
www.bmfbovespa.com.br

BRAZILIAN BUBBLE
http://brazilianbubble.com
Up-to-the-moment Brazilian business, economic, and financial news covered by Brazilian and American business professionals.

Communications

TELEPHONE, INTERNET, AND CABLE TV

CLARO
www.claro.com.br
Fixed, mobile, broadband, and cable TV service.

CTBC
www.ctbc.com.br
Fixed, mobile, broadband, and cable TV service.

EMBRATEL
www.embratel.com.br
National operator.

NET
www.netcombo.com.br
Fixed, broadband, and cable TV service.

OI
www.oi.com.br
Fixed, mobile, broadband, and cable TV service.

TIM
www.tim.com.br
Mobile and broadband service.

VIVO
www.vivo.com.br
Fixed, mobile, broadband, and cable TV service.

POSTAL AND COURIER SERVICES

CORREIOS/SEDEX
www.correios.com.br

DHL
www.dhl.com.br

FEDEX
www.fedex.com

MEDIA
Newspapers
ESTADO DE SÃO PAULO
www.estadao.com.br

FOLHA DE SÃO PAULO
www.folha.uol.com.br

JORNAL DO BRASIL
www.jb.com.br

O GLOBO
oglobo.globo.com

News Magazines
CARTA CAPITAL
www.cartacapital.com.br

ÉPOCA
revistaepoca.globo.com

ISTOÉ
www.istoe.com.br

VEJA
veja.abril.com.br

Travel and Transportation

AIRLINES

AVIANCA
www.avianca.com.br

AZUL
ww.voeazul.com.br

GOL
www.voegol.com.br

TAM
www.tam.com.br

TRIP
www.voetrip.com.br

AIRPORTS

INFRAERO
www.infraero.gov.br
Infraero is the government agency responsible for the operation of Brazil's major
airports. The bilingual site provides airport information and allows you to consult the status of all flights.

Prime Living Locations

RIO DE JANEIRO
Expat Resources

AMERICAN CHAMBER OF COMMERCE
Praça Pio X 15, 5 andar, Centro
Rio de Janeiro, RJ, 20040-020
tel. 21/3213-9200
www.amchamrio.com.br

AMERICAN CLUB OF RIO DE JANEIRO
Av. Rio Branco 123, 21 andar, Centro
Rio de Janeiro, RJ, 20040-005
tel. 21/2242-6105
www.clubeamericano.com.br

**ANGLICAN CHURCH OF RIO DE
JANEIRO**
Rua Real Grandeza 99, Botafogo
Rio de Janeiro, RJ, 22281-030
tel. 21/2226-7332
www.christchurchrio.org.br

**AMERICAN SOCIETY
OF RIO DE JANEIRO**
Estrada da Gávea 132, Gávea
Rio de Janeiro, RJ, 22451-260
tel. 21/2125-9132
www.americansocietyrio.org

**BRITISH AND COMMONWEALTH
SOCIETY OF RIO DE JANEIRO**
Rua Real Grandeza 99, Botafogo
Rio de Janeiro, RJ, 22281-030
www.bcsrio.org.br

**EXPAT BLOG COMMUNITY
OF RIO DE JANEIRO**
www.expat-blog.com

INTERNATIONAL CLUB RIO
www.incrio.org.br

INTERNATIONS'S RIO GROUP
www.internations.org/rio-de-janeiro-expats

**MEETUP.COM'S EXPATS
AND ENGLISH SPEAKERS
OF RIO DE JANEIRO**
www.meetup.com/riodejaneirobrazil

THE RIO TIMES
riotimesonline.com

RESOURCES

ST. ANDREW'S SOCIETY
Rua Real Grandeza 99, Botafogo
Rio de Janeiro, RJ, 22281-030
www.standrewrio.com.br

UNION CHURCH OF RIO DE JANEIRO
Av. Prefeito Dulcídio Cardoso 4351,
Barra da Tijuca
Rio de Janeiro, RJ, 22793-011
tel. 21/3325-8601
www.unionchurchrio.com

Education
THE BRITISH SCHOOL
www.britishschool.g12.br
Botafogo:
Rua Real Grandeza 99, Botafogo
Rio de Janeiro, RJ, 22281-033
tel. 21/2539-2717
Urca:
Av. Pasteur, 429, Urca
Rio de Janeiro, RJ, 22290-240
tel. 21/2543-5519
Barra da Tijuca:
Rua Mário Autuori 100, Barra da Tijuca
Rio de Janeiro, RJ, 22793-270
tel. 21/3329-2854

**ESCOLA AMERICANA
DO RIO DE JANEIRO**
www.earj.com.br
Gávea:
Estrada da Gávea 132, Gávea,
Rio de Janeiro, RJ, 22451-263
tel. 21/2125-9000
Barra da Tijuca:
Rua Martinho de Mesquita 301,
Barra da Tijuca
Rio de Janeiro, RJ, 22620-220
tel. 21/2495-2485
Macaé:
Rua Camboriu 257, Vivendas da Lagoa
Macaé, RJ, 27920-110
tel. 22/2773-5156

ESCOLA BLOOM
Rua Dom Rosalvo Costa Rego 400, Itanhangá
Rio de Janeiro, RJ, 22641-040
tel. 21/3344-1544
www.escolabloom.com.br

MAPLE BEAR BILINGUAL SCHOOL
Rua Martinho de Mesquita 136,
Barra da Tijuca
Rio de Janeiro, RJ, 22630-220
tel. 21 2480-1914
www.maplebearbarradatijuca.com.br

**PONTIFÍCIA UNIVERSIDADE
CATÓLICA DO RIO DE JANEIRO
(PUC-RIO)**
Rua Marquês de São Vicente 225, Edifício
Padre Leonel Franca, 8 andar, Gávea
Rio de Janeiro, RJ, 22451-900
tel: 21/3527-1578 (International Programs)
www.puc-rio.br

RIO INTERNATIONAL SCHOOL
Av. Prefeito Dulcídio Cardoso 4351,
Barra da Tijuca
Rio de Janeiro, RJ, 22793-011
tel. 21/3410-2807
www.riointernationalschool.com

**UNIVERSIDADE ESTADUAL DO
RIO DE JANEIRO (UERJ)**
Campus Francisco Negrão de Lima,
Rua São Francisco Xavier 524, Sala T030,
Bloco F, Maracanã
Rio de Janeiro, RJ, 20550-900
tel. 21/2334-0797 (International Programs)
www.uerj.br

**UNIVERSIDADE FEDERAL DO
RIO DE JANEIRO (UFRJ)**
Av. Pedro Calmon 550, Prédio da Reitoria,
2 andar, Cidade Universitária
Rio de Janeiro, RJ, 21941-901
tel. 21/2598-1609 (International Programs)
www.ufrj.br

Health Care
CASA DE SAÚDE SÃO JOSÉ
Rua Macedo Sobrinho 21, Humaitá
Rio de Janeiro, RJ, 22271-080
tel. 21/2538-7626
www.cssj.com.br

CENTRO PRÉ NATAL DE DIAGNÓSTICO E TRATAMENTO
Rua da Laranjeiras 445, Laranjeiras
Rio de Janeiro, RJ, 22240-002
tel. 21/2102-2300
www.cpdt.com.br

CLÍNICA GALDINO CAMPOS
Av. Nossa Senhora de Copacabana 492,
Copacabana
Rio de Janeiro, RJ, 22020-000
tel. 21/2548-9966
www.clinicagaldinocampos.com.br

HOSPITAL COPA D'OR
Rua Figueiredo de Magalhães 875,
Copacabana
Rio de Janeiro, RJ, 22031-011
tel. 21/2545-3600
www.copador.com.br

SÃO PAULO
Expat Resources
AMERICAN CHAMBER OF COMMERCE
Rua da Paz 1431, Santo Amaro
São Paulo, SP, 04713-001
tel. 11/3324-0194
www.amcham.com.br

AMERICAN SOCIETY OF SÃO PAULO
Rua da Paz 1431, Santo Amaro
São Paulo, SP, 04713-001
tel. 11/5182-2074
www.americansociety.com.br

ANGLO INFO SÃO PAULO
www.saopaulo.angloinfo.com

BRITISH COMMONWEALTH COMMUNITY COUNCIL
Rua Ferreira de Araújo 741, 1 andar, Pinheiros
São Paulo, SP, 05428-002
tel: 11/3813-7080
www.bcccsp.org.br

CANADIAN INTERNATIONAL SOCIETY
www.cisbrazil.org

EXPAT BLOG
www.expat-blog.com

EXPATS SÃO PAULO FACEBOOK PAGE
www.facebook.com/expatsaopaulo

INTERNATIONAL NEWCOMERS CLUB OF SÃO PAULO
www.newcomers-sp.com.br

INTERNATIONS'S SÃO PAULO SMALL BUSINESS GROUP
www.internations.org/activity-group/340

INTERNATIONS'S SÃO PAULO GET TOGETHERS
www.internations.org/activity-group/415

OUR LADY HELP OF CHRISTIANS CHURCH
Rua Vigária João de Pontes 537,
Chácara Flora
São Paulo, SP, 04748-000
tel. 11/2101-7400
www.chapelparish.org

ST. PAUL'S ANGLICAN CHURCH
Rua Comendador Elias Zarzur 1239,
Chácara Santo Antônio
São Paulo, SP, 04736-002
tel. 11/5686-2180

RESOURCES

Education

CHAPEL SCHOOL
Rua Vigário João de Pontes 537,
Chácara Flora
São Paulo, SP, 04748-000
tel: 11/2101-7400
www.chapelschool.com

GRADED - AMERICAN SCHOOL IN SÃO PAULO
Av. Presidente Giovanni Gronchi 4710,
Morumbi,
São Paulo, SP, 05724-002
tel. 11/3747-4800
www.graded.br

MAPLE BEAR BILINGUAL SCHOOL
www.maplebear.com.br
Moema:
Rua Inajaroba 88, Vila Nova Conceição
São Paulo, SP, 04511-040
tel. 11/3044-2851
Morumbi:
Av. Jorge João Saad 570, Morumbi
São Paulo, SP, 05618-001
tel. 11/3722-4522
Pinheiros:
Av. Padre Pereira de Andrade 575,
Alto de Pinheiros
São Paulo, São Paulo, 05469-000
tel. 11/3021-8664

PACA (THE CHRISTIAN AMERICAN SCHOOL OF SÃO PAULO)
Rua Cássio de Campos Nogueira 393,
Cidade Dutra
São Paulo, SP, 04829-310
tel. 11/5929-9500
www.paca.com.br

PONTIFÍCIA UNIVERSIDADE CATÓLICA-SÃO PAULO (PUC-SP)
Campus Perdizes
Rua Monte Alegre 984, Perdizes
São Paulo, SP, 05014-901
tel. 11/3670-8000
www.pucsp.br

ST. PAUL'S SCHOOL
Rua Juquiá 166, Jd. Paulistano
São Paulo, SP, 01440-903
tel. 11/3087-3399
www.stpauls.br

UNIVERSIDADE DE SÃO PAULO (USP)
VRERI-USP (International Relations)
Rua da Praça do Relogio 109, sala 603,
Bloco K, Cidade Universitária
São Paulo, SP, 05508-050
www.usp.br

UNIVERSIDADE ESTADUAL DE CAMPINAS (UNICAMP)
Cidade Universitária "Zeferino Vaz,"
Barão Geraldo
Campinas, SP, 13083-970
tel. 19/3521-4718 (International Relations)
www.unicamp.br

UNIVERSIDADE ESTADUAL PAULISTA (UNESP)
tel. 11/5627-0663; 11/5627-0273;
11/5627-0248 (International Students)
www.unesp.br

UNIVERSIDADE FEDERAL DE SÃO PAULO (UNIFESP)
São Paulo Campus:
Rua Sena Madureira, 1500, 5º andar,
Vila Mariana
São Paulo, SP 04021-001
tel. 11/5576-4000
www.unifesp.br

Health Care
HOSPITAL ALBERT EINSTEIN
Av. Albert Einstein 627/701, Morumbi
São Paulo, SP, 05652-000
tel. 11/2151-1233
http://apps.einstein.br/english

HOSPITAL ALEMÃO OSWALDO CRUZ
Rua João Julião 331, Bela Vista
São Paulo, SP, 01323-903
tel. 11/3549-1000
www.hospitalalemao.org.br

HOSPITAL SAMARITANO
Rua Conselheiro Brotero 1486, Consolação
São Paulo, SP, 01232-010
tel. 11/3821-5300
www.samaritano.org.br

HOSPITAL SÃO LUIZ
Rua Dr. Alceu de Campos Rodrigues 95,
Itaim Bibi
São Paulo, SP, 04544-000
tel. 11/3040-1100
www.saoluiz.com.br

HOSPITAL SÍRIO LIBANÊS
Rua Dona Adma Jafet 91, Bela Vista
São Paulo, SP, 01308-050
tel. 11/3155-0200
http://en.hospitalsiriolibanes.org.br

MINAS GERAIS
Expat Resources
MINAS INTERNATIONAL
www.minasinternational.com

Education
AMERICAN SCHOOL OF BELO HORIZONTE
Av. Professor Mário Werneck 3002, Buritis
Belo Horizonte, MG, 30575-180
tel. 31/3378-6700
www.eabh.com.br

ESCOLA DA SERRA
Rua do Ouro 1900, Serra
Belo Horizonte, MG, 30210-590
tel. 31/3263-6363
www.escoladaserra.com.br

MAPLE BEAR BILINGUAL SCHOOL
Central Branch:
Rua General Andrade Neves 601, Gutierrez,
Belo Horizonte, MG, 30441-119
tel. 31/2514-1101
www.maplebearbh.com.br

UNIVERSIDADE FEDERAL DE MINAS GERAIS (UFMG)
Av. Antônio Carlos 6627, Pampulha
Belo Horizonte, MG, 31270-901
tel. 31/3409-4025 (International Relations)
www.ufmg.br

Health Care
HOSPITAL DAS CLÍNICAS
Av. Alfredo Balena 190, Santa Efigênia
Belo Horizonte, MG, 30130-100
tel. 61/3409-9300
www.hc.ufmg.com.br

CENTRAL-WEST
Education
AFFINITY ARTS
SHIS,QI 9, Cj 16, Casa 7,
Brasília, DF, 71625-160
tel. 61/3248-2966
www.affinityarts.com.br

AMERICAN SCHOOL IN BRASÍLIA
SGAS 605, Cj E, Lotes 34/37
Brasilia, DF, 70200-650
tel. 61/3442-9700
www.eabdf.br

BRASÍLIA INTERNATIONAL SCHOOL
SGAS 914, Cj. C, Lotes 67/68
Brasília, DF, 70390-140
tel. 61/3346-1200
www.bischool.com.br

MAPLE BEAR BILINGUAL SCHOOL
SIG, Quadra 08, Lote 2225, Parte F
Brasília, DF, 70610-480
tel. 61/3961-4350
www.maplebear.com.br/brasilia

SCHOOL OF THE NATIONS
SHIS QI 21, Área Especial, Cj. C1
Brasília DF, 71619-970
tel. 61/3366-1800
www.schoolofthenations.com.br

SWISS INTERNATIONAL SCHOOL
SGA/SUL, Quadra 905, Cj. B
Brasilia, DF, 70390-050
tel. 61/3443-4145
www.swissinternationalschool.com.br

UNIVERSIDADE DE BRASÍLIA (UNB)
Campus Universitário Darcy Ribeiro,
Brasília, DF, 70910-900
tel. 61/3107-3300
www.alunoestrangeiro.unb.br

Health Care
HOSPITAL SANTA LÚCIA
SHLS, Qd 76, Cj. C.
Brasília, DF, 70390-700
tel. 61/3445-0000
www.santalucia.com.br

THE SOUTH
Expat Resources
CURITIBA EXPAT MEETUP GROUP
www.meetup.com/Curitiba-Expat

Education
AMERICAN SCHOOL OF FLORIANÓPOLIS
Rua Crispim Mira 351, Centro
Florianópolis, SC, CEP 88020-540
tel. 48/3025-1231
www.amesflorianopolis.com.br

INTERNATIONAL SCHOOL OF CURITIBA
Av. Dr. Eugênio Bertolli 3900,
Santa Felicidade
Curitiba, PR, 82410-530
tel. 41/3525-7400
www.iscbrazil.com

MAPLE BEAR BILINGUAL SCHOOL
Av. Nossa Senhora da Luz 695, Jardim Social
Curitiba, PR, 82510-020
tel. 41/3023-7177
www.maplebearcuritiba.com.br

PAN AMERICAN SCHOOL OF PORTO ALEGRE
Av. João Obino 110, Petrópolis
Porto Alegre, RS, 90470-150
tel. 51/3334-5866
www.panamerican.com.br

UNIVERSIDADE FEDERAL DO RIO GRANDE DO SUL (UFRGS),
Av. Paulo Gama 110, Farroupilha
Porto Alegre, RS, 90040-060
tel. 51/3308-6000
www.ufrgs.br

Health Care
HOSPITAL PRONTO SOCORRO
Largo Teodoro Herzl
Porto Alegre, RS,
tel. 51/3289-7999

HOSPITAL UNIVERSITÁRIO
Av. Beira-Mar Norte, Trindade
Florianópolis, SC,
tel. 48/3721-9100
www.hu.ufsc.br

HOSPITAL UNIVERSITÁRIO CAJURU
Av. São José 300, Cristo Rei
Curitiba, PR,
tel. 41/3271-3000
www.pucpr.br/saude/alianca/cajuru

THE NORTHEAST
Education
AMERICAN SCHOOL OF RECIFE
Rua Sá e Souza 408, Boa Viagem
Recife, PE, 51030-060
tel. 81/3341-4716
www.ear.com.br

MAPLE LEAF BILINGUAL SCHOOL
Salvador:
Rua General Bráulio Guimarães 76,
Jardim Armação
Salvador, BA, 41750-000
tel. 71/3016-2694
www.maplebear.com.br
Recife:
Av. Rosa e Silva 1510, Aflitos
Recife, PE, 52020-220
tel. 81/3427-8800
www.maplebear.com.br
Fortaleza:
Rua Rafael Tobias 2861, José de Alencar
Fortaleza, Ceará, 60830-105
tel. 85/3312-4058
www.maplebear.com.br

PAN AMERICAN SCHOOL OF BAHIA
Loteamento Patamares
Salvador, BA, 41680-060
tel. 71/3368-8400
www.escolapanamericana.com

Health Care
CENTRO HOSPITAL ALBERT SABIN
Rua Senador José Henrique 141, Ilha do Leite
Recife, PE, 50070-460
tel. 81/3421-5411
www.hu.ufsc.br

HOSPITAL BATISTA MEMORIAL
Av. Padre Antônio Tomas 2058, Aldeota
Fortaleza, CE, 60140-160
tel. 85/3224-5417
www.hospitalbatistamemorial.com.br

HOSPITAL ESPANHOL
Av. Sete de Setembro 4161, Barra
Salvador, BA, 41148-900
tel. 51/3264-1500

National Holidays

New Year's Day: January 1
Carnaval: February/March (Mon. and Tues. preceding Ash Wednesday, which is 46 days before Easter Sunday)
Good Friday and Easter Sunday: March/April
Tiradentes Day: April 21
May Day/Labor Day: May 1
Corpus Christi: May/June (60 days after Easter Sunday)
Independence Day: September 7
Nossa Senhora de Aparecida Day: October 12
All Saints Day: November 2
Republic Day: November 15
Christmas Day: December 25

Glossary

ambulante: street vendor

babá: nanny

bairro: neighborhood

barracas: simple kiosks (that often sell drinks or food)

bilhete de integração: integrated ticket (allowing transfers between Metrôs and buses)

Bolsa Família: federal program that pays poor Brazilian families to send their children to school

boteco/botequim: simple, neighborhood bar serving drinks and home-cooked food

cachaça: Brazil's national spirit made from fermented sugar cane

Cadastro de Pessoa Fïsica (CPF): Physical Person Registration card, necessary for carrying out financial and economic transactions in Brazil; the equivalent of the U.S. Social Security card

carro de luxo: luxury car

carro popular: economy car

cartório: public notary office

cartório de registro de imóveis: real estate registry office

Carteira de Trabalho e Previdência Social (CTPS): work permit that also serves as an employee's social insurance identity card

Carteira Nacional de Habilitação (CNH): Brazilian driver's license

Cédula de Identidade de Estrangeiro CIE: Foreigner's Identity Card, displaying a foreigner's RNE as proof of permanent residency

cidade: city

cidade históricas: Brazil's colonial cities, the most famous of which, the Cidades Históricas de Minas, are former mining towns located in central Minas Gerais

cobrador: collector (i.e., ticket collector on a bus)

conta corrente: checking account

conta de poupança: savings account

cultura popular: traditional popular (as in folk or street) culture

dar um jeito: literally "find a way," this expression refers to Brazilians' tendency improvise solutions in order to work their way around (often bureaucratic) obstacles

décimo terceiro salário: 13th salary; equivalent to a month's wages and paid to all workers at the end of the year

Diário Oficial da União: official journal, published daily, in which all government acts and legislation are announced

educação infantil: preschool

empregada: housekeeper

ensino fundamental: Brazilian equivalent of elementary school

ensino médio: Brazilian equivalent of secondary school

festa: festival or party

Fundo de Garantia por Tempo de Serviço (FGTS): unemployment insurance fund paid by private employers to the government and accessible when an employee is fired

fiador: guarantor

Indíce Geral de Preços do Mercado (IGP-M): general market price index used to calculate price increases (including annual rent increases)

Imposto de Renda das Pessoas Físicas (IRPF): personal income tax

Imposto sobre Propriedade Predial e Territorial Urbana (IPTU): property tax paid by owners and renters

Instituto Nacional do Seguro Social (INSS): National Institute for Social Security collects contributions made by both employees and employers to Previdência Social (social security)

LAN house: Internet café (LAN stands for local area network)

malandro: a type of wily rogue or scoundrel (both romanticized and marginalized) that is historically associated with a certain type of Carioca (resident of Rio)

nordestinos: inhabitants of the Brazilian Northeast

ônibus convencional: basic, no-frills bus

ônibus executivo: bus with amenities such as a/c

operadora: telephone company

plano de saúde: health insurance plan

pousada: B&B or guesthouse-style accommodation popular throughout Brazil

Previdência Social: Social Security, which covers illness, disabilities, maternity, unemployment, pensions, and death

Registro Nacional de Estrangeiro (RNE):

identity number for foreign residents featured on CIE permanent residency card
seguro: insurance
Sistema Único de Saúde (SUS): Unified Health System, which offers free universal public health care to Brazilians and foreign residents
união estável: stable union, whereby couples—both hetero- and homosexual—who have been living together have the same rights as married couples

Portuguese Phrasebook

Brazilian Portuguese is quite different from the Portuguese spoken in Portugal. In terms of speaking and comprehension, Brazilian Portuguese is easier because Brazilians pronounce words as they are written while the Portuguese tend to distort certain sounds. Depending on the region you are in, accents and expressions will be different. A wonderfully innovative language, Brazilian Portuguese is full of colorful expressions and sayings as well as borrowed words from diverse idioms.

PRONUNCIATION

Portuguese is spoken as it is written. However, things take a turn for the complex when confronted with the challenging vowel sounds.

Vowels

So-called non-nasal vowels are fairly straightforward:

a pronounced "ah" as in "father" in words like *garota* (girl).

e pronounced "eh" as in "hey" in words like *fé* (faith). At the end of a word, such as *fome* (hunger), pronounced "ee" as in "free."

i pronounced "ee" as in "free" in words such as *polícia* (police).

o pronounced "aw" as in "dog" in words such as *loja* (shop). At the end of a word, such as *minuto* (minute), it veers from "oh" as in "go" to "oo" as in "too."

u pronounced "oo" as in "too" in words such as *luz* (light).

Much more complicated are the nasal vowels. Nasal vowels are signaled by a tilde accent (~) as in *não* (no), or by the presence of the letters **m** or **n** following the vowel, such as *bem* (good) or *ponte* (bridge). When pronouncing them, it helps to exaggerate the sound, focus on your nose and not your mouth, and pretend there is a hidden "ng" on the end.

Consonants

Portuguese consonant sounds are a breeze compared with the nasal vowels. There are, however, a few exceptions to be aware of.

c pronounced "k" as in "catch" in words like *casa* (house). However, when followed by the vowels **e** or **i,** or when sporting a cedilla accent (¸) as in *caçar* (to hunt), it is pronounced "s" as in "soft" in words like *cidade* (city).

ch pronounced "sh" as in "shy" in words like *chá* (tea).

d usually pronounced as in English. The exception is when it is followed by the vowels **e** or **i** in words such as *parede* (wall); it acquires a "j" sound similar to "jump."

g pronounced "g" as in "go" in words like *gado* (cattle). However, when followed by the vowels **e** or **i,** it is pronounced like the "s" in "vision" in words like *gigante* (giant).

h always silent. Words like *horário* (schedule) are pronounced like "hour" in English, pronounced like the "s" in "vision" in words like jogo (game).

n usually pronounced as in English. The exception is when it is followed by **h** in words such as *banho* (bath), when it acquires a "ny" sound similar to "annual."

r can be pretty complicated. At the beginning of a word, such as Rio de Janeiro, or when found in twos, such as *carro* (car), it is pronounced as a very guttural "h" as in "home."

t usually pronounced as in English. The exception is when it is followed by the vowels **e** or **i** in words such as *morte* (death) when it acquires a "ch" sound similar to "chalk."

x pronounced like "sh" as in "shy" when found at the beginning of words such as *xadres* (chess). Otherwise, it is pronounced "z" as in "zoo" in words such as *exercício* (exercise).

Stress

Most Portuguese words carry stress on the second-to-last syllable. *Janeiro* (January), for example, is pronounced "ja-NEI-ro." There are, however, some exceptions. The stress falls on the last syllable with words that end in **r** (*falar* [to talk] is pronounced "fa-LAR") as well as words ending in nasal vowels (*mamão* [papaya] is pronounced "ma-MAO"). Vowels with accents over them (~, ´, `, ^) indicate that the stress falls on the syllable containing the vowel. As such, *inglês* (English) is pronounced "ing-LES" and *cardápio* (menu) is pronounced "car-DA-pi-o."

PLURAL NOUNS AND ADJECTIVES

In Portuguese, the general rule for making a noun or adjective plural is to simply add an "s." For example, the plural of *casa branca* (white house) is *casas brancas*. But there are various exceptions. For instance, words that end in nasal consonants such as "m" or "l" change to "ns" and "is," respectively. The plural of *botequim* (bar) is *botequins* while the plural of *hotel* (hotel) is *hotéis*. Words that end in nasal vowels also undergo changes: So "ão" becomes "ãos," "ães," or "ões," as in the case of *mão* (hand) which becomes *mãos* and *pão* (bread) which becomes *pães*.

GENDER

Like French, Spanish, and Italian, all Portuguese words have masculine and feminine forms of nouns and adjectives. In general, nouns ending in **o** or consonants, such as *cavalo* (horse) and *sol* (sun), are masculine, and those ending in **a**, such as *terra* (earth), are feminine. Many words have both masculine and feminine versions

determined by their **o** or **a** ending, such as *menino* (boy) and *menina* (girl). Nouns are always preceded by articles, *o* and *a* (definite) and *um* and *uma* (indefinite), that announce their gender. For example, *o menino* means "the boy" while *a menina* means "the girl." *Um menino* is "a boy" while *uma menina* is "a girl."

BASIC AND COURTEOUS EXPRESSIONS

Hello *Olá*
Hi *Oi*
Good morning *Bom dia*
Good afternoon/evening *Boa tarde*
Good night *Boa noite*
See you later *Até mais tarde/Até breve*
Goodbye *Tchau*
How are you? *Como vai?/Tudo bem?*
Fine, and you? *Tudo bem, e você?*
So so *Mais ou menos*
Not so good *Meio ruim*
Nice to meet you. *Um prazer.*
You're very kind. *Você é muito(a) simpático(a).*
Yes *Sim*
No *Não*
I don't know. *Não sei.*
Please *Por favor*
Thank you *Obrigado (if you're male)/ Obrigada (if you're female)*
You're welcome *De nada*
Excuse me *Com licença*
Sorry *Desculpa*
What's your name? *Como se chama?/ Qual é seu nome?*
My name is . . . *Meu nome é . . .*
Where are you from? *De onde vem?*
I'm from . . . *Sou de . . .*
Do you speak English? *Fala inglês?*
I don't speak Portuguese. *Não falo Portuguese.*
I only speak a little bit. *Só falo um pouquinho.*
I don't understand. *Não entendo.*
Can you please repeat that? *Por favor, pode repetir?*
What's it called? *Como se chama?*
What time is it? *Que horas são?*
Would you like . . .? *Gostaria de . . .?*

TERMS OF ADDRESS

I *eu*
you *você*
he/him *ele*
she/her *ela*
we/us *nós*
you (plural) *vocês*
they/them *eles/elas*
Mr./Sir *Senhor*
Mrs./Madam *Senhora* **or** *Dona*
young man *moço* **or** *rapaz*
young woman *moça*
guy/fellow *rapaz/cara*
boy/girl *garoto/garota*
child *criança*
brother/sister *irmão/irmã*
father/mother *pai/mãe*
son/daughter *filho/filha*
husband/wife *marido/mulher*
uncle/aunt *tio/tia*
grandfather/grandmother *avô, avó*
friend *amigo(a)*
colleague *colega*
boyfriend/girlfriend *namorado/ namorada*
single *solteiro(a)*
divorced *divorciado(a)*

TRANSPORTATION

Where is . . .? *Onde é . . .?/Onde fica . . .?*
How far away is . . .? *Qual é a distância até . . .?*
Which is the quickest way? *Qual é o caminho mais rápido?*
How can I get to . . .? *Como eu posso chegar . . .?*
Is it far? *É longe?*
Is it close? *É perto?*
bus *ônibus*
the bus station *a rodoviária*
the bus stop *a parada de ônibus*
How much does a ticket cost? *Quanto custa uma passagem?*
What is the schedule? *Qual é o horário?*
When is the next departure? *Quando é a próxima saida?*
What time do we leave? *Á que horas vamos sair?*
What time do we arrive? *Á que horas vamos chegar?*
first *primeiro*

last *último*
next *próximo*
Are there many stops? *Tem muitas paradas?*
plane *avião*
Is the flight on time? *O vôo está na hora?*
Is it late? *Está atrasado?*
I'd like a round-trip ticket. *Quero uma passagem ida e volta.*
I have a lot of luggage. *Tenho muita bagagem.*
Is there a baggage check? *Tem guarda volumes?*
boat *barco*
ship *návio*
ferryboat *ferry/balsa*
port *porto*
I want to rent a car. *Quero alugar um carro.*
Is it safe to drive here? *É seguro dirigir aqui?*
gas station *posto de gasolina*
Can you fill up the gas tank? *Pode encher o tanque?*
To drive fast/slowly *dirigir rapidamente/devagar*
parking lot *estacionamento*
stoplight *o sinal*
toll *pedágio*
at the corner *na esquina*
sidewalk *a calçada*
dead-end street *rua sem saida*
one-way *mão unica*
The car broke down. *O carro quebrou.*
I need a mechanic. *Preciso dum mecânico.*
Can you fix it? *Pode consertar?*
The tire burst. *O pneu furou.*
Where can I get a taxi? *Onde posso achar um taxi?*
Is this taxi free? *Está livre?*
Can you take me to this address? *Pode me levar para este endereço?*
Can you stop here, please? *Pode parar aqui, por favor?*
north *norte*
south *sul*
east *este*
west *oueste*
left/right *esquerda/direita*

straight ahead *tudo direito*
central *centro*
south central *centro-sul*
northwest *noroeste*
southeast *sudeste*

ACCOMMODATIONS

To stay in a hotel *Ficar num hotel*
Is there a guesthouse nearby? *Tem pousada perto daqui?*
Are there any rooms available? *Tem quartos disponíveis?*
For today? *Para hoje?*
I'd like to make a reservation. *Queria fazer uma reserva.*
I want a single room. *Quero um quarto simples.*
Is there a double room? *Tem quarto duplo?*
With a double bed or two singles? *Com cama de casal ou duas camas solteiras?*
With a fan or air-conditioned? *Com ventilador ou ar condicionado?*
Is there a view? *Tem vista?*
private bathroom *banheiro privado*
shower *chuveiro*
key *chave*
Is breakfast included? *O café de manhã é incluido?*
How much does it cost? *Quanto custa?*
Can you give me a discount? *É possível ter um desconto?*
It's too expensive. *É muito caro.*
Is there something cheaper? *Tem algo mais barato?*
for just one night *para uma noite só*
for three days *para três dias*
Can I see it first? *Posso dar uma olhada primeiro?*
quiet/noisy *tranquilo/barulhento*
comfortable *confortável*
change the sheets/towels *trocar os lençóis/toalhas*
soap *sabão*
toilet tissue *papel higiênico*
Could you please wake me up? *Por favor, pode me acordar?*

FOOD

to eat *comer*
to drink *beber*

I'm hungry. *Estou com fome.*
I'm thirsty. *Estou com sede.*
breakfast *café de manhã*
lunch *almoço*
dinner *jantar*
a snack *um lanche*
a light meal *uma comida leve*
I just want to nibble. *Só quero beliscar.*
Are the portions large? *As porções são grandes?*
Is it enough for two? *Dá para duas pessoas?*
Can I order a half portion? *Posso pedir uma meia-porção?*
Can I see the menu? *Pode dar uma olhada no cardápio?*
Is it all-you-can-eat? *Pode comer a vontade?*
Can you call the waiter over? *Pode chamar o garçom?*
Is there a free table? *Tem mesa livre?*
I'd like a cold beer. *Quero uma cerveja gelada.*
Another, please. *Mais uma, por favor.*
Do you have wine? *Tem vinho?*
Red or white? *Tinto ou branco?*
I'd like more ice, please. *Quero mais gelo, por favor.*
This glass is dirty. *Este copo está sujo.*
Can you bring me another? *Pode me trazer outro?*
Do you have juice? *Tem suco?*
I'd like it without sugar. *Quero sem açúcar.*
Do you have sweetener? *Tem adocante?*
carbonated mineral water *água mineral com gaz*
I'm a vegetarian. *Sou vegetariano.*
I'm ready to order. *Estou pronto para pedir.*
Can I have some more time? *Pode me dar mais um tempinho?*
well done *bem passado*
medium *ao ponto*
rare *mal passado*
hot *quente*
cold *frio*
sweet *doce*
salty *salgado*
sour *azedo*

utensils *talheres*
fork *garfo*
knife *faca*
soupspoon *colher de sopa*
teaspoon *colher de chá*
dessert *sobremesa*
Can you bring coffee please? *Pode trazer um cafezinho?*
with milk *com leite*
Can you bring the bill please? *Pode trazer a conta, por favor.*
It was delicious. *Foi deliciosa.*

MONEY AND SHOPPING

to buy *comprar*
to spend a lot of money *gastar muito dinheiro*
to shop *fazer compras*
for sale *à venda*
Until what time does the bank stay open? *Até que horas o banco fica aberto?*
I'm out of money. *Estou sem dinheiro.*
I don't have change. *Estou sem troco.*
ATM *caixa automática*
Do you accept credit cards? *Aceita cartão de crédito?*
Can I exchange money? *Posso trocar dinheiro?*
money exchange *câmbio*
Is there a discount if I pay in cash? *Tem desconto se pagar em dinheiro?*
That's too expensive. *É caro demais.*
That's very cheap. *É muito barato.*
more *mais*
less *menos*
a good price *um preço bom*
Let's bargain. *Vamos negociar.*
Is it on sale? *Está em promoção?*
It's a good deal. *É um bom negócio.*
What time does the store close? *A que horas fecha a loja?*
salesperson *vendedor(a)*
Can I try it on? *Posso provar?*
It doesn't fit. *Não cabe bem.*
too tight *muito apertado*
too big *grande demais*
Can I exchange it? *Posso trocar?*

HEALTH

Can you help me? *Pode me ajudar?*
I don't feel well. *Não me sinto bem.*
I'm nauseous. *Estou com nausea.*
I've got a headache. *Estou com dor de cabeça.*
I've got a stomachache. *Estou com dor de barriga.*
fever *um febre*
pain *uma dor*
infection *uma infeção*
cut *um corte*
burn *uma queimadura*
vomiting *vomitando*
I can't breathe. *Não posso respirar.*
I'm sick. *Estou doente.*
Is there a pharmacy close by? *Tem uma farmácia perto daqui?*
Can you call a doctor? *Pode ligar para um médico?*
I need to go to a hospital. *Preciso ir para o hospital.*
pill *pílula*
medicine *remédio/medicamento*
antibiotic *antibiótico*
ointment *pomada/creme*
cotton *algodão*
toothpaste *pasta de dentes*
toothbrush *escova de dentes*
condom *preservativo/camisinha*

SAFETY

Is this neighborhood safe? *Este bairro é seguro?*
dangerous *perigoso*
robbery *roubo*
thief *ladrão*
mugging *assalto*
mugger *assaltante*
Call the police! *Chame a polícia!*
Help! *Socorro!*

COMMUNICATIONS

to talk/to speak *falar*
to say *dizer*
to hear *ouvir*
to listen *escutar*
to shout *gritar*
to make a phone call *fazer um telefonema/ligar*

RESOURCES

What's your phone number? *Qual é seu numero de telefone?*

the wrong number *o numero errado*

collect call *uma chamada a cobrar*

international call *uma chamada internacional*

Do you have Internet here? *Tem Internet aqui?*

I want to send an email. *Quero mandar um email.*

What's your email address? *Qual é seu endereço de email?*

post office *os correios*

letter *carta*

postcard *postal*

package *um pacote*

box *uma caixa*

to send *enviar*

to deliver *entregar*

stamp *selo*

weight *peso*

NUMBERS

1 *um, uma*
2 *dois, duas*
3 *três*
4 *quatro*
5 *cinco*
6 *seis*
7 *sete*
8 *oito*
9 *novo*
10 *dez*
11 *onze*
12 *doze*
13 *treze*
14 *quatorze*
15 *quinze*
16 *dezesseis*
17 *dezessete*
18 *dezoito*
19 *dezenove*
20 *vinte*
21 *vinte e um*
30 *trinta*
40 *quarenta*
50 *cinquenta*
60 *sessenta*
70 *setenta*
80 *oitenta*
90 *noventa*
100 *cem*
101 *cento e um*
200 *duzentos*
500 *quinhentos*
1,000 *mil*
2,000 *dois mil*

TIME

What time is it? *Que horas são?*

It's 3 o'clock. *São três horas.*

It's 3:15. *São três e quinze.*

It's 3:30. *São três e meia.*

It's 3:45. *São três e quarenta-cinco.*

In two hours. *Daqui a duas horas.*

Sorry for being late. *Desculpe o atraso.*

Did I arrive early? *Cheguei cedo?*

before *antes*

after *depois*

DAYS AND MONTHS

day *dia*
morning *manhã*
afternoon *tarde*
night *noite*
today *hoje*
yesterday *ontém*
tomorrow *amanhã*
week *semana*
month *mês*
year *ano*
century *século*
Monday *segunda-feira*
Tuesday *terça-feira*
Wednesday *quarta-feira*
Thursday *quinta-feira*
Friday *sexta-feira*
Saturday *sábado*
Sunday *domingo*
January *janeiro*
February *fevereiro*
March *março*
April *abril*
May *maio*
June *junho*
July *julho*
August *agosto*
September *setembro*
October *outubro*
November *novembro*
December *dezembro*

SEASONS AND WEATHER

season estação
spring primavera
summer verão
autumn outuno
winter inverno
weather o tempo
sun sol
It's sunny. Está fazendo sol.

rain chuva
Is it going to rain? Vai chover?
clouds nuvens
cloudy nublado
It's hot. Faz calor.
It's cold. Faz frio.
a cool breeze uma brisa fresca
a strong wind um vento forte
dry air ar seco
wet molhado

Suggested Reading

TRAVEL LITERATURE

Bishop, Elizabeth. *One Art.* New York: Farrar, Strauss and Giroux, 1995. America's poet laureate, Bishop was also a steadfast and elegant letter writer. On a South American cruise, Bishop stopped off in Rio de Janeiro, fell ill after eating a cashew fruit, and was nursed back to health by Lota Macedo Soares, a wealthy and very clever Carioca with whom she fell in love. The subsequent years she spent in Brazil are chronicled with sharpness and affection in the letters published in this tome.

Grandin, Greg. *Fordlandia: The Rise and Fall of Henry Ford's Forgotten Jungle City.* New York: Picador, 2009. The surprisingly true story of the auto tycoon's misguided attempts to create a utopian Midwestern-style city in the heart of the Amazonian rain forest.

Haddad, Annette, and Scott Doggett, eds. *Travelers' Tales Brazil: True Stories.* New York: Travelers' Tales Guides, 2004. This great collection of travel essays—penned by a variety of writers and excerpted from books and magazines—offers a multifaceted view of Brazil through many lenses.

Lévi-Strauss, Claude. *Tristes Tropiques.* New York: Penguin, 1992. The famous French anthropologist supposedly hated traveling and explorers but quickly changed his mind when he traveled to Brazil in the 1930s and found himself face-to-face with the fascinating indigenous groups of the Amazon Basin. Lévi-Strauss's prose offers an engaging mixture of ethnographic description and autobiographical impressions.

Page, P. K. *Brazilian Journal.* Toronto: L. & O. Dennys, 1987. In the 1950s, Canadian poet P. K. Page found herself in Rio when her husband became Canada's ambassador to Brazil. Despite bouts of culture shock, Page fell in love with Brazil. Her descriptions of Rio's glamorous last days as the nation's capital are simple, lyrical, and ultimately moving.

Wallace, Alfred Russel. *A Narrative of Travels on the Amazon and the Rio Negro.* Whitefish, MT: Kessinger Publishing, 2006. Naturalist Alfred Russel Wallace was both a colleague and rival of Charles Darwin. Both men visited Brazil in the mid-19th century, but Wallace chose to slash and shoot his way through the Amazon Basin, taking minute and highly evocative notes of all the exotica that crossed his path.

RESOURCES

HISTORY AND SOCIETY

De Jesus, Carolina Maria. *Child of the Dark*. New York: Signet, 2003. Written between 1955 and 1960, these intimate journal entries by Carolina de Jesus offer a rare firsthand glimpse of the life of a single black mother of three who lived in a São Paulo *favela* and earned a living picking garbage. Through a chance encounter with a journalist, her diary was published in 1960, and de Jesus became something of a celebrity.

Fausto, Boris. *A Concise History of Brazil*. Cambridge, MA: Cambridge University Press, 1999. One of Brazil's leading historians and a professor at the University of São Paulo, Fausto does an admirable job of condensing five centuries of events and outsized personalities into one comprehensive and highly readable narrative.

Hemming, John. *Tree of Rivers: The Story of the Amazon*. New York: Thames and Hudson, 2008. This former director of the Royal Geographic Society is author of *Red Gold: The Conquest of the Brazilian Indians*, which is considered the definitive history of Brazil's indigenous peoples. In his most recent book, Hemming gives a fascinating account of life along the mythic river. His characters range from classic—native people, explorers, missionaries, and rubber barons—to contemporary—hard-core environmentalists, ecotourists, and soya and cattle agromillionaires.

Levine, Robert M., and John Crocitti, eds. *The Brazil Reader: History, Culture, Politics*. New York: Duke University Press, 1999. An intelligently edited volume of essays on myriad and often subtle aspects of Brazilian history, society, and daily life. The texts range from academic to alternative, but all are thought provoking and do a fine job of tackling Brazil's overwhelming diversity and complexity.

Mattoso, Katia M. de Queiroz. *To Be a Slave in Brazil, 1550–1888*. New York: Rutgers, 1987. Mattoso provides Balzacian details that movingly bring to life the harrowing existence of slaves in colonial Brazil as seen through the eyes of both slaves and their masters.

Morley, Helena. *Diary of Helena Morley*. Translated by Elizabeth Bishop. London: Virago, 2008. Alice Dayrell Caldeira Brant was a bright, rebellious, and imaginative girl of English ancestry. She grew up in Diamantina, Minas Gerais, in the late 19th century, when its once-glittering diamond mines were already in decline. In the 1940s, at age 62, Brant published her teenage diaries under the pseudonym Helena Morley. Immensely popular, the book became widely regarded as a fascinating record of life in a provincial mining town. The English version was translated by American poet Elizabeth Bishop.

Page, Joseph A. *The Brazilians*. New York: Da Capo Press, 1996. In an attempt to explain "Brazilianness," this highly readable cultural history of Brazil draws on politics, economics, sports, literature, pop culture, religion, and historic events and figures.

Rohter, Larry. *Brazil on the Rise: The Story of a Country Transformed*. New York: Macmillan, 2010. Former Brazilian correspondent to the *New York Times* who lived in Brazil for 14 years, Rohter's critical analysis of contemporary Brazil, organized by themes ranging from race relations to the Amazon, is peppered with lively personal anecdotes and interviews.

CULTURE AND MUSIC

Bellos, Alex. *Futebol: The Brazilian Way of Life*. London: Bloomsbury, 2002. A compelling look at Brazil's national pastime (some would say religion) that traces the fascinating history of soccer from its humble beginnings to its overblown present. Bellos is an accomplished journalist, and he mixes insightful reporting with highly entertaining anecdotes.

Castro, Ruy. *Bossa Nova—The Story of the Brazilian Music that Seduced the World*. Chicago: Chicago Review Press, 2003. One of Brazil's most prolific journalists, Castro conjures up the heady days of Ipanema in the late 1950s and early 1960s when fascinating characters such as João Gilberto and Tom Jobim pioneered the cool syncopated sound that took the world by storm. Aside from detailing the history of bossa nova, the book offers a slice of Carioca life from that time.

Guillermoprieto, Alma. *Samba*. New York: Vintage, 1991. A former dancer and contributor to the *New Yorker,* Guillermoprieto spent a year in Rio de Janeiro's Zona Norte neighborhood with Mangueira, one of the city's most traditional samba schools, as its 5,000 members prepared for Carnaval. The result is this vibrant, passionate, and beautifully written backstage narrative.

McGowan, Chris, and Ricard Pessanha. *The Brazilian Sound: Samba, Bossa Nova, and the Popular Music of Brazil*. Philadelphia: Temple University Press, 1998. A thorough and well-written compendium of popular Brazilian music styles and major performing artists, this book serves as a useful introduction to Brazil's rich musical world. The text is accompanied by photos and a vast discography.

Peterson, Joan, and David Peterson. *Eat Smart in Brazil: How to Decipher the Menu, Know the Market Foods & Embark on a Tasting Adventure*. Corte Madera, CA: Gingko Press, 2006. Illustrated with mouthwatering photos, this highly readable book acts as a culinary companion, introducing you to the ingredients, recipes, and diverse regional cooking traditions of Brazil.

Sullivan, Edward J., ed. *Brazil Body and Soul*. New York: Guggenheim Museum, 2003. Published to coincide with Brazil's 500-year anniversary and the subsequent "Best-of" survey exhibited by the Guggenheim Museum, this massive catalog provides a mesmerizing overview of Brazilian art. Included are early explorers' depictions of "paradise," Aleijadinho's baroque marvels, modernism, folk art from throughout the Northeast, and interesting sections on indigenous and Afro-Brazilian art. The thoughtful essays are illustrated with stunning high-quality photos.

Veloso, Caetano. *Tropical Truth: A Story of Music and Revolution in Brazil*. New York: Da Capo Press, 2003. Brilliant, charming, and sometimes aggravating, Bahian singer-composer Caetano Veloso is one of MPB's most creative figures. In this colorful memoir, he provides an insider's look at the generation-defining musical movement of the late 1960 and 1970s, which became known as Tropicália.

RESOURCES

Index

www.moon.com

DESTINATIONS | ACTIVITIES | BLOGS | MAPS | BOOKS

MOON.COM is ready to help plan your next trip! Filled with fresh trip ideas and strategies, author interviews, informative travel blogs, a detailed map library, and descriptions of all the Moon guidebooks, Moon.com is all you need to get out and explore the world—or even places in your own backyard. While at Moon.com, sign up for our monthly e-newsletter for updates on new releases, travel tips, and expert advice from our on-the-go Moon authors. As always, when you travel with Moon, expect an experience that is uncommon and truly unique.

f 🐦 KEEP UP WITH MOON ON FACEBOOK AND TWITTER
JOIN THE MOON PHOTO GROUP ON FLICKR